T0325157

Computing the Climate

How do we know that climate change is an emergency? How did the scientific community reach this conclusion, and what tools did they use to do it? This book tells the story of climate models, tracing their history from nineteenth-century calculations on the effects of greenhouse gases, to modern Earth system models that integrate the atmosphere, the oceans, and the land using the full resources of today's most powerful supercomputers. Drawing on the author's extensive visits to the world's top climate research labs, this accessible, non-technical book shows how computer models help to build a more complete picture of Earth's climate system. *Computing the Climate* is ideal for anyone who has wondered where the projections of future climate change come from – and why we should believe them.

STEVE M. EASTERBROOK is Director of the School of the Environment at the University of Toronto, where he teaches courses on environmental decision-making, systems thinking, and climate literacy. He received a PhD in Computing from Imperial College London in 1991. In the 1990s, he served as lead scientist at NASA's Katherine Johnson IV&V Facility in West Virginia, where he worked on software verification for the Space Shuttle and the International Space Station. He has been a consultant for the European and Canadian Space Agencies, and a visiting scientist at many climate research labs in the United States and Europe.

"While climate models are derived from first physical principles, they are developed by people and communities. This book's approach of the tracing of revolutionary ideas and Herculean efforts by generations of scientists to develop deep understanding and predictive capability for weather and climate does the topic justice. Many difficult concepts, including the greenhouse effect, chaos, computational instability, and the difference between predictions and projections are explained well and accessibly. This book will be compelling reading both for students and for people who simply want to know more."

Matthew Huber, Purdue University

"Easterbrook's non-technical survey of climate modelling uniquely expands the climate change genre. Students will benefit from its broad scope and equation-free conceptual explanations, and climate modellers will appreciate its historical approach linking nineteenth-century experiments and ideas to twenty-first-century breakthroughs."

Baylor Fox-Kemper, Brown University

"This is a very readable personal account of climate model development throughout history. It focuses on several individuals and modelling groups/countries. It often refers to 'you' and 'we.' I learned a lot and enjoyed the book, and I recommend it to anyone faced with making decisions involving the future climate."

Kevin Trenberth, University of Auckland,
author of *The Changing Flow of Energy Through the Climate System*

Computing the Climate

How We Know What We Know About Climate Change

STEVE M. EASTERBROOK

University of Toronto

CAMBRIDGE
UNIVERSITY PRESS

Shaftesbury Road, Cambridge CB2 8EA, United Kingdom

One Liberty Plaza, 20th Floor, New York, NY 10006, USA

477 Williamstown Road, Port Melbourne, VIC 3207, Australia

314–321, 3rd Floor, Plot 3, Splendor Forum, Jasola District Centre, New Delhi – 110025, India

103 Penang Road, #05–06/07, Visioncrest Commercial, Singapore 238467

Cambridge University Press is part of Cambridge University Press & Assessment, a department of the University of Cambridge.

We share the University's mission to contribute to society through the pursuit of education, learning and research at the highest international levels of excellence.

www.cambridge.org
Information on this title: www.cambridge.org/9781107133488

DOI: 10.1017/9781316459768

© Steve M. Easterbrook 2023

This publication is in copyright. Subject to statutory exception and to the provisions of relevant collective licensing agreements, no reproduction of any part may take place without the written permission of Cambridge University Press & Assessment.

First published 2023

A catalogue record for this publication is available from the British Library.

A Cataloging-in-Publication data record for this book is available from the Library of Congress

ISBN 978-1-107-13348-8 Hardback
ISBN 978-1-107-58992-6 Paperback

Cambridge University Press & Assessment has no responsibility for the persistence or accuracy of URLs for external or third-party internet websites referred to in this publication and does not guarantee that any content on such websites is, or will remain, accurate or appropriate.

Contents

Preface

A century is a long time, longer than most of us expect to live. A hundred years ago, Europe had just emerged from the First World War, a War that was fought mainly on the ground, by soldiers sheltering in trenches. There were cars, but they weren't yet mass produced. There were planes, but no passenger airlines. And a computer was not a machine but a job description, a person who did mathematical calculations by hand.

By the end of this century, the world will be very different again. But exactly how it will change is hard to say. In the last few decades, an alarming view of that future has emerged, produced by computer models of the Earth's climate. These future scenarios are hard for many of us to comprehend. They sound more like the product of a science fiction writer's imagination than the output of serious scientific research. Few of us can think that far ahead, and we're certainly not used to the idea of a computer that can foretell the future. It's much easier for us to dismiss these forecasts than it is to find out where they come from.

For most people, climate change is easier to talk about if we focus not on the distant future, but on the signs of change we can already see today. Those signs are now all around us: disrupted weather patterns bring flooding to some places and heat waves and drought to others. Hotter summers and earlier springs affect the seasonal growth of plants and animals. Melting glaciers are already causing a discernible rise in sea levels. But it's still hard to see these phenomena as part of a larger pattern of change, and especially to comprehend the causal links that drive such changes, and to understand how those changes will play out over time.

Perhaps it would be better if climate models could tell us more about the immediate future, rather than what it will be like by the end of this century. For example, will next summer be hotter than this summer? When can we expect the next big heat wave, or another superstorm? Which year in the coming decade will be the warmest? What changes should farmers make in their crop planning in the next few years? Unfortunately, computer models are poor at forecasting weather months in advance, which only serves to increase our suspicions about their longer-term forecasts. To put it bluntly, how can we say what the climate will be like in 100 years, if we can't forecast the weather for next month?

In this book, I want to take you on a journey to the scientific labs where climate models are built. I want to take you inside the models themselves. I want to show you how they compare with the most incredible feats of human engineering, on a par with the Golden Gate Bridge, or the Space Shuttle. I want to explain how it's possible to do science with computer models. Most of all, I want to explore what it is that climate scientists do, when they do what they do.

Just like those other engineering marvels, climate models are large and complex. But the principles on which they are based are not hard to explain, and the ways in which scientists use them are fascinating.

If we don't know what's in a climate model, we have no basis for judging whether to believe them. We're left with having to accept the opinion of an expert. And if you spend time on the Internet, you quickly discover it's not hard to find one or two "experts" to support almost any position on climate change.

Which brings me to the three main goals I have in writing this book. I hope to take something that's normally invisible – a complex piece of computer software – and make it understandable. I hope to convince you that a science based on simulation models makes sense and produces valid results. And I hope to give you a sound basis to judge for yourself whether a computer projection for the Earth's climate for the rest of this century is believable.

Acknowledgements

This book took a long time to write, and I had a lot of help and encouragement along the way. First, a huge thank you to the team at Cambridge University Press for their enthusiasm for the idea, especially my editor Lauren Cowles, who sharpened my writing and pointed out when my digressions got in the way of the story. I left a few in. Sorry! Thanks also to Johnathan Fuentes at CUP for his help navigating the publishing process and helping me with permissions for the images. At the outset of the project, Clive Thompson, Paul Edwards, and Trudy Ledsham helped me navigate the world of publishing and book contracts.

The book would not have been possible without the support of all the climate scientists who welcomed me into their labs, showed me what they do, and corrected all my misunderstandings. They include Dick Peltier at U of T, who first set me on this journey, and my wonderful hosts at each of the labs I visited: Tim Johns at the UK Met Office, Mariana Vertenstein and David Bailey at NCAR, Claire Lèvy, Marie Alice Foujols, and Sylvie Joussaume at IPSL, Reinhard Budich at MPI-M, and John Scinocca at CCCMa. Extra special thanks for Tim, Mariana, Claire, Marie-Alice, and Reinhard for detailed readings of the relevant chapters to fix my mistakes!

I also owe a big thanks to all the climate scientists and software engineers I interviewed over the years. Even though I couldn't fit you all into the book, you all helped me figure out what to write. At UKMO: Phil Bentley, Dan Bernie, Ben Booth, Mick Carter, Bill Collins, Dan Copsey, John Edwards, Colin Johnson, Chris Jones, Adrian Lock, Andy Malcolm, Gill Martin, Steve Mullerworth, Paul Selwood, Cath Senior, Len Shaffrey, Julia Slingo, Rachel Stratton, Allyn Treshansky, Pier Luigi Vidale, Stuart Webster, Keith Williams, Damian Wilson, and Nigel Wood. At NCAR: David Bailey, Gordon Bonan, Antony Craig, Gokhan Danabasoglu, Rocky Dunlap, Brian Eaton, Jim Edwards, Steve Goldhaber, Jim Hurrell, Erik Kluzek, Peter Lauritzen, Sam Levis, Keith Lindsay, Rich Loft, Matthew Mayernik, Rich Neale, Nancy

Norton, Keith Oleson, Bill Sacks, Isla Simpson, Warren Washington, and Jon Wolfe. At MPI-M: Marco Giorgetta, Helmuth Haak, Christian Hovy, Thomas Jahns, Christian Jakob, Johan Jungelaus, Stephan Kindemann, Daniel Kloche, Luis Kornblueh, Stephanie Legutke, Robert Pincus, Christian Reick, and Bjorn Stevens. At IPSL: Rachid Benshila, Sandrine Bony, Patrick Brockman, Sebastian Denvil, Jean-Loius Dufresne, Laurent Fairhead, Frederic Hourdin, Claire Levy, Gurvan Madec, Oliver Marti, Seb Masson, Laurent Nguyen, and Denys Quesneau.

Along the way a number of other scientists have helped me develop my understanding of climate modelling, including Dave Randall at Colorado State University, Balaji at GFDL, Gavin Schmidt at NASA GISS, Bryan Lawrence and Ed Hawkins at Reading University, Sophie Valcke at Cerfacs, Graham Riley and Rupert Ford at Manchester University, Michael Tobis at UT Austin, Amy Dahan and Helen Guillemot at Centre Alexandre-Koyré, and Cecelia DeLuca and Sylvia Murphy at NOAA.

Others have written parts of the story in this book before, particularly Paul Edwards, Peter Lynch, and Spencer Weart, all of whom were exploring and writing about the history of climate science long before I started. I have followed in your footsteps, so I hope my work measures up to yours. Thanks also to Jennifer Barton who helped me trace the history of the Bretherton diagrams.

Many thanks to all my students who accompanied me on this journey. Thanks especially to Kaitlin Naughton, who found an interesting new way to visualize climate model architectures; Jon Pipitone who figured out how to measure their software quality; and Sami Fassnacht and Alex Hurka, who re-implemented Arrhenius's model. Thanks to all the colleagues and students who read and commented on various chapter drafts: Miriam Diamond, Zoe Chakraborty, Kaitlin Naughton, Harshit Gujral, Soukayna Mouatadid, Stephanie Knill, Zoe James, Julien Emile-Geay, Andre Erler, Steve Goldhaber, Isla Simpson, Claire Levy, Nigel Wood, and John Edwards.

Finally, huge thanks to my family for always being there for me, and for tolerating my absences when I disappeared off to write. My kids Toby, Harriet, and Jamie hadn't started high school when I began writing this. The three of you were always my target audience whenever I was stuck, wondering how to get the key ideas across. And finally, most importantly, I couldn't have done this without my wife, Sarah, who is my best friend, fiercest critic, and greatest morale booster. I love you!

1

Introduction

How certain can we be about projections of future climate change from computer models? In 1979, President Jimmy Carter asked the US National Academy of Science to address this question, and the quest for an answer laid the foundation for a new way of comparing and assessing computational models of climate change. My own work on climate models began with a similar question, and led me to investigate how climate scientists build and test their models. My research took me to climate modelling labs in five different countries, where I interviewed dozens of scientists. In this chapter, we will examine the motivating questions for that work, and explore the original benchmark experiment for climate models – known as Charney sensitivity – developed in response to President Carter's question.

A Question from the White House

A few miles north of the Woods Hole Oceanographic Institute on Cape Cod, Massachusetts, perched on a bluff of land overlooking Quissett Harbour, the Jonsson Center is an imposing Victorian house, with a wrap-around verandah, where guests can eat their meals looking out over the harbour. The centre serves as the summer retreat for the US National Academy of Sciences,[1] hosting weekly workshops on many different areas of science (see Figure 1.1). It was here, for one brief week in the summer of 1979, that a small group of scientists gathered to answer an urgent question from the White House, and in doing so, changed the way we understand and evaluate computer models of climate change.

The question they were called upon to answer wasn't *whether* the planet would warm in response to rising carbon dioxide emissions – by the late 1970s, that was no longer in dispute in the scientific community. The question was: *how certain can we be about the numbers?* President Jimmy

Figure 1.1 The entrance to the Jonsson Center at Woods Hole. (Photo: Steve M. Easterbrook)

Carter wanted to understand the policy implications, and for that he needed to know how confident the scientists were that the computer models were correct.

The question was posed to the National Academies by Frank Press, science advisor to the president. He was reacting to a report that landed on President Carter's desk from an elite group of physicists, known as the JASONs,[2] who regularly advised the president on matters of national defence, particularly concerning the risks from nuclear weapons. To explore the implications of rising levels of carbon dioxide, the JASON group had developed their own computer model of the Earth's climate. Their model showed that by the second half of the twenty-first century, the planet would warm by several degrees. The implications were stark: this would reduce the world's food supply, cause the oceans to rise, and lead to new "dust bowl" conditions across large parts of America, Asia, and Africa, with serious political consequences as people migrate away from affected regions. The JASON report concluded, with dramatic understatement, "the impact of the projected changes on man is unknown, but unlikely to be wholly favourable."[3]

Very little about the JASON report was new – throughout the 1960s and 1970s a steady stream of papers from climate research labs had reported similar results.[4] Many scientists used computer models to study weather and climate,

Figure 1.2 Jule Gregory Charney. (Courtesy MIT Museum)

ever since 1948, when John von Neumann, widely regarded as the father of the modern computer, hired a promising young meteorologist named Jule Charney to develop a weather forecasting program to show off the capabilities of the first programmable electronic computer. Their work laid the foundations of computational weather forecasting and climate modelling – we'll explore their story in detail in Chapter 3.

So the JASON computer model wasn't particularly innovative. In fact, it was fairly simple compared to other models around at the time. But the JASON group was highly regarded in government circles, and their report caught the attention of the president. It prompted deep concern at the White House, and hence a serious question about scientific confidence in the results.

That summer, the National Academy convened a small working group of experts,[5] under the leadership of Jule Charney, by now widely considered to be the father of computational weather forecasting (see Figure 1.2). So it was here, in this quiet corner of Cape Cod, where the seeds of a new way of thinking about computer models were sown, one that would weave together the ad hoc efforts of individual research groups into a new, systematic scientific enterprise.

How Sure Are We?

When politicians ask big questions that matter to society, there is usually a gap between what the politician is asking and what science can answer. For climate change, politicians want answers about the future, while scientists are more comfortable analyzing data from the past and present. Climate models represent the bridge between the two: they are developed to simulate behaviours of the climate system that have been observed in the past, but can also be run forward in time, to explore future scenarios.

Can we be sure the computer models are any good? It's a common question, especially when confronted with descriptions of how difficult life might become on a hotter planet. And anyway, why would we trust a computer? After all, our everyday experience of computers can be very frustrating. Computer software often crashes, or corrupts our data. Some days we can't even get the machine to work in the first place.

It's also a vitally important question because our responses are likely to lead us down very different paths. If we cannot be confident about what the models say, we're likely to support a wait-and-see attitude.[6] Cheap fossil fuels have delivered many of the comforts of modern life, and replacing them with alternatives may be expensive. Perhaps the most natural reaction is to avoid thinking about it at all, and hope that the scientists are wrong. We now know that lobbyists for the fossil fuel industry have been exploiting this doubt for years, paying people to exaggerate the uncertainty, to undermine efforts to phase out fossil fuels.[7]

But if the models are accurate, we have to accept their forecasts. And that means acknowledging climate change is a very serious and urgent problem, and will require us to re-think almost every aspect of how we live.

Stories about science in the media rarely answer this question. New discoveries and new results are usually presented as disconnected facts, with very little insight into where the results come from and how they were generated. If it sounds like good news ("new treatments for cancer!"), or if they don't seem to affect us directly ("new advances in quantum theory!"), we tend to accept them as true. Conversely, if the results sound like bad news ("sugar is really bad for you"! "glaciers are melting much faster than we thought"!), we're more likely to filter out parts that challenge our view of the world.[8]

Could the Models Be Wrong?

My own work in climate research was motivated by a similar question. For most of my career, I had been vaguely aware of the issue of climate change, but, like many people, I pushed it to the back of my mind, and got on with life.

But in 2006, while reading yet another newspaper article about alarming projections from the computer models, I started to realize how important this question was. How *would* I know if the models are any good?

As a computer science professor, I felt I might have some relevant expertise. I'd been teaching software engineering all my career, and I had plenty of practical experience of how difficult it is to get software correct. In the 1990s, I was lead scientist at NASA's software verification research lab, where we investigated how NASA and its contractors develop flight software used on the Space Shuttle and the International Space Station. While I was at NASA, several robotic missions to Mars had failed because of software bugs. At conferences, I had given talks on the reasons for these failures. It was clear to me that no matter how clever our technology, human mistakes always occur. Success does not depend on eliminating mistakes – with complex systems that's all but impossible. Success depends on putting in place a whole series of engineering practices that ensure we can find and correct such mistakes before they lead to catastrophic failure.

Some organizations have become exceptionally good at this, especially in places where human lives are at stake. The Space Shuttle, for example, never had a serious software failure[9] in 30 years of operation. Software errors are extremely rare in flight control software for aircraft and for the tracking systems in flight control towers. They're also extremely rare in cars, despite the fact the software in today's cars is far more complex than the shuttle flight software. But even in these systems, nobody has found a way to eliminate mistakes completely, and the cost of the engineering processes that catches and corrects these mistakes is phenomenal. The aircraft manufacturer Boeing estimates that more than half the cost of developing a new aircraft is spent on developing the software, and half of that is just the cost of testing it.

Outside of these safety critical software systems, software errors are far more common. The newspapers are full of reports of software errors bringing down stock markets, airline booking systems, government services, power grids, online games, the core arithmetic of Intel's processor chips, and, occasionally, NASA's unmanned space missions. The more we rely on software, the more it seems that the software lets us down. So it seemed natural to me to ask whether the scientific models used by climate scientists suffer from the same kinds of problem.

Getting the Big Picture

One of the great things about being a university professor is that cutting-edge research is a part of our job description. We're expected to come up with new research questions, and to conduct studies to answer them. But coming up with good research questions turns out to be much harder than most people realize. Too often, what appears to be an interesting question has already been answered by other researchers, and if it hasn't, it's usually because there is no obvious way to answer it (yet). Good research questions lie in that narrow gap between *already known* and *impossible to answer*. I needed to find out whether I was asking a good research question.

Luckily, another pleasure of life at a big research university is that it's not hard to find experts on almost anything. I contacted Prof Dick Peltier, perhaps the most renowned atmospheric physicist in Canada, who happens to work in the next building to mine. Dick is famous for his work on the advance and retreat of glaciers since the ice ages, and in particular, our ability to measure the rates that they are currently melting and contributing to sea level rise. Although his team doesn't develop their own global climate models, they regularly use the outputs of climate models in their work, and sometimes run their own experiments on the models.

We met for beer in the faculty pub, and Dick was eager for me to get involved. He told me that global climate models are usually developed in large government research labs, rather than universities, because most universities don't have the resources: you need a big team of scientists and technicians, and, preferably, your own supercomputer. Most developed countries have at least one major climate research lab, and each has developed its own computer model. The Canadian team, at the Canadian Centre for Climate Modelling and Analysis (CCCma), is based at a federal government research lab in Victoria, out on the west coast. Dick told me that the Canadian team is much smaller than those in other countries, but their model is often regarded as one of the better models, scientifically speaking. But from an engineering point of view, there is plenty of room for improvement. The team do the best they can, but they don't have the resources for a careful engineering process. So the program code is messy, and people outside of CCCma have a hard time working with it. Dick gave me one of his infectious smiles: they could use my help – I could help them re-engineer the Canadian model!

That sounded like a worthwhile challenge. But to do that, I'd need to understand more about what it takes to engineer a good climate model. I needed to know whether anyone was getting it right, and if so, what they were doing? I needed to start at the top. Which team, I asked, were doing this the best? Dick suggested I should start with the UK Meteorological Office (or, as those who work there call it, the Met Office). If anyone was getting it right, they were. The Met Office provides some of the most accurate weather forecasts in the world, although you might not think so, given the criticism they get in the British tabloid newspapers on the very few occasions they get it wrong.

Interestingly, their climate simulation models are built from the same program code as their weather forecast models. As this code runs every day to compute the weather forecasts, this seemed like an excellent place to look for good engineering practices.

I contacted Tim Johns, who was then the manager for the UK Met Office coupled climate model, and asked if I could come and visit. After I explained what I wanted to do, he readily agreed to host me for a visit. I ended up spending the entire summer at the Met Office, and Tim I and wrote a paper[10] together about how climate models are developed there. And then, when scientists at other labs heard about the work, I started getting invitations to visit more labs. My journey into the heart of climate modelling had begun.

When I started out, I thought it would be easy for me to suggest improvements to the software engineering practices for these models. But I was in for a surprise – many surprises, in fact. The first surprise was how eager climate modellers were for me to get involved. In lab after lab, I was welcomed with open arms, with scientists eager to find out how to improve their software. When I presented the results of my initial study of the UK Met Office at the European Geophysical Union conference in Vienna, I had a line of scientists from other labs imploring me to visit them next. But the deeper I got into the field, the more I realized there was very little I could teach them, and I gained a new appreciation of the breadth and depth of expertise needed to build a simulation of the Earth's climate. What I discovered was humbling and awe-inspiring.

Perhaps the biggest surprise of all was that the labs I visited had already developed the engineering processes they needed to prevent errors in the software from affecting their science. Without realizing it, they had built an impressive engineering enterprise that easily rivals the ones I had seen at NASA. Their achievement is largely invisible – it exists in the program code inside their supercomputers. But over the course of half a century, these scientists have figured out how to build and test some of the most ambitious scientific simulations ever attempted. Starting from a set of mathematical equations that express the physical properties of planet Earth – its gravity, rotation, how it is heated by the sun, and how air and water flow when subjected to heat and pressure – they were able to build simulations to capture how the atmosphere and oceans and ice sheets and vegetation and weather systems interact, with all the right patterns of the daily and seasonal cycles of winds and ocean currents.

The visualizations of these simulated climates are stunningly beautiful. At the National Center for Atmospheric Research (NCAR) in Boulder, Colorado, the software team showed me the output from one of their models (see Figure 1.3). As I watched the simulation, summer cyclones formed in the

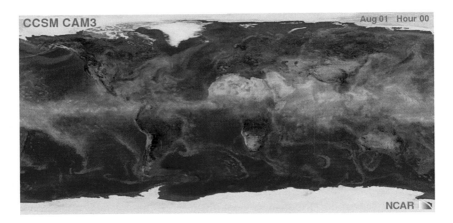

Figure 1.3 A screenshot from NCAR's visualization of the CCM3 model output for precipitation.[11] The white areas represent rain, with very heavy rain shown in orange. The full visualization spans a whole year, but does not represent any specific year; rather it shows what's typical over the course of a year. (© 2022 UCAR)

North-West Pacific and pounded the coast of Japan. Dust blown by the winds from the Sahara desert blew across the Atlantic to the Amazon, where it helps seed the daily cycle of rainfall over the rainforests, which, with the simulation speeded up, make the Amazon jungle appear to pulse with cloudbursts. Rainclouds formed in the Mid-Atlantic and flowed steadily North-East, bringing warmth and rain to the British Isles. But none of these patterns are programmed into the models. They emerge when you get the basic physics right, and when you succeed in coupling of the different parts of the physical climate system to mimic how energy and mass move around the planet.

These scientists always work at the leading edge of their field, worrying about the parts of the model they haven't yet got right. They're continually pushing the boundaries of what's possible – scaling the simulations to run on parallel supercomputers with tens of thousands of processors, dealing with programs that generate terabytes of data per hour, and working new science into the models. Which means, at a technical level, continual frustration. Code rarely works first time when you're trying to make it do something new, and as soon as one technical challenge is overcome, it's on to the next. There isn't much time to perfect the existing code, because the scientific questions always take priority. In such circumstances, it's easy to be critical of design decisions buried in the code, because most of those decisions were taken before anyone even knew whether the model would work. So the modellers spend their time obsessing over the weaknesses in their code, looking for ways to improve it.

But a lot happens to the program code on the long journey from "*I wonder if the model can do this ...*" to "*Here are our latest scientific results.*" It turns out climate modellers have built a remarkable set of design and testing practices that look quite unlike anything I've observed in commercial software companies. If you have a large enough community of experts who run the models over and over again, treating each run as though it were a scientific experiment, treating every quirk of the model with the utmost suspicion, it's possible to produce remarkably high quality software.

My aim in writing this book is to explain what that process is, and why it works. Climate models are now so large and complex that no one person understands the entire model. Taken together, the thousands of scientists who help build and test these models produce something that's much more than the sum of its parts.

The models enable a new approach to doing science, which threads together the contributions of experts around the world, from many different disciplines, and allows them to explore how their ideas interact, in a way that previously would have been impossible. Massive inter-disciplinary teams work together, sharing data, program code, and experimental results. Scientists from around the world regularly get together to design a large set of standardized experiments – I think of them as benchmarks, but the scientists call them *model intercomparison projects* – so that models can be directly compared with one another. And the results from these runs are made freely available on the Internet for anyone to explore. The result is a quality control process that I believe is unique in the world of computational modelling. We'll explore it in more depth in Chapter 8.

Climate Modelling Grows Up

Climate modelling didn't used to be like this. As we will see in Chapter 2, the first computational model of climate change was created in the 1890s, by a Swedish chemist, Svante Arrhenius, long before we had electronic computers. Arrhenius got many of aspects of the climate system right, and his predictions are remarkably similar to the best computer models today. Unfortunately, his work was largely ignored for 50 years, as few other scientists at the time really understood how the greenhouse effect works.

The advent of electronic computers revived interest in his work. In the 1960s and 1970s, several research groups built their own climate models, each running their own experiments and presenting their results in journals and conferences, in much the same way that most scientific fields operate.

But there was no way to directly compare the different models, and no easy way for labs to share their expertise, other than through the occasional visiting scientist. Most importantly, there was no way to assess the reliability of their results, even when they appeared to agree with one another.

It was in this context that Charney's group pondered the questions posed by the White House at their meeting at the Jonsson Center in the summer of 1979. Climate change was becoming an important policy issue, and the questions asked by politicians were changing rapidly. President Carter's science advisor, Frank Press, asked Charney's group to address three specific questions: "What is the basis for our scientific understanding of climate change; can the adequacy and uncertainty of this knowledge be quantified; and what are the key issues that policymakers need to be aware of?"[12]

In the decades since, scientists have collected a wide range of evidence that the climate is changing in ways that are unprecedented in human history. In 1979, observational data wasn't clear enough to be certain whether such warming was occurring, but we did have many pieces of the puzzle. Experimental evidence dating all the way back to the mid-nineteenth century showed that carbon dioxide slows the rate at which heat can escape from the planet, creating what we now call the *greenhouse effect*. Scientists had begun precise, regular measurements of carbon dioxide in the atmosphere in 1958 (see Figure 1.4). By 1979, it was obvious that CO_2 levels were steadily rising, and the rate was

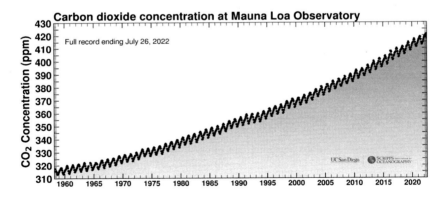

Figure 1.4 Continuous measurements at Mauna Loa in Hawaii since 1958 show the steady rise of carbon dioxide in the atmosphere. The dots show monthly averages. The saw-tooth shape of the graph is due to the annual cycle of plant growth in the extensive forests of the northern hemisphere, which absorb CO_2 in the summer and release it in the winter. (Scripps Institution of Oceanography)

accelerating, as a result of emissions from our growing consumption of coal, oil, and natural gas, and the clearing of forests to create farmland. But to put all of this evidence together to quantify *how quickly* rising CO_2 levels will alter global temperatures you have to build a model.

Charney's group began by clarifying precisely which questions computer models could answer. To quantify how the climate will change as a result of human activity, we can split the question into three parts (see Figure 1.5). The first part of the question is about *greenhouse gas emissions* – specifically, how will pollution from human activities alter the atmosphere over time? You could simply extend the trend shown in Figure 1.4 into the future. But that assumes society will continue to develop (and industrialize) in same way it has in the past. What if renewable energy becomes cheaper and replaces fossil fuels? Or we find ways to use less energy, or to limit the emissions of greenhouse gases? So to answer this question accurately, we would need to know how the global economy is likely to develop, how much energy we will use, and how we will generate that energy. This is not a question for climate science; it is a question for economists and technologists.[13] Today's climate scientists rely on such experts to generate plausible scenarios by

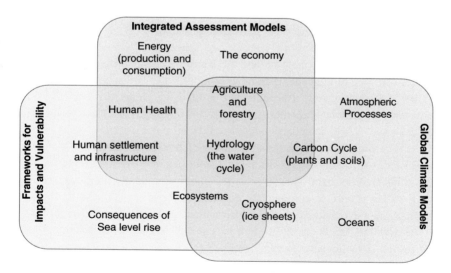

Figure 1.5 Three distinct research communities have sprung up around three parts to the question identified by Charney: how fast will emissions rise? (Integrated Assessment Models); how will the climate system respond? (Global Climate Models), and how will this affect us? (Impacts and Vulnerability). In this book, we'll focus on the second of these. (Adapted from Moss et al. (2010))

which human society might develop in the future, and how much greenhouse gases we will produce in each scenario.

Another part of the question is about the *impacts* of climate change – how will the inhabitants of planet Earth (including humans) be affected by rising global temperatures? This is also hard to answer. The world's climate is a complex system, and impacts may play out over many different timescales. Ecosystems may be damaged or destroyed, and the impact on human society might vary in different parts of the world, depending on how resilient they are to flooding, heat waves, wildfires, droughts, sea level rise, and so on. Climate models are unable to calculate these impacts directly. The best Charney's group could do in 1979 was to point to summaries by experts in other fields, although research since then has filled in many gaps in our knowledge.

So a climate model cannot predict how much humans will pollute the atmosphere, nor can it quantify how much humans will suffer from the resulting climate change. But it can answer the question that connects them: what, precisely, is the relationship between rising greenhouse gases and rising temperatures? A rough estimate can be made using a few basic equations describing the balance between incoming energy from the sun, and the rate at which that heat is lost back into space. But many complicating factors can affect this answer. For example, warmer air holds more moisture, which can then trap more heat, and further increase the warming. Clouds play an important role, reflecting some of the sun's rays back into space, so if warmer air produces more clouds, this could help reduce the warming at the surface. The oceans can absorb a lot of heat energy, and so will delay the rate at which the planet warms. Weather systems transport heat around the planet, so some regions may warm a lot more, and others may even cool slightly. The computer models are designed to help scientists understand how all these factors interact.

As is common in science, the scientists in each research lab choose different parts of this question to explore, putting into their models whichever factors they think are important. This diversity is a major strength of scientific research, but it makes it hard to compare results from different groups, and frequently confuses people outside the field. By investigating (or ignoring) different parts of the problem, scientists in different labs sometimes appear to offer conflicting results. This happens in many areas of science. Newspapers love to write stories about new research showing something that was previously thought to be good for our health is actually bad for it (or vice versa). The truth is rarely quite so simple. Cause-and-effect relationships are complex, and many factors affect how they will play out. Usually, when results don't agree, it's because the scientists are investigating subtly different versions of a research question – a treatment that's good for arthritis might be bad for your heart.

Charney's group could have picked whichever model they thought was the "best" – perhaps the most complete, or the most accurate – and summarized its results. But that wouldn't have answered the president's question of *how sure* we are about the results. Instead, they tried something new: a systematic comparison of several different models.[14] They began by defining an idealized experiment, and compared what happens in each model during that experiment. By setting up the same experiment[15] in each model, they could then explore how and why the results differed, and hence assess how well each model captured the underlying science.

It would have been tempting to conclude that where the models agreed, we could be sure of the answers, and where they disagreed, those were the unknowns. But that merely avoids the problem: what if all the models contain the same mistakes? What matters is that any similarities or differences in the model outputs can be explained in terms of how the models were constructed. We will return to this crucial point later in this book.

Charney Sensitivity

The Charney report created a framework that has been used to evaluate climate models ever since. The most immediate impact was a definition of the first *benchmark test* for climate models. That benchmark – to compute what is now known as *Charney Sensitivity* – is still used as one of a growing set of standard experiments for comparing climate models today. The experiment simulates what happens if you instantaneously double the amount of carbon dioxide in the atmosphere. Because temperatures tend to rise fairly slowly in response to increased CO_2, the experiment keeps the model running, typically for a few decades of simulation time, until the climate simulated in the model stabilizes, and settles to a new equilibrium temperature. The test is entirely artificial – an instant doubling of carbon dioxide in the atmosphere is impossible in the real world. But the experiment tells us a lot about how different models simulate a changing climate, and how much they agree or disagree about the magnitude of climate change.

Actually, the idea of measuring how the model reacts to a doubling carbon dioxide wasn't new – climate modellers in the 1970s often included the temperature response to a doubling of CO_2 when presenting model results in published papers. Unfortunately, each group would set up the test differently, and then report just a single number – the size of the change in global temperature when they ran this scenario in their model – and the answer from each group was different.

When it comes to forecasting how the climate will change in the future, a single definitive answer isn't plausible, because the climate is such a complex system.

We need to know a full range of likely outcomes, taking into account what we know and what we don't know. This was what the White House was really asking: how big is the margin of uncertainty?

Applying the same test to each computer model will give a range of different answers, which can then be analyzed based on what each model includes and what it leaves out. And if there is something all the models leave out, we need a way to estimate its effect. In the 1970s, the models included what climate scientists call "fast feedbacks" – changes in cloud cover, snow and ice cover, and heat exchange between layers of ocean, all of which affect the rate of warming. But they didn't include slower feedbacks – geological processes that play out over thousands of years, and which can store or release vast amounts of carbon dioxide. So the model outputs need to be interpreted carefully, to estimate the size of the uncertainty range.

In doing this, Charney's group concluded that doubling the concentration of carbon dioxide in the atmosphere would eventually result in a global average temperature increase between 1.5°C and 4.5°C, with a most likely value of 3°C. This answer has proved remarkably robust. In the four decades since the report was written, with huge advances in our understanding of Earth systems, the availability of data from modern satellites, and huge advances in computing power, this answer has barely changed at all.[16] The most recent IPCC Assessment Report,[17] published in August 2021, has narrowed the likely range to 2.5°C to 4.0°C, and still gives a "best estimate" of 3°C.

Charney's report also provided new insights about *when* this warming would occur. If our use of fossil fuels keeps growing we're on track to double the CO_2 in the atmosphere sometime in the 2030s or 2040s. Much of the heat would initially be absorbed by the oceans, so the warming at the surface would be delayed by several decades: "We may not be given a warning until the CO_2 loading is such that an appreciable climate change is inevitable."[18] This conclusion captures the biggest dilemma for climate policy. If we wait and see how bad climate change is before we decide what to do about it, we will have left it too late to act. If we are to make wise policy choices, we need a way to assess the likely impacts of those choices many decades into the future. We need accurate computer models.

Things Left Out

The range and sophistication of climate models have grown dramatically since the Charney report. The models Charney assessed focused on the physical climate system, particularly the global circulation patterns of winds and ocean currents that transport heat around the planet. Such models were originally known as General Circulation Models (GCMs). The acronym is also sometimes interpreted as Global Climate Model, which is equally apt. In the last decade or so, these models have evolved further to incorporate simulations of the formation, movement, and melting of ice sheets at the poles, the interaction of vegetation with the climate, and chemical reactions that take place in the atmosphere and oceans. Because they incorporate so much more than just the climate, this new generation of models are referred to as Earth System Models (ESMs).

In this book, I will tell the story of how these models of the physical climate system came to be, what scientists do with them, and how we know they can be trusted. There is much more to be told than I can fit into one book, so I will leave out many things. I will ignore another whole class of models used to understand the social and economic responses to climate change, known as Integrated Assessment Models (IAMs), which focus on questions such as how our demand for energy is likely to grow over the coming century, what this means for the economy, and how much of that demand might be met with clean energy technologies. These models form the basis for estimates of the likely costs of climate change versus the costs of taking action to avoid it.

The distinction between these two classes of models is important. In this book, I have chosen to focus on models that are grounded in the physical sciences, and for which the assessment practices developed by Charney's group work well. Part of my aim in writing the book is to bring together in one place a detailed description of what these practices are and why they work. As we shall see, these practices draw heavily on the way scientists conduct controlled experiments and submit their work to peer review, as well as the use of *hind-casting*[19] pioneered by the meteorologists to test their the weather forecasting models on data from the past, and a sophisticated benchmarking process that performs detailed model intercomparisons following the example set in the Charney Report.

It appears that none of these practices[20] are used for the economics models. So while physics-based models provide an excellent basis for our understanding of the speed and magnitude of climate change in response to our use of fossil fuels, the same cannot be said for our understanding of the economic costs and consequences. Recent research suggests economics models have vastly *under*estimated the likely costs of rapid climate change.[21] Unfortunately, valid criticism of the *economic* models is sometimes taken to mean that *all* climate models are useless, especially by those with a vested interest in blocking action on climate change.

The term *climate model* itself is sometimes used to describe any and all of these models, although it is more commonly used to describe just the physics models I cover in this book. To be clear then, when I use the term climate model in this book, I do *not* include models of social and economic factors related to climate change.

I will also leave out much of the story of how observational data about the climate is collected, and what climate scientists do with it. Paul Edwards's book, *A Vast Machine*,[22] covers this very well, from the hard-won efforts to standardize data collection methods in the nineteenth century, through to the huge volumes of data about the planet that are now collected from satellites and remote sensing instruments today. Most of our knowledge about climate change comes from this observational data. You don't need a climate model to tell you that the first two decades of the twenty-first century were hotter than any time since records began. Nor that carbon dioxide levels in the atmosphere have risen steadily over the last 60 years. We know from experiments the role that carbon dioxide plays as a kind of heat-trapping blanket in the atmosphere. So climate models represent only one of many sources of knowledge about climate change. But they do help fill in many of the gaps in the data, and they provide a testbed for asking "what-if" questions about how the climate system works.

Finally, I will leave out the work of paleo-climatologists, who study evidence from the distant past that shows us how the climate changed before modern humans were around on planet Earth. Michael Bender's book *Paleoclimate*[23] gives an excellent introduction to their work. These scientists study fossil records, cores of ice extracted from deep in the ice sheets at the poles, and layers of sediment under the oceans, to reconstruct a very long-term record of climate change, particularly over the course of ice ages that mark the last million years. The amounts of different gases in the atmosphere can be measured directly from bubbles trapped in the ice when it was frozen many thousands of years ago.[24] Temperatures can be reconstructed from analysis of the oxygen[25] in the trapped bubbles as well as evidence about the growth rate of trees, plants, and corals that are known to be sensitive to temperature change. Paleo-climatologists frequently use climate models to test how well these ancient records agree with our current understanding of the climate system. Some of these models – referred to as Earth Models of Intermediate Complexity (EMICs) – tend to be simpler than the models used to study modern climate change, as it would take far too long to run a full GCM for a simulation spanning hundreds of thousands of years. However, EMICs are directly comparable with their more complex cousins, the GCMs, because both can be run over the same scenarios, at least for shorter periods, to assess their consistency with each other. We'll explore this interplay between simple and complex models more in Chapter 6.

What This Book Is About

Today, the wealth of evidence from direct observation and from measurements of the distant past shows the climate is changing in the way climate scientists predicted, and we've already warmed the planet beyond anything previously experienced by modern humans. Computer models tie together the various strands of this evidence, and allow us to test our understanding of cause-and-effect relationships in the global climate system. My goal in this book is to explain how and why they are able to do this.

We will begin, in Chapter 2, with the work of the nineteenth-century scientists who discovered the greenhouse effect and first attempted to measure it. Central to this story is the work of Svante Arrhenius, who developed the first global climate model, before there were computers. We'll explore how his model worked, and how well it compares to modern models.

Climate modelling didn't get much further until the invention of the digital computer during the Second World War. Almost immediately, a number of people saw the potential for computers to predict (and perhaps modify) the weather. After the War, John von Neumann assembled a team of meteorologists, led by the young Jule Charney, to develop the first numerical weather prediction program. Chapter 3 tells the story of their model. Their success led, within a few years, to the establishment of operational weather forecasting by computer, and to the development of the first generation of global circulation models, which became a testbed for climate research.

The comparison of weather and climate models provides an apparent paradox: weather forecasts are only good for a few days into the future, while climate models simulate changes that occur over decades to centuries. In Chapter 4, we tackle this issue, focusing on the work of one of the early weather modellers, Ed Lorenz, who discovered that his model appeared to produce different results, even when started from the same conditions. Lorenz's experiments turned out to be the first practical demonstration of *chaos theory*, which offers deep insights into the nature of complex systems, and helps us reason about why some things are predictable while others are not. As we'll discover, chaos theory gives us an explanation for why we can be confident about our predictions of climate change over the coming century, but can't really say for sure whether it will rain next Thursday.

In the next few chapters, we will visit some of the major climate modelling labs around the world and meet with the scientists who build and work with the models. In Chapter 5, we'll visit the UK Met Office and get inside the models, to explore how they work, while in Chapter 6, we'll visit NCAR in Colorado, to explore what experiments scientists run on them.

Perhaps the most remarkable aspect of climate modelling is the huge number of scientists from many different disciplines who participate. Over the years, the computational models have come to play a crucial role in facilitating this collaboration. I've often observed that cross-disciplinary collaboration in the sciences is hobbled by misunderstandings, due to a myriad of small differences in how key terminology is used, and the amount of tacit knowledge each scientist has about their own area of specialty. But computational models overcome these barriers, because they force scientists to be explicit about every little detail – after all, when you want a computer to do something, you have to be explicit about *everything*. Chapter 7 will explore how this massive collaboration works as an elegant demonstration of *open science* and we'll visit IPSL in Paris, to see how this collaboration works.

In Chapter 8, we will visit the Max Planck Institute in Hamburg and return to the question of how scientists know they can trust their models, and the observations that lead me to describe climate modelling as a remarkably high-quality engineering process. We'll explore how climate scientists connect their models with the wealth of observational data on the climate system, and we'll explore why, surprisingly, when today's models disagree with the data, it's often the data that are wrong. The reasons are fascinating.

I close the book with a "so what?" chapter. A model is only ever a simplification of the real world. There are still things the models leave out, and they can't do all they are asked. But in political arguments, criticism of the models is always wide of the mark; you don't even need a computer model to establish many of the basic findings in climate science, but the models allow us to put those findings together and explore their consequences.

Remaining weaknesses in the models should not give us any comfort that climate change might not be as bad as projected. The problem isn't that we don't know whether the climate is changing: we do. Nor is it that we're uncertain whether the changes are significant to human life and well-being: they are. The problem is that the further we shift the climate away from the stable patterns that have existed over the entire history of human civilization, the less certain we can be that the models will tell us what happens next. In other words, we know the initial trajectory of climate change, and we know that over the next century, carbon emissions from the industrialized world will take us to a climate unlike any experienced on Earth in the last million years.[26] What we don't know, and what models cannot tell us with any certainty, is what other unpleasant surprises lie in wait for us as the world warms. Such surprises are, in the words of the JASON team, "unlikely to be wholly favourable."

As we will see, the models show us that because we've largely wasted more than four decades since the Charney report, we've missed the opportunity to stabilize the climate by cutting emissions. While the politicians argue, and the public worries, the industrial engine that drives our modern way of life grinds on. In the media, climate change is often portrayed as a debate between one group of experts who think it's a crisis and another group of experts who think it's nothing to worry about. But in the community of climate scientists, and especially, among those who build climate models, there is no longer any debate about the seriousness of the crisis. Where there is debate, it tends to be about how bad the worst-case scenarios are, and what kinds of pathway will allow us to avoid them. I end the book with an exploration of what the models tell us about these possible pathways into the future, and the urgent choices that face us.

Notes

1 The National Academy is a venerable institute, founded by Abraham Lincoln to provide the nation, and especially the US president, with advice on scientific issues. See Olson (2014) for a detailed history, including a section on the Academy's role in advice on climate change.
2 Named after Jason and the Argonauts, the JASONs were a group of about 40 of the most famous physicists in the United States, hired as regular consultants at the Institute for Defence Analyses, reporting to the Pentagon. The group was set up in 1959 to ensure the United States remained ahead of the Soviet Union in terms of technological warfare. Much of their work remains classified. See Finkbeiner (2006).
3 MacDonald et al. (1979, p. 28).
4 A few studies in the early 1970s had also warned of a global cooling effect as industrial pollution blocks out the sun. These studies were widely reported in the media, but were outliers from mainstream climate science, and were rapidly proven wrong. See Peterson et al. (2008).
5 The report is a remarkably succinct 17 pages, and well worth reading. See Charney et al. (1979) for the report, and Bony et al. (2013) for a retrospective on it.
6 See Lamb et al. (2020) for a summary of all the arguments people use for delaying action on climate change.
7 See Oreskes and Conway's (2010) book, "Merchants of Doubt."
8 This is known as motivated reasoning, and nearly everyone is susceptible to it. See Lewandowsky (2020) for an overview of how climate science communication has worked to overcome it.
9 NASA did lose two Space Shuttles: Challenger and Columbia. In both cases the immediate cause of failure was a hardware problem: for Challenger, the O-rings sealing the joints in the fuel tanks failed, and for Columbia, the tiles under the wing that protect from the heat of re-entry failed. But there's a bigger lesson that's just as important: in both cases, the accident could have been prevented if NASA had been able to use the available data more effectively during critical decisions. We'll explore this in more detail in Chapter 8. See Leveson (1995) for more insights.
10 Easterbrook and Johns (2009).

11 See: https://scied.ucar.edu/learning-zone/how-climate-works/visualizing-earth

12 See Charney et al. (1979) for the original wording of the three questions.

13 See Moss et al. (2010) for an explanation of how this is done today.

14 The report compares five global circulation models, and several simpler models, three from the Geophysical Fluid Dynamics Lab (GFDL) at Princeton and two from NASA's Goddard Institute for Space Studies (GISS). See Charney et al. (1979) for details.

15 Because of the speed at which Charney's team worked, they relied on existing data from the modelling teams as much as possible, rather than re-running the tests. For one of the models, the only data available was for a quadrupled CO_2 scenario, so they scaled this accordingly, noting that this is less than ideal, as some of the effects of climate change might not scale linearly. See Charney et al. (1979).

16 Bony et al. (2013) summarize what has been learned since then.

17 IPCC Sixth Assessment Report, Working Group 1, summary for policymakers, August 2021.

18 Charney et al. (1979, p. 2).

19 Hindcasting is a process of using the model to reproduce phenomena that occurred in the past, where we already know what happened next. We'll meet hindcasting as a key technique in Chapter 3.

20 See Weyant (2009) for a list of the good modelling practices from physical climate science that are *not* used in the IAM community.

21 See Ackerman et al. (2009) for a detailed critique. More recently, Pindyck (2013) calls IAMs "close to useless as tools for policy analysis," and a 2017 National Academies report recommends big changes in how these models are applied.

22 Edwards (2010).

23 Bender (2013).

24 The oldest available ice core was drilled to a depth of more than 3 km into the ice in Antarctica. The ice in this core dates back nearly 800,000 years, spanning eight distinct ice ages. See Jouzel et al. (2007).

25 Different isotopes of oxygen vary at different temperatures, so the ratio of isotopes trapped in the ice correlates with the average air temperature at the time.

26 See Snyder (2016).

2

The World's First Climate Model

The first computational climate model was built by a Swedish scientist in 1895, 50 years before the invention of programmable electronic computers. All the calculations had to be done by hand. Despite this, the model shares many similarities with today's computer-intensive climate models, and is a good introduction to how modern models work. The model also provided the first ever prediction of how our use of fossil fuels would lead to global warming, but that wasn't why it was built. So what was it built for, and were its predictions any good?

The Stockholm Cosmic Physics Society

In the late nineteenth century, Sweden was considered a backwater by most European scientists. Promising students hoped for positions in research labs in Germany, France, or Austria. But in Stockholm, in the early 1890s, a small group of scientists were laying the foundations for a new field of science. They met every fortnight at the Stockholm Cosmic Physics Society, to consider big questions about our planet – how geological and cosmic processes help shape the conditions for life on Earth (see Figure 2.1).

This group of scientists was remarkably diverse. Geologists from the Swedish Geological Survey came to discuss the geological eras of the past. Weather forecasters from the Meteorological Office came to discuss the forces that shape weather patterns. Biologists from the Museum of Natural History came to discuss fossil records and evolution. Astronomers came to discuss comparisons between the Earth and other planets and moons.

In the group were two remarkable young scientists, Svante Arrhenius and Vilhelm Bjerknes. Both served as lecturers in the early 1890s at the Stockholm Högskola (which later became the University of Stockholm) and both were promoted to professors of physics in the same year: 1895. Bjerknes was a mathematical physicist, with interests in magnetic fields and fluids – we'll come back

21

Arvid Högbom   Nils Ekholm   Svante Arrhenius   Vilhelm Bjerknes

Figure 2.1 Members of the Stockholm Cosmic Physics Society: Arvid Högbom (Geologist, mapped fluxes of CO_2 in the atmosphere); Nils Ekholm (Meteorologist, studied causes of the ice ages); Svante Arrhenius (Chemist, developed first model of climate change); Vilhelm Bjerknes (Physicist, worked out the equations for weather prediction).

to his work in more detail in Chapter 3. Arrhenius was a chemist who went on to win a Nobel Prize for his research on acids. Both were inspired to apply their work to weather and climate by the discussions at the meetings of the Society.

Arrhenius was particularly intrigued by a series of talks by the geologist Arvid Högbom about carbon, the basic building block for all life on Earth. Högbom had mapped out what was, at the time, the most complete account of the carbon cycle, and had taken detailed measurements of the amount of gaseous "carbonic acid" in the atmosphere.[1] Today we call it carbon dioxide (or CO_2 for short). Högbom had studied where carbon dioxide comes from and where it goes. He had identified six different sources: erupting volcanoes; meteorites burning up in the upper atmosphere; vegetation as it decomposes or burns (in which he included the burning of coal and oil); release of carbon trapped in rocks by chemical reactions; rock fracturing; and seawater as it warms under the sun. He had identified three ways carbon dioxide is removed: rock weathering (in which carbon dioxide dissolves in rainwater and reacts with limestone to produce calcium bicarbonate); absorption by plants; and absorption by the oceans.

Högbom thought these sources and sinks would balance each other, so the amount in the atmosphere wouldn't change much over time. But he couldn't be sure, because there was no easy way to measure some sources, such as meteorites. This suggested a rather radical idea: perhaps the amount of carbon dioxide in the atmosphere did change over time. When the society members pressed him on the question, Högbom thought only one of his sources would be big enough to radically change things: volcanoes. He never imagined that human use of fossil fuels would eventually far outstrip anything volcanoes produce, because, in the nineteenth century, the human contribution to CO_2 in the atmosphere was too small to measure.

Early in 1893, the society turned its attention to one of the biggest scientific mysteries of the time: what had caused the ice ages? Nils Ekholm, from the Swedish Meteorological Office, had just returned from an expedition to Spitsbergen, a large island halfway between Norway and the North Pole. He came to the society to give a talk on the latest findings about the ice ages, when the world was on average 5°C to 6°C cooler, and Northern Europe was covered in ice sheets. The topic was particularly salient for Scandinavian scientists: evidence of the retreat of the glaciers was all around them. Ekholm's talk was followed by a lively discussion of the latest hypotheses about possible causes of the ice ages. Some members thought that changes in the height of the land were to blame, but others pointed out this wouldn't explain why ice ages seemed to come and go on a regular basis, nor why the temperature changes affected the whole planet.

It was Svante Arrhenius who connected the dots between Högbom's work on the carbon cycle and Ekholm's question about the ice ages. It was well known at the time that gases such as carbon dioxide help keep the planet warm. What if there was less CO_2 during the ice ages? Wouldn't that explain everything? The idea was largely dismissed by the society, as none of them believed the carbon in the atmosphere could change enough to affect the temperature of the planet. But Arrhenius was undeterred. Inspired by Högbom's observations of how carbon dioxide enters and leaves the atmosphere, he built a climate model to show that his idea was plausible.

Climate Science in the Nineteenth Century

Arrhenius was an unusual scientist, at least by today's standards.[2] His curiosity took him from an early career in chemistry, through physics and cosmology, to a study of toxins. As a student, he was always interested in big conceptual questions, which sometimes led him to neglect his laboratory work, much to the dismay of his professors. When he received his PhD, his professors didn't think much of his work, and gave him the lowest possible passing grade. He, in turn, thought his professors were stuffy traditionalists, resistant to the latest ideas in the field. He spent the next few years as a research fellow at several labs in Germany and Holland, where he developed the theories of ionization of acids in water that would later earn him a Nobel Prize. He returned to Sweden in 1891 for a teaching job at the Stockholm Högskola. His German friends thought this was a bad move – all the interesting work was being done in Western Europe. But it was at the Högskola that Arrhenius found the rich intellectual environment he craved. He shifted his interests from chemistry to physics, driven, no doubt, by the broad set of topics discussed at the Cosmic Physics Society, of which he was a founding member.

We tend to think of science as advancing mainly through the work of lone geniuses, but this is largely because it's easier to tell the story if we can give credit to just one person. Arrhenius himself was clearly a brilliant scientist. But, as is usually the case, his achievement was only possible because it built on the work of many others. The basic theory behind his model wasn't new. Nor was the data he used for the calculations. But his obsessive pursuit of an answer to a very specific question drove him to tie together the work of physicists, astronomers, and meteorologists in a remarkable new way. In his 1896 paper, Arrhenius phrased the question as: "Is the mean temperature of the ground in any way influenced by the presence of heat-absorbing gases in the atmosphere?" The answer he sought was a precise quantification of how much ground temperatures would change if the amount of CO_2 in the atmosphere changed.

The idea that the temperature of the planet could be analyzed as a mathematical problem dates all the way back to the work of the French mathematician, Joseph Fourier,[3] in the 1820s. Fourier had studied the up-and-down cycles of temperature between day and night, and between summer and winter, and had measured how deep into the ground these heating and cooling cycles reach. It turns out they don't go very deep. At about 30 metres below the surface, temperatures remain constant all year round, showing no sign of daily or annual change. Today, Fourier is perhaps best remembered for his work on the mathematics of such cycles, and the *Fourier transform*, a technique for discovering cyclic waveforms in complex data series, was named in his honour.

For a planet as a whole, Fourier reasoned as follows. The temperature of any object is due to the balance of heat entering and leaving it. If more heat is entering, the object warms up, and if more heat is leaving, it cools down. For planet Earth, Fourier pointed out there are only three possible sources of heat: the sun, the Earth's core, and background heat from space. His measurements showed that the heat at the Earth's core no longer warms the surface, because the diffusion of heat through layers of rock is too slow to make a noticeable difference. He thought that the temperature of space itself was probably about the same as the coldest temperatures on Earth, as that would explain the temperature reached at the poles in the long polar winters. On this point, he was wrong – we now know space is close to absolute zero,[4] a couple of hundred degrees colder than anywhere on Earth. But he was correct about the sun being the main source of heat at the Earth's surface.

Fourier also realized there must be more to the story than that, otherwise the heat from the sun would escape to space just as fast as it arrived, causing night-time temperatures to drop back down to the temperature of space – and yet they don't. We now know this *does* happen on the moon, where temperatures drop by hundreds of degrees after the lunar sunset. So why not on Earth?

The Greenhouse Effect

The solution lay in the behaviour of "dark heat," an idea that was new and mysterious to the scientists of the early nineteenth century. Today we call it infra-red radiation. Both Fourier and Arrhenius referred to it as "radiant heat" or "dark rays" to distinguish it from "light heat," or visible light. But really, they're just different parts of the electromagnetic spectrum (see Figure 2.2). Any object that's warmer than its surroundings continually radiates some of

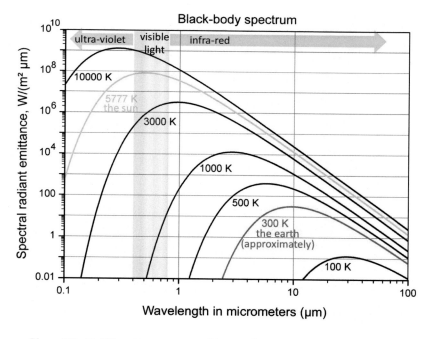

Figure 2.2 At different temperatures, objects radiate energy in different parts of the spectrum. A hotter object radiates more heat at shorter wavelengths on the electromagnetic spectrum than a cooler object. The sun radiates across the ultra-violet, visible, and infra-red, with the peak of its emissions in the visible spectrum. The Earth, being much cooler, emits only in the infra-red part of the spectrum. The shorter the wavelength, the more energy the rays carry, which is why very short wavelength ultraviolet light is dangerous to human health. (CC-BY-SA Wikimedia Commons user: Sch)

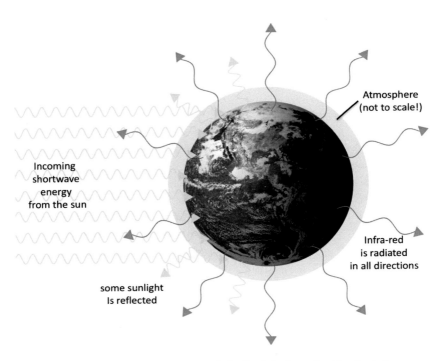

Figure 2.3 The surface temperature of the Earth is determined by the balance between the incoming heat from the sun (shortwave rays, mainly visible light and ultra-violet) and the outgoing infra-red, radiated in all directions from the Earth. The incoming short-wave rays passes through the atmosphere much more easily than the long-wave outgoing rays.

its heat to those surroundings. If the object is hot enough, say an oven, you can feel this "dark heat" if you put your hand near it, although we can only feel infra-red rays when the oven is pretty hot.[5] But even objects that we think of as pretty cold still radiate a small amount of infra-red to their surroundings. When you heat up an object, it radiates more energy, and the kind of energy it radiates spreads up the spectrum from infra-red to visible light – it starts to glow red, and then, eventually white hot.

Fourier's theory was elegantly simple. Because the sun is so hot, much of its energy arrives in the form of visible light, which passes through the atmosphere relatively easily,[6] and warms the Earth's surface. As the Earth's surface is warm, it also radiates energy. But the Earth is a lot cooler than the sun, so the energy the Earth radiates is in the form of dark heat (see Figure 2.3). Dark heat doesn't pass though the atmosphere anywhere near as easily as light heat, so this slows the loss of energy back to space.

To explain the idea, Fourier used an analogy with a hotbox, a very well-insulated wooden box, painted black inside, with three layers of glass in the lid, used by explorers as a solar oven. The sun would heat the inside of the box to over 100°C, even on high mountains, where the outside air is much colder. The glass lets the sun's rays through, but slows the rate at which the heat can escape. Fourier argued that layers of air in the atmosphere play a similar role to the panes of glass in the hotbox, by trapping the outgoing heat; like the air in the hotbox, the planet would stay warmer than its surroundings. A century later, Fourier's theory came to be called the "greenhouse effect," perhaps because a greenhouse is more familiar to most people than a hotbox.[7]

Experimental Evidence

While Fourier had observed that air does indeed trap some of the heat from the ground, it wasn't clear why until the 1850s, when scientists began to experiment with the heat trapping effects of different gases (see Figure 2.5). The first of these was Eunice Foote, an American scientist who set up a series of experiments to discover why air in a valley is warmer than air up a mountain. Foote's experiments showed that denser air absorbs more of the sun's heat. She then went on to show that air with more moisture and air with more carbonic acid also absorb more heat, and retain it longer. These remarkable experiments, reported in Scientific American[8] in September 1856, led her to hypothesize that if, for planet Earth, "at one period of its history the air had mixed with it a larger proportion [of CO_2] than at present, an increased temperature ... must have necessarily resulted."[9] Unfortunately, her experiments appear to have been largely forgotten, until her work was rediscovered in 2011, but she is now credited as the first scientist to discover carbon dioxide is responsible for global changes in climate.

In Foote's experiment, she pumped the gases into glass cylinders, heated directly by the sun. But glass is largely opaque to infra-red – dark heat – so her experiment missed an important piece of the puzzle. A few years later, the English scientist John Tyndall devised a more elaborate experiment[10] to find out if different gases would absorb dark heat. Tyndall's experiments put different gases into a four foot brass tube, sealed at both ends with disks of salt crystal, because, unlike glass, salt is transparent to dark heat. Two pots of boiling water provided sources of heat, and a galvanometer compared the heat received directly from one heat source (A) with heat from the other (B) after it had passed through the tube of gas. Figure 2.4 shows a drawing of his apparatus.

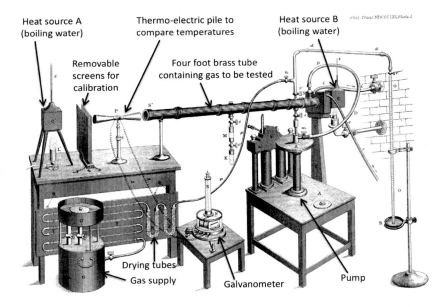

Figure 2.4 Tyndall's experimental equipment for testing the absorption properties of different gases. The brass tube was first evacuated, and the equipment calibrated by moving the screens until the temperature readings from the two heat sources were equal. Then the gas to be tested was pumped into the brass tube, and change in deflection of the galvanometer noted. (Adapted from Tyndall (1861))

When Tyndall filled the tube with dry air, or oxygen, or nitrogen, there was very little change. But when he filled it with the hydrocarbon gas ethene, the temperature at the end of the tube dropped dramatically. This was so surprising that he first suspected something had gone wrong with the equipment – perhaps the gas had reacted with the salt, making the ends opaque? After re-testing every aspect of the equipment, he finally concluded that it was the ethene gas itself that was blocking the heat. He went on to test dozens of other gases and vapours, and found that more complex chemicals such as vapours of alcohols and oils were the strongest heat absorbers, while pure elements such as oxygen and nitrogen had the least effect.

Why do some gases allow visible light through, but block infra-red? It turns out that the molecules of each gas react to different wavelengths of light, depending on the molecule's shape. A good analogy is the way sound waves of just the right wavelength can cause a wine glass to resonate. Each type of molecule will vibrate when certain wavelengths of light hit it, making it stretch, contract, or rotate. So the molecule gains a little energy, and the light rays lose

Joseph Fourier   Eunice Foote   John Tyndall   Samuel Pierpont Langley

Figure 2.5 Nineteenth-century scientists who contributed to the discovery of the greenhouse effect.

some. Scientists use this effect to determine which gases are in distant stars, because each gas makes a distinct pattern of dark lines across the spectrum from white light that has passed through it, marking the wavelengths at which that gas absorbs energy.

Tyndall noticed that gases made of more than one element, such as water vapour (H_2O) or carbon dioxide (CO_2), tend to absorb more energy from the infra-red rays than gases made of a single type of element, such as hydrogen (H_2) or oxygen (O_2). He argued this provides evidence of atomic bonding: it wouldn't happen if water was just a mixture of individual oxygen and hydrogen atoms. He was clearly on the right track here. We now know that what matters isn't just the existence of molecular bonds, but whether the molecules are asymmetric[11] – after all, oxygen gas molecules (O_2) are also pairs of atoms bonded together. The more complex the molecular structure, the more asymmetries it has, and the more modes of vibration and spin the bonds have, allowing them to absorb energy at more wavelengths. Today, we call any gas that absorbs parts of the infra-red spectrum a *greenhouse gas*. More complex compounds, such as methane (CH_4) and ethene (C_2H_4), absorb energy at even more wavelengths than carbon dioxide, making them stronger greenhouse gases.[12]

Tyndall's experiments showed that greenhouse gases absorb infra-red even when the gases are only present in very small amounts. Tyndall concluded that, because of its abundance in the atmosphere, water vapour is responsible for most of the heat trapping effect that keeps the Earth warm, with carbon dioxide second.[13] Some of the other vapours he tested have a much stronger absorption effect, but are so rare in the atmosphere they contribute little to the overall effect. Like Foote, Tyndall clearly understood the implications of these experiments for the Earth's climate, arguing that it explains why, for example, temperatures in dry regions such as deserts drop overnight far more than in more humid regions.[14] In the 1861 paper describing his experimental results,

Tyndall argued that any change in the levels of water vapour and carbon dioxide, "must produce a change of climate." He speculated that "such changes in fact may have produced all the mutations of climate which the researches of geologists reveal."[15]

A Model Needs Data

Although the greenhouse effect was known by the time Arrhenius developed his model, what was missing was a way to calculate the size of the effect. Some scientists had already attempted this. For example, in 1837, the French physicist Claude Pouillet invented an instrument known as a pyrheliometer to measure the heat energy we receive from the sun, and obtained the remarkably accurate measurement of 1.76 calories per minute per square cm. He later attempted to calculate how much of the Earth's outgoing infra-red energy is absorbed by the atmosphere, but, as Arrhenius discovered, Pouillet got these calculations wrong.[16]

So in one sense, Arrhenius was merely replicating the work of earlier scientists, checking they were correct, and finding errors. But he went well beyond what anyone else had attempted in his quest to explain the cause of the ice ages.

For precise calculations, Arrhenius needed data. Tyndall's experimental data didn't help, because measurements of the absorption effect in a four-foot tube don't really tell you how the effect works when infra-red rays pass through the full height of the atmosphere. Arrhenius needed data on how much of the existing greenhouse effect could be attributed to each of water vapour and carbon dioxide, the two main greenhouse gases – he called them "selective absorbers" – when they are mixed in the exact proportions that occur in the atmosphere. And he needed data on what happens if you vary the amount of each gas.

Today, we measure the outgoing infra-red at the top of the atmosphere directly, using satellites (see Figure 2.6), and we have excellent data showing how absorption levels have changed over time, from the beginning of the satellite era in the 1970s to the present day. Analyzing the contribution of water vapour and CO_2 is now relatively straightforward, because we can compare the heat emitted in wetter and drier regions, and we can compare changes over the last few decades, as carbon dioxide levels have risen. These satellite readings demonstrate not only that Fourier's theory is correct, but also (spoiler alert) increasing levels of carbon dioxide have indeed reduced the rate at which the planet loses heat to space.[17]

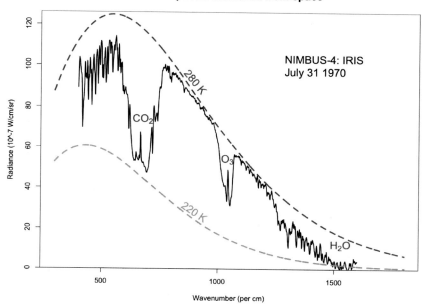

Figure 2.6 The fingerprint of greenhouse gases, as detected by the Nimbus 4 satellite on July 31, 1970, with theoretical radiation curves (dashed lines) shown for comparison. With no greenhouse gases, the satellite would see infra-red rays from the ground, matching the upper dashed line for expected radiation at 280 K (about 7°C), the local ground temperature when these measurements were made. The dips in the solid line show parts of the spectrum where each greenhouse gas blocks the infra-red from the ground. In these parts of the spectrum, the satellite only sees rays from higher in the atmosphere, where the air is cooler (lower dashed line). (Gavin Schmidt/NASA GISS)

But Arrhenius was working long before we had satellites – even before the Wright brothers had demonstrated a working airplane. Luckily, he had access to observational data collected by an American, Samuel Pierpont Langley, one of the Wright brothers' fiercest competitors. A remarkable inventor, Langley might have beaten the Wright brothers to the first working airplane if he hadn't chosen to use a catapult for the take-off. Langley had also invented an instrument for making very precise measurements of infra-red energy. His "bolometer" was widely admired; it was accurate enough to measure the heat from a cow at a quarter of a mile away.

As director at the Allegheny Observatory in Pittsburgh, Langley put his bolometer to good use measuring the temperature of the moon. When we see the moon shining in the night sky, what we actually see is sunlight reflected from the moon's surface. But as the sun heats the surface of the moon, the moon also radiates its own "dark rays" – infra-red energy. As we saw in Figure 2.2, objects at different temperatures emit energy across different parts of the spectrum. If Langley could measure the amount of energy the moon gave off at each wavelength, he could calculate its temperature. He used a prism made from a pure crystal of salt to separate the wavelengths of infra-red coming from the moon, in the same way that a glass prism can separate sunlight into the colours of the rainbow. Readings from the bolometer could then be used to calculate the energy received at each of 21 different wavelengths across the infra-red spectrum.[18]

Between 1883 and 1888, Langley and his colleague, Frank Very, used the bolometer to take detailed measurements of the infra-red spectrum from the moon, at different times of day and night. In 1890 they published the first detailed estimate of its surface temperature. The full moon was, they found, around 100°C – the temperature of boiling water. During a full moon, the whole of the side of the moon that is visible from Earth is bathed in sunlight, so this is actually the hottest the moon gets. Modern measurements show the moon's surface temperature varies dramatically, as hot as 120°C, during the lunar day, but dropping as low as −150°C on the dark side of the moon,[19] much colder than anywhere on Earth. The Apollo astronauts' spacesuits had to protect them from both extreme heat and extreme cold.

These measurements solved one of Arrhenius's biggest challenges. He needed data on how much heat from the Earth's surface is absorbed as it passes up through the atmosphere. Langley and Very's measurements were almost as good: the infra-red rays from the moon had passed *down* through the Earth's atmosphere, and so would be absorbed by about the same amount. Not only that, but they had measured the rays from the moon when it was at different heights in the sky. This meant the rays had passed through different amounts of atmosphere for each reading. The more atmosphere they passed through, the more greenhouse gases they encountered (see Figure 2.7). Furthermore, Langley and Very had carefully recorded the humidity for each reading; in drier air there was less water vapour to absorb the infra-red. This gave Arrhenius the range of absorption data he needed. By comparing the measurements for each wavelength of infra-red in drier and wetter air, and in different thicknesses of atmosphere, Arrhenius could calculate "absorption coefficients" for varying amounts of H_2O and CO_2.

As with any observational data, there are many potential sources of error in the readings, from human mistakes in recording the measurements, to problems with the instrument and the way it is used. Arrhenius picked the readings

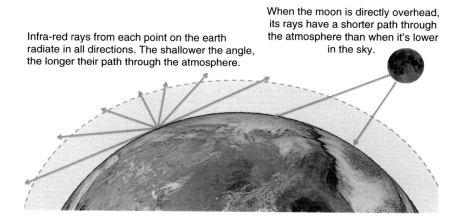

Infra-red rays from each point on the earth radiate in all directions. The shallower the angle, the longer their path through the atmosphere.

When the moon is directly overhead, its rays have a shorter path through the atmosphere than when it's lower in the sky.

Figure 2.7 The length of the path of an infra-red ray as it passes through the atmosphere depends on its angle. On longer paths, the ray passes through more greenhouse gases. Most of the paths taken by outgoing infra-red from the surface of the Earth are longer than the vertical height of the atmosphere. Arrhenius calculated the average length of these paths to be about 1.6 times the vertical height of the atmosphere. Similarly, the moon's rays pass through different amounts of atmosphere as the moon crosses the sky. (Diagram not to scale!)

that appeared to be most consistent with one another, and used the changes in humidity and angle of elevation to deduce the absorption fraction for each of the two gases at each of Langley's 21 measured wavelengths of infra-red. Today we call this a *line-by-line analysis*, and it has become a standard technique in satellite data analysis. The result is an absorption "fingerprint" for each gas across the infra-red spectrum. Arrhenius tested his results by checking them against the rest of Langley and Very's data,[20] which again is now a standard technique in data analysis: use some of the data to compute a relationship, and the remainder of the data to test it.

With this data, most of the puzzle pieces were in place (see Figure 2.8). Fourier provided the theory, from basic physics, that the sun warms the Earth during the day, and the atmosphere slows the loss of this heat, keeping the planet warm. Tyndall provided the experiments that demonstrated why: some gases, such as water vapour and carbon dioxide, "selectively absorb" parts of the infra-red spectrum. And finally, Langley and Very had detailed observations of how much infra-red is absorbed along different paths through the atmosphere, at various levels of humidity. By putting these pieces together in the right way, Arrhenius could build a computational model of the Earth's energy balance.

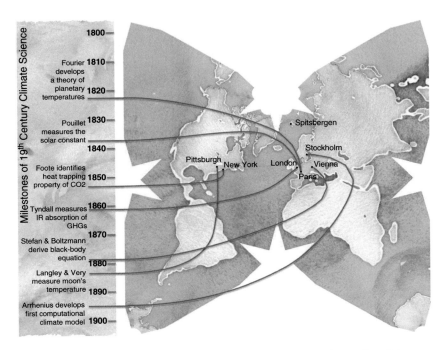

Figure 2.8 Timeline of key milestones in nineteenth-century understanding of the greenhouse effect. (Watercolour map by Stamen Design)

Putting the Model Together

In essence, a model is just a set of equations that capture the relationships described in a scientific theory. Running a model means putting some observational data into these equations, to calculate other values that cannot be observed directly.

The starting point for Arrhenius's model was an equation that captures the key idea in Fourier's theory: for the average temperature of the planet to be stable over the years, the incoming energy from the sun must equal the outgoing energy lost at the top of the atmosphere. Temperatures do rise and fall across the planet, because different regions receive more or less sunlight at different times of the year, and the winds and ocean currents move the heat around. But overall, these exchanges of heat balance out, so that, at least during the nineteenth century, no part of the planet was experiencing a year-on-year warming or cooling trend. The planet was in *radiative balance*.

The equation needed to express this was first worked out in 1879 by the Austrian physicist Jožef Stefan, who discovered the relationship between the temperature of an object and the energy it radiates.[21] Stefan found that the rate at which an object radiates heat is proportional to its temperature (in Kelvin) raised to the power of four.[22] The fact that there's a power of four in the equation means the rate at which energy is radiated grows very rapidly with small increases in temperature. For example, if you put a pan on the stove and turn on the heat, the temperature of the pan rises, but as it does, the amount of heat it radiates rises even faster. The pan heats up only until it is losing energy as fast as it is receiving it from the stove: it finds a new equilibrium.

Stefan's equation describes an "ideal" object, one that absorbs perfectly all the radiative heat it receives, and radiates heat out again with no impediment. Such an object reflects no light, so would appear completely black – in thermodynamics, it's called a *blackbody*. But most objects don't absorb and emit radiative heat perfectly – an object with a paler surface will reflect some heat, rather than absorbing it. Shiny surfaces do this well: they reflect incoming heat and light away from the object (which is why they look shiny), and, perhaps less obviously, they reflect internal heat back towards the inside, which means they cool down more slowly. So shiny materials make good coat linings and emergency survival blankets. Stefan's student, Ludwig Boltzmann, found the original equation still works for such objects (known as "grey bodies") if you adjust[23] for the fraction of incoming rays that are reflected rather than absorbed. For a planet, the percentage of sunlight reflected back to space is called the *albedo*. The Earth currently reflects around 30% to 35% of the incoming sunlight, due to all the white snow and clouds. For other things, including gases, it's more usual to talk about what fraction of heat they absorb, which is the inverse of albedo – it's the fraction of rays (at each wavelength) that will pass into them. Arrhenius called this their *absorption coefficient*. Today we call it *emissivity* – because any insulating effect that hampers how an object absorbs heat also hampers the heat being emitted again.

With the surface and the atmosphere acting as grey bodies, it's possible to write equations for the flows of energy between them. The key insight is the energy balance at the top of the atmosphere – as shown in the schematic of the model in Figure 2.9. If the climate doesn't change from one year to the next, then the total input of energy from the sun – over the course of a year – must be the same as the total output of energy lost to space. Inputs and outputs must balance.[24] The Stefan–Boltzmann equation then allows you to work out what temperature the ground and atmosphere must to be to make all these energy flows balance.

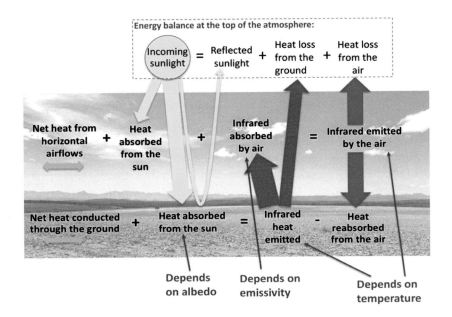

Figure 2.9 Schematic of Arrhenius's model, for a patch of the Earth's surface and the column of air above it. All energy flows are in "watts per square meter" of ground surface. The diagram shows heat received from neighbouring columns in green, incoming (shortwave) sunlight in yellow, infra-red emitted by the ground in red, and infra-red emitted by atmosphere in blue. The three equations express that in-flows and out-flows in each part of the system must balance. The detailed equations appear in Arrhenius (1896).

The model has the sun as the main source of heat. Some of the sun's heat warms the air, and some warms the Earth's surface. Of the sunlight that reaches the surface, some is absorbed, and some reflected directly back out to space. The latter depends on the Earth's albedo, which varies across the planet. Arrhenius spent considerable effort coming up with estimates for the albedo of different types of surface: fresh snow, old snow (which is darker because it gets dirty), ocean, vegetation, and soils. His estimates were remarkably close to modern measurements. Because some parts of the surface are obscured by clouds, which reflect sunlight directly back into space, Arrhenius estimated the "average cloudiness" of the sky, and adjusted his albedo values to account for this too.

The complication is that different locations on the planet receive different amounts of sunlight. Surface temperature, albedo, and humidity all vary by location too. So the energy balance will be different at each location. To

The Arrhenius Model Grid

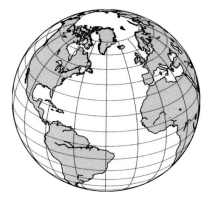

Figure 2.10 The grid used in Arrhenius's model. The grid has 13 bands of latitude from 60° South to 70° North, each divided into 18 cells around the planet
(covering 20° of longitude each). This grid covers nearly all the major landmasses
except Antarctica and Northern Greenland, as reliable weather data for the polar
regions wasn't available in the nineteenth century. This 13 × 18 grid has 234 cells.

address this, Arrhenius divided up the surface of the planet into a regular grid,
with grid cells each spanning 10° of latitude and 20° of longitude (see Figure
2.10) – but omitting the polar regions, where very little data had been collected. He could then apply the energy balance equation to each grid cell.

This choice of grid was convenient because it was also used in published
weather maps[25] compiled by the Scottish meteorologist Alexander Buchan,
who had calculated the average temperature for each grid cell, for each month
of the year. Arrhenius converted these to seasonal averages, to reduce the
amount of data he had to deal with, but without losing the ability to study
whether seasonal changes mattered. This gave him four seasonal temperature
values for each of the 234 grid squares – a total of 936 data points. He then did
the same for humidity data.[26]

Like modern climate models, Arrhenius's model is built from the laws of
physics. However, it's much simpler than modern models: it treats the vertical
column of air in each grid cell as though it were a single unit, with a single
average temperature. In reality the higher you go, the colder the air gets. To
check how much this simplification mattered, Arrhenius tested a calculation
for a two-layer version of his model, with a lower warmer layer of air that
exchanges heat with the surface, and a higher, cooler layer that loses heat to
space. He concluded the results were similar enough that he could just work
with a one-layer version to cut down the number of calculations. Nowadays,

we have supercomputers to do the work, so modern climate models use much smaller grid cells, and divide the air into dozens of different layers to calculate the exchange of heat between each layer and those above and below it.

Despite all the data Arrhenius had collected from existing weather maps, there were still many unknowns. These include, for each grid cell, heat received from the sun, the fraction absorbed directly by the air, and horizontal heat exchanges with neighbouring grid cells. To simplify things, Arrhenius assumed none of these values would change when you vary the amount of greenhouse gases, so he could treat them as constants in each grid cell, for each season. Today, we would call these *model parameters* – values that cannot be calculated, so must be estimated from observational data. Obtaining accurate measurement for parameters like these is still tricky in today's models. For Arrhenius it was impossible. Instead, he re-arranged the equations to collect all of these unknown values together as a single (unknown) parameter, which he called K.

This new form of the equation could calculate surface temperature for any location on the planet, as long as you had the local values for surface albedo, the atmospheric emissivity, and the parameter K.[27] In Arrhenius's experiments, emissivity would be the main input to the model. To test the effect of different concentrations of the two main greenhouse gases, you would select the relevant values from his tables of absorption coefficients to provide this input.

The unknown constant parameter K in Arrhenius's equation is different for each location, and each season, because it depends on the amount of sunlight received (which is larger closer to the equator, and closer to summer), and the amount of heat exchanged horizontally (which depends on prevailing winds and ocean currents). However, Arrhenius realized he could calibrate the model to find each value for K by running his model "backwards" – given he knew the average surface temperature for each location at each time of year. He could then run the model "forwards" to calculate how the temperature would change with different levels of CO_2.

Using the Model

The key equation in Arrhenius's model calculates how the surface temperature (at a particular location and a particular time of year) will change if the levels of water vapour and carbon dioxide in the atmosphere change. Because his original question was about the cause of the ice ages, Arrhenius was mainly interested in what happens if there is less of these greenhouse gases. But the model works just as well for increases.

Of the two gases, water vapour is by far the more abundant in the atmosphere. On average, about 4% of the atmosphere is water, while carbon dioxide is around 0.04%.[28] So there are roughly a hundred times more H_2O molecules in the atmosphere than there are CO_2 molecules. So why did Arrhenius focus on carbon dioxide rather than water vapour? Why, for that matter, do modern climate scientists also focus on carbon dioxide?

The answer is that natural cycles of evaporation and precipitation tend to stabilize the amount of water vapour in the atmosphere, so that the average amount only varies when the air temperature changes – hotter air can hold more moisture. In contrast, the amount of carbon dioxide in the atmosphere can vary almost without limit. So the atmosphere can retain large changes in the amount of CO_2 over long time periods, but not large swings in the amount of water.

In fact, any given molecule of CO_2 might only stay in the atmosphere for a few years, as CO_2 is regularly absorbed by plants and soils, and some of it dissolves in the surface waters of the ocean.[29] But plants and soils also emit CO_2 as they decompose over the winter. And the ocean re-emits CO_2, especially when it warms up. So, over a period of a few years, any additional CO_2 gets shared out, with plants, soils, oceans, and atmosphere each taking a share. The atmosphere's share is, roughly speaking, about half of any new CO_2 produced, for example from burning coal and oil. Högbom's other carbon sinks all operate much more slowly – on a geological timescale – taking thousands of years to absorb CO_2 from the atmosphere.

Thinking this through led to one of Arrhenius's most important insights: changes in water vapour don't *cause* climate change, but are a *result* of it. In other words, water vapour forms a feedback loop. If something else warms the atmosphere, the air will hold more water vapour, which will then produce more warming. Similarly, if something else causes cooling, the resulting loss of water vapour will accelerate that cooling. This water vapour feedback loop would amplify any change in global temperature. This insight was both exciting and frustrating. Exciting, because it helped his hypothesis about carbon dioxide causing the ice ages – a smaller change in carbon dioxide would be amplified by the water vapour feedback to cause a bigger change in temperature. But frustrating, because it would complicate the model.

Arrhenius handled this feedback loop by applying the model in two steps. First he "ran" the model once, to calculate the temperature change from a decrease (or increase) in carbon dioxide, with no change in water vapour. Then, for each output, he calculated how this temperature change would affect water vapour, assuming no change in *relative humidity* – the fraction of moisture the air actually holds, compared to how much it could hold. This assumption isn't perfect, but is close enough to give reasonable results. Then he "ran" the model again to calculate how much more the temperature would change in response to this increased water vapour.

To do this for his entire grid would require 936 calculations at each step: 2,808 calculations in all – and when repeated for each season that would mean 11,232 calculations! All of these would have to be done by hand, so Arrhenius saved himself a lot of effort by first calculating an average seasonal temperature for each latitude band, leaving him with 624 calculations for each "run" of the model. Today, we would call this a one-dimensional model, where the dimension is latitude – a full three-dimensional model would include longitude and height in the atmosphere too.

Water vapour feedback is not the only feedback loop in the global climate system, and understanding these feedbacks is important for developing good models. Arrhenius was aware of some of them, but could not include them without making the calculations unmanageable. Instead, he dealt with them by reasoning about how they might affect the model results. For example, snow and ice create a feedback loop, because they alter the surface albedo. A little warming would melt some of the ice and snow, replacing it with darker ocean or soil, which absorbs more heat. This amplifies the warming. Similarly, a little cooling allows ice and snow areas to expand, raising the albedo to reflect more heat directly back to space, and hence amplifying the cooling. This ice-albedo feedback is strongest at the edges of existing ice fields, so Arrhenius reasoned the temperature changes would be bigger in the polar regions if he had included this effect.

Today's models incorporate more of these feedback effects, but modellers still have to make similar trade-offs between computability and completeness. Expert judgment is needed to identify feedbacks that might matter, and to decide whether they can be included in the model. This also illustrates another feature of both Arrhenius's work and today's models: the output of a computer model has to be interpreted very carefully, based on an understanding of what the model includes and what it leaves out.

The Results

Arrhenius laid out his results in a table (shown in Figure 2.11), giving the computed temperature change for each latitude, for each season of the year, under various scenarios for decreased or increased carbon dioxide. The rows correspond to the 10° latitude bands. The five main columns show scenarios for five different levels of CO_2: reduced by one third (0.67), and increased to 1.5, 2, 2.5, and 3 times the current level. Within each major column is a

TABLE VII.—*Variation of Temperature caused by a given Variation of Carbonic Acid.*

Latitude	Carbonic Acid=0·67.					Carbonic Acid=1·5.					Carbonic Acid=2·0.					Carbonic Acid=2·5.					Carbonic Acid=3·0.				
	Dec.–Feb.	March–May.	June–Aug.	Sept.–Nov.	Mean of the year.	Dec.–Feb.	March–May.	June–Aug.	Sept.–Nov.	Mean of the year.	Dec.–Feb.	March–May.	June–Aug.	Sept.–Nov.	Mean of the year.	Dec.–Feb.	March–May.	June–Aug.	Sept.–Nov.	Mean of the year.	Dec.–Feb.	March–May.	June–Aug.	Sept.–Nov.	Mean of the year.
70	-2·9	-3·0	-3·4	-3·1	-3·1	3·3	3·4	3·8	3·6	3·52	6·0	6·1	6·0	6·1	6·05	7·9	8·0	7·9	8·0	7·95	9·1	9·3	9·4	9·4	9·3
60	-3·0	-3·2	-3·4	-3·3	-3·22	3·4	3·7	3·6	3·8	3·62	6·1	6·1	5·8	6·1	6·02	8·0	8·0	7·6	7·9	7·87	9·3	9·5	8·9	9·5	9·3
50	-3·2	-3·3	-3·3	-3·4	-3·3	3·7	3·8	3·4	3·7	3·65	6·1	6·1	5·5	6·0	5·92	8·0	7·9	7·0	7·9	7·7	9·5	9·4	8·6	9·2	9·17
40	-3·4	-3·4	-3·2	-3·3	-3·32	3·7	3·6	3·3	3·5	3·52	6·0	5·8	5·4	5·6	5·7	7·9	7·6	6·9	7·3	7·42	9·3	9·0	8·2	8·8	8·82
30	-3·3	-3·2	-3·1	-3·1	-3·17	3·5	3·3	3·2	3·5	3·47	5·6	5·4	5·0	5·2	5·3	7·2	7·0	6·6	6·7	6·87	8·7	8·3	7·5	7·9	8·1
20	-3·1	-3·1	-3·0	-3·1	-3·07	3·5	3·2	3·1	3·2	3·25	5·2	5·0	4·9	5·0	5·02	6·7	6·6	6·3	6·6	6·52	7·9	7·5	7·2	7·5	7·52
10	-3·1	-3·0	-3·0	-3·0	-3·02	3·2	3·2	3·1	3·1	3·15	5·0	5·0	4·9	4·9	4·95	6·6	6·4	6·3	6·4	6·42	7·4	7·3	7·2	7·3	7·3
0	-3·0	-3·0	-3·1	-3·0	-3·02	3·1	3·1	3·2	3·2	3·15	4·9	4·9	5·0	5·0	4·95	6·4	6·4	6·6	6·6	6·5	7·3	7·3	7·4	7·4	7·35
-10	-3·1	-3·1	-3·2	-3·1	-3·12	3·2	3·2	3·2	3·2	3·2	5·0	5·0	5·2	5·1	5·07	6·6	6·6	6·7	6·7	6·65	7·4	7·5	8·0	7·6	7·62
-20	-3·1	-3·2	-3·3	-3·2	-3·2	3·2	3·2	3·4	3·3	3·27	5·2	5·3	5·5	5·4	5·35	6·7	6·8	7·0	7·0	6·87	7·9	8·1	8·6	8·3	8·22
-30	-3·3	-3·3	-3·4	-3·4	-3·35	3·4	3·5	3·7	3·5	3·52	5·5	5·6	5·8	5·6	5·62	7·0	7·2	7·7	7·4	7·32	8·6	8·7	9·1	8·8	8·8
-40	-3·4	-3·4	-3·3	-3·4	-3·37	3·6	3·7	3·8	3·7	3·7	5·8	6·0	6·0	6·0	5·95	7·7	7·9	7·9	7·9	7·86	9·1	9·2	9·4	9·3	9·25
-50	-3·2	-3·3	—	—	—	3·8	3·7	—	—	—	6·0	6·1	—	—	—	7·9	8·0	—	—	—	9·4	9·5	—	—	—
-60	—	—	—	—	—	—	—	—	—	—	—	—	—	—	—	—	—	—	—	—	—	—	—	—	—

Figure 2.11 Raw results from Arrhenius's model, showing expected temperature change in degrees centigrade, for each latitude (the rows), and each season, for a range of scenarios from reducing CO_2 ("carbonic acid") by a third, up to increasing it by a factor of three. (Reproduced from Arrhenius (1896))

sub-column for each season, followed by an annual average. The numbers represent changes in surface temperature, in degrees centigrade.

Despite the many simplifications, developing and using the model was hard work. The data he had gathered for his grid consisted of more than 3,000 data points, and the five scenarios shown in Figure 2.11 required 3,120 separate calculations. The work took Arrhenius over a year, from December 1894 to January 1896. In his letters at the time he commented on how tedious the work was, but also expressed his determination to complete it, so he could answer his original question about the ice ages.

The table suggests that changing levels of carbon dioxide could indeed cause the kinds of temperature swing Arrhenius had hypothesized. He also realized the relationship between CO_2 levels and temperature isn't linear – you get about the same rise (or fall) in temperature for each doubling (or halving) of carbon dioxide, which is why today we use doubling of CO_2 – the Charney sensitivity – as a benchmark for comparing models.

Arrhenius's model also predicts that the effect would be different in different parts of the world. The temperature changes are larger over land than over the ocean, and larger in the northern hemisphere than the southern – because the southern hemisphere has a lot more ocean. The model predicts larger temperature changes wherever and whenever it is currently coolest: towards the poles, and during the winters. Arrhenius also predicted larger changes for nighttime temperatures than daytime, although this isn't shown in the table – Arrhenius did a separate "run" of the model for day versus night.

These effects all arise directly from the basic physics represented in the model. Greenhouse gases work by trapping outgoing heat. Therefore they have the biggest impact when there is more heat leaving the Earth's surface than arriving: after the heat of the day; after the summer has ended; and on the parts of the planet that receive less sunlight anyway. Arrhenius summarized his results: "If carbonic acid content rises, temperature differences between land and sea, between summer and winter, between night and day, and between equator and temperate zones will be levelled out, at least for habitable parts of the Earth's surface. The reverse will be true if the carbonic acid content diminishes."[30] This is quite a remarkable set of predictions, as none of these effects had been worked out before Arrhenius built his model. And every one of them turned out to be correct.

But what of the question that drove him to develop the model in the first place: could carbon dioxide be responsible for the ice ages? The results suggest that CO_2 would need to drop to nearly half its late nineteenth-century level to produce the global cooling of about 5°C that occurred during the last ice age.[31] Arrhenius took this as a very encouraging result, as there is no physical reason why it couldn't have happened, given Högbom's analysis of carbon flows into and out of the atmosphere. However, the model only says what would have happened *if* carbon dioxide levels fell this much; it doesn't help answer *why* they would fall in the first place.

What about the scenarios for increased CO_2? It seems odd that he would have included results for doubled and trebled CO_2, given his primary interest was in explaining the ice ages. But Högbom had pointed out the amount of carbon in the atmosphere is insignificantly tiny compared to the vast stocks tied up in limestone rocks. The idea that geological processes might, over time, release these to the atmosphere was certainly worth exploring.

And Arrhenius lived during the age of steam. There were no cars and no planes; the dominant modes of transport, other than the horse, were steam trains and steam ships. Coal was the magic fuel that powered the industrial revolution, and the effects of coal smoke in cities across Europe was easy to see: smog swirled around the cities, and bigger cities such as London were known for their intense fogs, known as "pea-soupers," in the second half of the nineteenth century. Högbom had included burning of coal as a source of atmospheric carbon dioxide, so it made sense for Arrhenius to explore where this might lead. He took Högbom's measures of carbon emissions from coal burning, and projected them into the future. At the time, the best estimate was that each year about 0.7 giga-tonnes of carbon were being released globally from coal use – about 1/900th of the total amount already in the atmosphere. As a chemist, Arrhenius also knew that increased levels of CO_2 in the atmosphere would increase the rate at which it dissolves in seawater. He calculated that about five sixths of these emissions from coal would eventually be absorbed by the oceans. That left an annual increase of CO_2 in the atmosphere that would, at the time, be too small to measure.[32]

Using these numbers, he calculated it would take 54 years to increase atmospheric CO_2 by 1%, and about 3,000 years to increase CO_2 levels by 50%, for which his model indicated global temperatures would rise by about 3.4°C. His reaction to this might resonate today with anyone who lives in a cold climate: "we would have some right to indulge in the pleasant belief that our descendants, albeit after many generations, might live under a milder sky and in less barren natural surroundings than is our lot at present."[33] He had no way to foresee the imminent and dramatic rise in the use of fossil fuels.

A Sceptical Audience

Unfortunately, Arrhenius's work was largely ignored by other scientists at the time. His closest colleagues were full of admiration: Högbom and Ekholm, whose work had inspired Arrhenius to set off on this path in the first place, were delighted with his model. But others in the Stockholm Society were not so impressed. Nobody attempted to replicate his calculations, as the effort would have been too great, and the results didn't seem plausible enough to warrant it. While the idea that water vapour and carbon dioxide play an important role in keeping the Earth warm was widely accepted, the notion that changes in these gases might explain the ice ages was dismissed as ridiculous. Besides, another theory about the ice ages was rapidly gaining ground: regular changes in the Earth's orbit appeared to be the best explanation.

Perhaps the biggest reason that few people took the work seriously was a devastating critique by another Swedish scientist, Knut Ångström. Ångström's father, Anders, was renowned for his work developing the science of spectroscopy. Knut was following in his father's footsteps. He had held a lectureship in physics at the Stockholm Högskola before Arrhenius, and was now a professor at the University of Uppsala, 70 km north of Stockholm, where he was working on making precise measurements of the sun's energy. By comparison, Arrhenius was the newcomer, seen to meddle in fields in which he hadn't been trained.

Ångström argued there were two key problems with Arrhenius's model. First, Langley's data wasn't reliable enough, and indeed, Langley himself had warned his spectroscopic analysis of the moon's heat wasn't to be trusted. But it didn't matter anyway, argued Ångström, because of another problem. Tyndall's experiments had showed when he kept adding more CO_2 in his tube, eventually there is no more change in how much energy it absorbs. At very high concentrations, all of the rays in a gas's absorption bands have been blocked, and rays of other wavelengths pass through unaffected. Today, we call this *saturation*.

To prove the point, Ångström asked his assistant to conduct a simple experiment, similar to Tyndall's, with a short tube containing enough CO_2 to represent the amount the Earth's rays would pass through in full height of the atmosphere. When one third of the gas was pumped out, there was virtually no difference in absorption of infra-red. It seemed that all the infra-red that could be absorbed was already being absorbed. The implication was clear: Arrhenius's model must be wrong. A review of Ångström's critique[34] appeared in the widely read Monthly Weather Review in 1901, and to most scientists, the matter was settled.

We now know Ångström's argument is wrong – for subtle reasons, as we will see shortly – but it seemed compelling at the time. We're used to the idea that climate is a stable thing: Stockholm winters are very cold and always have been. North Africa is hot and dry, and stays that way. Somehow or other, these patterns persist. So presumably, it would require something extraordinary to shift them – and shifts in the concentration of an invisible gas seemed an unlikely candidate. So Ångström's simple experiment was far more believable than Arrhenius's complicated model.

Arrhenius continued to give talks about this work even after the turn of the century, and he later published some revised estimates of the temperature change. But the lack of interest from others led him to turn to other problems. He went on to do pioneering work in how toxins work in the human body, and his work on climate change remained almost entirely forgotten for half a century.

Orbital Variations

Meanwhile, new evidence was emerging in favour of the hypothesis that the ice ages were caused by changes in the Earth's orbit. In the 1920s, the Serbian scientist Milutin Milankovic developed a mathematical model of the relationship between the Earth's climate and small variations in its orbit.[35] Milankovic's model included three different kinds of shift in the Earth's orbit. First, the shape of the Earth's orbit varies on roughly a 400,000-year cycle, from nearly circular to somewhat egg-shaped. This variation is caused by gravitational pull from other planets, and is known as *eccentricity*. It mainly affects the relative lengths of the seasons. Second, like a spinning top, the Earth's rotational axis wobbles, changing its tilt by about 2.4° over a 41,000-year cycle. This is known as *obliquity*, and it affects the intensity of summers and winters, especially towards the poles. Cooler summers at the poles mean that less of the winter ice melts, allowing ice sheets to grow over the long term. Finally, the direction of the Earth's tilt changes, on roughly a 26,000-year cycle, so that the seasons – which occur when one or other pole is turned towards the sun – occur at different times in the annual orbit around the sun. This is known as *precession*, and it affects the intensity of the winters and summers, because it changes, for example, whether the northern hemisphere summer occurs at the point in the orbit when the sun is closer or further away.

By putting all these cycles together, Milankovic hypothesized a correlation with the cycles of ice ages and inter-glacial periods. Each of Milankovic's three cycles causes small changes in the amount of sunlight the Earth receives at the poles, and hence affects whether ice builds up or melts, over periods of tens of thousands of years. When the cycles coincide, it can trigger an ice age. The argument was good enough that for most of the twentieth century, the mystery was considered solved. Not only that, these cycles were completely predictable using a fairly simple mathematical model. It removed all the uncertainty: another ice age would be inevitable, but not for another 50,000 years. There was obviously no point worrying about it.

There were, however, problems with Milankovic's theory, and by the end of the twentieth century it was clear that there must be more to the story. While the cycles help explain the timing of the ice ages, they don't really explain the large global temperature changes. Milankovic cycles have an impact that is mostly regional and seasonal. Around the Arctic and Antarctic circles, they change the amount of sunlight received in the summers. But over the course of the entire year these changes balance out, and for the planet as a whole, the amount of energy from the sun remains more or less unchanged. The mystery deepened when, in 1998, scientists managed to drill more than 3 km down into the glaciers of Vostok in Antarctica, to extract a column of ice, which, like layers of rock studied by geologists, captured a slice through the pre-historical record. The layers of ice went back as far as 400,000 years, spanning the last four ice ages.[36] Bubbles trapped in the ice offered evidence of what the air was like over this period. And sure enough the levels of CO_2 in the bubbles went up and down in perfect harmony with the cycle of the ice ages. During the last ice age, these ice cores showed that the level of CO_2 fell to around 180 to 190 ppm,[37] almost exactly the level that Arrhenius's model had predicted. Arrhenius's theory was correct after all.

Was Arrhenius's Model Correct?

We can directly compare Arrhenius's results with today's models, because he gives a value of 5.7°C for a doubling of CO_2 – the standard Charney sensitivity metric we met in Chapter 1. The Charney report, comparing 1970s models, gave a range of 1.5°C to 4.5°C. The Intergovernmental Panel on Climate Change (IPCC), which regularly assesses modern climate models, reports the latest generation of global climate models give a range of 2.5°C to 4.0°C.[38] So Arrhenius's result is higher than modern models, but is remarkably close, given the large number of simplifications he made in his model, and the fact that he did all the calculations by hand.

That doesn't necessarily mean the model is good – it's possible to get the right result for the wrong reasons. Also, agreement with other models isn't the only way to judge the quality of a computer model. An accurate model that tells us nothing new would not be very useful. Does the model offer a promising new approach to a problem? Does the model surprise us in any way, and if so, do those surprises lead to new hypotheses about the world? Does the model provide predictions that turn out to be correct? Arrhenius's model does well on all of these questions.

Even just completing these calculations and getting a set of results that are physically plausible and internally consistent is a remarkable achievement, given the available technology at the time. Very few programmers today can code up a set of calculations this complex and get the program working right on the first run. Yet Arrhenius didn't have the luxury of running the entire model and then fixing up the algorithms: if he made mistakes early in the process and didn't immediately spot them and fix them, the entire year's work would have been wasted.

He also lacked an important ingredient that today's computational scientists tend to take for granted: a community of other scientists around the world, each developing similar models, who can check the results of each other's work. It would take another 60 years, until the invention of the electronic computer, before anyone would attempt to build a comparable model. And when they did, almost immediately, they realized Arrhenius had most of the science correct.[39]

A computer model is not just a calculation engine. It's also a conceptual structure – a way of thinking about a problem that brings together existing theories and data, usually from other scientists, and connects them in a new way. But to make a computer model work, every detail has to be worked out, and that demands a new level of rigour. The conceptual structure is sometimes the most important scientific contribution of a computer model, because it offers an explicit step-by-step way to analyze a problem that avoid errors in earlier approaches.

This was certainly true of Arrhenius's model. The rigour of his analysis led Arrhenius to discover serious flaws in previous attempts to calculate the Earth's energy balance. And perhaps the single most important contribution in his model is the idea that the incoming and outgoing heat to the Earth must balance at the top of the atmosphere, rather than at the ground level. It wasn't until the satellite era, when we were able to look down at the atmosphere instead of up from the ground that the significance of this really became clear.

It turns out the greenhouse effect isn't as simple as most scientists thought. The determining factor isn't the saturation effect that Ångström had attempted to test. In fact, some wavelengths of infra-red from the surface are indeed entirely absorbed within the first 30 metres of air above the ground, just as Ångström had argued. But this is looking at the problem upside down. The issue isn't what happens at ground level, it's what happens in the upper atmosphere, where the air gets thin, and the concentrations of greenhouse gases are low enough that infra-red radiation can finally escape into space. Adding more greenhouse gases in the upper atmosphere will cause warming, no matter what is happening at ground level.[40]

The greenhouse gases in the layer of air just above the ground absorb some of the infra-red energy emitted from the ground. But anything that's good at absorbing infra-red is equally good at radiating it, so these gas molecules then radiate infra-red energy again, both upwards and downwards. And that energy is absorbed and re-emitted by each layer of air in the atmosphere. In the layer of the stratosphere where greenhouse gases are finally thin enough for these rays to escape to space, the air is very dry, so carbon dioxide is the dominant greenhouse gas. Adding more CO_2 makes it harder for heat to escape from this layer, and the height from which the heat eventually escapes is pushed upwards. Pushing the "heat loss" layer upwards means the Earth loses heat more slowly.[41]

Arrhenius's papers show he understood this. He didn't use a multi-layer atmosphere directly in his model, as it would have taken too long to do the calculations, but he did experiment with a two-layer version, to explore how much this simplification would matter. Unfortunately, few other scientists at the time understood this point, and it wasn't until the 1960s, with the benefit of new computer models, that scientists finally realized why the interaction between different layers of atmosphere is important.

So Ångström was wrong and Arrhenius was right: Ångström's experiment was based on a misunderstanding of how the greenhouse effect works in the real atmosphere. Unfortunately, Ångström's misunderstanding is widespread, and some people today still use his argument to try and "disprove" climate change.

How Accurate Was Arrhenius's Model?

Arrhenius's input data contained many inaccuracies, but most didn't matter at all. For example, the weather data he used didn't have to be accurate, because the model computes temperature *change*, not the weather that would result from this. You could re-run the model with different starting temperatures, and get approximately the same results.[42] This is also true of today's climate models.

Most of the simplifications he used reduce the precision of the model, but don't change the overall results. For example, he treated the horizontal movement of heat from winds and ocean currents as constants in his model. Today's models simulate these heat exchanges explicitly, because they affect how heat is transported around the planet, and therefore how different climates respond to changing levels of greenhouse gases. He also treated cloudiness as a constant factor, even though he acknowledged that global climate change would almost certainly affect clouds. As we saw in Chapter 1, clouds remain the biggest source of uncertainty even in today's models, because the computational power needed to simulate cloud-climate interactions is still beyond today's fastest supercomputers.

However, his model did have two huge weaknesses – inaccuracies in Langley and Very's absorption data,[43] and the simplification of treating the atmosphere as a single layer. Purely by luck, these weaknesses roughly cancel each other out. As a summer research project a few years ago, two of my students, Samantha Fassnacht and Alexander Hurka, re-built Arrhenius's model in a modern programming language. Using his original data, our model produces the same results as Arrhenius did. But when we used modern data for infra-red absorption, the model only gave very small temperature changes – around $0.1\,^{\circ}C$ for a doubling of CO_2. A single layer atmosphere model cannot capture the full extent of the greenhouse effect. We then created a multi-layer version, with 17 layers of atmosphere, and the model showed more warming – around $1\,^{\circ}C$ per doubling of CO_2. This is still lower than it should be. To model the greenhouse effect properly, you have to include the full vertical structure of the atmosphere, including vertical heat exchanges by convection. Nobody attempted this until the work of another Nobel Prize winning scientist, Sykuro Manabe, in the 1960s. We'll explore his work in Chapter 6.

Despite these serious weaknesses, virtually all the predictions from Arrhenius's model have turned out to be correct. As the climate has warmed over the last few decades, we have seen night time temperatures rise faster than daytime, temperatures over land rise faster than over the oceans, and the polar regions warm about twice as fast as the rest of the planet. Although Arrhenius couldn't include the ice albedo effect in the model, his hypothesis about this was also correct – it provides a further boost to the warming in the polar regions. Arrhenius got these predictions correct, even with inaccurate data and a grossly simplified model, because his intuitions were correct, and he got the basic physics right.

Even more surprising is that by the end of the twentieth century, it was clear Arrhenius was right about the ice ages after all. We now know that the cooling experienced during the ice ages can only be explained through a combination of both the Milankovic cycles *and* a dramatic reduction in CO_2 levels. The orbital changes mapped out by Milankovic trigger local changes in formation of ice in the polar regions. But then CO_2 becomes a feedback. As the ice sheets grow, carbon dioxide gets trapped in frozen vegetation and soil under the ice, preventing it from re-entering the atmosphere, and hence triggering a further cooling effect. Similarly, at the end of an ice age, the orbital changes trigger a local thaw in the polar regions, which unlocks these stores of CO_2, returning it to the atmosphere to cause a much larger warming. Most of the global temperature change over this cycle is due to CO_2, just as Arrhenius's model showed.

While Arrhenius's predictions all turned out to be correct, he couldn't have anticipated how quickly we would see them play out.[44] His calculations suggested it would take more than 50 years for CO_2 levels to rise by 1%. But in those 50 years, while Arrhenius's model remained largely forgotten, the world saw dramatic technological advances: from the invention of the internal combustion engine to dominance of cars and trucks for transport; from the invention of flight to the existence of commercial airlines; from experiments in electricity transmission to nationwide power grids driven by coal-fired power stations; and from stone and brick buildings to poured concrete. As a result, by 1950, CO_2 levels had risen not by 1% but by 10%, and by the end of the twentieth century, they had risen by more than 30%.

The warming Arrhenius thought would take thousands of years is now happening in decades, and far from being benign, the rapid changes are likely to make life dramatically harder for much of the world's population. We often suffer from a failure of imagination on this. But think about it this way – if a cooling of −5°C is the difference between today's climate and an ice age, then a warming of +5°C is likely to be as different again – a planet we would barely recognize.

Notes

1 See Högbom (1894).
2 See Crawford (1996) for detail on his life, and on the meetings of the Stockholm Physics Society.
3 See Archer and Pierrehumbert (2011) for a detailed commentary on the significance of Fourier's insights to climate science.
4 Absolute zero means zero on the Kelvin scale, which is about −273°C. This is as cold as anything can ever get – the point when molecules have no more energy.
5 Some night vision goggles work by shifting the infra-red light into the visible spectrum, so you can see the heat from warm objects like people and animals.
6 See Pierrehumbert (2004). The atmosphere does scatter some of the incoming sunlight, mostly at the blue end of the spectrum, which is why the sky appears blue during the day. Also, the Earth's ozone layer blocks a lot of the ultraviolet portion of the sun's rays.
7 While Fourier did mention the sun heating enclosed spaces such as greenhouses ("Les Serres") in his classic book (Fourier, 1827), he never used the term when talking about the atmosphere (see Fleming, 1999). Arrhenius used the Swedish word drivbänk, which usually translates as hotbed. Ekholm appears to be the first to use the English word "greenhouse" to describe the effect, in his 1901 paper (Ekholm, 1901), and the term "Greenhouse Effect" was introduced by John Henry Poynting (Poynting, 1907).

8   See Ortiz and Jackson (2022) for a detailed account.

9   Foote (1856).

10 It's not clear whether Tyndall was aware of Foote's research. If he was, he never cited it. Arrhenius gives Tyndall the credit for discovering the properties of these "heat trapping gases."

11 More specifically, it depends on imbalances in the number of electrons either side of the atomic bond. The electromagnetic waves vibrate the electrons on either side of the bond, causing them to bounce around like balls on a spring.

12 Even more complex molecules, such as the man-made chlorofluorocarbons (CFCs), are tens of thousands of times more powerful as greenhouse gases than carbon dioxide. These gases do not occur naturally in the atmosphere, and were entirely due to industrial production for refrigerants, household spray cans, and to make bubbles in foam.

13 It's hard to completely distinguish the effects of H_2O and CO_2, because their absorption bands overlap, but roughly speaking, H_2O is responsible for 2–3 times as much of the total greenhouse effect as CO_2. See Schmidt (2005).

14 During the day, surface temperatures are determined mainly by the amount of sun received. But at night, the temperature is determined by how quickly the heat of the day can escape. Dryer regions have less water vapour to trap the heat in the lower atmosphere.

15 Tyndall (1861, p. 29).

16 He'd forgotten to take into account that some of the rays are scattered rather than absorbed. See Dufresne (2008).

17 See Feldman et al. (2015).

18 Langley used a salt prism for the same reason that Tyndall had used salt: it is transparent to infra-red, while glass is not. His instrument made 21 readings across the spectrum from the prism, separated by deflection angles of only one quarter of a degree. This covers only a part of the infra-red spectrum, wavelengths from around 1 μm to 30 μm. This range covers most of the heat given off by anything that's warm but not glowing hot, including cows and moons.

19 There is, unfortunately, no evidence that Langley's bolometer inspired Pink Floyd to put a prism on the album cover of Dark Side of the Moon. However the inclusion of an infra-red photo of the pyramids inside the sleeve notes should give conspiracy theorists something to work with.

20 Arrhenius also tested his result against similar, but less detailed measures of infra-red absorption calculated by other scientists, such as Ångström and Paschen, and again found a good agreement.

21 Here we're only talking about heat exchange by radiation. Heat can also move around by conduction and convection. But neither of these can occur in a vacuum, so at the top of the atmosphere, the only incoming and outgoing heat is via radiation.

22 The actual equation is $W = \sigma(T^4 - T_c^4)$, where W is the outgoing radiation in watts per square metre of surface from an object at temperature T to its surroundings at the temperature T_c (both in Kelvin), and σ is the Stefan–Boltzmann constant.

23 The modified equation is $W = \alpha\varepsilon\sigma(T^4 - T_c^4)$, where ε is the emissivity of the object, and α is the emissivity of its surroundings. At each wavelength, absorbance is equal to emissivity, as rays of that wavelength are equally good at entering or leaving an object. But an object can have different absorbance/emissivity at different wavelengths, as in the example of gases that are transparent to light, but absorb infra-red.

24 To be clear, it's the annual average of the energy flows for the whole planet that must balance; at the poles the Earth loses more heat than it gains, while the reverse is true at the equator. Just like money flows, if you don't balance the budget each year, you start to accrue a deficit or a surplus. Global warming is due to an unbalanced energy budget, year after year.

25 The temperature maps he used are printed in Tait et al (1889). Unfortunately, there were no corresponding global data for humidity, so Arrhenius calculated how much water vapour there was in each grid cell by plotting a large number of humidity measurements from around the globe onto the charts, and computing their averages.

26 In his longer 1896 paper, written in German and published in the Papers of the Royal Swedish Academy of Sciences, Arrhenius devotes 12 full pages to presenting the gridded data for temperature and absolute and relative humidity.

27 His resulting equation is $T^4 = K / (1 + (1 - a)(1 - e))$, where T is the surface temperature, K is the unknown constant, a is surface albedo, and e is emissivity of the atmosphere. From the Stefan–Boltzmann equation, there should be another variable, the average air temperature, but Arrhenius treated this as irrelevant, and eliminated it from his equation.

28 In Arrhenius's time, CO_2 was about 300 parts per million (ppm), which is around 0.03% of the atmosphere by volume. It's risen by more than one third since then, reaching 420 parts per million in 2022.

29 As we'll see in Chapter 6, the discovery in the 1950s that dissolved CO_2 mainly stays in the upper layers ocean water marked a major step forward in our understanding of climate change. It turns out it takes centuries for carbon dissolved in the surface waters to make its way to the seabed, mainly through shellfish using it to build their shells, which then drop to the ocean floor when they die. Over an even longer time period, this carbon can eventually make its way back into the atmosphere via volcanic eruptions.

30 From a lecture by Arrhenius given on February 3, 1896. Translation by Rohde et al. (1997).

31 In his paper, Arrhenius puts the numbers at 0.5–0.6 of then current levels of CO_2 of 300 ppm. That would mean that, according to the model, concentrations of around 150–180 ppm would be sufficient to explain the drop in global temperatures during an ice age.

32 He figured about 0.055 ppm (parts per million) would be added to the atmosphere per year.

33 Quoted in Rohde et al. (1997).

34 Very (1901).

35 Milankovic started this work just before the First World War, and was in Hungary on his honeymoon when the War broke out. As a Serbian national, he was immediately arrested as a prisoner of War. Luckily, his Austrian colleagues negotiated a release from prison and an office in the Hungarian Academy of Sciences, where he continued his work until the end of the War.

36 See Petit et al. (1997). Ten years later, an even older core was extracted in Antarctica, stretching back nearly 800,000 years (Jouzel et al., 2007).

37 See Monnin et al. (2001).

38 IPCC Sixth Assessment Report, Working Group 1, summary for policymakers, August 2021.

39 See Plass (1956)

40 It also turns out that air pressure matters: when you compress a gas, it broadens the wavelength bands in which the gas will absorb infra-red. This means that air at different pressures across the vertical height of the atmosphere have a different

absorption profile than the gas in the short tube that Ångström's experiment tested. Arrhenius's data from the moon's rays avoided this problem.

41 More precisely: if the layer where heat finally escapes to space is higher, it is also cooler. And cooler air loses heat more slowly than warmer air.

42 The opposite is true for weather forecasting: errors in the initial conditions are the biggest factor in forecast errors.

43 See Archer and Pierrehumbert (2011) for a more detailed analysis of this in their intro to Arrhenius's work. Recent analysis by Dufresne (2009) shows that Langley and Very's data missed an important CO_2 absorption band entirely, around 15 μm.

44 Arrhenius also didn't realise how long the ocean would take to absorb our carbon dioxide emissions. He was correct that eventually the ocean will absorb five sixths of all anthropogenic emissions. But it takes thousands of years to do so, because the surface water of the ocean mixes only very slowly with the deeper ocean.

3

The Forecast Factory

Climate and weather are intimately connected. Weather describes what we experience day-to-day, while climate describes what we expect over the longer term. So it's not surprising the models used to understand weather and climate share much of the same history. While Arrhenius's model ignored weather altogether, focusing instead on the energy balance of the planet, modern climate models grew out of the early work on numerical weather forecasting – the basic equations for how winds and ocean currents move energy around, under the influence of the Earth's rotation and gravity. The equations for these circulation patterns were first worked out by Arrhenius's colleague, Vilhelm Bjerknes, in 1904, but it wasn't until the invention of the electronic computer that John von Neumann put them to work forecasting the weather. The approach developed by von Neumann's group now forms the core of today's weather forecasting models.

The First Electronic Computer

The invention of the electronic programmable computer in the 1940s unleashed a technological revolution that is still unfolding today. It took many decades before computers found their way into our homes, but in some branches of science, the computer revolution was much faster. Meteorology was one of the fastest – the first successful computational weather forecast was made within five years of the invention of electronic computers, and within ten years, the US Weather Bureau was issuing regular weather forecasts from its computer models. These weather forecasting models revolutionized the field of meteorology, and provided the basis for the general circulation models that lie at the heart of today's climate science.

The seeds of the revolution in digital electronic computing were planted during the Second World War. While electric calculators had been around for a few decades before the War, they were not programmable, and they used mechanical switches to store numbers, making them very slow. The War effort drove a great leap forward in the technology. Scientists and engineers on both sides of the War were put to work on figuring out how to design faster, more flexible machines to provide computational support for problems ranging from code breaking to calculating weapons trajectories.

These computers needed to be fully automatic, fully electronic, and programmable, so that the same machine could be used to solve a variety of problems. The first machine to achieve all three was the Colossus,[1] designed and built, in secret, by Tommy Flowers at Bletchley Park in the United Kingdom, to help crack the codes used by German high command. However, while it could be programmed using switches and pluggable wires, it was designed only for code-breaking, which means it was not a *general purpose* programmable computer.

That honour belongs to ENIAC, designed by John Mauchly and J. Presper Eckert at the University of Pennsylvania in 1946, with funding from the US Army, who wanted a computer to produce ballistics tables for heavy artillery weapons (see Figure 3.1). ENIAC was a thousand times faster than the best

Figure 3.1 ENIAC, showing the pluggable wires used to program it. (US Army Photo)

electro-mechanical calculators at the time, although its vacuum tubes were much less reliable than mechanical switches. Like the Colossus, ENIAC didn't store its programs in memory. Programming ENIAC involved a laborious process of plugging in wires and setting switches, so it could take several days to set up a new calculation, and the Army eventually modified it to add a stored program component in September 1948.

As well as being the first general-purpose computer, ENIAC scored another first, when, in 1950, it ran the world's first weather forecasting program.

The First Weather Forecasting App

During the development of ENIAC, most experts were sceptical that it could ever work. One of the few people who understood its potential was the mathematician John von Neumann, an expert on complex mathematical problems, such as the movements of fluids. These problems could readily be described using a set of equations, but were almost impossible to solve by hand. von Neumann was one of the few mathematicians of his generation who thought a solution was possible, and he dedicated much of his career to pursuing it. During the War years he developed what he described as "an obscene interest in computation."[2] He had a consulting role in the Los Alamos atomic bomb program, building mathematical models of explosions, and he toured the United States and Britain on a quest for a computational machine that could run his calculations fast enough to be useful.

von Neumann heard about ENIAC almost by accident, when an army captain[3] who was working on the project recognized him at a railway station and struck up a conversation. He immediately arranged to work with the ENIAC team in Philadelphia. His involvement had an immediate and unexpected impact: the first program run on ENIAC wasn't, as the Army had intended, a ballistics calculation at all. In December 1945, von Neumann arranged for the physicists at Los Alamos to use ENIAC for a thermodynamics calculation they needed for the design of a hydrogen bomb. They encoded the program, along with the data it needed, onto half a million punched cards, which were shipped from Los Alamos to Philadelphia. The program took six weeks to run, but completed successfully. The era of computational science had begun.

von Neumann wrote a report[4] in early 1946, to help guide the development of a successor to ENIAC. He described a "logical" design with five separate components: a central arithmetic unit, a central control unit, a memory to store numerical data as well as the program itself, and input and output units, to transfer programs and data to and from punched cards. This is now known as the von Neumann architecture,[5] and has shaped how we think about computer design ever since.

However, von Neumann was never really interested in designing computers; his real interest was the computational science that computers would enable. There are several classes of mathematical problem that, up until the 1940s, were considered to be unsolvable. Among these were the equations for the flow of fluids and heat – hydrodynamics and thermodynamics. Oil companies needed to solve such problems when considering what flow rates to expect if they drill into an oil field at a particular location. Nuclear scientists needed to solve them to calculate the dispersion of heat and nuclear fallout during an explosion. And meteorologists needed them to attain the holy grail of weather forecasting – the ability to calculate how a particular weather pattern would evolve over days or weeks.

Numerical weather forecasting particularly captured von Neumann's imagination. It would be an excellent demonstration of the value of electronic computers for science, and would build on his work on numerical solutions to fluid flow equations. The theory was already well understood – all that was missing was a machine to run the calculations fast enough to be useful. After the War, von Neumann returned to the Institute of Advanced Study (IAS) at Princeton, where he set about developing a new computer using his design principles, and recruited a team of experts in meteorology to design a weather forecasting program, to demonstrate what the machine could do. The development of the IAS computer proceeded much more slowly than von Neumann had planned, and it didn't enter operation until 1952. The meteorology project also began rather slowly, but achieved a major boost in 1948, when von Neumann hired the young Jule Charney to lead the effort. Within a year, they had several promising weather models ready to test. As there was no prospect of the IAS computer being ready, von Neumann once again pulled strings with the army to allow them to try a test run on ENIAC, which was by now installed in an army facility doing the ordinance calculations it was originally intended for.

Designing the program code took nearly six months.[6] Charney's group didn't attempt to forecast *future* weather; instead, they picked dates in the recent past for which they had excellent observational data of different weather patterns. Because they already knew the correct answer before the program was run, they could use it to make a detailed assessment of the model's accuracy. Today we call this a *hindcast*, and it has become a standard testing technique in climate and weather model development.

By March 1950, the programs were ready, and the team operated ENIAC around the clock for 33 days with a series of tests of their model (see Figure 3.2). The tests were somewhat disappointing. Many programming errors had to be caught and corrected before a successful run could be completed, and as a result, the team only managed to complete a few of

Figure 3.2 The ENIAC weather modelling team. Left to right: Harry Wexler, John von Neumann, M. H. Frankel, Jerome Namias, John Freeman, Ragnar Fjörtoft, Francis Reichelderfer, and Jule Charney. (Courtesy MIT Museum)

the hindcast runs they had prepared. Eventually, they successfully ran two 12-hour hindcasts and four 24-hour hindcasts using real weather data. The results were rather mixed – only one of the runs gave anything close to an accurate result. ENIAC was also much slower than they expected: it took 36 hours to compute 24 hours' worth of weather, which made it rather useless for real weather forecasting.

Despite these disappointments, von Neumann and Charney were enthused. Most of the time had been spent on manual support – taking the stacks of punched cards output during one step in the calculation, and re-ordering them ready to provide input for the next step. Machines with more internal memory and faster processors were already being developed at Princeton and elsewhere, so it was easy to foresee that within a few years a computer would be able to run a weather simulation faster than real-time, making real weather forecasting possible. And the model was one of the simplest the team had developed – a better model would surely produce better forecasts. Most importantly, they had overturned a widely held belief among meteorologists at the time that calculating the weather directly from a set of equations was impossible.

So how did this computational model work? To understand that, we have to go back to the beginning of the twentieth century, when the equations Charney and von Neumann used were first worked out, and explore why the only previous attempt to apply them to weather forecasting had produced a result so ridiculous that nobody else had tried it since.

Weather Forecasting as Science

Before the birth of modern computing, weather forecasting was very haphazard. Many nineteenth-century scientists took up recording weather data as a hobby, but their observations weren't particularly systematic – each tended to develop their own scheme for how to measure and record weather data. Forecasting relied on maps, experience, and a lot of guesswork. And very little science.

By the end of the nineteenth century, three distinct traditions in meteorology had developed,[7] with very little interaction between them:

The *empirical* tradition focused on the collection of weather data. These were the "big data" scientists of their day. Their goal was to improve how weather was measured and recorded, and they regularly published detailed tables of weather data from around the world, along with analyses of statistics and patterns in the weather of the past.

The *theoretical* tradition focused on explaining the properties of the atmosphere using the laws of physics, without concern for whether these explanations had any predictive power. The theoreticians lacked the tools to make detailed comparisons of their theories with the detailed data collected by the empiricists, so they largely limited themselves to logical deduction from basic principles.

The *prognostic* tradition focused on creating forecasts of future weather. New mapping techniques in the nineteenth century had inspired a novel approach: plot the current conditions on a map, and compare it to catalogues of weather maps from the past. When you find one that closely resembles the current conditions, use it to reason about what will happen next. Physics played no role in this approach: forecasters used a combination of extrapolation, guesswork, and knowledge of local conditions. They used maps to plot air pressure and other variables, and to identify patterns such as depressions, anticyclones, troughs, and ridges. They then used experience, memory, and various rules of thumb to predict how such patterns might evolve. But most forecasts were hardly any better than guesses, and the empiricists and theoreticians looked down on these forecasters as "unscientific."

By the end of the nineteenth century, several prominent meteorologists pushed for a unification of these traditions. But the biggest step forward came from outside the field, in the work of the Norwegian physicist, Vilhelm Bjerknes, who was then a colleague of Arrhenius in Stockholm. Bjerknes felt that meteorology could become an exact science, based on principles from physics. In 1904, he published a manifesto for scientific weather forecasting, suggesting a two-step process: first a diagnostic step, in which data about current conditions were collated and analyzed to provide a starting point. Then, a prognostic step would compute a forecast from this initial state by solving a set of mathematical equations describing the physics of the atmosphere. The right set of equations would enable the weather to be forecast in much the same way that scientists had learned to predict the movements of the planets.

Bjerknes's equations and manifesto led to a revolution in weather forecasting methods, but he was, at first, a reluctant leader for such a revolution. During the early part of his career, he was strongly influenced by his father, who had made an extensive study of the properties of electrical and magnetic fields. A key problem at the time was to explain how magnets seemed to cause instantaneous "action at a distance."

In the mid-nineteenth century, the Scottish scientist James Clerk Maxwell had shown electricity, magnetism, and light were all aspects of the same phenomena. At the time, a common way of explaining this was to assume there was an invisible fluid, the "luminiferous aether," on which light and electrical and magnetic fields were carried. Vilhelm's father, Carl Anton Bjerknes, had developed an explanation for the effects of magnetic fields from the mechanical properties of this supposed fluid, and wanted his son to continue the work. In 1890, Carl Anton sent his son to study in Germany with Heinrich Hertz, who had demonstrated Maxwell's ideas in practice. Here, Vilhelm Bjerknes began a promising line of research on electromagnetic waves. But his father wanted him to come home to Norway to publish their ideas on the mechanical theory of magnetism as a book. As a compromise, Bjerknes took a faculty position at the Stockholm Högskola in 1893, where he worked on the manuscript for the book throughout the 1890s. It took much longer than he expected, and by the time the book appeared, in two volumes in 1900 and 1902, research on electromagnetism had moved on.

Within a few years, in 1905, the young Albert Einstein published his special theory of relativity, which made the equations work without the need to assume an invisible fluid. The idea that electromagnetic fields were like fluids was no longer useful to theoretical physicists.

Bjerknes was bitterly disappointed at the lack of interest from other physicists in his work on electromagnetism. But while working on the book, Bjerknes had developed two new equations for fluid motion, describing how a vortex can develop when a fluid is heated, causing some of it to expand and rise. This work solved a problem in the mathematics of fluid flow, which had previously only worked for "ideal fluids," which had a uniform density.[8] His equations united thermodynamics and hydrodynamics, and are now known as Bjerknes's General Theorem of Circulation.[9] This work had a profound impact on his future career.

Bjerknes presented his circulation theorem at the Stockholm Physics Society in 1897, without mentioning any possible applications. Unlike his colleague and friend, Svante Arrhenius, Bjerknes hadn't really shown much interest in geoscience. But Arrhenius and the other the members of the Stockholm society saw remarkable potential in Bjerknes's results, and persuaded him to explore several new applications.

One of these applications was inspired, in part, by a tragic accident. In 1896, Nils Ekholm, the meteorologist whose work on the ice ages had inspired Arrhenius to build his climate model, was helping to plan an expedition using a hydrogen balloon to travel to the north pole, to plant the Swedish flag and conduct scientific experiments. The mission was financed by King Oscar II and Alfred Nobel, and was to be "the greatest ballooning adventure of all time." Ekholm was in charge of selecting a launch date when the prevailing winds would take them over the pole. He would also accompany them on the expedition and collect detailed weather data. But the weather was too unsettled through the summer of 1896, and the expedition was called off. Meanwhile, Ekholm became increasingly concerned about flaws in the balloon that would cause it to leak. Unfortunately, his concerns were ignored, and the following summer the expedition set off to great media fanfare, but without Ekholm. The expedition disappeared without a trace.[10]

Ekholm and Arrhenius worked on a rescue plan, but were unable to put it into action because they couldn't calculate the likely path of the balloon. They had wind measurements only at the ground level, and couldn't deduce the corresponding currents in the upper air. Ekholm realized the circulation patterns in the atmosphere matched the conditions described in Bjerknes's equations, and felt that the equations would enable them to add a vertical dimension to their weather maps. Bjerknes began to include the fate of the lost balloon expedition as an example application in his lectures, and Ekholm started a campaign to measure pressure and density gradients in the vertical dimension using kites and balloons. The Cosmic Physics Society rapidly embraced the idea, raised funds for it, and established the program "in Bjerknes' honour."

Meanwhile, Otto Petterson, a professor of chemistry at the Högskola, was building a research program into precise analytical methods for understanding the oceans. He was particularly keen to explain the sudden return of herring to the Swedish west coast. There had been no herring to catch in that region for 70 years, and their disappearance had devastated the local fishing communities. Understanding what caused the fish stocks to disappear and then reappear became a pressing question for the local economy. Petterson discovered that the herring depend on ocean currents that bring warmer, saltier water. If they could determine the circulation properties in the ocean, they could predict these flows. Peterson immediately saw that Bjerknes's theorem provided a mathematical basis for this work, and began to talk about a science of "rational fishery." Collaboration with the other Baltic states would be essential, so Petterson organized a major conference to plan a coordinated international study in 1899, and invited Bjerknes as a guest of honour, to talk about possible applications of his theorem.

The attention Bjerknes's work received from meteorologists and oceanographers was in marked contrast to his experiences in theoretical physics, and he was increasingly drawn into studying applications in the geosciences, particularly weather forecasting. Funding for this research was much better than theoretical physics, and his students were all immediately in demand.

As he was drawn into the geosciences, Bjerknes began advocating a new idea: meteorology should become an exact science, based on the laws of physics. His public lecture in 1903, entitled "A Rational Method for Weather Prediction" received a lot of press attention. Bjerknes argued that accurate weather forecasting would be possible if two conditions were met: "1. A sufficiently accurate knowledge of the state of the atmosphere at the initial time; 2. A sufficiently accurate knowledge of the laws according to which one state of the atmosphere develops from another."[11] He argued that the first condition was, in essence, already met, given the huge advances in collecting observational data. For the second condition, he felt that the physical principles were well understood, and all that was needed was to codify these principles to make calculations possible.

A year later he formulated a set of seven equations that did exactly this. Today they are known in meteorology as the *primitive equations*. He declared a new research program for predicting weather using mathematics, and devoted the rest of his career to making it a reality. In 1917, he started a new geophysical institute in Bergen. It was the work of Bjerknes and the Bergen school that von Neumann and Charney drew on to develop their first computerized weather forecast.

Getting the Data

The first of Bjerkness's two conditions for successful forecasting depends on how well we know the current state of the atmosphere. By the end of the nineteenth century, it was possible to give a detailed characterization of the atmosphere at a given place and a given time. What was missing was the ability to do this routinely for enough locations to cover an entire region. At the Bergen School, Bjerknes persuaded the Norwegian government to build a dense network of observation stations to provide the data needed for his forecasting work.

Instruments for accurately measuring temperature, air pressure, and humidity have been around since the seventeenth century, along with a variety of ways of measuring rainfall, wind direction, and wind speed. In the nineteenth century, with the introduction of the telegraph, the idea of coordinated measurements became important.[12] Amateur meteorologists realized they needed to agree on basic questions such as what time of day to take readings, what units to use, and even whether to tie their readings to local time or to a global standard such as Greenwich Mean Time. National weather services began to spring up in the 1870s, and in 1874, an international commission designed standard forms for recording and summarizing weather data, which were used around the world for many decades afterwards. Numerical tables were published, to make it easier to convert units, and to translate between related values such as humidity, mass density, vapour pressure, and so on. Coverage of the ocean improved as ships started to report weather data rapidly using wireless telegraphy.

Most of the data up until this time described weather conditions at the surface of the planet – the state of the atmosphere higher up was still largely unknown. New data from kites and balloons were beginning to fill this gap, and by the 1890s, major efforts were underway to do this systematically. An international agreement to launch weather balloons on the same day each month ("Balloon Days") began in 1896, and lasted until the First World War. Another international program, started in 1896, measured the heights and movements of clouds. The new data provided a much better understanding of the vertical structure of the atmosphere, and led to the discovery of the stratosphere – a layer of the upper atmosphere starting about 8 km to 12 km above the surface, where temperatures no longer drop with height, but begin rising again.

Bjerknes identified seven key measurements that he would need for his forecast calculations. Three were wind speed (velocity) in three dimensions: North-South, East-West, and vertically. The other four were pressure, temperature, density, and water content. The technology existed to measure each of these seven variables at different heights in the atmosphere. Each reading had to be labelled with a precise location (latitude, longitude, and height), and the time it was taken. The observational data wouldn't cover every possible location and time, but if the readings were close enough together in space and time, the readings for any specific point could be inferred by averaging its neighbours.

A complete account of the state of the atmosphere would consist of a value for each of these seven variables for every point in space and time. Bjerknes believed that any property of the atmosphere could either be determined from these seven variables, or safely ignored for the purposes of forecasting the weather.

The Primitive Equations

The first of Bjerknes's conditions – accurate knowledge of the current state – could be met with existing technology. But what of the second condition – accurate knowledge of the laws that determine how the atmosphere evolves from one moment to the next? Bjerknes believed that a theoretical account of this was also complete, and that the laws of physics could provide a complete mathematical account of large-scale atmospheric phenomena. In other words, he believed he could build a mathematical model to generate explicit solutions to meteorological questions. Bjerknes wasn't the first try to model the motions of the atmosphere mathematically,[13] but he was the first to assemble a complete set of equations from which weather forecasts might be calculated.

Where did Bjerknes's equations come from? Once he had identified his seven key variables, he needed an equation for each variable, to describe how its value would change over time. These equations would capture relationships between the variables, and the boundary conditions of the system. The boundary conditions include the force of gravity and rotation of the Earth, energy received from the sun, and conditions at the top and bottom of the atmosphere. A more complex model might include more detail, such as the exchange of water between the oceans and the air, and the way clouds form in the presence of dust in the air. But for large-scale weather phenomena – which focuses on the way winds move storms around – these could be ignored.

The equations themselves come from basic physics. For example, the ideal gas law, formulated by Émile Clapeyron in 1834, captures the relationship between pressure, density, and temperature of a gas. If you heat up a gas, it expands. Or, if there's no room for expansion, its internal pressure increases. So for example, if you throw a sealed container on a fire, the air pressure in it will increase until it explodes. And if you reduce the pressure, air will expand and cool. So a barometer, which measures changes in air pressure, can be used as a simple weather forecasting tool – if the air pressure is falling, it usually means colder weather is on the way, and if the pressure is rising, warmer weather is coming.

The ideal gas law is the simplest of the seven equations Bjerknes needed. The remaining equations express constraints on the system. For example, by Newton's laws of motion, momentum must be conserved – moving air will tend to keep moving in the same direction, unless another force acts on it.[14] By the first law of thermodynamics, energy must be conserved – if energy is gained from elsewhere, the temperature must rise accordingly, and if energy is lost, the temperature must drop. By the second law of thermodynamics, energy tends to flow from hotter things to cooler things, until they reach equilibrium. And finally, mass must be conserved – air and moisture cannot spontaneously appear or disappear. These physical laws determine how the key variables can change over time – the velocity of the wind, or the change in flow of heat. They can be formulated as a set of equations giving the rate of change of each variable over time, in terms of the other variables – a set of *partial differential equations*. Altogether, these constraints give six more equations: three for conservation of momentum (in each of three dimensions), one each for conservation of mass and energy, and one for dispersal of energy according to the second law of thermodynamics.

Meteorologists now refer to Bjerknes's original seven equations as the *primitive equations*. They capture the basic physical principles of how the atmosphere works, but on their own are too simplistic (primitive) for detailed weather forecasting. Today's weather models use variants of these seven equations, but also include a lot more detail about physical and chemical processes in the atmosphere, and how the atmosphere interacts with land and ocean surfaces.

Bjerknes was confident his equations are correct because he was confident that the laws of physics are correct. In principle, these equations could be used for weather forecasting by first measuring the current conditions at a number of locations, at ground level and at various heights in the atmosphere. Starting from these initial conditions, the equations could be used to calculate the "next" value for each variable, typically for a few hours into the future. Then the calculations could be repeated to generate longer and longer forecasts. Unfortunately, because the equations are complex, there is no easy way to solve them by hand. Bjerknes estimated that it might take about three months to calculate three hours of weather in this way, so they couldn't be used directly for forecasting.

However, even without access to modern computers, Bjerknes was able to establish a successful weather forecasting program using a kind of graphical calculus. He would plot current observations for the seven variables on a set of weather maps (including maps for multiple levels of height in the atmosphere) and connect them with lines to show gradients. He would then use the principles in the equations to estimate the "next state" – how the variables would change over the course of a few hours. He would generate another set of maps by estimating the future state for a few selected points, and filling in the points in between using either "graphic interpolation or visual judgment."[15] This next set of maps would then be used as the starting point for the next iteration, and so on. The approach was slow and labour intensive, but it worked. For weather forecasters, this was more useful anyway, because they need to see the overall pattern of weather as it changes far more than they need precise solutions for each variable at each location.

After he moved to the University of Bergen in 1917, Bjerknes set up a department of meteorology, where he developed the graphical calculus over the next few decades. The Bergen school was soon established as one of the most successful weather forecasters in the world. Their approach treated weather systems as a collection of air cells, whose boundaries (fronts) cause a change in the weather. They became experts in predicting the paths of storms (cyclones), and their techniques became standard training for an entire generation of meteorologists.

Is It Really That Simple?

There is, of course, more to the story than this. Long before Bjerknes's time, scientists had pondered whether the laws of physics could be used to predict the weather, in the same way that astronomers could predict the movements of planets and moons. If you think of the atmosphere as a moving body of air, then its main function is to transport local properties (heat, storms, rainclouds, etc.) from one location to another. This movement of local weather properties is known as *advection*. If you can predict large-scale advection, then you can predict what kind of weather is headed to each region.

Newton's Laws of motion are the obvious starting point to study advection, and had already been explored for this purpose during Newton's lifetime, by the astronomer, Edmond Halley (of Halley's comet fame). In 1686, Halley published detailed maps of the trade winds, along with an explanation for why, in the northern tropics, these winds blow steadily from the north-east to the south-west. Halley reasoned that the heat from the sun is greatest near the equator. As the heated air rises, colder, denser air from further away is pulled in to replace it, creating a rotating mass of air. This air obeys Newton's laws: once it starts moving, it tends to keep moving in the same direction. Halley also thought that as the sun progresses from east to west through the day, the rising edge of hotter air is always further east than the flow of cooler air that it sucks in, giving the characteristic pattern of tradewinds from the north-east in the tropics north of the equator, and from the south-east in the tropics south of the equator (see Figure 3.3). In 1735,

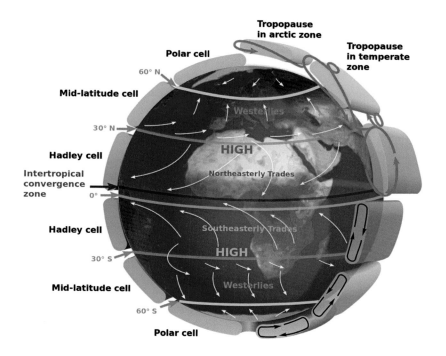

Figure 3.3 Hadley cells are vertical circulation patterns, created when the heat from the sun in the equatorial regions warms the air, causing it to rise and spread north and south away from the equator. Meanwhile at the surface, cooler air replaces it. Eventually the warm air flowing away from the equator cools and falls, completing the loop. Two similar cells, the mid latitude cell and the polar cell create similar patterns closer to the poles. The prevailing winds at the surface are driven largely by these cells. (CC-BY-SA 3.0 Wikimedia User: Kaidor)

the meteorologist George Hadley produced a better account of these patterns by taking into account the inertia from the rotation of the Earth. Hence, these large-scale movements of air in the atmosphere are now known as Hadley cells, rather than Halley cells.[16]

However, while Newton's laws explain the motion of the atmosphere, they do not provide a suitable mathematical basis for predicting that motion. Newton's laws were formulated to describe the movement of solid objects, with fixed centres of mass. They apply to planets and moons much more readily than they apply to a complex moving fluid, such as the atmosphere. In a fluid, the centre of mass will change as the fluid sloshes about. In principle, one could apply Newton's laws to each molecule, and aggregate these to work out the overall flow. This, of course, is completely impractical, but it's possible to achieve something similar by working with larger "parcels" of a fluid, while assuming any difference in behaviour between two adjacent parcels varies smoothly over the distance between them. But there is a trade-off. Smaller parcels give more realistic results, but the amount of computation goes up dramatically, because there are so many more parcels to keep track of.

Another complication is that if parts of the fluid move at different rates, there is internal friction as the molecules move past each other. This friction exerts another force on the fluid – slowing down any movement – and is known as *viscosity*.

The core mathematics for how all these factors affect the movements of fluid were worked out by Claude-Louis Navier and Gabriel Stokes in the 1830s. The three basic Navier–Stokes equations adapt Newton's second law (Force equals mass times acceleration) to calculate acceleration of a parcel of fluid in each of three dimensions, depending on the inertia of the fluid, the forces applied to it, the mass of the fluid, and its viscosity. A fourth equation, known as the continuity equation, represents conservation of mass.

The Navier–Stokes equations are widely used today in the field of *computational fluid dynamics*, for problems as diverse as the design of aircraft wings to the realistic rendering of liquids in animated movies. They are usually applied not to the fluid itself, but to the space through which it moves. The idea is to divide the space into a series of cubes, and use the equations to compute the changes in mass and velocity of the fluid in each cube, at each moment in time, as the fluid flows through it.[17] This is convenient if you're reasoning about liquids flowing through pipes, air moving through a wind tunnel, or the atmosphere moving over mountains and valleys.

To apply the Navier–Stokes equations to the atmosphere, terms have to be added to account for two additional forces: the force of gravity, and the spin caused by the rotation of the Earth. The latter, now known as the *Coriolis force*,[18] is what causes hurricanes to spin clockwise in the northern hemisphere, and counter-clockwise in the southern hemisphere, and also tends to make them curl away from the equator.[19]

So although I presented Bjerknes's equations as a direct expression of Newton's laws, in reality, many other scientists contributed ideas to adapt Newton's equations into the form Bjerknes was able to use. And although meteorologists call them "primitive equations," to the layman they don't seem very primitive at all. Bjerknes's contribution was to realize these seven equations contain enough detail to describe the mathematics of a fluid atmosphere on a rotating planet.

Richardson's Forecast Factory

While Bjerknes's approach represented a big step forward in theoretical meteorology, it largely failed to bring together the theoretical and practical branches of the field. Bjerknes himself acknowledged the equations were too complex to work with directly, and many meteorologists remained sceptical that they would give sensible forecasts, even if the calculations could be done. This skepticism was greatly reinforced in the 1920s by the publication of a book containing a bold attempt to use Bjerknes's equations in a practical weather forecasting method. The book, now regarded as a classic in early meteorology, was the work of a quiet-spoken English scientist called Lewis Fry Richardson, who did more than perhaps any other scientist to develop the numerical techniques now used in all modern weather forecasting models (see Figure 3.4).

Richardson only ever made one attempt to produce a weather forecast using the equations, and it was spectacularly wrong. But as is often the case with computational models, a well-thought out model that gives the wrong results is often far more interesting than one that is right. Unfortunately, in this case, Richardson was too far ahead of his time, and the insights from his model remained unexplored until after the invention of the electronic computer.

Figure 3.4 Lewis Fry Richardson.

Early in his career, Richardson held a short-term research job with the National Peat Industries, choosing optimal places to cut drainage channels to remove the water from peat bogs. Realizing that the flow of water through the bogs could be represented by a series of partial differential equations, he invented a method to solve them, the method now known as *finite differences*. The key idea is to plot values on a regular grid, and then calculate rates of change by looking at the differences between adjacent values.

The method is tedious to compute, because the timesteps have to be small compared to the rate of flow between grid points, but it can be used to produce good, if approximate, solutions to many kinds of flow problem. For weather, you can calculate wind speed and direction from the pressure differences between adjacent locations. And if you know the wind speed into and out of a location, you can calculate how its pressure will change over time.

Figure 3.5 shows Richardson's scheme for weather forecasting. For each shaded cell, he would collect a measurement for air pressure, and for the unshaded cells around it, he would take a measurement for wind speed. The rate of change in pressure at each shaded cell could be calculated from the differences in wind speed in the surrounding cells, and the rate of change in wind speed at each unshaded cell could be calculated from the differences in pressure in the surrounding cells. Once he had a measurement and a rate of change for each cell, he could just combine them to calculate the next value, after a suitable timestep (say, one hour). The new values then act as the starting state for a repeat of the calculation, with each repeat extending the forecast by another hour.

Richardson published details of his method in 1910, and at about the same time, began to think about how to make it work for practical weather fore-casting. One significant problem with the method is what to do at the edges of the grid. Because you need to know the values either side of each grid cell to calculate its rate of change, the method cannot be applied to the cells at the edges of the region for which measurements are available. For weather, one might have good measurements of air pressure, say, over Europe, but beyond that a set of unknowns. Each time you apply the method, you calculate new values for all the interior grid points, but not the edges. Which means if you apply the method repeatedly, to calculate a forecast forward in time, it is as though you trim the edges off your map at each step. Eventually there will be nothing left.

The problem would go away if you could calculate the weather for the entire globe – the grid wraps all the way around the planet so there is no edge. This led Richardson to propose a bold plan for calculating global weather forecasts.

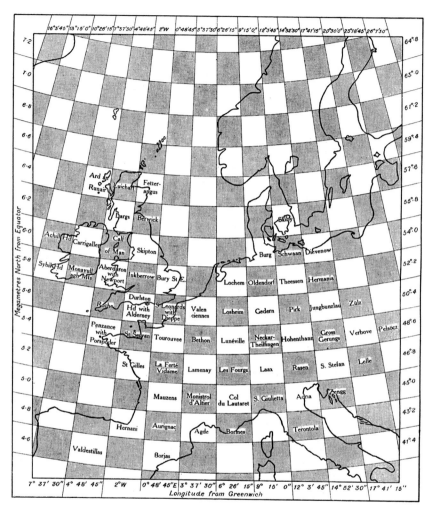

Figure 3.5 Richardson's idealized grid. The idea was to measure air pressure at the centre of each shaded grid cell, and wind speed at the centre of each unshaded grid cell. The cells are labelled with towns that are closest to the centre of each cell, from which the relevant data would be collected. Where there is no town near the centre of the grid, he used the average from two different towns – for example, "St Leonards with Dieppe." (Reproduced from the frontispiece of Richardson (1922))

He imagined a grid with points spaced out about 200 km apart, covering the entire globe. If he assigned 32 people to each grid point, between them they would be able to calculate the equations quite a bit faster than the real weather, and hence produce a viable forecast. For reasonably localized forecasts, he estimated his grid would need about 2,000 gridpoints to cover the entire globe, and hence a team of 64,000 people would be needed for a full global weather forecast. To organise this team, he imagined stationing them inside a massive hollow sphere, with a map of the world painted on the inside, and each group of 32 people positioned on a balcony next to their own grid point (see Figure 3.6). A conductor on a large podium in the centre would keep everyone to the same speed, shining a flashlight on any group who were getting too far ahead or behind their colleagues:

> Imagine a large hall like a theatre, except that the circles and galleries go right round through the space usually occupied by the stage. The walls of this chamber are painted to form a map of the globe. The ceiling represents the north polar regions, England is in the gallery, the tropics in the upper circle, Australia on the dress circle and the Antarctic in the pit. A myriad computers are at work upon the weather of the part of the map where each sits, but each computer attends only to one equation or part of an equation. The work of each region is coordinated by an official of higher rank. Numerous little "night signs" display the instantaneous values so that neighbouring computers can read them. Each number is thus displayed in three adjacent zones so as to maintain communication to the North and South on the map. From the floor of the pit a tall pillar rises to half the height of the hall. It carries a large pulpit on its top. In this sits the man in charge of the whole theatre; he is surrounded by several assistants and messengers. One of his duties is to maintain a uniform speed of progress in all parts of the globe. In this respect he is like the conductor of an orchestra in which the instruments are slide-rules and calculating machines. But instead of waving a baton he turns a beam of rosy light upon any region that is running ahead of the rest, and a beam of blue light upon those who are behindhand.[20]

In Richardson's day, the term "computer" meant a person who did these kinds of calculation as a job, and so his forecast factory was literally a design for a massively parallel computer. When you consider that today's weather forecasts are indeed calculated on massively parallel supercomputers, with tens of thousands of processors, using the kinds of numerical method that Richardson invented, it's perhaps not that fanciful – today, we just use silicon chips rather than people.

In 1913, Richardson took a position with the UK Meteorological Office, hoping he would have the chance to put his ideas into practice. He was assigned duties as the superintendent of a remote observatory at Eskdalemuir in Scotland, a position that suited him well, as he wanted somewhere quiet to work, to try out his calculations. The following year, War broke out across Europe, leaving Richardson with a dilemma. As a Quaker and a lifelong pacifist, he would not sign up to fight, but he found a way to help the wounded

Figure 3.6 An artist's impression of Richardson's forecast factory. For a detailed look at this painting, see Lynch (2016). (Painting: "Weather Forecasting Factory" based on Richardson (1922) and on advice from Prof. John Byrne, Trinity College Dublin. © Stephen Conlin 1986. All Rights Reserved.)

by volunteering to drive ambulances behind the lines in France. It was here, working between shifts, that Richardson finally attempted to calculate a real weather forecast.

During the two years he worked on the western front, he was able to calculate a 6-hour "forecast" (actually a hindcast) for two locations in France. He selected May 20, 1910[21] – an international balloon day. Detailed weather data for central Europe for this period had been collected and published by Bjerknes during his time in Leipzig. Richardson had analysed Bjerknes's primitive equations, modifying them slightly. He realized the equation for the second law of thermodynamics was unnecessary, as the dispersal of energy expressed in this law can be ignored at the timescale of most weather processes. Instead, he used an equation for conservation of moisture, which is essential if changes in humidity are to be captured correctly. He also realized that accurate forecasts would need to account for differences in weather patterns at different heights in the atmosphere. He eventually settled on a five-layer model, with all his measurements and calculations in each grid cell repeated five times, for different heights in the atmosphere.

According to Bjerknes's manifesto, the first step was a diagnostic step, to work out the initial state. Richardson plotted the observational data for each of the seven variables on maps of Europe, averaging the measurements to get the value of each variable for each square on his grid. He then used his finite differences method between adjacent grid squares to calculate how each variable varied across the region, and from these, a similar process to calculate how each of these varied across time. By plugging these values back into the original equations, he was able to calculate a new value for each grid cell at the next hour. These then became the initial state for the next step of the method.

With six weeks of labour,[22] Richardson managed to calculate a 6-hour forecast for 20 May 1910 for two grid points. The work was remarkable, all the more so because, as he put it "My office was a heap of hay in a cold rest billet."[23] Unfortunately, his forecast was, in his own words, "absurd" – it showed a rise in air pressure of 145 millibars over the 6 hours – in reality it only rose by 1 millibar. Even in the fiercest hurricane, the air pressure might only change by around 30 mb.[24] However, Richardson was undeterred. He correctly diagnosed that the problem lay with the initial data, and devoted a chapter of his book to methods to address the problem through smoothing. The core problem is that measurement of wind speed at any one moment is subject to short-term oscillations, like gusts and eddies. If you want to know the longer-term tendency, you need to smooth the data to remove this short-term noise. A recent reconstruction of Richardson's work,[25] by Peter Lynch, did the appropriate smoothing, and demonstrated that, in essence, Richardson's methods work just fine.

Richardson's notes on this work were lost during the War, but remarkably they were re-discovered under a coal heap after the War ended, and returned to him. He then turned these notes into the book, "Weather Prediction by Numerical Process," published in 1922, which was widely read by meteorologists for its insights into theoretical meteorology. The reasons for the failure of Richardson's forecast became a frequent discussion topic among the meteorological community for decades afterwards. It persuaded many not to use numerical methods, but a handful of meteorologists remained convinced that there ought to be a way to correct Richardson's mistake and get the approach to work.

Convergence

The debate over Richardson's methods raged on in the meteorological community for decades, while theoretical work on the physics of the atmosphere proceeded steadily. During this time, practical weather forecasting remained little more than an art, with very little improvement in forecast accuracy. Most meteorologists didn't expect any.

The importance of weather for military planning in the Second World War changed things dramatically. Training centres for practical meteorologists were set up at a number of universities, and by the end of the War, almost every developed country had established a national weather bureau. Collection of observational data improved enormously, especially in the upper atmosphere. Rockets and jet aircraft allowed collection of new data, to add to measurements from weather balloons. Radar was used to track cloudiness, precipitation, cyclones, and storm fronts.

It was no coincidence that it was John von Neumann who revived Richardson's work, and used it as a demonstration of numerical computing. As mathematicians, they were both fascinated by the same set of problems, particularly the mathematics of fluid flow. With the advent of electronic computing in the 1940s, von Neumann had access to a tool that could actually implement Richardson's bold visions, and along with it, a much more sophisticated set of mathematical methods.

von Neumann also had another vital piece of information necessary for reliable computer simulations. In the late 1920s, even before he had completed his PhD, von Neumann was invited to the University of Göttingen, on a Rockefeller fellowship. There, he met Richard Courant, who had developed a sound mathematical basis for solving differential equations using numerical approximations. Courant and his colleagues proved that methods like those proposed by

Richardson would produce correct (but approximate) solutions, but there was a catch: the methods only converge on correct solutions if the timestep used in the solution isn't too large. The key idea is that any disturbance happening at one grid location at a particular timestep cannot have moved beyond the next grid location before the next timestep. In mathematical terms, the *Courant Condition*[26] puts a fixed limit on the ratio of the timestep to the size of the grid. If this convergence criterion is not met, the errors grow to unmanageable proportions, and the simulation becomes unstable.

This condition now plays an important role in ensuring what we now call *numerical stability* in modern computer simulations. But in the 1940s, before the era of computer simulation, few people had any experience of solving partial differential equations using numerical methods, and fewer still understood the importance of numerical stability. von Neumann was an exception – this was his specialty. He had built on Courant's work by developing methods to calculate the constraints on the grid size and timestep for each numerical method for any given problem in fluid flow, along with a smoothing technique to eliminate fast moving waves by including an artificial viscosity in the equations.

In 1946, von Neumann used these methods to test the feasibility of running Richardson's approach on the computer he was designing at the Institute for Advanced Studies. He was encouraged in this work by one of the leading meteorologists of the time, Carl Gustaf Rossby, who had been a student of Bjerknes in Norway, and was now a professor at the University of Chicago. Together, they concluded the new computer[27] would be able to handle the required number of calculations, and submitted a proposal to the US Navy to fund the construction of the machine and a team of meteorologists to develop the forecasting methods to run on it. von Neumann couldn't persuade Rossby to move to Princeton to join the project – Rossby was in the process of moving back to his native Stockholm, as director of the newly established Swedish Meteorological and Hydrological Institute. However, Rossby did help[28] von Neumann recruit an outstanding team of young meteorologists to push the work forward, among them, two new recruits from the University of Oslo: Arnt Eliasson and Jule Charney.[29]

Selecting Approximations

With the arrival of Charney and Eliasson, the meteorology team made rapid progress. A central question was to find out which things *really* matter for practical weather forecasting. Bjerknes (and Richardson) had narrowed it down to seven key variables – with seven equations to express how each of these variables change over time. But this was still too complex for the available computers. How simple could they go, while still outperforming existing forecasting methods?

Because the primitive equations are derived from basic physics, they capture the physical properties of all sorts of phenomena, many of which are irrelevant for weather prediction. For example, movements of air and water on the smaller scale – sound waves and ocean waves – are captured in the equations just as well as the movement of winds and storms. But these small-scale waves would, according to the Courant Condition, require an infeasibly short timestep. The only practical approach for weather modelling was to re-write the equations to filter out waves that are too small to matter.

How do we know which phenomena are too small to matter? Much of the hard work in computational modelling is figuring out practical ways to separate "signal" from "noise." Modellers frequently have to make judgments about which kinds of phenomenon they are interested in studying, and then select an appropriate mathematical framework to describe these phenomena, while filtering out everything else. What counts as signal and what counts as noise depends on what you're trying to study. One scientist's "noise" is another scientists "signal" – what happens at a subatomic level is irrelevant to a biologist, but crucial to a quantum physicist. And it's important to regularly check that the noise you're ignoring really doesn't affect the things you're trying to study. One way to do this is to use a hierarchy of models, to simulate the phenomena of interest at different space and timescales. Simple models that focus on what appear to be the key phenomena can provide fast results on a coarse scale, while more detailed models can be used, selectively, to check that the main results hold up when you remove the simplifying assumptions. This is exactly the approach Charney advocated.

At the surface of the planet, geography gets in the way. Surface features, such as hills and mountains (and even buildings and trees) disrupt the airflow, creating swirls and eddies as the wind finds its way through this obstacle course. But as measurements of the upper atmosphere improved during the early twentieth century, it become clear our weather is largely determined not by surface features, but by the pattern of global circulation in the upper atmosphere. If you go up high enough, the influence of the surface disappears. Here, in what meteorologists call the upper troposphere,[30] or the *free atmosphere*, there are just two dominant factors that shape the movement of air: heat from the sun and the rotation of the planet.

Because of the shape of the Earth, the equatorial regions receive the majority of the sun's heat. This creates vertical circulation patterns, such as the

Hadley cells we saw in Figure 3.3. These cells act as heat pumps, transporting the sun's energy away from the equator and towards the poles.[31]

Lateral movement of air in the free atmosphere is largely due to the Earth's rotation. This causes winds to curve away from a straight line, with the effect being stronger the further you move away from the equator. Or at least that's how it looks to us, as inhabitants of a rotating planet. In reality, the winds are trying to travel in straight lines, but appear to curve because the Earth rotates underneath them. Imagine setting off in a plane from the north pole and flying slowly south. You fly straight, but the Earth rotates beneath you, from west to east. To someone on the ground, it looks like your flight path is curving westwards, as though you were steering to your right.

Now imagine you were to fly from the equator to the North Pole. You set out in Northern Brazil, and head for Greenland, due north of you. Before you take off, you're already travelling pretty fast, because you're rotating with the planet. The equator is about 40,000 km long, and rotates once every 24 hours, so on the ground before you start, you're already moving east with the planet at about 1600 km/h. You just don't notice it, because everything else around you is also moving at the same speed. As you fly north, the Earth curves in, and the lines of latitude get progressively shorter. The ground below you has less distance to travel each day, so it's moving slower than the equator. But you still have the eastward momentum from when you took off, which means you're moving eastward faster than the ground beneath you. Despite your effort to fly in a straight line, you're drifting to the right again. At the 60th parallel, which runs through the southern tip of Greenland, the ground beneath you is only rotating half as fast as the equator – the 60th parallel is only 20,000 km long. To observers on the ground, it looks like you've been steering steadily to the right throughout your flight. You could argue you've been flying straight, and it's the observers on the ground who moved, and you'd be correct. But your destination moves with them, so you miss Greenland altogether.

This tendency for things to curve as they move across the planet is the Coriolis effect (see Figure 3.7). In the northern hemisphere things curve to the right, and in the southern hemisphere they curve to the left, no matter which direction they're heading in, and the curvature is strongest closer to the poles. It only affects things that aren't anchored to the surface, and they have to travel quite some distance for the effect to be noticeable. But ocean currents, winds, and long distance aircraft are all affected. Pilots on long flights have to take this effect into account when planning their flight paths, or they'll end up in the wrong place. The effect can also be demonstrated with a pendulum, if you leave it swinging for long enough – as the physicist Léon Foucault famously demonstrated in the Panthéon in Paris, in 1851. In Paris, it takes a pendulum

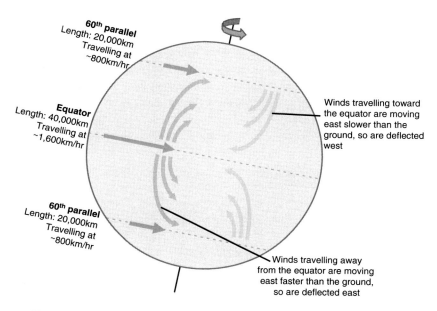

Figure 3.7 The Coriolis force is a result of the rotation and curvature of the Earth. While all parts of the Earth rotate once every 24 hours, the equatorial regions have much further to travel in this time than the polar regions, hence are moving much faster. So winds and ocean currents tend to curl as they move. They curl to the right in the northern hemisphere, and to the left in the southern hemisphere.

about 32 hours to rotate completely, as each swing back and forth is deflected very slightly to the right. At the equator, it wouldn't rotate at all, and at the poles, it would rotate once every 24 hours.[32]

The Coriolis effect causes storms to rotate, but not, perhaps, in the direction you might expect. A casual glance at Figure 3.7 would suggest storms should rotate clockwise in the northern hemisphere, and counter-clockwise in the southern hemisphere. Yet hurricanes – also known as cyclones – do the exact opposite. This is because hurricanes are areas of low air pressure, created when air is heated by the warm ocean, causing it to expand and rise, leaving a low pressure area below it. So the dominant direction of the surface winds in a hurricane are inwards towards the centre, as air rushes in to replace the rising warm air. As they flow towards the centre, these winds are deflected to the right (in the northern hemisphere), which is in the counter-clockwise direction. In the southern hemisphere, they are deflected to the left, creating a clockwise spin (see Figure 3.8). For a large storm, which can be hundreds of kilometres across, the Coriolis force can create very high wind speeds.

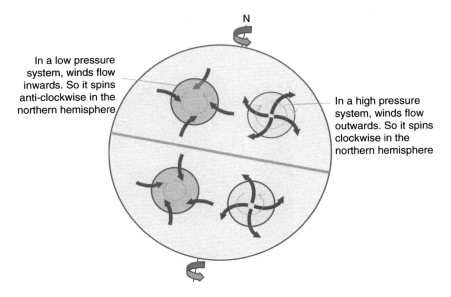

Figure 3.8 Because of the way the Coriolis force deflects winds, low pressure storms (hurricanes/cyclones) rotate anti-clockwise in the northern hemisphere, and clockwise in the southern hemisphere. Areas of high pressure rotate in the opposite direction. Hurricanes can't cross the equator, because they would lose their spin.

The Coriolis effect is also responsible for a distinct, persistent feature of the Earth's atmosphere: the jet streams. These are massive "rivers" of air that flow in a circle from west to east all the way around the globe. The Coriolis effect deflects the currents of warmer air as they flow away from the equator at the top of the Hadley and Ferris cells, bending them eastward. By the time they reach the poleward edge of their cells, these winds are mainly flowing east, creating a constantly moving airflow around the planet, one at about the 30th parallel, and another at about the 60th parallel, with a similar pair in the southern hemisphere.

These airflows tend to meander in distinct wavy patterns. Rossby had studied these waves in the jet streams, and called them as *planetary waves,* because of their size (see Figure 3.9). Today we call them Rossby waves.[33] Usually, there are around three to five complete waves in the polar jet stream as it traverses the planet, although the number can change from season to season. Rossby also showed these waves determine much of the weather in North America, Europe, and northern Asia – because the waves bring regions of high and low pressure with them. The polar jet stream acts as a barrier separating

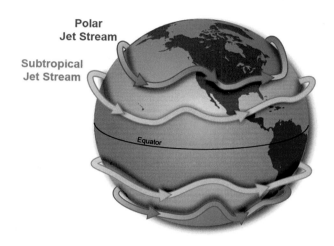

Figure 3.9 The jet streams. These are rivers of air that flow all the way around the planet, caused by the Coriolis effect, which creates an eastward deflection of the winds at the top of the Hadley and Ferris cells. Wind speeds at the centre of the jet stream can reach 400 km/h. The characteristic meander of the jet streams are known as Rossby waves. (NOAA)

cold air at the poles from the warmer air of the subtropics. When the jet stream meanders further south, it brings cold air from the polar regions, and when it meanders further north, it brings warmer air from the tropics.

Rossby's work on these waves provided an intriguing hypothesis for Charney's team. Could a computer model of these waves, initialized from measurements of the current conditions, provide useful weather forecasts, at least for some parts of the globe? In the late 1930s, Rossby had identified the causes of these waves, and in the 1940s, experiments with rotating "dishpans" of water had confirmed that Rossby's explanation was correct. But nobody had tried simulating them numerically.

Step by step, Charney simplified Richardson's equations, until he had reduced them to just a single equation. He did this by ignoring temperature and water vapour, and focusing instead just on air pressure. Whereas Richardson's model included five distinct levels in the atmosphere, Charney reduced this to one, by assuming air behaves the same at all heights, and that the density of the air depends only on the pressure of the air above it.[34] This gave him what he called a *barotropic* model – "baro-" for pressure, and "-tropic" for varying uniformly. In the real atmosphere, heating and cooling complicates things, but Charney was curious to find out how much this would matter.

The resulting model has a single variable, representing, at each grid point, the height in the atmosphere at which the air pressure is 500 millibars. As the average air pressure at sea level is about 1,000 millibars, the 500 millibar level can be thought of as "halfway up" – half the mass of the atmosphere is above this point, and half is below it. If you imagine the bottom half of the atmosphere is made of something other than air, the 500 millibar point would represent the "surface" of this substance. Areas of low pressure would appear as dents or troughs in this surface, and areas of high pressure would appear as peaks or ridges. Rossby waves would look like meandering ridges that circle the planet.

Many large-scale weather effects are a result of the shape of this 500 millibar surface, or changes in its shape. When air flows from high pressure peaks to neighbouring low pressure troughs, it is deflected by the Coriolis effect. Hence, the wind can be assumed to flow along the contour lines of this 500 millibar surface, at a speed proportional to the steepness of the slope. If a trough is approaching you, a mass of low pressure air is coming your way, bringing colder, unsettled weather. If a ridge of high pressure holds still over a region, it's called a blocking pattern, and tends to cause an extended period of hotter weather. So if a model could calculate the movement of this surface over time, it could give useful weather predictions.

Two questions remained: was Charney's equation good enough to capture how the 500 millibar surface behaves, and could the calculations be done fast enough to give timely weather forecasts? The new IAC machine wasn't ready yet, so Charney and von Neumann had to negotiate access to ENIAC to run their tests. Before they did this, they tried one, even simpler test by hand. They reduced the two-dimensional barotropic model to a single dimension, by selecting a single latitude band – the 45th parallel, which stretches for 28,000 km around the planet, halfway between the equator and the North Pole. The idea was to analyze the progression of Rossby waves around the planet at a single latitude, without considering what was happening north and south of it. A forecast using this "one-dimensional" model could be calculated using detailed air pressure data as a starting point. To initialize the model, they converted the air pressure readings into an estimated height for the 500 mb surface at each 10 degrees of longitude, giving them 36 data points spaced out about 800 km apart. The barotropic equation would give new values for these points, 24 hours later, and the result could be compared with the actual readings for the next day, to determine whether the "forecast" was any good.

The calculations for this were handled by a team of three women, led by Margaret Smagorinsky, who was, at the time, a meteorological statistician[35] with the US Weather Bureau. The three women hand-calculated over a hundred

24-hour forecasts for this one-dimensional model, using data from the Weather Bureau to initialize the forecasts. They found many of the 24-hour forecasts to be surprisingly realistic,[36] although longer forecasts (e.g., over five days) were essentially useless. The model tended to perform better where the initial data was the most reliable: over Europe, the Atlantic, and North America, and it worked better for some 24-hour periods than others. Charney and von Neumann were enthused. They declared the experiment a success, and began to make plans for a full-scale experiment using ENIAC. The rest is, as they say, history. But in all the celebrations of the ENIAC program as the foundation of modern numerical weather forecasting, most people seem to forget that credit for performing the first successful numerical weather forecast doesn't belong to ENIAC at all: it belongs to three "human computers:" Margaret Smagorinsky, Norma Gilbarg, and Ellen-Kristine Eliasson.[37]

All We Need Is a Faster Machine

The results from this one-dimensional model were encouraging enough to try the same calculations for a two-dimensional grid, with an electronic computer – computing it by hand could take years. von Neumann pulled strings with his military sponsors, to arrange to "borrow" ENIAC for a month. The army readily agreed, persuaded by von Neumann of the importance of weather forecasting for military applications. And so, in March 1950, a team of five scientists, headed by Charney, set off for the US Army base in Aberdeen, Maryland, where they would spend the next five weeks working around the clock to run the model on ENIAC.

For the experiment with ENIAC, the team used the same equation as the one-dimensional model, but on a two-dimensional grid, with 16 by 19 grid points over North America (as shown in Figure 3.10). Initially, they used a 1-hour timestep, repeatedly, to create a 24-hour forecast for the whole area, although in later runs, they switched to a 3-hour timestep to save computation time, when they found the results were very similar. Once again, they initialized the model using air pressure data from existing weather charts, and the boundary conditions were held constant throughout the runs. Charney chose two kinds of test for the model: a set of 24-hour hindcasts from real data, and a set of hypothetical simulations, with specific patterns of vortices, to explore how the model handled these situations. He chose four different dates from the previous year's weather records that had quite different types of weather condition: January 5, 30, and 31, and February, 13, 1949. Some were conditions where the model might work well, because they matched the simplifying

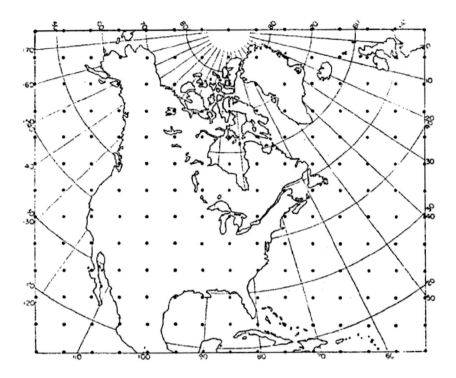

Figure 3.10 The grid used for the ENIAC forecast runs in 1950. The complete grid was 16 × 19, with the grid points spaced about 700 km apart, although the distances vary because the grid makes no allowance for the curvature of the Earth. In this figure, one strip of grid points has been removed from the southern edge, and two strips from the other edges – these were held fixed during the calculations, to eliminate spurious boundary conditions. (Reproduced from Charney et al. (1950))

assumptions in the model – no major vertical variations in the atmosphere – and some where these assumptions were not[38] met, which would offer an extreme challenge for the model.

Running the program itself was extremely labour intensive. Because ENIAC's internal memory would only hold 15 ten-digit numbers, the calculations required a huge amount of input and output on punched cards. Solving the barotropic equation for each timestep required a program with 16 distinct operations, some of which the team performed manually by re-ordering the punched cards printed out from the previous step, and feeding them back in again. They would then run the program again for each timestep. The entire procedure took more than 24 hours to complete a 24-hour simulation, but, as von Neumann commented at the time, most of this was the manual effort: if they could automate the card sorting, the entire run would have taken less than an hour. Better yet, a machine with more memory could hold all the intermediate results internally, without needing punched cards until the end of the run.

A faster machine would easily outpace the weather itself. Two years later, the team re-computed the ENIAC forecasts using the new IAS computer, and it took about 90 minutes to do a 24-hour forecast. Still, most of this time was for input and output, and once they replaced the input device with a faster one, they were able to reduce the computation time to about 10 minutes. This is, of course, how the history of computing goes; every year, faster computers become available. A recent reconstruction of the ENIAC weather model in 2008 ran in less than one second on a Nokia cellphone.[39]

Perhaps the biggest surprise with the ENIAC experiments was that any of the runs were realistic at all. The model was so simple that it missed many of the significant features of real weather. It could not simulate the formation and dissipation of storms, because of the barotropic assumption – that vertical movements of air are small enough to be ignored. But when cold and warm air masses meet, large amounts of energy are transferred between sinking cold air and rising warm air. A model would need to incorporate this vertical move-ment to get the energy transfer right, and in unsettled weather conditions, the energy flows are important. But the basis for Charney and von Neumann's optimism about the results of the ENIAC experiment wasn't so much that it did okay for one of the forecasts. Rather, the experiments showed that their theory was correct: some of the time the atmosphere behaved barotropically, and dur-ing these times, a simple barotropic model works reasonably well.

This meant that the simplified barotropic model was a good starting point for constructing more sophisticated models. Another young meteorologist, Norman Phillips, joined the group in 1951. His dissertation focused on the simplest way to capture some of the vertical structure in the atmosphere: a two-layer model consisting of two barotropic layers, each with air at different densities. The team called this a "two and a half dimension" model, because it didn't quite capture the full three-dimensional structure of the atmosphere. But Phillips showed that this model could provide many of the features of a full three-dimensional model, including the ability to forecast the locations of clouds and rain, if given the initial state of water vapour in the atmosphere.

At Thanksgiving in 1950, a huge, unforeseen storm blanketed much of the east coast of the United States with snow. Immediately, it became an impor-tant test case for the new science of numerical meteorology: could the new computer models have predicted this storm, given that traditional forecasting

methods had all failed? The simpler barotropic models also failed to produce the storm when initialized with the conditions of the previous day. But
Phillips's two-layer model succeeded. Even more importantly, the model still
gave reasonable forecasts for 48 hours ahead, while the simpler models rapidly
became useless beyond 24 hours. In 1953, Charney tested a three-layer model
which did even better. From there, Charney's group at Princeton proceeded to
develop models with more and more layers.

Operational Computer Weather Forecasting

In the summer of 1952, their work was advanced enough that the US Weather
Bureau started the process of transitioning these models into operational fore-
casting, and Charney's group at Princeton took on the job of training the staff.
By 1955, the US Weather Bureau and US armed forces had established a Joint
Numerical Weather Prediction Unit, and in May 1955, it began publishing
real-time forecasts in advance of the weather, using a new IBM 701 computer.

The revolution in weather forecasting was now underway. Early results
from the US Weather Bureau were encouraging, and within a decade their
computed forecasts were significantly better than traditional forecasts by experienced meteorologists. Today's weather models are based on the same principles as these early models – they capture the physical laws that determine the
thermodynamics of the atmosphere, using a set of numerical equations – but
are run on much higher resolution grids (with grid points only a few kilometres
apart), and include detailed simulations of many more physical processes that
affect the weather.

Today's supercomputers make this easier using massively parallel machines.
Just as Richardson imagined nearly a century ago, the weather can be forecast
by a very large number of computers, each calculating the equations for a specific grid point, and sharing results at each timestep with its neighbours. But
today's supercomputers go well beyond Richardson's imaginings. Fifty years
of advances in computing speed have produced computers that are billions of
times faster than the forecast factory that Richardson imagined. And 50 years of
advances in meteorological modelling have produced models that go far beyond
the primitive equations, as they now take into account chemical processes and
pollution, the physics of clouds, the evaporation of water from plants and soils,
and the movements of ocean currents and ice sheets. Machines are fast enough
that instead of picking a single model to work with, today's meteorologists can
run hundreds of models on the same data, to make up for uncertainties in the
data, and to analyze probabilities when precise predictions aren't possible.

This revolution in weather forecasting also kicked off an interest in other uses of numerical models of the atmosphere. What if, instead of trying to predict how current weather conditions will evolve over the space of a few days, you could use a similar model to explore why patterns such as Rossby waves occur in the first place? What if you added equations for the heating and cooling effects, when the Earth receives energy where it faces the sun, and loses energy back to space? Would such a model eventually simulate *typical* weather patterns experienced on planet Earth? These are questions about *climate*, rather than *weather*. Simulating these things in a model would be a tremendously powerful demonstration that theories about atmospheric circulation patterns were correct, and it would enable scientific experiments that cannot be done for real on planet Earth. And it could help explain why each region on Earth has the climate it does, and how stable those climate patterns are over time. In the next chapter, we will explore what happened when scientists began to explore such questions.

Notes

1 The work at Bletchley was kept secret for many decades after the War, so the invention of the Colossus is missing from many histories of the early computers.
2 Quoted in Asprey (1990, p. xv). Few mathematicians at that time thought that computation was worthy of study. Mathematics concerned itself with elegant conceptual structures, not the tedious work that electronic calculators could do.
3 This was Captain Herman Goldstein, who had helped secure the funding for ENIAC, and was, at the time, the army's chief liaison with the ENIAC engineering team. Goldstein and von Neumann later collaborated on developing some of the numerical methods now used in weather simulation.
4 The document was later the focus of a legal dispute over intellectual property, as Eckert and Mauchly argued it contained their ideas, while von Neumann argued it was a synthesis of the ideas of the entire team. Eckert and Mauchly resigned from the university and set up their own company to commercialize their ideas. This infuriated von Neumann, who wanted the designs to be freely available so other scientists could develop their own machines, and he would not have participated had it been clear that his contributions would be used for commercial purposes. In the end, von Neumann won the legal battle, and the ideas became public domain.
5 One of von Neumann's key requirements was to compute iterative solutions to partial differential equations. For this, the machine had to operate entirely autonomously, and store many intermediate results in memory. ENIAC was poorly suited to this, as it had only 20 internal registers. Von Neumann's new design was based on his estimates for typical hydrodynamic problems: he wanted 30-bit numbers, and 2^{18} bits of memory. See Asprey (1990).
6 See Platzman (1979) for a schematic of the program algorithm.
7 See Nebeker (1995).
8 More specifically, in an ideal fluid, density would depend solely on pressure. Under a planet's gravity, density increases with depth, because of the weight of

the fluid above. If this is the only thing that affects density, the fluid is said to be *barotropic*. If other things, such as heating and cooling can cause pockets of different density, then the fluid is *baroclinic*.

9 See Thorpe et al. (2003).

10 The expedition was finally re-discovered in 1930, along with log books describing a perilous journey after the three men crashed onto the ice floes. The actual cause of death is still a mystery.

11 Quoted in Friedman (1993).

12 See Edwards (2010) for a detailed history.

13 For example, in 1890, Cleveland Abbe (US meteorologist) argued "meteorology is essentially the application of hydrodynamics and thermodynamics to the atmosphere," and proposed a mathematical approach to forecasting. See Lynch (2008).

14 The key equation is $F = ma$, or Force equals mass times acceleration, although for weather forecasting, it's normally expressed as $a = F/m$.

15 Bjerknes (1904, p. 665).

16 See Persson (2006).

17 Following the parcels of fluid is known as the Lagrangian method, while focusing on the space through which it moves is known at the Eulerian method. We'll return to this choice in Chapter 5.

18 The Coriolis force was first worked out by Gaspard-Gustave de Coriolis in 1835, who was studying fluid flow in rotating systems like water wheels.

19 As the force of gravity and the Coriolis force depend only on the shape of the planet, in a weather simulation model they are usually combined together to provide a single constant force in each direction at each point in the atmosphere.

20 Richardson (1922, p. 219).

21 The international balloon days were normally the first Thursday of each month. However in May 1910, the balloon day was delayed so it would coincide with the passage of Halley's comet later in the month, to see if there was any detectable effect on the weather of the passage of the Earth through the tail of the comet.

22 Lynch (1993) notes that from Richardson's own arithmetic in his description of the Forecast factory, he must have meant six weeks of effort (working 24 hours a day), so it probably took closer to two full years for him to do all the calculations – most of his stay in France.

23 Richardson (1922, p. 219).

24 See Harper (2008), p100. In a hurricane, the air pressure drops, rather than rises.

25 See Lynch (2014).

26 Today, it's known as the Courant–Friedrichs–Lewy condition, in recognition of the three authors on the original paper, although von Neumann referred to it at the Courant Criterion.

27 The IAS computer would be built according to von Neumann's design, and would be much faster than ENIAC. The IAS team referred to it as "Johnniac," in tribute to von Neumann.

28 Harper (2008) makes it clear that Rossby's support was absolutely central to the eventual success of the project, given von Neumann's lack of expertise in meteorology.

29 Charney had only been in Oslo for a few years. He had completed his PhD at UCLA, in the research group founded by Bjerknes's son, and was a postdoc in Chicago where he began a long running collaboration with Rossby.

30 The troposphere extends from the surface to about 20 km up, although it thins to less than 10 km towards the poles. Above it is the stratosphere, where there

is very little air, virtually no water vapour and so not much weather either. The troposphere itself can be divided into two parts: the boundary layer close to the ground, where surface features create a lot of turbulence, and the "free atmosphere" above it, where surface friction no longer matters. You can sometimes see the top of the boundary layer, when cumulus clouds have flat bottoms. It can extend from a few hundred metres to about 2 km, depending on local conditions.

31 This heat pump effect helps explain Arrhenius's prediction that the poles would warm faster than the equator when you increase greenhouse gases. The Earth tends to gain heat from the sun near the equator, and lose heat near the poles. As increasing GHGs traps more of this escaping heat, the warming effect is strongest near the poles where there is more escaping heat to trap.

32 This was demonstrated by a team at the South Pole in 2001, who constructed a Foucault's Pendulum in the stairwell of the Amundsen–Scott South Pole Station.

33 Similar waves have been observed on other planets, particularly Jupiter, which has a very distinct jet stream, because it rotates much faster than Earth.

34 The assumptions in the model include: the atmosphere has uniform density, and motion is purely horizontal; density and pressure variation coincide ("barotropy"); pressure gradients are approximately balanced by the Coriolis force ("quasi-geostrophy"); vorticity is conserved over time; wind is parallel at all levels; and the system is thermodynamically closed. See Charney et al. (1950).

35 Margaret Smagorinsky (née Knoepfel) was, at the time, a graduate student in meteorology at NYU. She had just married another graduate student, Joseph Smagorinsky, who was working with Charney on the equations. Joseph went on to find fame as the head of the GFDL lab in Princeton, while Margaret stayed at home to raise their five children. See Harper et al. (2006).

36 The full results are presented in Charney and Eliasson (1949), although the paper fails to give any credit to the three women who did the calculations.

37 See Dyson (2012, p. 166). The movie *Hidden Figures* celebrates a similar story of the role of women in calculating the rocket trajectories for the space program. I'd like to think one day we'll see a similar movie about the early days of weather forecasting.

38 In technical terms, they selected dates that exhibited three different types of condition: essentially barotropic, essentially baroclinic, and with a pronounced blocking of the jet stream.

39 See Lynch and Lynch (2008).

4

Taming Chaos

Climate models are often presented as tools to predict future climate change. But that's more a reflection of the questions that politicians and the general public ask of the science, rather than what the science does. Climate scientists prefer to use their models to improve our understanding of the past and present, where more definitive answers are possible. Predicting the future is notoriously hard. It requires some careful thinking about what can be predicted and what cannot. On this question, early experiments with climate models led to one of the most profound scientific discoveries of the twentieth century – chaos theory – which gave us a new understanding of the limits of predictability of complex systems. The so-called butterfly effect of chaos theory helps explain why a computer model can predict the weather only for a few days in advance, while the same model can simulate a changing climate over decades and even millennia. To find out why, read on!

Predictions from Models

One thing most people want to know about climate change is: how will it affect us? By "us," we may mean our local communities, or human society in general. But either way, we want to know about things that happen on a human timescale: what should we expect within our lifetimes and those of our children and grandchildren? Many impacts of climate change can already be observed around the world, but the biggest impacts still lie some way into the future. So for non-scientists, a *useful* climate model would give us detailed predictions over a range of scales from "next year" to perhaps 100 years from now.

Computational models often work with very different timescales, so we should ask, for each model, over what timescales can it give reasonable predictions? A hurricane model created to track storms over a few days is unlikely to give sensible results over months or years. And a model created to simulate the cycle of ice ages over hundreds of thousands of years is not likely to tell us what next summer might be like. So how can a climate model make predictions for the rest of this century?

In Chapters 2 and 3, we met two important models, the global climate model developed by Svante Arrhenius in Stockholm in the 1890s, and the numerical weather forecast model developed by Jule Charney and colleagues at Princeton in the 1940s. Weather and climate are different things, and operate on different timescales. Charney's first model struggled to forecast the weather beyond a day or two. Arrhenius built his model to answer questions about the ice ages, so the timescale he was exploring was geological, rather than human. He did use his model to speculate about possible future climate change from burning coal and oil, but he also expected this would take thousands of years.

When I first visited the UK Meteorological office in 2008, I was surprised to learn they have one big model,[1] called the Unified Model, which they use for both weather forecasting and climate prediction. We'll explore this model in depth in Chapter 5. While most other climate research labs don't combine their modelling efforts quite this closely, all global climate models incorporate ideas from both Arrhenius's and Charney's models, along with a whole lot more.

How do these models overcome the limits of weather forecasting for longer timescales? As we'll see, climate turns out to be easier to predict than weather. My favourite saying about the difference between weather and climate is that climate is what you expect, and weather is what you get. When we talk about our local climate, we mean the kind of weather that would be typical at each time of year: expected maximum and minimum temperatures, average rainfall, and whether the region experiences hurricanes, tornados, droughts, etc. The weather itself can vary dramatically, but over time, those variations fall within a predictable statistical distribution, with an average and an expected spread. You could say that climate is the statistics of weather.

So how can we predict *changes* in these statistics over months, years, or decades? How will those averages change? And what will happen to the distributions of cold days versus warm days, rainy days versus dry days, or the number of extreme weather events? It turns out that climate models can give good answers to this type of question, but to understand why, we have to understand what makes some things predictable and others not.

The answers can be found in chaos theory. The story of chaos theory is very much the story of how we learned what you can and can't do with computer models. And because weather and climate modelling were always at the forefront of advances in computational modelling, much of our understanding of chaos theory arose from attempts to model the atmosphere.

Figure 4.1 Edward Norton Lorenz during a visit to NCAR, in Boulder, Colorado.
(Curt Zukosky / © 2022 UCAR)

The roots of chaos theory lie in pure mathematics,[2] but a colleague of Charney's, the applied mathematician and meteorologist Edward Lorenz (see Figure 4.1), stumbled across the key ideas almost by accident in the 1960s, when one of his weather models did something very unexpected. This illustrates another important point in computer modelling: model surprises are often extremely valuable. When a model does exactly what you expect, it probably doesn't tell you anything you didn't already know. But when it surprises you, that's when the learning starts. If your model never surprises you, it might not be a very useful model.[3]

Chaos theory is perhaps best known through the idea of the Butterfly Effect, after Lorenz gave a talk entitled *"Predictability: Does the Flap of a Butterfly's Wings in Brazil Set off a Tornado in Texas?"*[4] at the American Advancement of Science meeting, in Washington DC, in December 1972. At the time, he was a professor of meteorology at MIT, highly regarded by his colleagues, and immensely popular with his students, but largely unknown outside his own field. But Lorenz was never happy with the butterfly metaphor. His answer to the question, at least in the way it was phrased in the title of the talk, was a fairly confident "no."

Nevertheless, many books and movies latched onto the idea that the butterfly's flutter – a minuscule change in conditions – could over the course of time, lead the world down an entirely different path. In chaos theory, we call this *sensitivity to initial conditions*, and it refers, not so much to a butterfly's wing flaps, but to small errors or gaps in our measurements, which over time, grow to become enormous, and guarantee that a computer simulation of the weather will eventually diverge from the real weather. The real villain in Chaos theory isn't a capricious butterfly. It's our inability to know the world precisely.

Before we examine Lorenz's work and what it tells us about climate prediction, we should step back in time to understand what scientists thought about predictability before chaos theory was discovered.

Arrhenius versus Charney

What does predictability mean in each of the two models we have already met? Arrhenius's model could calculate the expected change in the Earth's surface temperature if you vary the amount of greenhouse gases in the atmosphere. In essence, this is an *equilibrium model*. It uses the principles of thermodynamics to calculate a new equilibrium surface temperature for the planet – how much warming or cooling would be needed to bring the incoming and outgoing energy to the planet back in balance – after a change in the amount of greenhouse gases. The model doesn't say how long it would take to reach this new equilibrium. And because it doesn't include weather at all, it can't account for possible changes in weather patterns, which might shift the extra heat around in new and unexpected ways.

Charney's model could calculate how the weather over North America would evolve over a 24-hour period, from a specific observed starting state. This is a *discrete time simulation* model. It starts with a given state of the atmosphere – in this case, air pressure at each point on a two-dimensional grid, at a particular moment – and uses the equations of motion and heat to calculate how these values will change after a short timestep, for example, 1 hour later. By repeating the calculations with the computed new state as the starting point, longer simulations can be run.

The two models focus on different things, but share many similarities. Both were developed to improve our understanding of how the atmosphere works. Both were based on long established physics principles, particularly the laws of thermodynamics, drawing on decades of prior work that had established and tested these principles. The underlying theory in both cases was sound, and the models were intended as new applications of existing knowledge, rather than novel theories. Both models also relied on a large number of simplifying assumptions, in order to make the calculations tractable. And both models needed good data about observed conditions at each point on a grid, covering a large area of the planet, and suffered because the available data wasn't anywhere near as good as the model required.

Modern climate models combine ideas from both models. Today's climate scientists distinguish them as *"the physics"* – the equations that express how incoming sunlight and outgoing infra-red interact with the atmosphere, like Arrhenius's model, and *"the dynamics"* – the equations representing how weather systems move air and energy around the planet, like Charney's model.

Predictability

Perhaps the biggest difference between these two models is in the *predictability* of the things they were designed to study. Some things are relatively easy to predict. For example, prediction of times for high and low tides are so accurate we tend to think of them as facts.[5] Tides are caused primarily by the gravitational pull of the moon dragging the water in the oceans towards it. Since we know the relative movements of the Earth and moon, we can predict the tides years ahead using a simple model of the moon's orbit and a precise measurement of its initial position. The gravitational pull of the sun has an effect too, although it is smaller. This can be easily added to the model because the Earth's movement around the sun is also very predictable. The biggest complication is the tides are also affected by the shape of the shoreline and the prevailing winds, so we need more data to adjust our predictions for each location. But once we've worked out these local parameters, we can make good predictions of the tides at any location for decades in advance.

Eventually, however, this simple model would be wrong. When we say that the tides are easy to predict, we need to specify over what timescale, and how precisely. In billions of years' time, the sun will burn out, most likely expanding to swallow the Earth before collapsing. Over millions of years, the moon will gradually spiral away from the Earth, and slow in its orbit. Other planets in the solar system also perturb the orbits of the Earth and moon in small ways, allowing a little bit of chaos to creep in. If we wanted to predict the tides in future millennia, we would have to model all these interactions, which means we would have to solve the notoriously tricky *three-body problem*.[6] But fishers and sailors can download tidal tables for a whole year ahead, and rely on them completely.

In contrast, predicting the local weather a year in advance is impossible. Early weather modellers didn't know this, and their optimism about long-term weather forecasting was unbounded. But weather depends on the interaction of a very large number of parcels of air, and small differences in their arrangement can lead to very different outcomes. So we can build models to predict large-scale patterns like the path of the jet stream weeks and sometimes months ahead, and fine-grained models to predict the formation of a cloud on the scale of a few minutes. But in each case, any small difference between the simulation and the real world will, over time, grow to the point where they diverge completely, and once they do, there's no way to get the simulation back on track.[7] This is the butterfly effect – sensitivity to initial conditions – and it cannot be overcome just by developing better models.

Predicting climate change is nowhere near as hard as predicting the weather, but is harder than predicting the tides. Just as the movement of the tides are almost entirely dominated by the gravitational pull of the moon and the sun, the average temperature of the Earth is almost entirely dominated by the equilibrium between the incoming energy from the sun and outgoing energy lost to space from the upper atmosphere. The fact that this is an equilibrium problem greatly helps – a climate model can calculate the equilibrium point for any conditions, at any point in time. Of course, if the conditions – greenhouse gases in the atmosphere, for example – continually change, that complicates matters. There are more complicating factors to this problem than there are for planetary motion, including feedback loops that trigger other changes in the Earth's atmosphere. Today's models take far more of these factors into account than Arrhenius's original model did, and accordingly give us more confident predictions. But there's always the possibility that something important is missing in the model.

First Signs of Chaos

There is another big difference between Arrhenius's climate model and Charney's weather model. From a mathematical perspective, they belong to different classes of problem. The key equation in Arrhenius's model gives an exact solution, and can be solved using the same number of steps, no matter what inputs it is given – using an *analytical* method. But the equations of motion in Charney's model are too complex to have an analytical solution. Instead, Charney used a *numerical* method – Richardson's technique of finite differences, in which equations expressing a rate of change are replaced by approximations for the actual change over a small(ish) timestep – like replacing a smooth curve with a large number of short straight lines. The calculation takes more and more steps for longer forecasts, and small errors introduced by the approximation will accumulate as the calculation proceeds.

We saw in the last chapter that John von Neumann was one of the few mathematicians of his generation to see the potential of numerical methods to solve problems mathematicians had previously been unable to handle. And indeed, as computers have become more powerful, the use of numerical methods has proliferated in applications throughout science and engineering.

The distinction between analytical and numerical methods is well illustrated in the story of the solution to the three-body problem and the origins of chaos theory. In theory, Newton's equation for the law of gravity should allow astronomers to calculate more accurate paths for each planet, taking into account the gravitational effect not only of the sun, but also the other planets and their moons. In practice, this turns out to be really hard. The solution for two bodies is simple – the orbit of a lone planet around its sun is an *ellipse*. But as soon as you add a third body, the equations become incredibly complex. The problem of finding a precise, analytical solution to this became known as the *three-body problem*, or, more generally, the *n-body* problem.

Astronomers and mathematicians in the nineteenth century considered the *n*-body problem so important they suggested it as a topic for a mathematics prize to celebrate the 60th birthday of King Oscar of Norway and Sweden, in 1889. The prize was to be awarded for an analytical solution, or failing that, for work that made significant progress towards a solution. Twelve entries were submitted, but only five actually tackled the *n*-body problem, and none of them solved it. The jury decided to award the prize to a brilliant young French mathematician named Henri Poincaré, as his paper was packed with new ideas, including a proof that the three-body problem could not be solved using the standard method of "looking for first integrals".[8] Many people have since assumed Poincaré's proof showed the problem cannot be solved at all, but this is not so.

In fact, *numerical* solutions had already been discovered long before. The planet Neptune was discovered in 1846 using one such technique, in which you start with simple elliptical orbits, and then systematically add in the perturbations from each of the other planets to get closer and closer to an accurate solution.

In 1913, a Finnish mathematician, Karl Sandman found an *analytical* solution to the three-body problem that works for all cases in which the bodies never collide. And in 1991, a Chinese mathematician, Quidong Wang found a similar solution for the *n*-body problem. Unfortunately, while both of these analytical solutions are correct and precise, they are also entirely useless, because you would have to add up millions of terms to calculate the motions of objects even for tiny intervals of time. These solutions add little to our understanding of the n-body problem.[9]

Poincaré's prize-winning paper was far more interesting than these eventual solutions, because it laid the groundwork[10] for the discovery of chaos theory. Poincaré analyzed a simplified version of the three-body problem, in which two of the bodies are constrained to orbit one another in a circle, while the third can move freely around them – like a planet orbiting twin suns (see Figure 4.2). To reason about whether there is any regularity in the path of the third body, he used a brilliantly simple thought experiment. Imagine a huge ocean in space, cutting across the orbit of this planet, so some parts of its orbit are underwater. Then ignore all of the complex movements of the planet, and focus instead just on the points on the surface of this ocean where the planet dives in – and ignore the places where it re-surfaces again. If the object has repeating behaviours, it must pass through the same sequence of diving locations on this surface more than once. In a very simple case, say a stable elliptical orbit, it will always dive in at the same point. More complicated orbits might pass through a series of points that form a closed shape on the surface. But Poincaré found in some cases the pattern never repeats. If there is no repetition, finding mathematical solutions would be much harder. What he had found was an example of chaotic behaviour, and today we call this way of thinking about it a Poincaré map.[11] Curiously, Poincaré never pursued these chaotic behaviours further, perhaps because to him they were nothing more than an inconvenience that messed up the quest for an elegant analytical solution.[12]

Poincaré believed, like many mathematicians and astronomers of his time, that the motions of the planets were stable and predictable. It seemed likely that chaotic patterns should be rare, and most n-body systems would have simple, repeating patterns. But as chaos theory developed in the 1960s and 1970s, it became clear that regular patterns are rare, and chaotic ones are in the vast majority. From most starting points, the three bodies will produce a chaotic pattern, as illustrated in Figure 4.2. Even the apparent stability of the solar system is an illusion. Over millions of years, chaotic interactions between the planets will distort their orbits in complex ways, and we have no way of predicting their paths on this timescale.

But that doesn't mean chaotic systems are *never* predictable. In fact, knowing that a system is chaotic makes some things easier, because the behaviours that occur in chaotic systems are not random. We can predict the paths of the planets for decades ahead with incredible accuracy, using numerical methods – if we couldn't, then spacecraft navigation would be impossible. We can also quantify the limits of predictability in a chaotic system. By measuring the

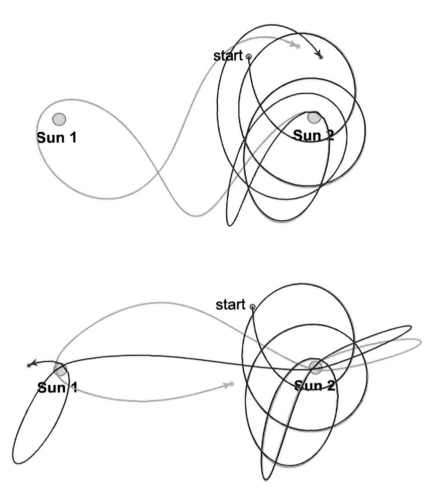

Figure 4.2 Two simulations of chaotic behaviour in the simplified three-body problem. Each simulation shows a pair of paths (one light blue, one dark blue) for a planet orbiting the two suns, but with a tiny difference in their starting points – so close they appear identical at the start. In each case, the orbits appear to be the same, at first. But over time, their paths slowly separate, and eventually each follows an entirely different path. (Images courtesy of David M. Harrison)

rate of growth of small differences in starting conditions, we can measure the growth of errors, and calculate how long a prediction will still be reliable. And chaotic systems often have characteristic patterns of similar behaviours, even when they never repeat exactly.

A Very Artificial Model

To understand what causes a particular pattern of events to occur, a useful strategy is to find the simplest model in which the pattern occurs. One of the most successful simple models in meteorology consisted of a dishpan of water, with drops of ink in it, to simulate Rossby waves in the upper atmosphere. As an illustration of how an unrealistic model can offer important scientific insights, this one is hard to beat.

We met Carl Gustaf Rossby briefly in Chapter 3. He was instrumental in helping von Neumann hire a team of bright young meteorologists to develop the first computer weather forecast model. At the end of the War, in 1945, Rossby became the first head of the newly formed department of meteorology at the University of Chicago. In the 1920s, he had experimented with the idea of using a rotating tank of water to simulate the rotation of the Earth, so that he could study how the Coriolis effect affected the flow of a fluid. These early experiments hadn't been very successful, but the discovery of the jet stream in the 1940s renewed his interest in this work – would it be possible to simulate a jet stream in a tank of water?

Rossby suggested the idea to one of his graduate students, Dave Fultz, who took up the challenge with great enthusiasm, and eventually developed a hydrodynamics laboratory of his own to carry out such experiments. Fultz's first model[13] consisted of two spherical glass flasks, cut off at the "equator," to give a pair of glass hemispheres, one inside the other (see Figure 4.3). Fultz filled the space between the two flasks with water, to represent the thin layer of atmosphere around the Earth, and used a heater at the neck of the outer flask to supply a steady source of heat to the water at the bottom. At the top, heat could escape from the open surface of the water at the "equator," but it could also escape through the inner and outer surfaces of the flasks. He placed the entire apparatus on a rotating platform, to simulate the rotation of the Earth.

The correspondence between this model and the Earth's atmosphere was relatively poor. It was only a hemisphere rather than a sphere,[14] and the heating arrangement was backwards: while the Earth receives most of the heat from the sun at the equator, and loses most of it at the poles, the model had the heat at the South Pole, with cooling at the equator. Nevertheless, the model demonstrated turbulent effects similar to the real atmosphere. Traces of ink injected through the outer shell made these easy to see. Bands of fluid at different latitudes moved at different speeds and eddies a few centimetres wide would form at the boundaries between these bands. The patterns were reminiscent of photos of the planet Jupiter, with its swirling bands of colour. The combination of

Figure 4.3 David Fultz's original rotating hemispherical model, which had a thin
layer of water trapped between two concentric glass hemispheres. The rods across
the top stop the inner hemisphere floating up. (Reproduced from Fultz (1949).
Published 1949 by the American Meteorological Society.)

just a rotating fluid and a heat source seemed to be enough to induce some of
the complex patterns seen in the atmosphere of real planets.

Meanwhile, in a different lab in the department, another scientist, Ferguson
Hall, had also built a rotating model, to try and simulate the formation of hurricanes. Hall's model was much simpler, consisting of a cheap metal saucepan
(or *dishpan*), filled with water, heated underneath with a bunsen burner, and
mounted on a rotating platform. To see what patterns the water would form, he
would sprinkle aluminium powder on the surface of the water. For Hall, it was
just a side project, and it failed to show anything resembling miniature hurricanes. But Fultz thought the patterns on the water were intriguing, and when
Hall left to join the Weather Bureau in Washington in 1949, Fultz moved the
equipment into his own lab, to experiment further.

Fultz made a number of modifications to the dishpan setup. He thought of
the dishpan as a flattened hemisphere, and moved the bunsen burner to the
outer edge of the dishpan to simulate heating at the equator. Later he added a
jet of cold water at the centre, to simulate cooling at the pole. He also developed a complex overhead camera that rotated with the dish, to take regular

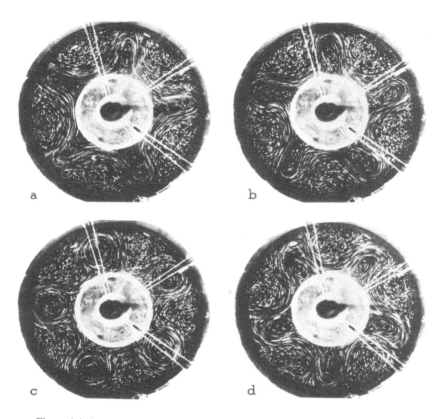

Figure 4.4 A sequence of four photographs of David Fultz's dishpan experiment, showing vacillation. A Rossby wave forms, then splits off into separate eddies and finally re-forms again. (Reproduced from Pfeffer and Chiang (1967))

photographs of the patterns of the aluminium particles on the surface of the water. Using a long exposure with a big flash at the end, the camera could capture the movements of the particles, with the flash creating an "arrowhead" at the end to show which way they were moving.

Fultz had been hoping to re-create the familiar wave pattern of the meandering jet stream, around the circle of the pan. What he found was far more interesting. The dishpan would produce two quite distinct patterns, one with a regular, symmetrical flow, with the particles travelling in concentric circles around the dish, and the other a characteristic pattern of Rossby waves, with vortices shearing off from the waves (see Figure 4.4). The patterns would flip from one to the other as the speed of rotation and amount of heat applied were altered. The transition points were perfectly predictable: the pattern would always flip at the same combinations of rotation speed and heating level.

These patterns demonstrated another key idea in chaos theory: *bifurcation*.[15] Many complex systems exhibit what appears to be a stable pattern of behaviour, but when conditions are slowly altered, this will suddenly flip to an entirely different pattern, which then also appears to be stable. The flip is called a *phase transition*. Each pattern endures, until changes in conditions flip the system back again. In this case, the dishpan had two distinct patterns that depended only on the rotation speed and the rate of heating. A similar effect crops up everywhere: from the way the Earth flips between ice ages and warmer interglacials, as the planet slowly wobbles on its axis, to the way water flowing around an obstacle will flip from one path to another when the rate of flow slowly changes. What makes bifurcation remarkable is that the flips are dramatic and sudden relative to the slowly changing variable that induces them. Small changes in the conditions seem to do nothing at all for a while, and then suddenly cause a massive change all at once.

Later in 1950, Fultz travelled to the University of Cambridge on a Guggenheim scholarship, leaving the dishpan experiments in the hands of his colleagues. On his travels, he visited labs across Europe to find many other meteorologists experimenting with physical models of rotating fluids. At the University of Göttingen, scientists had an entire rotating room, about ten feet across, but found it was hard to use for experiments, as anyone in the room would tend to get motion sickness. In Cambridge, he met a young geologist, Raymond Hide, who wanted to use Fultz's approach to simulate patterns of the magnetic fields in the Earth's core. Hide ended up with a similar experimental set up to the dishpan experiment, but with an additional cylinder within it, so that the water was constrained in a ring-shaped dish, between an outer wall and an inner wall. In Hide's experiments, the Rossby wave patterns were sharper and more regular, and would slowly travel around the ring while maintaining their shape. Hide also noticed the waves would alter their shape in unison without any changes in the conditions, passing through a series of different shapes over the course of several complete rotations of the ring, and finally back to their original shape, from where the cycle would repeat. Hide called this *vacillation*.

When Fultz returned to Chicago, he discovered he could observe vacillation in his dishpan setup, but the patterns were more complex. The waves would evolve in a predictable way over a number of rotations. At one stage, a single wavefront formed around the dish. Each loop of the wave would then spin off vortices, causing the wave to break up into a set of swirling circles, spaced around the dish, which would then coalesce back into a single wavefront again.

The pattern behaved very much in the way storm systems spin off from the air flows in the upper atmosphere. Part of the sequence is shown in Figure 4.4.

These discoveries were exciting to meteorologists because they meant that the characteristic patterns of flow observed in the upper atmosphere – jet streams and travelling vortices – didn't depend on the shape of the planet and the existence of continents and mountains, nor on water vapour, which is responsible for much of the movement of heat in the real atmosphere. Nor did it even depend on the fact that the atmosphere is made of air – the patterns could be simulated in any fluid. The models had shown the complexity of the system could be reduced to just a few variables that mattered: rotation, heating and cooling, and gravity. Because the rotation speed mattered, it was clear that the duration of a day on Earth also mattered. If the Earth spun at a different rate, Rossby waves might disappear. The rate of heating and cooling also mattered, so atmospheric patterns could shift dramatically under different climate conditions – during the ice ages for example. But it would take several more decades for the full implications of these experiments for predictability became clear, as nobody had yet threaded together all the ideas that became chaos theory.

The Birth of Global Circulation Models

Charney's team of meteorologists at Princeton was intrigued by the results of the dishpan experiments. Could their simple computer models also exhibit some of the same patterns? von Neumann and Charney were keen to figure out how to extend the range of their forecasts. Their early weather models had produced some reasonably good forecasts for 24 hours, and sometimes even 36 hours. To extend the forecasts, they would need better models and better data. Getting a realistic simulation of the jet stream over the longer term would help tremendously.

Because of limited computing power, and limited observational data, their early models were designed to cover only a part of the globe – the region over North America. If a storm system from elsewhere moved into the region, the model could not simulate this, because it had no information on what is happening beyond its boundaries. In his initial models, Charney ignored this problem. He simply added an extra strip of grid points at each edge of the model's grid, where conditions were treated as constant. When the simulation calculated the next state for each point within the grid, the edge points just kept their initial values. This simplification limits the accuracy of the weather forecasts. As the simulation proceeds, the values at these edge points become less and less like the real conditions, and the errors propagate inwards, across the grid. To get longer forecasts – say for weeks, instead of days – a better solution was needed. The computer would need to "think outside the box."

The obvious way to do this is to extend the grid to cover the entire globe, making it a "closed" system.[16] This would leave only two, simpler boundaries – the top and bottom of the atmosphere. At the top of the atmosphere, energy arrives from the sun, and is lost back to space. But no air mass crosses this boundary, which means there are no significant boundary disturbances. At the bottom, where the atmosphere meets the surface of the planet, things are a little more complicated. Here both heat and moisture cross the boundary, with water evaporating from the land and oceans, and eventually being returned as rain and snow. But this effect is small compared to movements within the atmosphere, so it could be ignored in the coarse-grained models of the 1950s – later models would incorporate this exchange between surface and atmosphere directly in the simulation.

Among the group at Princeton, Norman Phillips was the first to create a working global model. Because the available computer power was still relatively tiny, extending the grid for an existing forecast model wasn't feasible. Instead, Phillips took a different approach. He removed so many of the features of the real planet, the model barely resembled the Earth at all. In fact, his model was more a simulation of the dishpan experiments than it was of planet Earth.

To simplify things, he treated the surface of the Earth as smooth and featureless – like the bottom of a dishpan. He used a 17×16 grid, not unlike the original ENIAC model, but connected the cells on the eastern edge with the cells on the western edge, so that instead of having fixed boundaries to the east and the west, the grid wrapped around, as though it were a cylindrical planet. At the north and south edges of the grid, the model behaved as if there were solid walls – movement of the atmosphere against the wall would be reflected back again. This overall shape simplified things: by connecting the east and west edges, the model could simulate airflows that circulate all the way around the planet, but Phillips didn't have to figure out the complex geometry where grid cells converge at the poles.

The dimensions of this simulated cylindrical planet were similar to those of Charney's original weather model, and it used the same equations. Phillips's grid points were 375 km apart in the east-west direction and 625 km apart in the north-south. This gave a virtual planet whose circumference was less than one sixth of the circumference of the Earth, but whose height was almost the same as the height of the Earth from pole to pole.

Like the dishpan, Phillips' cylindrical model represented only one hemisphere of Earth. He included a heating effect at the southern end of the grid, to represent the equator receiving the most energy from the sun, and a cooling effect at the northern end of the model, to represent the Arctic cooling as it loses heat to space.[17] The atmosphere itself had two layers, each a version of Charney's original one-layer model. The grid therefore had 17×16×2 cells in total, and it ran on a machine with 5 Kbytes of RAM and 10 Kbytes of magnetic drum memory. The choice of this grid is not an accident: the internal memory of the IAS machine could store 1,024 numbers.[18] Phillips' choice of grid meant a single state of the global atmosphere could be represented with about 500 variables,[19] thus taking up just under half of the machine's memory, leaving the other half available for calculating the next state.

Phillips decided not to bother with observational data at all. That would have been hard anyway, as the geometry of his model didn't resemble planet Earth. Instead, he started his model with a uniform atmosphere *at rest*. Every grid point started with the same values, as though there was no wind anywhere. Starting a simulation model with the atmosphere at rest and hoping the equations would generate realistic weather patterns was a bold, and perhaps crazy idea.

It is also the ultimate test of the equations in the model: if they *could* get the virtual atmosphere moving in a realistic way, it means nothing important has been left out. Today, we call this a *spin-up* run. The ocean and atmosphere components of today's global climate models are regularly started in this way. Spin-up runs for today's models are expensive though, because they require a lot of time on the supercomputer, and until the model settles into a stable pattern the simulation results are unusable. Oceans in particular have tremendous inertia, so modern ocean models can take hundreds of years of simulation time to produce stable and realistic ocean currents, which typically requires many weeks of processing time on a supercomputer. Therefore, the spin-up is typically run just once, and the state at the end of this spin-up is used as a start state for all the science experiments to be run on the model.

By 1955, Phillips had his global simulation model running successfully.[20] Once the run started, the simulated atmosphere didn't stay at rest. The basic equations in the model included terms for forces that would move the atmosphere: gravity, the Coriolis force,[21] expansion and contraction when air warms and cools, and the movement of air from high pressure areas to lower pressure areas. With heat entering the atmosphere towards the southern edge, the equations in the model made this air expand, rise, and move northwards, just as it does in real life. Under the effect of the simulated Coriolis force, this moving air mass slowly curled towards the east.

In his early tests, Phillips was able to run the model for a month of simulation time, during which the model developed a realistic jet stream and gave good results for monthly and seasonal weather statistics. Unfortunately, getting the model to run longer than a month proved to be difficult, as numerical errors in the algorithms would accumulate. In later work, Phillips was able to fix these problems, but by then a whole generation of more realistic global climate models were emerging.

Phillips's model didn't attempt to match any real conditions of the Earth's atmosphere. But because it could simulate realistic patterns, it opened the door to the use of computer models to improve our understanding of the climate system. The model could generate typical weather patterns from the basic principles of physics, meaning models like this could help answer questions about the factors that shape the climate and drive regional differences. Clearly, long-range simulation models were possible for overall atmospheric patterns – the *climate* – but not the actual *weather* on any specific day.

Extending the Weather Forecast

Despite its huge over-simplifications, Phillips's model was regarded as a major step forward, and is now credited as the first General Circulation Model. John von Neumann was so excited that within a few months he persuaded the US Weather Bureau, Air Force, and Army to jointly fund a major new research program to develop the work further. The new research program, initially known as the General Circulation Research Section,[22] and housed at the Weather Bureau's computing facility in Maryland, eventually grew to become today's Geophysical Fluid Dynamics Lab (GFDL), one of the world's leading research labs for climate modelling. von Neumann then convened a conference in Princeton, in October 1955, to discuss prospects for General Circulation Modelling. Phillips's model was the highlight of the conference, but the topics also included stability of the numerical algorithms, how to improve forecasting of precipitation (rain and snow), and the need to include in the models the role of greenhouse gases.

In his speech to the conference, von Neumann divided weather prediction into three distinct problems. Short-term weather prediction, over the span of a few days, he argued, was completely dominated by the initial values. Better data would soon provide better forecasts. In contrast, long-term prediction, like Phillips's model, is largely unaffected by initial conditions. von Neumann argued that by modelling the general circulation patterns for the entire globe, an "infinite forecast" would be possible – a model that could reproduce the large-scale patterns of the climate system indefinitely. But the hardest prediction problem, he suggested, lay in between these two: intermediate-range forecasts, which are shaped by both initial conditions and general circulation patterns. His assessment was correct: short-term weather forecasting and global circulation modelling both developed rapidly in the ensuing decades, whereas intermediate forecasting – on the scale of months – is still a major challenge today.

Unfortunately, von Neumann didn't live long enough to see his prediction play out. That same year he was diagnosed with cancer, and died two years later in February 1957, at the age of 53. Charney and Phillips left Princeton to take up positions at MIT, in the meteorology department where Ed Lorenz was working as an assistant professor. The Princeton meteorology project that had done so much to kick-start computerized weather forecasting was soon closed. However, its influence lived on, as a whole generation of young meteorologists established new research labs around the world to develop the techniques. The UN had established a World Meteorological Organization (WMO) in 1950, aimed at better coordination for data collection and knowledge sharing, and began discussions about an international research project to improve the models. The Global Atmospheric Research Program, GARP, was eventually launched in 1967 under Charney's leadership, with 20 nations participating, from both sides of the cold war.

As weather forecasting models improved, it rapidly became clear sensitivity to initial conditions was more of a problem than even von Neumann had foreseen – far more important than weaknesses in the models.

Lorenz's Surprise

In the late 1950s, Ed Lorenz was appointed as head of the statistical meteorology project at MIT. Lorenz never felt quite suited to the role, as he believed statistical weather forecasting was too limited, and that dynamical simulations like those developed by Charney and colleagues would be far more reliable. The statistical methods at the time would predict that what was happening already was likely to continue to happen, but shifted slightly in time and space – like a storm of constant intensity moving across the ocean.

Lorenz wanted to demonstrate that for realistic weather systems, a dynamical model could capture weather patterns that the statistical models could not, and hence was a better forecasting tool. For this he came up with a clever experiment. He would generate a set of data from a dynamical weather model, and treat this as though it was real weather data. He would then show the statistical methods were unable to reproduce this data. But the dynamical model could be re-run at any time to create a perfect "prediction" of the generated data, demonstrating the statistical approach is inferior. To generate the data, he needed a plausible simulation of real weather. However, it also needed to be simple enough so that the comparison was straightforward. That meant using as few variables as possible.

He chose a simplified model with 12 variables. His first attempts generated weather patterns that repeated at regular intervals, making it too easy for both methods to predict. What he needed was chaos – a pattern that never repeated – although he didn't realize it at the time.

By changing the way the equations handled heating and cooling, he eventually arrived at a model that, like the real weather, had none of these regularities. He programmed it to print out a graph of a chosen variable while the simulation proceeded. The computer took about a minute to simulate a day's worth of weather, so the graph would slowly emerge from the printer, and his colleagues would gather round, placing bets on what the next day's weather in the model would do.

One day, he wanted to repeat a portion of one of the runs, to study how it behaved in more detail. He stopped the computer, and used the set of values it had printed out earlier in the run as the new starting point. He then went off for coffee. When he returned, he was startled to discover the new run looked nothing like the old one. A weather forecasting model is, like most computer programs, an entirely deterministic algorithm. Run it twice on the same inputs and you should get exactly the same answers. Lorenz suspected that one of the valves in the computer had failed, and he compared the two runs to see if he could pinpoint when the error had occurred. Surprisingly, the two runs started out looking the same, but after some time, the curves differed slightly. The size of the gap doubled roughly every four days of simulation. Eventually the two curves diverged completely, showing very different behaviours (see Figure 4.5).

It took a while for Lorenz to realize what had happened. The numbers he had typed in – from the printout – were rounded to three places of decimals, and were therefore slightly different from the numbers stored in memory. These tiny roundoff errors were enough to ensure that eventually the two runs would end up simulating completely different weather. The implications were enormous: the errors in observational weather data would be orders of magnitude bigger than the roundoff errors in Lorenz's program. His discovery – sensitivity to initial conditions – meant that long-term weather forecasting would be impossible.

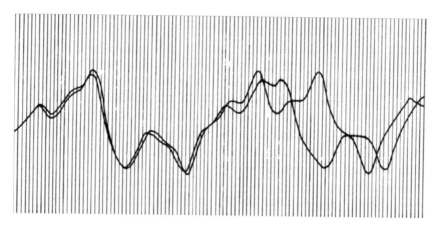

Figure 4.5 An example graph from Lorenz's experiment. At first the two curves are indistinguishable. But slowly, they start to diverge, and eventually show wildly different behaviours. (Reproduced from Gleick (1987))

Doubling Time

Model accuracy isn't the biggest issue in today's leading weather forecast models, as I discovered on one of my visits to the UK Met Office, when the lab was getting ready for delivery of a new, faster supercomputer. The meteorologists were looking forward to it, because the new machine would give them an instant improvement in the quality of their weather forecasts. Naïvely, I asked what improvements to the model they would be making on the new computer to achieve this. On no, they told me – the exact same model run on a faster machine would give them better forecasts. I asked them to explain.

As von Neumann had pointed out, the quality of a short-term weather forecast depends primarily on having accurate measurements of the current conditions as a starting state. The Met Office's customers need their weather forecasts by a certain deadline: TV companies need it to prepare their weather bulletins, while newspapers need it in time for their print deadlines. On a faster machine, the forecast model takes less time to run, which means the meteorologists can delay the start of their runs, giving them more time for the diagnostic step – analyzing the data about current conditions to provide a high quality start state for the model. Better initial data means better forecasts.

When we measure the current weather conditions, there are always gaps and inaccuracies in the data. So the initial state for a weather forecast model is always slightly different from reality. As the simulation runs, as Lorenz discovered, tiny differences get steadily magnified. Sooner or later, the differences grow so large that the simulation bears no relation to what will happen with real weather. Meteorologists assess this problem by talking about the *doubling time* in their simulations – how long does it take for small differences in the initial state to grow to double their size.

With more powerful computers becoming available, modellers could reduce the spacing between grid points in their models, and divide the atmosphere into more than two layers. In the early 1960s, several research groups discovered they could get more accurate forecasts by switching to the original primitive equations described by Richardson in 1922, in place of Charney's filtered equations, which smooth out noise at every step in the simulation, making it less responsive to changes in the weather. A better solution is to smooth once, at the start, by removing inconsistencies in the observational data used for the initial state. In meteorology, the process of "cleaning" the observational data to get a consistent state is known simply as *analysis*. Getting the analysis right is crucial to producing good weather forecasts.

Switching to the primitive equations gave better forecasts, but made errors grow faster. Doubling time for errors in these newer models shrank to three days, and by the 1970s, with steady improvements in the fidelity of the models, it was down to two days. A two-week forecast would involve *seven* doublings of errors in the initial state – small errors would be 128 times bigger. Two-week forecasts were unlikely to ever be much better than guesswork.

The doubling time for errors in a simulation isn't a fixed number – it depends on which phenomena we are trying to predict, and under what circumstances. In most models, thunderstorms occur at too small a scale: they happen in between adjacent grid points, and can start and end between timesteps. So rather than simulating them directly, the model would include estimates – *parameters* – for the typical number of thunderstorms expected under different atmospheric conditions. Very high resolution models can simulate a thunderstorm directly, but the doubling time for errors in such a model is very short – less than an hour. Adding finer grained detail to the model produces better forecasts, but only over shorter timescales.

In contrast, some weather phenomena can be predicted months ahead. For example, high winds in equatorial regions exhibit a very large-scale global vacillation pattern, like those observed by Fultz and Hide in their water tanks. Before the 1950s, meteorologists assumed that winds at 20–25 km above the equator flow from east to west. But sometimes they noticed this flow appeared to be missing. We now know that they blow east for about a year, then switch and blow west for about a year, so the entire vacillating pattern takes about two years. There's some variability over when the transitions occur, but within the steady part of the cycle, the flow can be predicted months ahead with reasonable accuracy.

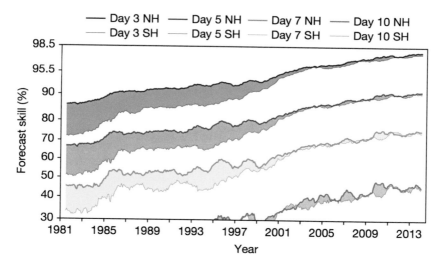

Figure 4.6 Steady improvements in weather forecast skill over the last few decades. Today, five-day forecasts are as good as three-day forecasts were 20 years ago, and seven-day forecasts are as good as five-day forecasts were. But the skill of a forecast drops rapidly the longer we peer into the future. Note that forecasts for the southern hemisphere (SH) were consistently worse than for the northern hemisphere (NH) until about 2000, when satellite coverage for the whole globe improved dramatically. (Reproduced from Bauer et al. (2015) by permission from Springer Nature)

Modern weather forecasting models have improved steadily over the years, but perhaps more importantly, so has the data collection and analysis. Today, three-day forecasts are accurate about 98% of the time, and five-day forecasts are accurate about 90% of the time. Figure 4.6 shows how forecasts have improved over time.

What happens if you keep running a weather forecast model long after it diverges completely from the real weather? A poorly designed model might start to produce unrealistic weather – weather that would never happen on planet Earth. But if the physics is correct in the model, and it obeys laws of conservation of mass and energy, it should continue to produce "typical" weather – the kinds of weather system one might expect at each location, given its climate. General circulation models are designed to do exactly this – they can simulate typical patterns for decades and even centuries, because they don't depend on initial conditions, and don't attempt to simulate what the weather will actually do. This makes them an ideal testbed for long-term climate experiments – for example, by checking whether typical patterns observed in the past can be reproduced in the model, and testing hypotheses about the causes of observed variations in the climate. However, that doesn't mean they escape from the challenges posed by chaos theory. As we shall see, chaotic processes affect them in quite a different way.

The Attractor

When studying some of the early weather forecasting models, Lorenz realized that you could start a weather model with almost any state of the atmosphere – even one that could never exist in reality – and by the physics of the model, it should rapidly evolve to a realistic atmosphere, like the spin-up run Phillips had used for his cylindrical model. The set of realistic weather states acts as an *attractor*: simulations starting in unrealistic states would eventually be pulled to realistic patterns.

To study this further, Lorenz decided to find a much simpler set of equations that still exhibited this behaviour. By 1961, he had found a system of three equations in three variables, which could be plotted fairly easily on a graph, but which exhibited all the properties of a chaotic process: the pattern they traced out never repeated, tiny differences in starting position would eventually lead to very different paths, but the overall pattern of those behaviours was always similar. Coincidentally, when plotted in three dimensions, the shape of this pattern vaguely resembles a butterfly (see Figure 4.7).

Attractors are an important feature of chaotic systems. For the atmosphere as a whole, attractors exist because of the *boundary conditions*: the Earth's gravity stops the atmosphere drifting off to space, and the Earth's rotation and heat from the sun keep the atmosphere moving in particular ways. On a smaller scale, hurricanes (and other storm systems) are also attractors – once they get going they form a characteristic pattern that can persist for many days. And on the global scale, the jet stream is an attractor, pulling the atmosphere into a flow that circles the globe, marked by waves that form and then break off into areas of high and low pressure. If you know what the attractors are, you can describe typical behaviours of the system, even if you can't say precisely what will happen when.

Lorenz's simplified set of equations has two very distinct attractors: the surfaces of each of the two wings of the butterfly (see Figure 4.7). From any starting point, the equations gradually move the system into orbit around one of the two attractors, where it spirals in until, suddenly, the system flips towards the other attractor. This pattern recurs repeatedly, although never in exactly the same way. The number of orbits it makes around each attractor before flipping

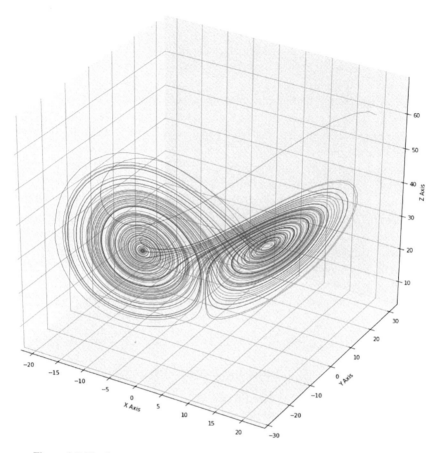

Figure 4.7 The Lorenz attractor. Lorenz's three equations are plotted on a three-dimensional graph. As the simulation runs, two distinct attractors appear, and the curve occasionally flips from orbiting one to orbiting the other, without ever repeating itself. I started this plot in the top right-hand corner ($x = 20$, $y = 30$, $z = 60$), and ran it for 10,000 steps, to show how quickly the attractor pulls the trajectory into the distinct butterfly pattern. No matter how long you run it, the trajectory never repeats.

to the other varies widely. The overall shape of the graph looks roughly the same, no matter where you start. But two starting points very close together – but not identical – will lead to two different sequences of orbits and flips.

It's not hard to describe an attractor in statistical terms – for example, the average time the system spends on each wing before it flips to the other, the typical size of the orbits, and so on. But a precise description is hard.

The attractor isn't any specific point on the surface of the wings, as the system never repeats any of its paths. Nor is it the entire "wing surface," as there are many parts of each wing it will never reach. The attractor is more like an infinitely nested series of curves. Today, we call this a *strange* attractor.

Lorenz wrote up his observations, including his visualizations of the attractor, in a paper[23] for the Journal of Atmospheric Sciences. His colleagues, particularly Charney, were enthused, and circulated the paper widely in the meteorological community. But his paper was largely unknown outside the field until Lorenz's now famous presentation at the 1972 conference[24] – the talk that gave us the term *butterfly effect*. Today, Lorenz's paper is widely recognized as the first clear description of a strange attractor.

In fact, Lorenz didn't choose the title of his famous butterfly talk, and he took the time to explain why the metaphor is a poor one: *"over the years, minuscule disturbances neither increase nor decrease the frequency of occurrence of various weather events such as tornados; the most they may do is to modify the sequence in which these events occur,"*[25] and he went on to explain why a butterfly might be too small to do even that. The key point of his talk was that small errors in our ability to measure the precise state of the atmosphere would always put a strict limit on the length of reliable weather forecasts.

Chaos Isn't Random

Chaotic systems are characterized by complicated, non-repeating behaviours, which makes them hard to study without the help of a computer model. But they also show a remarkable orderliness, best visualized using Poincaré's approach: instead of looking at the trajectory a chaotic system traces in the space of all possible behaviours, focus instead on the pattern of dots it traces on a surface that cuts across this space. These patterns may involve intricate curves that repeatedly fold in on themselves, but they are not random.

In everyday English, the term *chaos* is usually taken to mean an absence of order – a mess where there shouldn't be one. For example, if my office has been burglarized, and things have been strewn about randomly, I might say it's chaos. But the scientific meaning of chaos is almost the opposite of this: a very clear order even when none might be apparent.

Chaotic systems are not random. In a random system, the next state doesn't depend on the current state. For example, if you roll dice, your previous roll does not affect the next one in any way – the dice have no memory. But in a chaotic system, neither the attractors, nor the path taken are random. At any moment, the next state always depends on the previous state and the governing rules of the system – and the rules determine the shape of the attractors. It is only the complexity of the behaviours that makes them appear random.

In Lorenz's simplified model (shown in Figure 4.7) the current point of the curve at any moment is like day-to-day weather, while the attractors are like the climate. This particular model could represent a region that has two stable phases; perhaps a dry season and a wet season. If you observe the system for long enough, you can describe the attractors – the climate – in great detail, and characterize their statistics: how long each season typically lasts, how wet (or dry) it normally is, etc. But you can accurately predict the actual path – the weather – only for a short distance, and it can be very hard to predict when the system might flip from one phase to the other.

A system can exhibit different kinds of chaotic pattern on different times-cales. For example, an individual hurricane is a self-sustaining attractor that persists for perhaps a week or so. El Niño and La Niña are two opposite phases of a vacillating pattern that persists for months or years, bringing markedly different weather patterns to the Pacific coast of the Americas. And the ice ages represent another vacillating pattern where the Earth cycled through a pattern of freezing and warming roughly every 100,000 years for the last half million years, triggered by orbital variations – but with a carbon cycle feedback responsible for most of the temperature change.

If you want to predict a specific future state of a chaotic system, your prediction will be limited by two things: your knowledge of the starting state (the current conditions), and your ability to model the rules that determine how each state produces the next state. Even if your model approaches perfection, tiny changes in the initial conditions will place a limit on how many steps into the future your model can reliably predict things, and we can quantify this limit by exploring how fast errors in the model grow. We call this an *initial value problem* – successful prediction depends primarily on how well you know the initial value (see Figure 4.8).

On the other hand, if you only want to study the attractors in a chaotic system, you don't ever need to predict the exact state of the system, and initial conditions are largely irrelevant. In this case, you can start the model in any state you like. Your ability to map the attractors will depend only on how accurately your model captures the internal dynamics of the system. With a computer model, you can try many different starting states, and compare the statistics of its attractors with the statistics of the real system. Such a model may be excellent at simulating the climate (the attractors) but useless at predicting weather (the exact state at any moment). We call this a *boundary value problem*: if you get the overall conditions right – the boundaries – then you should be able to predict typical patterns of behaviour – the attractors – very well.

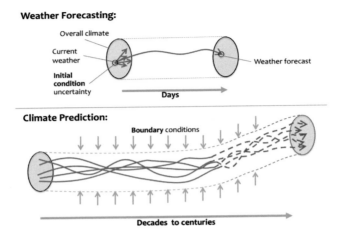

Figure 4.8 The difference between weather forecasting and climate prediction. For weather forecasting, the goal is to predict the exact state of the weather at some point in the future, from a given starting state. For climate prediction, the goal is to predict how the overall envelope of climactic conditions will shift in response to changing boundary conditions, such as a change in the amount of greenhouse gases in the atmosphere.

Forcings and Feedbacks

Long-term predictions of climate change aren't particularly useful to a climate scientist, because by the time we know whether they are right, the models that made them will be obsolete. You can't test a model that way, because it takes too long to see if we're getting the science right. Modern climate scientists build models not to predict the future, but to test their understanding of how the climate system works, and to help make sense of data from the past and present.

The fact that climate models *can* produce long-term predictions for planet Earth is, to some extent, a bonus feature. But they're not really predictions in the sense that a weather forecast for tomorrow is a prediction – something that will probably happen. A simulation of future climate change in a climate model is an *if-then* experiment: *if* humans continue to add greenhouse gases to the atmosphere at a particular rate, *then* the model will tell you the likely effect on the climate, taking into account everything we know about how the climate system works. It's better to call them *projections*. Humans rarely do what we expect, so comparing a climate model projection to what actually happened is tricky – the actual emissions of greenhouse gases over any time period won't exactly match the model inputs. We'll come back to this question in more detail in Chapter 8.

Another way of making this distinction is to examine whether the thing we're trying to predict is the result of internal variability or an externally imposed change. Weather prediction is all about internal variability. In a weather model, the external inputs – for example, heat from the sun – don't change much, beyond the usual daily and seasonal cycles. In contrast, climate prediction focuses on external change: variations in the Earth's orbit or the sun's intensity, greenhouse gases produced by human activity, volcanoes erupting, and so on. Climate scientists call these *forcings*, because each of them can force a change to the equilibrium temperature of the planet. In terms of chaos theory, forcings alter the position and shape of the attractors.[26]

You can sometimes turn an external forcing into internal variability by expanding the scope of your model, but it's not always easy. And if you want to study the impact of specific forcings, they need to be external to the model, so that you can specify them as inputs. For example, global climate models always treat human emissions of greenhouse gases as an external forcing, so that we can study how human activity affects the climate system.

Bringing more external factors into the model allows scientists to study how they interact, which is especially important if they form *feedback loops*. A simple example is the feedback loop between global warming and melting sea ice. Because ice is white, it reflects a lot of sunlight directly back into space, contributing to the relatively high albedo of planet Earth. But when it melts, it is replaced by darker seawater, so more of that energy from sunlight will be absorbed by the ocean, rather than reflected. This creates a feedback loop that leads to more warming and more melting.

There are many climate-related feedbacks in the Earth system, operating on different timescales. The ice-albedo feedback is very rapid – as soon as the ice melts, the feedback effect kicks in. The water vapour feedback that Arrhenius identified is another example: when the air warms, it holds more water vapour, which is itself a powerful greenhouse gas. But there are also slower feedbacks, which might take decades or centuries. An example is the slow release of other greenhouse gases – including methane and nitrous oxide – from the soil as it warms up, especially in sub-polar regions where the soils are normally frozen year round. Such slow feedbacks complicate assessments of future climate change, because they are missing from some of the models, and continue to operate well beyond the timescale in which most model simulations are done.

Many climate feedbacks in the Earth system are *amplifying feedbacks* –
once a change begins, they push that change further in the same direction.[27]
They need an initial change to get started – in an unchanging system they
do nothing. But the presence of amplifying feedbacks can make a system
unstable, as any small change will accelerate, often leading to chaotic behaviour. Such feedback loops can cause a system to escape from one attractor and
move toward another, by accelerating any small perturbation in that direction.
In contrast, *balancing feedbacks* tend to slow down a change. An example
is the cloud albedo feedback. Warming air holds more moisture, leading to
more cloudiness. But clouds reflect more sunlight back into space, which cools
things down again. Balancing feedbacks tend to keep a system stable – they are
the reason attractors exist in the first place.

Accurate prediction in climate science depends on getting these feedbacks
correct: a missing feedback can make a big difference in identifying how the
system will react to a forcing. However, as Phillips demonstrated with his virtual dishpan model, if you can get a simulation to produce the same attractors
that occur in the real world, and if these patterns persist over the course of a
long run, that's an encouraging sign the model is getting the feedbacks right.
If the amplifying feedbacks are too strong, the model won't produce a stable
simulation at all, and if the balancing feedbacks are too strong, the model will
end up being too static.

We know a lot about these feedback loops from simulations of their effect
in the recent past, and from reconstructions of the distant past, over millions of
years. Climate scientists often move back and forth between simplified models
and complex global models. The simple models, like that built by Phillips,
improve our understanding of a particular feedback loop or chaotic behaviour
on its own, while global Earth system models explore how these phenomena
interact with the rest of the climate system. By experimenting with different
models, and comparing their results, scientists explore how well each feedback
loop is understood, and hence how much uncertainty it contributes to climate
change projections.

As with any chaotic system, there is still room for surprise. The models tell
us what is likely to happen, based on all the information we currently have
about how the Earth system works. But the more the climate diverges from
anything we've been able to observe before, the higher the chances that feedback loops missing from the models will start to matter. In other words, the
more we push the climate away from the attractor that has kept it relatively stable throughout human history, the less we can be sure about what new attractor
it is heading towards.

Notes

1   Technically speaking, it's really a family of models, built from the same code base, where each model might include different aspects of the Earth system. The shared code base requires a lot of coordination, but it brings some significant advantages for the Met Office. See Easterbrook and Johns (2009).

2   See Abraham and Ueda (2000) for an overview of the discovery of the mathematics of chaos theory.

3   I like to think that many of the greatest scientific discoveries were preceded by someone saying "oops, that's not supposed to happen," rather than "Eureka!" But such moments are probably safer when you're talking about a computer model than when you're building, say, a nuclear reactor.

4   The full text of the talk is given as an appendix in Lorenz's book "The Essence of Chaos" (Lorenz, 1993).

5   Lorenz (1993) makes this point in his book.

6   More precisely, we'd have to solve the more general n-body problem. See Diacu (1996) for an entertaining account of how this problem was solved, and why many mathematicians still think it's unsolvable. We'll return to this problem shortly.

7   Actually, you could nudge the simulation back on track at each timestep with real data. This is known as data assimilation. It's no good for making predictions, as we don't have the data about the future. But it's very useful for studying the past, as the model can then fill in missing detail from past observational datasets.

8   Roughly speaking, this method tries to simplify the differential equations that express changes in motion by finding constant relationships between the variables. Poincaré's proof shows that there are too many degrees of freedom for this method to work.

9   See Diacu (1996) for a more detailed argument on this point.

10   The original version of his paper, submitted for the prize, missed the chaotic behaviours of the three body problem, and he only discovered them when working through questions from a reviewer. Poincaré eventually paid more than the prize was worth to have the first print run destroyed and replaced with the corrected version.

11   Technically speaking, a Poincaré map is the mathematical function that relates each point of intersection on the surface to the next point of intersection. The surface itself is known as a Poincaré section.

12   It's not clear why Poincaré never explored the chaotic solutions he had encountered, although you really need a computer to investigate chaos theory properly. Lorenz (1993) speculates that to Poincaré, the chaotic solutions to the three-body problem were nothing more than inconveniences – the spaces where his solutions didn't work.

13   Details of these experiments can be found in an interview with Dave Fultz. See Frenzen (1993). A preliminary report of the work, along with photos of the apparatus, can be found in Fultz (1949).

14   Well, the Earth's not quite a sphere either, but you get the point.

15   The term *bifurcation* was first coined by Poincaré in his prize-winning paper on n-body problems.

16   Physicists distinguish between "open," "closed," and "isolated" systems. In a closed system, energy can cross the system boundary, but matter cannot. In an isolated system, energy cannot cross the boundary either. For planet Earth, some

matter does cross the boundary – spaceships, meteorites, etc. – but the amounts are tiny compared with the size of the planet. In effect, the Earth can be treated as a closed system, but not an isolated system, as we continually receive energy from the sun.

17 This was implemented in the model using a heating parameter as a linear function of latitude, with maximum heating at the southern edge, and maximum cooling at the northern edge, with points in between scaled accordingly. As Phillips points out, this is not quite like the real planet, nor the dishpan experiments he was mimicking, but it was sufficient to generate stable circulation patterns similar to those in the real atmosphere. See Phillips (1956) for details.

18 More precisely, it had 1,024 words, each 40-bits long.

19 Actually, the grid was only 17×15, because it wrapped around, with the westernmost grid points being the same as the easternmost ones. So each of the two atmospheric levels could be represented as a geopotential array of 255 elements (see Lewis, 1998).

20 Details of his early experiments with the model are given in Phillips (1956).

21 Strictly speaking, a cylindrical planet, if it could exist at all, wouldn't have a Coriolis force, as the effect comes from the curvature towards the poles. Phillips included it in the equations anyway, to see if it would still produce a jet stream. He used a variable Coriolis factor – the Coriolis force would get stronger, the further north you moved. This is essential for the formation of a jet stream (see Lewis, 1998).

22 Joseph Smagorinsky, another member of the team that had run the ENIAC forecasts, was appointed head of this project. See Aspray (1990). von Neumann's original proposal is reproduced in full in Smagorinsky (1983).

23 The paper title, "Deterministic Non-periodic Flow," might also have been a factor in the paper being ignored outside meteorology. See Lorenz (1963).

24 As the conference approached, the session chair needed a title for the talk, and when he couldn't get hold of Lorenz, he made up a catchy title, to reflect the buzz that was building up in the community about Lorenz's work: "Predictability: Does the Flap of a Butterfly's Wings in Brazil Set Off a Tornado in Texas?" Lorenz points out another member of the original ENIAC weather modelling team, Joe Smagorinsky, originated the butterfly metaphor in his 1969 Wexler Lecture. See Lorenz (2006).

25 Lorenz (1993, Appendix 1).

26 As Stainforth et al. (2007) point out, if you continually alter the forcing (e.g., by steadily increasing the levels of CO_2 in the atmosphere), the attractors keep mutating; it's not clear whether a chaotic system experiencing transient forcing can be said to have attractors. It's certainly much simpler to study where the attractors ended up once you stop applying the forcing, which is what most climate models experiments attempt to do.

27 Engineers prefer the terms positive and negative feedback. I've avoided this terminology as we tend to associate value judgments with the terms positive and negative. For climate feedbacks, negative (balancing) feedbacks are a very good thing, as they help to counteract some of the warming humans are causing.

5

The Heart of the Machine

Today's climate models trace their lineage to the global circulation models of the 1950s. The core equations are the same, but the algorithms that implement them have evolved, and scientists have taken advantage of each new generation of faster computers to improve their models. The models I've studied often weigh in at more than a million lines of code, contributed over many years by hundreds of scientists. And they keep evolving; every climate model is a work in progress. Even the beating heart of a climate model – its "dynamical core" – gets replaced every once in a while. In this chapter, we'll examine one model in particular, the UK Met Office's Unified Model, and explore its dynamical core and the design decisions that shaped it.

A Visit to Exeter

The UK Meteorological ("Met") Office occupies a large purpose-built building on the outskirts of Exeter, in the southwest of England, a 2-hour train ride from London. The first time I visited, in 2007, I got off the train one stop before Exeter itself, in the tiny village of Pinhoe, and set off on foot. It was a warm summer day, and the walk was glorious – down one of those narrow Devon county lanes where the hedgerows rise steeply on both sides to create a tunnel of greenery.

Eventually, the lane opens out onto the main road of the industrial estate, and the Met Office building emerges out of the trees, a four-storey glass front with a swooping curved roof suspended above it (see Figure 5.1). The inside of the building is as spectacular as the outside – a huge central atrium known as "The Street" runs the length of the building, its floor split in two by a stream that runs right through the centre of the building. On each floor, balconies overlook the central atrium, on which the staff of the Met Office would gather every Thursday afternoon with their mugs of tea, to hear a weekly weather briefing from the senior meteorologists.[1]

Figure 5.1 The UK Met Office building in Exeter, United Kingdom. (CC-BY-SA 3.0 William M. Connolley)

The Met Office is one of the largest weather forecasting centres in the world, employing around 2,000 staff, and operates its own purpose-built super-computer centre in Exeter's new science park, about 2 km away. It also boasts one of the world's leading climate research labs – the Hadley Centre – which occupies a huge office on the top floor of the building, sharing it with other scientific research groups. The Hadley Centre itself is home to around 200 climate scientists.

Shortly after that first visit, I arranged with my host, Tim Johns, to spend an entire summer at the Met Office, interviewing climate scientists, and observing how they work. At the time, Tim was the manager of the Hadley Centre's coupled climate model, and we had many long conversations about what it takes to build and maintain one of the world's leading climate models. Tim organized more than 30 interviews for me with Met Office scientists, and invited me to sit in on many key meetings. He even arranged a few road trips for me to other labs that collaborate with the Hadley Centre.

I had chosen to begin my studies of climate modelling here because the Hadley Centre had been recommended to me as the best climate modelling centre in the world.[2] My studies of climate modelling eventually led me to visit many other climate research labs, along with many conferences and workshops where climate modellers discuss their work. The four models I studied most closely come from the United Kingdom, France, Germany, and the United States.

Surprisingly, the labs I contacted welcomed the idea of me studying their efforts, and two of them invited me to come and study them even before I had asked! The four research labs I describe in this and the next few chapters are four of the largest climate research labs in the world – big enough that having a computer scientist wandering around taking notes wouldn't disrupt their research too much. I've also had invitations to visit many of the smaller research labs, and hope to do so eventually. But for my initial studies, the bigger labs were the ideal place to start.

All of these models have a substantial history. One of the most dramatic changes over the decades is the increase in computational power available. This has enabled a steady evolution in the design of climate models, including improvements in the numerical algorithms, the level of detail, and the scope of these models. So what does a climate model do, and how does it do it?

A Unified Model

The Met Office is unique[3] in the world for having merged its climate models with its operational weather forecasting models, to create a single body of program code, which they call the Unified Model (or UM for short). The UM consists of well over 1 million lines of program code, and can be used to construct a huge variety of models, including the weather forecast models used every day at the Met Office, as well as a large number of models used for scientific research in both meteorology and climate science.[4] The code used in the UM has been under continuous development for many decades – the models were first unified in 1990, and some of the models involved in that merge already had a long pedigree, as numerical modelling at the UK Met Office dates back to the late 1960s.

Despite its age, the UM is very much a work in progress – the software engineers I met estimate they update about a quarter of the code each year, with contributions from more than 50 different scientists in any given year. Along with the model itself, the Met Office has developed a sophisticated set of tools[5] for configuring each model, extracting the relevant code from the shared code repository, setting up the runs, and creating visualizations of the model outputs.

Each individual model built from the UM code has its own name. The climate model names all start with "Had," a reference to the Hadley Centre. When I first visited, HadCM3 was the current workhorse global climate model, having evolved out of HadCM2 which was used in the 1990s. But climate modelling was undergoing a change in emphasis, growing to incorporate more of Earth's systems, all of which interact with the climate – ice sheets, soil and vegetation, atmospheric chemistry and pollution, and the biogeochemistry of the oceans. Accordingly, the Met Office renamed their next generation of climate models, calling them Global Environmental Models – HadGEM1, HadGEM2, etc. – in recognition of the broader set of environmental issues they could analyze.

For weather forecasting, the Met Office builds both global and regional models from the UM code. They also run a complex forecasting system called MOGREPS – the Met Office Global and Regional Ensemble Prediction System – which runs many variants of the model at the same time to help assess uncertainties in the forecasts. This overcomes the problem of sensitivity to initial conditions in a chaotic system. A single run of a model might just be a shot in the dark. What you really want to know is how robust your forecast is. So instead, you run different versions of the model – an *ensemble* of runs – and systematically vary the inputs to see if all the runs converge on roughly the same forecast, or end up with a spread of different forecasts. This is the basis for modern weather forecasts, which include probability estimates for the likelihood of rain, and likely paths of an approaching hurricane. And increasingly, the same approach is also used to explore uncertainties in our understanding of climate change.

Each of the Met Office and Hadley Centre models can be built from the UM code base by selecting a set of relevant code modules,[6] along with the data they need to operate. Today, software engineers would call this a *software product line* – a family of related software programs managed as a single code-base. While members of a product line share many common elements, each member of the family has a slightly different purpose, and so will need some alternative code modules. Product lines are now common across the software industry: car manufacturers use this approach to manage the software used in the different vehicles they build, and cellphone companies use it to manage the software used in all the different types of cellphone they sell. But in 1990 when the UM was created, the approach was almost unheard of.[7] As in so many areas, the Met Office was ahead of the curve.

Unifying climate models with the weather forecast models brings many advantages and a few drawbacks. For the Met Office, the approach saves a lot of duplication of effort, and ensures that advances in modelling are rapidly shared across the entire lab. Because the core model elements are run every day for weather forecasts, and analyzed carefully afterwards for how well they did, the meteorologists continually identify areas where the model performs poorly, and come up with improvements. The approach also means the same code is run at many different scales – from days to centuries, and from local regions to global scales. This gives the scientists tremendous insight into how the assumptions in their models hold up under different circumstances.

The scientists at the UK Met Office call this approach *seamless prediction*. The vision is a bold one: a scientist could explore a question at different timescales within the same model, switching back and forth between short-term weather patterns and longer-term climate change. For example, if you're studying the link between climate change and flooding, you might run a global climate model at a fairly coarse resolution to generate a century-long climate projection, and then zoom in at regular intervals – say once each decade – to generate a higher resolution weather simulation, to see how patterns of rainfall shift as the climate changes. Ideally, you would use exactly the same model, to be sure that that the simulations at different timescales are consistent with one another. However, that's not always possible yet. Some of the model components don't scale as well as they should, and have to be turned on or off as you shift across scales. But exploring what happens when you change these model configurations tests the strengths and weaknesses of each part of the model.[8]

The shared code also means the teams of scientists need a set of careful engineering practices, to ensure their work is coordinated, and that nobody can break anybody else's model with an ill-considered change to the code. As with most large software projects, the Met Office scientists use a version control system which allows each person to create their own experimental version of the UM, to test their ideas for changes to the code. But the decision for when (and whether) to incorporate their proposed change into an upcoming release of the UM depends not just on whether the change works on its own – it has to work in all the various models built from the UM, without messing up how fast it runs and how accurate its forecasts are.[9]

This also forms the main drawback of the approach: there are often changes that one modelling team would like to make to their version of the model, to optimize it for their own purposes, but which may cause problems elsewhere. A performance enhancement to speed up the weather models might affect the stability of the climate models on very long runs, or a change that makes the model more scientifically accurate for long-term climate processes can make weather forecasts less reliable, if it replaces finely tuned empirical parameters. The climate modellers tell me that sometimes they save up such changes, and introduce them alongside other changes that improve the weather forecasts, so that overall forecast accuracy doesn't drop. And all these changes can only be added to the model after a long process of performance testing, scientific assessment, and consensus building across the teams.

Which Components Are Shared?

The weather and climate models built from the code of the Unified Model share many components,[10] but not everything. The largest and oldest part of the Unified Model code is its atmosphere model, and this constitutes most of the sharing across the Met Office's family of models.

The ocean model, on the other hand, isn't usually included in the daily weather forecast runs.[11] Ocean temperatures and currents change on a much slower scale than the atmosphere, so there's little benefit from running a full ocean simulation for a short-range weather forecast. But for longer-term forecasts – anything from a season to a century – the role of the ocean becomes essential, and these kinds of model need a detailed ocean simulation model.

Many other processes that matter for climate science have little or no impact on a short-range weather forecast – such as the dynamics of ice sheets, chemical reactions in the atmosphere from industrial pollution, and the absorption of carbon dioxide by plants and soils. The relative importance of these processes for climate versus weather also affects the choices at the Met Office for where to invest time and expertise. Historically, the Met Office has devoted far more of its resources to atmospheric modelling than to other aspects of the climate system, and the climate scientists at the Hadley Centre collaborate with other groups across the United Kingdom to help build other model components that are relevant to climate. For example, the atmospheric chemistry component of the model is developed by a consortium of six universities, supported by the Hadley Centre.

Conceptually, the scientists at the Met Office divide their atmosphere model into two distinct parts, which they call the "dynamics" and the "physics." *Dynamics* refers to the movement of atmosphere, caused by changing air pressures, the effect of gravity, and the rotation of the Earth. This part of the model derives directly from the work of Vilhelm Bjerknes and Lewis Fry Richardson in the early twentieth century, and the primitive equations that calculate the next state of the atmosphere given its current state. *Physics* refers to the processes that aren't captured in these primitive equations, such as heating and cooling via radiation – downwards radiation as the sun's rays pass through the atmosphere, and upwards radiation as the heat from the surface is gradually lost back to space – and the way in which gases and particles in each layer of air interfere with downwards and upwards radiation. The physics components also include the exchange of water with the surface – precipitation and evaporation – along with the formation of clouds, and the friction on the atmosphere as it moves over the landscape.

I like to think of the dynamics as the beating heart of every model. Atmospheric modellers call this component a *dynamical core*.[12] This component controls the entire simulation, as it calculates how the atmosphere changes from one timestep to the next, and calls on relevant parts of the physics code to make adjustments to the state of the atmosphere, before beginning the calculations again for the next timestep. Running the entire model is so computationally demanding that every climate modelling centre needs access to a supercomputer to run the models on. If you're going to calculate the state of the global atmosphere at 30-minute intervals over the period of a century, you need a pretty powerful machine.

The Need for Speed

Each time I visit a climate research lab, my hosts offer me a tour of their supercomputer facility. These look very impressive – housed in a room the size of a supermarket, full of rows of cabinets, each the size of a grocery store freezer cabinet, covered with blinking lights, accompanied by the roar of the air-conditioning that keeps them from overheating (see Figure 5.2). The only discernible movement comes from the robotic arms in the data archiving units, travelling along metal rods, retrieving and replacing magnetic tape cartridges. But I now find these tours rather dull – once you've seen one supercomputer room, you've seen them all.

Nevertheless, the supercomputers are the tangible evidence of a massive scientific enterprise. Politicians are invited to cut ribbons for new supercomputer facilities, because they're expensive and look good in photographs. But politicians don't cut ribbons for new versions of the computer models, because the model itself is invisible. And yet the program code for a global climate model is an engineering marvel, more complex than the buildings that house the research groups, more expensive[13] than the supercomputers it runs on, and more central to the scientists' work than either.

Figure 5.2 The UK Met Office's new Cray XC40 supercomputer. (UK Met Office)

But the scientists couldn't do what they do without access to a supercomputer, and the available computers constrain the model in many – perhaps unexpected – ways. In the last chapter, we learned about the very first global circulation model, developed in 1955 by Norman Phillips at Princeton. His simple model simulated the Earth as a cylinder rather than a globe, using two 17×15 grids – for two layers of atmosphere. This choice of grid allowed him to store the entire state of the atmosphere using only half the internal memory of the Princeton computer, leaving the other half available for calculating the next state. The IAS computer took about 12 hours to compute a 31-day simulation, with a 1-hour timestep.

Since the 1950s, computer speeds and computer memory have grown exponentially, and with them the computational power available to climate modellers. This exponential growth is known as Moore's law, named after one of the founders of the Intel Corporation, Gordon E. Moore, who pointed out in 1965 that increasing miniaturization meant the number of circuits that fitted onto a computer chip was doubling every year.[14]

Most of us don't care how many components can be squeezed onto a silicon chip. But we do care how fast our computers run. Smaller circuits mean faster computers, because the electronic signals take time to travel from one transistor to the next. Increasing miniaturization means the speed of the fastest available computers has doubled approximately every 18 months since the 1950s (see Figure 5.3). Today's computers are a thousand times faster than those of 15 years ago. As consumers, we've been trained to throw out our computers and mobile devices every few years to buy faster ones.

Many Processors in Parallel

Like most of us, the Met Office regularly replaces its computers with faster ones. At the time of writing, it operates the fastest supercomputer[15] in the world dedicated to weather and climate modelling, the Cray XC40, shown in Figure 5.2, which has a peak speed of 8 thousand trillion operations per second.[16] When it was first installed, in 2017, it was the 11th fastest machine in the world overall,[17] although, as with all supercomputers, it is slowly sliding down the rankings, as other, even faster machines come online around the world. The Met Office also has two smaller versions of this machine, each about half as powerful, which are used mainly for the operational weather forecast model runs. They use two identical machines for this so the next version of the model can be tested alongside the current version – every day, for several months – before eventually supplanting it. This also provides a backup so that if one machine fails for any reason, weather forecasts can still be run.

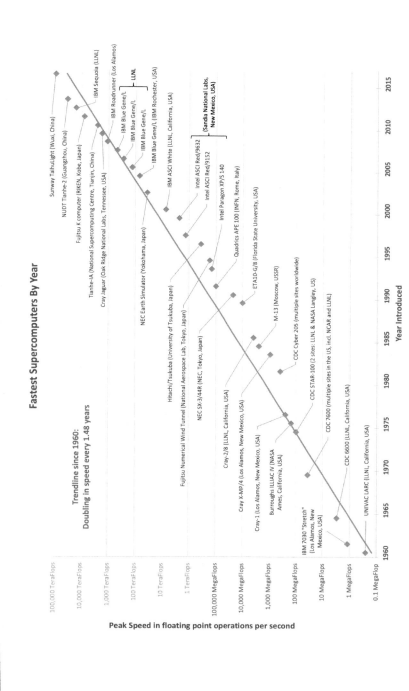

Figure 5.3 The processing speed of the fastest supercomputer in the world each year. Note the logarithmic scale on the Y axis: each point on this scale is ten times the speed of the previous one. Speeds are measured in floating point operations per second (FLOPS). Most of these machines were installed in government labs, typically dedicated to energy and weapons research. Climate and weather models have been run on many of these machines, and some, such as the NEC Earth Simulator, were installed specifically for this purpose.

In the mid-2000s, the computing industry found it was reaching the limits of further miniaturization. For companies like Cray and IBM that sell supercomputers, this led to an important change in strategy – adding more processors[18] became the main way to speed things up. Today's supercomputers have hundreds of thousands of processors working in parallel, each doing a small part of the overall computation. Currently, the Met Office's three Cray supercomputers have nearly half a million processors between them.

In theory, climate models are perfect for such machines. Just as Richardson foresaw in 1921 with his idea for a forecast factory, the calculations for each grid point could be given to a different processor, to be done in parallel. Unfortunately, it's not that simple.[19] Before the 2000s, climate models weren't designed to run on massively parallel machines. Each time a climate research lab acquires a new supercomputer, the code has to be adapted to run efficiently on the new machine, and this usually means finding ways to restructure the code to run on a much larger number of processors. When I first visited the UK Met Office, the lab was gearing up for delivery of three new IBM computers, to replace their old NEC machines. They would be switching from machines that had just over 100 processors each to machines with tens of thousands of processors. The technical support teams were expecting several months' worth of effort to adapt the models to the new machine – optimizing the code and then testing and re-testing it to make sure everything would still work correctly.

If the new machine was similar to the old machine, but just faster, the code wouldn't have to change. But when the extra power comes from parallel processors, this is no longer the case. If any part of the code has to wait for another part to complete, or has to wait to access the data it needs, the benefits of parallelization will be lost. The more processors we add, the harder it is to find ways to spread the calculations between them. And the data have to be untangled, so that each processor gets just the data it needs for its part of the job. In theory, if a model were perfectly scaleable, spreading it over twice as many processors should halve its run time.[20] But restructuring the code usually gives only a small fraction of this potential speed up, because the algorithms depend on things being done in a particular order. The only solution is to completely redesign the core algorithms.

But there's another problem. In a climate model, the computations for each gridpoint need data from surrounding locations. And if we want to save detailed information during the run, huge amounts of data need to flow from the individual processors to a data archive. The biggest barrier to faster models these days typically isn't the speed of the processors at all – it's the bottleneck of moving petabytes of data around within a massively parallel supercomputer.

Quicker Runs or Better Models?

As our hardware gets faster and faster, we can run more and more complicated software on it, meaning the software gets slower and slower.[21] Today's word processors and spreadsheets have so many extra features, they are hardly any more responsive than they were 20 years ago, despite the computers we run them on being many times faster. Although you can buy a machine today that's several thousand times faster than what was available 20 years ago, it can still take just as long to reboot your computer, or to lay out a page of text.

Climate models have their own version of this. As Figure 5.3 shows, today's supercomputers are about a trillion times (12 orders of magnitude!) faster than the machines available in the mid-1950s. So while Norm Phillips had to wait 12 hours for his model to simulate a single month, on today's machines, his model would run in a few nano-seconds.[22] So it might seem that today's climate scientists no longer have to wait around for their runs to complete. But in fact, their waiting times have grown rather than shrunk.

In weather forecasting, the focus is on accurate simulation from the current conditions, at a very high resolution, simulating only a week or so forward in time. A typical 5-day weather forecast might take about 45 minutes to run on the supercomputer, after several hours to prepare the latest data, to ensure the run starts with as much information as possible about current conditions. Faster runs help, because it means more time to prepare the data, although, as we'll see, it's often just as effective to increase the model resolution and keep run times the same.

For climate models, shorter run times aren't so important. Rather than using the faster machine to shorten the run times, climate modellers simply add more detail to their models. Their models get better and better, year after year, but the run times rarely change. A typical experiment might simulate the global climate for an entire century – for example, a simulation of the twentieth century, to explore how well the model matches observed conditions, or a simulation of the twenty-first century, under different scenarios for human-caused carbon emissions. A typical century-long simulation will take a couple of weeks to run on the supercomputer.

These run times impose a certain rhythm[23] on the work of each team. The weather forecasting teams set up forecast runs each day, to complete in time for the deadlines of their various customers, such as broadcast TV channels, newspapers, and weather apps. This daily cycle is very evident at the Met Office, beginning with a briefing by the chief forecaster at 9 am each day. The scientists in the Hadley Centre, up on the top floor, occasionally attend these briefings. But the rhythm of their work is very different.

The weeks spent waiting for each run of the climate model are occupied with analyzing the results of the previous runs, writing up findings, preparing experiments for the next set of runs, and deciding how to allocate precious compute time to different experiments. A massively parallel machine can be devoted to a single run, but it's usually more effective to partition it to do several different runs at once. Of course, some runs are more urgent than others, depending on who is waiting for the results. Lower-priority experiments might be run on older machines, which means waiting even longer for the results. And on average, about half of the available computing time is taken up just with testing new versions of the models.

Enhance!

There are many ways of using more processing power to improve a climate model, but the most obvious way is to increase the number of grid points – a higher resolution grid. Early global circulation models used very coarse grids. The key idea, as we saw in Chapter 3, is that the computer calculates values for the equations that describe the movements of the atmosphere at each of a number of discrete points on the planet. The original weather forecast that Charney's team ran on ENIAC covered only part of North America, with grid points 700 km apart, while in Phillips's original global circulation model, the grid points were 375 km apart in the East-West direction, and even further apart in the North-South direction. These scales are far too coarse to capture local weather conditions, especially at the surface of the planet – but can simulate very large-scale wind patterns higher in the atmosphere.

To capture more detail, you need higher resolution, ideally in all three dimensions – more vertical layers as well as more grid points horizontally. As you increase resolution, the contours of the coastlines become steadily more accurate (see Figure 5.4), and the equations are able to capture smaller-scale weather patterns. Perhaps the most dramatic example of this is the sudden emergence of tropical cyclones (hurricanes), once the model resolution is fine enough. Cyclones are not programmed into the models. Having them appear – in the right parts of the world – when you increase the resolution of a climate model is an excellent demonstration that the models get the physics of the atmosphere correct.

A steady improvement in the resolution of the grid is one of the most obvious features of the history of computational climate models. Figure 5.4 shows the effect of successively doubling the resolution, from the crude models of the 1960s, with grid points hundreds of kilometres apart, to recent models

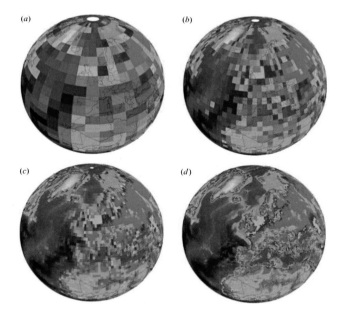

Figure 5.4 Effect of increasing grid resolution. These models show successive doubling of grid resolution, with grids of (approximately) 500 km, 300 km, 150 km, and 75 km. Land cells are coloured green to brown to show density of vegetation, while ocean cells are coloured turquoise to blue to show ocean depth. Country outlines are for illustration only. Note that when climate modellers give a size for their grids, they usually mean the effective grid size near the equator, where the grid cells are biggest – grid cells near the poles are much smaller. (Reproduced from Washington et al. (2009). Used with permission of The Royal Society through Copyright Clearance Center, Inc.)

with grid points only dozens of kilometres apart. Weather models benefit from increasing resolution too – the Met Office's highest resolution global weather model runs on a 10 km grid, while the regional model for the United Kingdom runs on a 1.5 km grid.

But increasing the resolution takes a lot of extra computation. If you halve the distance between the grid points in all three dimensions[24] in your model, that's eight times as many grid points, and you'll need shorter timesteps too, to capture how disturbances pass from one grid point to the next. So when a climate research centre installs a machine that's ten times faster than the old one, just doubling the resolution of the simulation can eat up all the extra speed. For climate modelling labs, decades of Moore's Law has enabled decades of steadily improving resolution, rather than faster runs.

The World Isn't Flat

The simplest grids – like those in Figure 5.4 – use lines of latitude and longitude to divide the globe into the kinds of grid we're used to seeing on world maps. Climate modellers call this a *Lat-Lon grid*. But flat maps lull us into a false sense of geography. On the curved surface of the Earth, none of these grid cells is a perfect square. The distortion is especially acute as you approach the poles. The lines of longitude converge, and the grid cells get thinner. This means the simulations are much higher resolution in the polar regions than they are near the equator – which could be useful if you're particularly interested in polar climates, but a waste of computer resources if you're interested in parts of the planet where most humans live.

Smaller grid squares need shorter timesteps. The numerical algorithms used in many climate models make use of a finite differences method, like the one we met in Chapter 3, developed by Lewis Fry Richardson. For these algorithms, the timestep used in the calculations must be short enough to ensure the phenomena you are modelling (e.g., waves of high and low pressure in the atmosphere) cannot travel beyond the next grid point in a single timestep,[25] otherwise the simulation becomes unstable. In a modern high resolution grid, that might mean a timestep of just a few minutes. So the smallest grid cells constrain the timestep for the entire simulation, and shorter timesteps means a lot more computation.

These kinds of problem have pushed the modellers to explore alternative ways to do the numerical calculations. The early models all used Richardson's approach – compute the rates of change of wind speed and air pressure at each grid point, based on what is happening in neighbouring grid points. This is known as an *Eulerian method*, after the eighteenth-century mathematician Leonhard Euler, who used a similar technique in his work developing calculus.

The Eulerian method is akin to sitting on a dock (a fixed grid point) and keeping track of the speed and direction of the water as it flows past you. But you could also jump in, and ride the waves instead, keeping track of where you go, and how fast. This is like the *Lagrangian method*, named after Joseph Louis Lagrange, who succeeded Euler as director of mathematics at the Prussian Academy of Sciences in Berlin, and who pioneered the application of calculus to engineering problems. Rather than using a fixed grid, the Lagrangian method calculates where each parcel of air or water will end up at the next timestep. With this method, longer timesteps don't cause the simulation to become unstable, although they are less accurate.

You can't track every molecule of air in the Earth's atmosphere, so you still need a three-dimensional grid to divide the atmosphere into parcels of air.

But these parcels then move and distort as they swirl around the planet. After many timesteps, some of the parcels end up clustered together, leaving large gaps in other places. So atmosphere modellers often use a compromise – *semi-Lagrangian* methods. In these methods, each parcel of air is tracked only for one timestep. At the end of the timestep you revert to a regular grid, to select new parcels of air for the next timestep. Semi-Lagrangian methods were first used by the Irish Meteorological Service in the early 1980s, and were widely adopted into climate and weather modelling by the 1990s.

The simplest algorithms, used in early models, use *explicit* methods, where the next value of a variable – for example, wind speed – is calculated by extrapolating its current value, using its current rate of change. But the rate of change itself varies over time, and if it varies a lot, explicit methods can become unstable, as each timestep overcorrects for errors in the previous timestep.

A better solution is to first work out the rate of change *over the next timestep*, and use that to calculate the new value for the wind speed. But now we have a chicken-and-egg problem – to calculate the new rate of change, you need to already know the wind speed at the next timestep. *Implicit* methods solve this problem by iteratively zooming in on both values at once. Implicit methods help make climate modelling more accurate, without restricting the length of the timestep. But they need many more computational steps, so are much slower to compute.

Each of these choices has advantages and drawbacks, and the best way forward is often to combine the techniques, applying each where it fits best. So the Met Office's dynamical core uses a mix of explicit and implicit methods – explicit for the slower moving variables where longer timesteps are stable, and implicit for the faster moving variables. Similarly, it uses a mix of Eulerian and Lagrangian methods. The resulting numerical method is known as a *semi-implicit semi-Lagrangian* (SISL) scheme.[26]

Polar Problems

None of these choices solve the pole problem. In a Lat-Lon grid, the calculations at each grid point only need data from four neighbours. But all the lines of longitude meet at the poles, causing a data bottleneck – in a very high resolution model, the polar cell will have thousands of neighbours, and they all have to exchange data at every timestep. Where the grid points converge, the shape of the grid itself creates spurious patterns in the simulation – a problem known as *grid imprinting*. Models that use the Lat-Long grid need a *polar filter* to remove these spurious patterns around the poles.

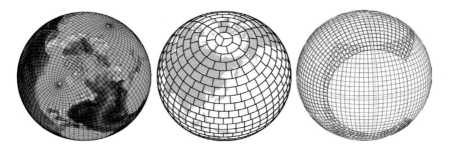

Figure 5.5 Three creative solutions to the grid convergence problem. (a) A tri-polar grid used in the ocean model MPIOM, developed at the Max-Planck Institute for Meteorology in Hamburg, Germany, which has the grid converge to two points over land in the northern hemisphere. The third convergence point is over Antarctica; (b) a reduced grid, designed by Yoshio Kurihara in the 1960s, in which fewer cells are used in the bands of latitude as you approach the poles; (c) a Yin-Yang grid, designed by Kageyama and Sato in the early 2000s, in which two partial rectangular grids are overlapped. (a: Irina Fast, MPI-M; b: Reproduced from Washington et al. (2009). Used with permission of The Royal Society through Copyright Clearance Center, Inc.; c: Reproduced from Li and Peng (2018) by permission from Springer Nature, © 2018.)

Over the years, modellers have come up with many other ingenious ways of avoiding these problems. Norm Phillips's solution was probably the most creative: if you model the Earth as a cylinder rather than a globe, the grid lines never converge! Ocean modellers sometimes use another clever solution: they rotate the grid so that the points of singularity end up on the continents, where there is no ocean, and so no calculations needed. But if your ocean model has a different grid[27] than the atmosphere model, coupling them together is harder – as we'll see in Chapter 7. Figure 5.5 shows other creative suggestions for avoiding the problem, but each solution introduces irregularities that make the computation more complex.

Gridding the Planet

Finding a better grid might seem a fairly straightforward – decide how many grid points you want in your model, based on how fast your computer will run, and then just lay them out evenly across the globe. But if you want the distance between every pair of neighbouring points to be the same, you're out of luck. By a quirk of spherical geometry, the highest resolution grid you can create this way has only 20 grid points. If you want more, the distances between them will have to vary.

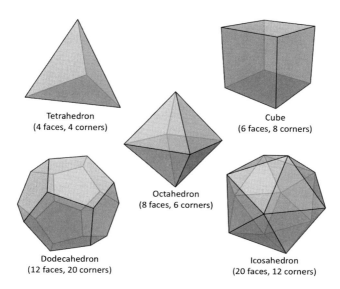

Tetrahedron
(4 faces, 4 corners)

Cube
(6 faces, 8 corners)

Octahedron
(8 faces, 6 corners)

Dodecahedron
(12 faces, 20 corners)

Icosahedron
(20 faces, 12 corners)

Figure 5.6 The platonic solids. Note the duality. If you switch faces and corners, for example by slicing off all the corners on one shape to turn them into faces, each shape has a dual. The cube pairs with the octahedron, the icosahedron pairs with the dodecahedron, and the tetrahedron pairs with itself.

Why 20? The easiest way to explain this is via a mathematical conundrum that fascinated both Plato and Pythagoras in ancient Greece. Plato was enchanted with the idea of perfection. To him, there was something magical about the set of shapes we now name after him – the platonic solids. For each of these solids, the faces are the same shape, the edges the same length, and the angles all match. Pythagoras gave a proof that only five such solids can exist – the tetrahedron, cube, octahedron, dodecahedron, and icosahedron, as shown in Figure 5.6.

Imagine you want to make a model platonic solid out of card. You pick a shape with all edges the same length, and prepare a bunch of them – all the same size – to make the faces of your solid. At each corner[28] of your solid, at least three faces must meet. So you start by joining two of your faces together along one edge and folding that edge a little, so it is no longer flat. You need to add at least one more face into the angled corner, so the angle of your fold must be big enough to fit the corner(s) of more faces. With squares, you can fold the joined edge to 90 degrees, to add in a third square. But if you try to add a fourth square, it will push the card out flat – which won't make a solid shape. For triangles, this happens when six meet, and if you try it with hexagons, the sheet is already flat when only three of them meet – because hexagons tessellate, in a honeycomb pattern. So you cannot make a regular polyhedron from a hexagon, nor any shape with more sides. And for both the pentagon and cube, the most shapes that can meet at any corner is three. So the five shapes shown in Figure 5.6 are the only ones possible.

What does this have to do with placing grid points on a sphere? If the distances between adjacent points must all be the same, then the problem of laying out the grid points evenly on a sphere is the same as fitting a platonic solid inside the sphere so its corners just touch the sphere at the grid points. As you can't make a platonic solid with more than 20 corners, you can't make a regular grid for a sphere using more than 20 points.

To create a higher resolution grid, we have to allow some irregularity – some of the points will have to be closer together than others. One way to do this is to start with one of the platonic solids, and divide each of its faces into a regular grid. Imagine a cube with a square grid inscribed on each of its faces, like a huge Rubik's cube. Then inflate this cube until it bulges out into a sphere. What you get is something like Figure 5.7a. The grid is not entirely regular – there are eight places where only three cells meet instead of four, at the corners of the original cube. And all of the grid cells are a little distorted, some more than others. But overall, the distortions are much smaller than at the poles in the traditional Lat-Lon grid, making it a good choice for higher resolution climate models. This approach is known as the *cubed sphere*, and will be used as the basis for the next version of the Met Office's Unified Model, in place of its current Lat-Lon grid.

A similar approach is used in the *icosahedral grid*, shown in Figure 5.7b. For this grid, we start with the icosahedron, inscribe a triangular grid on each of its faces, and then inflate it to a sphere. The resulting triangular grid has even less distortion than the cubed sphere. Over most of the sphere, six triangles meet at each grid point, except at the twelve points corresponding to the corners of the icosahedron, where only five triangles meet. The icosahedral grid is particularly interesting to climate modellers because it lends itself nicely to variable resolution grids – each triangular grid cell can be subdivided into four smaller triangles without changing the geometry. This means we could subdivide the grid for some parts of the planet and not for others. For example, the version in Figure 5.7b has higher resolution over Europe than for the rest of the globe. For climate modellers interested in studying specific regions, this is very useful, as it allows them to devote the available computational power where they most want it.

The ability to add extra resolution just where it's needed is also attractive to ocean modellers, as they can capture the complex shapes of coastlines better by

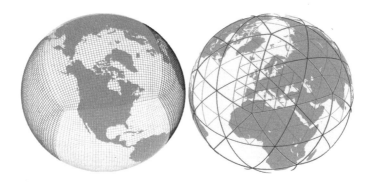

Figure 5.7 Grids derived from the platonic solids. (a) A cubed sphere grid; (b) an icosahedral grid, showing how each triangular face can be subdivided into smaller and smaller triangles to increase resolution. (a: NASA; b: Leonidas Linardakis/ MPI-M.)

adding more resolution in coastal regions. An ocean modeller using a regular grid must label each cell as ocean or land, so coastlines can only lie on boundaries between cells. Unless the grid resolution is very fine, this leads to very unrealistic coastlines, and messes up the way the model simulates coastal currents. Variable resolution grids help overcome this problem.

Off the Grid

There are other ways to solve the problem of grid convergence at the poles. One is to avoid having a grid in the first place. The need for a regular grid comes from using finite difference methods to solve the primitive equations, as the rate of change at each point is calculated from the differences between its neighbouring points. However, it's also possible to convert the primitive equations into a set of *wave-form* equations that can be solved directly. The approach is known as a *spectral method*, and it became popular for weather forecast models in the 1970s. By the 1990s, it became the dominant method used in atmospheric models.[29]

The key idea is that any curve – say, representing a value that fluctuates over time – can be broken down into a set of waves of different wavelengths (see Figure 5.8). The *Fourier transform* is a mathematical technique for doing this. It decomposes any complex curve into a (possibly infinite) set of sine waves, which, when added together, will accurately reproduce the original curve.

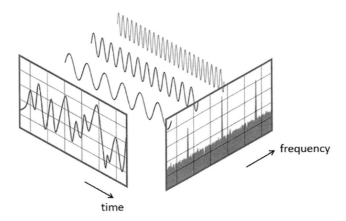

frequency

time

Figure 5.8 Example of the Fourier Transform. The graph on the left, representing a variable that changes over time, can be decomposed into the sum of many
sine waves, each at a different frequency. A curve of any shape – no matter how
complex – can be decomposed in a similar way into an infinite series of waves of
different frequencies. Higher frequencies add more and more detail to the shape.
(CC-BY-SA Wikimedia User: Phonical)

A graph of changing temperatures can be decomposed in the same way – we
just have to specify the amplitude and offset for each sine wave. And if we
write the terms of the series in order of increasing frequency, the first few
terms capture the overall shape of the graph, and the later terms add further fine-grained detail, each at a smaller scale than the previous one. To cut
down on computing time, we could truncate the series at any point, ignore
the remaining terms, and still have a reasonable approximation of the original
graph – the choice of truncation point will determine how much of the fine-
grained detail is included.

This idea can be adapted to work on a sphere by using *spherical harmonics*
instead of sine waves. Think of these as three-dimensional sine waves – wave
forms that propagate around the planet in all directions, such that there are
always a whole number of wavelengths in each direction around the sphere.[30]
Figure 5.9 shows an example of how a global variable – say, temperature – can
be decomposed into the sum of these terms. The series of terms is infinite, and
must be truncated somewhere to make it computable. Adding more terms to
the equation gives a higher resolution, and so captures more fine-grained detail
in the temperature map. But it also means higher computational cost, and the
number of terms needed rapidly grows with increasing resolution. In a global
climate model, 100 terms will give a resolution of about 125 km. But to get this
down to 25 km requires around 800 terms.

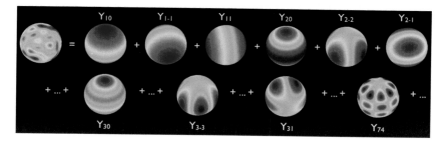

Figure 5.9 An example of how a spatially varying value can be represented as the sum of a series of spherical harmonic functions. (Reproduced from Petrov (2012))

Spectral methods are excellent for capturing the dynamically evolving variables that represent mass and energy of the atmosphere – air pressure, temperature, wind speed, etc. – but they cannot be used for computing the physics components of a climate model – radiation, convection, evaporation, etc. All models that use spectral methods for their dynamical cores have to convert back to a grid space representation at each timestep to compute the physics components. The repeated conversion back and forth becomes computationally expensive as the resolution of the models increases. So while spectral methods were very popular in the 1990s, many of the labs that used spectral methods in earlier versions of their models are now starting to ditch them, and return to finite difference algorithms.

Design Decisions

Figure 5.10, which appeared in the IPCC's Third Assessment Report, published in 2001, shows how the scope of climate models has steadily increased to cover more processes that affect the climate, as computers became more powerful, and as our understanding of these processes has matured. The original general circulation models represented only the atmosphere, while additional processes have been added steadily since then, each developed by a separate community of experts, and incorporated into the climate models once they were considered to be mature enough.

The diagram suggests climate models evolve mainly by accumulating additional functions. This has led some people to suggest that the core elements of the models have becomes steadily buried, like layers of sediment at the bottom of the ocean, with their assumptions and limitations no longer open

The Development of Climate models, Past, Present and Future

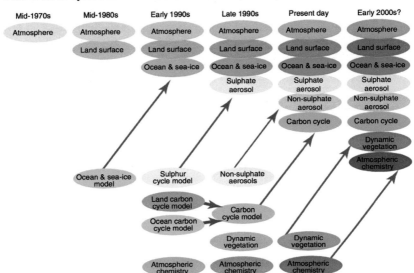

Figure 5.10 The development of global climate models, as depicted in the IPCC Third Assessment Report. "Present Day" refers to 2000–2001, when this report was written and published. Deepening colours represent increasing improvements in the model components over time. The diagram shows how different specialist communities develop components separately, and these additional components are coupled to the models once they are sufficiently mature. (IPCC TAR WG1, TS, Box 3, Figure 1)

to question. For example, Lenhard and Winsberg argue that design decisions built into these core elements become deeply buried within the model over time – that is, *entrenched* – which means those decisions can no longer be understood or critiqued.[31]

But you only have to step into a climate modelling lab and talk to the modellers to realize this isn't the case at all. One of the first people I interviewed on my visit to the UK Met Office in the summer of 2008 was Dr Nigel Wood, then head of the Dynamics Research group at the Met Office. Nigel was leading a team of nine scientists responsible for the dynamical core of the model. In the early 2000s, in one of the biggest single changes to the Unified Model, Nigel and his team stripped out the heart of the model and replaced it with a new numerical scheme, known, appropriately enough, as New Dynamics (ND). The changes to the model were substantial, and it took several years to get the new version working effectively in all the different versions of the

Met Office family of models. When I interviewed him, Nigel reflected on that experience, and talked about an ongoing project – Even Newer Dynamics[32] – to replace it again. A few years after we first spoke, work began on yet another replacement, known as Gungho,[33] to improve scalability by replacing the Lat-Lon grid with a cubed sphere grid, along with new numerical algorithms that will scale to hundreds of thousands of processors.

So at any moment, Nigel and his team are at work on at least two generations of dynamical core for the Unified Model: the current operational version, which occasionally needs tweaks to improve its performance on different supercomputers; and a new research project to create an even better one.

Nigel also shared with me the documentation his team wrote for the New Dynamics core – a 500-page, painstakingly exhaustive discussion of all the decisions that have to be made to design a dynamical core.[34] Many of these focus on the differences between an ideal, mathematical model of planet Earth and the reality – and the decision-making needed to handle such differences.

For example, the Earth, like most planets, isn't quite spherical. The rotation of the planet creates enough centrifugal force that the surface of the planet has settled into a slightly flattened sphere, bulging towards the equator – a shape known as an *oblate spheroid*. This has some interesting consequences. Over most of the planet, the force of gravity doesn't quite point to the centre of the Earth (see Figure 5.11). Another similar complication arises from the fact that as well as spinning on its own axis, the Earth and the moon rotate together around their common centre of mass, which introduces a secondary centrifugal force. But in both cases, the adjustment needed to the gravitational forces in the model would be very small, and would greatly complicate the computation. So climate models ignore both factors, and treat the Earth as a sphere, spinning only on its polar axis. Nigel's design document carefully weighs up such decisions, explaining the rationale for each.

The Heart of a Climate Model

Many of the decisions that go into the design of a dynamical core focus on the need to balance the accuracy of the model with what is feasibly computable, given the available computers. There is no right answer, and each modelling centre decides for itself how best to do this. A walkthrough of some of the decisions Nigel's team had to address when they built the New Dynamics core – and its replacement, ENDGame – will help show why developing a state-of-the-art climate model is hard, and why it takes years of testing before a new dynamical core is ready for deployment.

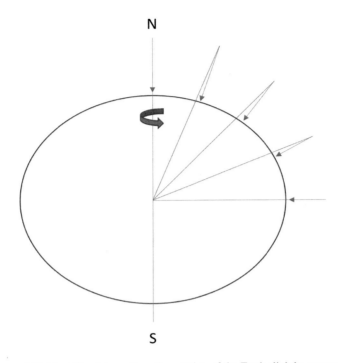

Figure 5.11 Centrifugal force from the rotation of the Earth slightly counteracts gravity, so the Earth is an oblate spheroid, rather than a sphere. This means apparent gravity (shown as arrows) does not point to the centre of the Earth, except at the poles and equator. The effect is exaggerated on this diagram, to show the concept. For the Earth, the difference amounts to about 0.1° at its greatest, which is at the 45th parallel.

The starting point for a dynamical core is to decide on an appropriate set of governing equations.[35] These equations derive from the set of seven primitive equations originally identified by Bjerknes, and adapted for numerical weather forecasting by Richardson. The first six equations define the properties of dry air (momentum, density, pressure, and temperature), and we can use these to build and test a *dry core*. Once this works satisfactorily, we can add additional equations to handle water, and hence build a *moist core*.

The term "primitive" to describe Bjerknes's equations is somewhat misleading.[36] It doesn't mean they're inferior; quite the contrary. As we saw in Chapter 4, the primitive equations are derived directly from the physical laws – such as conservation of mass, momentum, and energy. In their raw form, they proved to be too sensitive to noise in the initial data, as Richardson first discovered. For his first weather forecast model in 1949, Charney adapted the equations to ensure poor input data would still produce a stable simulation, by filtering out fast moving dynamics such as sound waves. For several decades after this, meteorologists adopted various versions of Charney's filtered equations in their models. But by the 1960s, it was clear the filtered equations were producing too much damping, which particularly showed up in longer runs. So attention turned back to primitive equations themselves, and modern weather and climate models now use some form of the unfiltered primitive equations.[37]

The primitive equations only have a single variable for water in the atmosphere. But water occurs in the atmosphere in three forms: water vapour, liquid water (as droplets in clouds), and ice (as frozen crystals in clouds). To keep track of how water moves between these three states, and ensure that the total amount of water is conserved, we need to add equations for the rate of change for each state. These additional equations must take into account air pressure, temperature, and how much dust, smoke, and other particles there are – as water vapour condenses into clouds much more readily when there are particles to condense around.

Once we have selected an appropriate set of equations, we need to adapt them for the geometry of planet Earth. To do this, we need to translate from the three-dimensional space described in the equations to a spherical coordinate system, so each point is identified by three coordinates: distance from the centre of the Earth, angle of latitude, and angle of longitude – usually measured from the Greenwich Meridian. The terms in the equations for gravity and the Coriolis force (from the rotation of the Earth) have to be adjusted for this spherical coordinate system.

The choice of grid over which to apply the equations is important, as it affects all other aspects of the model. The changing nature of supercomputer architectures increasingly drives this decision. In the early 2000s, when New Dynamics was introduced, a Lat-Lon grid was still a good choice. The next generation of dynamical core at the Met Office – the Gungho project – is switching to a cubed sphere to avoid the grid convergence problems we met earlier.

We then need to decide how high to go in the atmosphere. There is no definitive "top" to the atmosphere – air just gets thinner and thinner until eventually there's too little to measure. Early climate models, in the 1960s, omitted the stratosphere, which led to large inaccuracies. The air is thin and there is no water vapour in the stratosphere, but there is ozone and carbon dioxide. The ozone absorbs some of the incoming sunlight – especially the ultraviolet rays that cause sunburn – and the CO_2 absorbs outgoing infra-red from lower in the atmosphere. These play a crucial role in moderating the climate, so modern climate models usually extend to the top of the stratosphere. To simplify things, they treat this as a "lid," above which no air can go. The upper edge of the stratosphere, at about 50 km above sea level, is a reasonable boundary[38] to choose, because 99.99% of all the planet's air is below this height. From our vantage point on the surface, this might seem a long way up, but compared to the size of the Earth, the entire atmosphere is very shallow. At 50 km, the atmosphere is less than 1% of the radius of the Earth – if the Earth were an apple, the atmosphere would be roughly the thickness of the apple skin.

This relative shallowness allows us to make some simplifying assumptions. For example, the area of each grid square should increase as you move away from the surface. But the atmosphere is shallow enough compared to the Earth's radius that you could ignore this and use a fixed grid size at all heights.[39] Similarly, the force of gravity gradually reduces as you move further away from the Earth – at the top of the stratosphere, gravity is about 1% weaker than at the surface. But again, you could choose to ignore this. Early weather and climate models all used such simplifications – adopting a *shallow atmosphere assumption*. However, Nigel and his team chose to discard these assumptions for the Met Office's dynamical cores, making the calculations more complex, but the model more accurate.

We also need to decide how to divide the atmosphere into layers. We could divide the atmosphere into layers of equal height, but this is a poor choice because there's a lot more going on in the lower layers, near the surface, than the upper layers, where there is very little air. A simple alternative is to use air pressure instead of height above sea level as the vertical coordinate. At sea level, air pressure is approximately 1,000 millibars,[40] reducing steadily with height, to zero at the top of the atmosphere. The pressure at any point is really a measure of how much air there is above that point,[41] pushing down – so if we divide the atmosphere into, say, ten layers, at every 100 millibars, each layer will contain the same mass of air, but the lower layers are squashed much thinner by the weight of the layers above them. The result is more layers near the Earth's surface.

However, there is another problem. The lower layers are interrupted by mountains, which would mean complex calculations to deal with layers of air with gaps in them. A simple solution is to have the layers of the atmosphere follow the terrain. This can be done by expressing air pressure as a *fraction* of the ground level air pressure in each grid cell, rather than the actual pressure – a technique known as *sigma-coordinate*s (see Figure 5.12). In this scheme, 1 represents the normal local air pressure at ground level, and 0 represents the pressure at the top of the atmosphere. Each fraction in between captures how much of the vertical mass of air is above that point, pressing down on it. Modern weather and climate models typically use some variant of a sigma scheme, often with further adjustments to improve how the model captures the air flow over mountains.[42]

Before developing the numerical algorithms that implement the equations over this three-dimensional grid, we should also consider whether to *stagger*

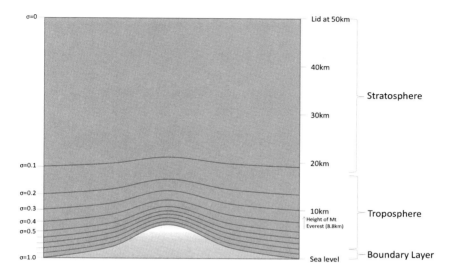

Figure 5.12 Schematic for a Sigma (terrain-following) vertical coordinate system over a tall mountain, with a ten-layer atmosphere. More layers can be added to increase vertical resolution. Because air pressure drops exponentially with height, the sigma-coordinate system provides a lot more resolution in the first few layers above the ground, which is useful, as this is where most of the action is. Curved lines show fractional mass, so for example at σ = 0.5, half the mass of the atmosphere is above you and half below. Note that heights shown on the right are for the atmosphere in the tropics. At the poles, the troposphere is much thinner,[43] with a height of only 7–8 km.

the variables in the grid. The finite difference algorithm used in gridded models calculates the rate of change for each variable by comparing neighbouring values. When Lewis Fry Richardson developed this method in the 1910s, he used a chequerboard pattern for his grid (see Chapter 3, Figure 3.5), with air pressure and wind speed measured in alternating cells. A simpler solution is to evaluate some variables at the edge of the grid cells, and others at the centre. In a classic paper in 1977, Arakawa and Lamb set out a number of different ways of doing this, with different variables evaluated at different places on the centres, edges, and corners of the grid cells. The most common choice – now known as the Arakawa C grid – calculates air pressure and temperature at the centre of each grid cell, and wind velocities on the cell boundaries (see Figure 5.13).

Having selected our grid, it's time to design a numerical scheme for solving the governing equations. Over the years since the first numerical weather forecast models were developed, there has been a blossoming of research

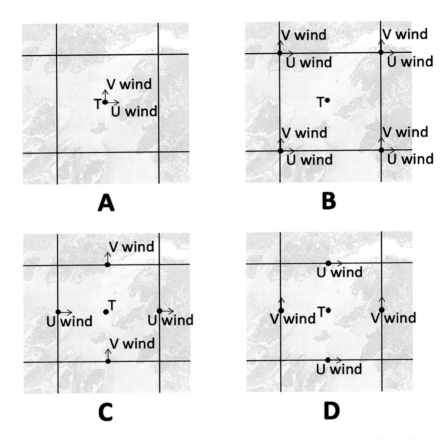

Figure 5.13 Simplified view of Arakawa and Lamb's four grid choices. Here, T represents a quantity we need to compute at each grid cell, such as Temperature. U and V are the wind velocities in the east-west and north-south directions.

into alternative algorithms. We met some of the choices earlier in the chapter: explicit versus implicit, Eulerian versus Lagrangian. The UK Met Office dynamical cores use semi-implicit semi-Lagrangian (SISL) algorithms.

Testing Time

Extensive testing is needed to determine whether the chosen numerical scheme captures the same dynamical structure as the real atmosphere. Testing is usually done step-by-step, starting with simplified versions of the model – for example, a one-dimensional and then a two-dimensional version; the dry equations before adding water; and so on. But testing a dynamical core is hard because there is no way to determine correct solutions to the equations, except for very trivial examples. So we cannot determine what the "right" answer should be for each test. The modellers look for other clues that the simulation is realistic.

Many of the tests focus on how well the model simulates different kinds of waves, when you introduce a disturbance into the atmosphere – a bit like adding a drop of water to a pond and checking that the ripples it generates are realistic. Standard tests include a symmetry test – do waves propagate the same in each direction – and a steady state test, in which the core has to maintain a stable atmosphere over a long period of time when there are no disturbances. Another useful technique is to compare the new dynamical core with other models, using reference test cases. And when something is wrong in the model, this is sometimes the only way to debug it. Nigel told me a story of a particularly tricky bug in an early version of the dynamical core that was only diagnosed when a professor[44] at Exeter University built his own version of the code, and discovered problems in the way the detailed equations had been programmed.

Building a high performance dynamical core is quite an achievement. Judging by the successive projects at the UK Met office, it takes an expert team many years to build and test a working dynamical core, able to run on highly parallel supercomputers at the kind of speeds needed for operational weather forecasting. Each replacement core started as a five-year research project, in which the team tried out different ideas, and explored different kinds of algorithm. For the ENDGame core, this phase ran from 2001 to 2006. By 2006, Nigel and his team had developed several prototypes, including a one-dimensional and two-dimensional version. Work on the three-dimensional version started in 2007, and the core was finally incorporated into the UM in 2014. Much of the last few years of the project were spent testing and tweaking the new core, as it has to perform well in all the different models built from the UM. During this phase, available time for testing on the supercomputer becomes a major bottleneck.

Just Add Physics

Getting a working dynamical core is only half the story. A dynamical core focuses on how the atmosphere transports mass and energy around, under the influence of air pressure, gravity, and the Earth's rotation. But there are many other physical processes in the atmosphere – affecting both weather and climate – which are not captured in the governing equations of a dynamical core. These processes happen at a scale smaller than the grid used in the model – things that happen within a single grid cell, but which can affect the dynamical core's calculations for that grid cell. Collectively, these processes are referred to by the modellers as "the physics."

Take for example, the effect of friction as air moves over rough ground – mountains and valleys. Mountains act as barriers to the flow of air, and the effect of this "drag" propagates upwards from the lowest levels of the atmosphere in a series of waves of air, known as *mountain waves*. The shape of these waves depends on the shape of the mountains and the direction of the prevailing winds over them – and often cause spectacular cloud shapes downwind from the mountains. If the grid cells are too large to resolve these effects, they have to be worked out in advance,[45] and incorporated into the model as a set of adjustments for each grid cell in the model.

These physics processes are represented in the model using what the modellers call *parameterizations*. These reduce what would be a complex set of equations to a small set of parameters to adjust for processes that happen within each grid cell. A simple example would be to reduce complex effects like cloud formation to a single parameter for "cloudiness." More often, a parameterization is like a mini-model in its own right, with its own hypotheses, its own equations, and its own algorithms. Most of these mini-models represent something that happens within a single column of air the size of one grid cell, typically ignoring any horizontal effects from neighbouring columns. And each mini-model handles a different physical process, so they can be tested on their own, before being coupled into the dynamical core. These parameterizations are regularly updated or replaced, as the modellers improve their understanding of the processes involved, and find better ways of including them in the simulation.

The physics processes that matter to weather and climate models operate on a number of different timescales, so the modellers sometimes distinguish between "fast physics" and "slow physics." Friction with mountains and valleys is an example of slow physics – the effect is small enough that it can be handled as a one-time adjustment in each grid cell at each timestep. The dynamical core just calls the surface friction model to make the necessary adjustments before starting the dynamics computation for the next timestep.

In contrast, the fast physics processes move air around enough to distort the calculations of the dynamical core during a single timestep, and they may also affect each other. Examples include convection, small-scale turbulence, and cloud formation.

Convection currents are particularly important for weather forecasting. Air expands when it is heated, becoming lighter, which makes it rise, carrying the heat upwards. These upwellings of warm moist air create clouds and thunderstorms. On a larger scale, convection currents are responsible for much of the large-scale structure of the atmosphere, such as the Hadley Cells we met in Chapter 3. Some aspects of convection can be calculated directly in the equations of conservation of energy and mass. But because convection processes operate over a wide range of scales, they are tricky to get right. Most models use a mix of theoretical and empirical approaches for convection – simulation from the basic physics equations, with parameters chosen to match observed convection patterns in different parts of the world. Improvements to how the model represents convection can make a big difference in its ability to get the detail right, especially in the tropics where large convection currents are a dominant factor in shaping tropical storms.

In the UM, fast physics processes are interleaved with the dynamical core's calculation of the state of the atmosphere for each timestep. In the newer versions of the UM core, accuracy is improved by iterating these, so at each timestep, the dynamics and fast physics calculations are run several times each, allowing them to converge on a more accurate representation of the next state of the atmosphere.

What About Radiation?

If you want to study climate change, the most important physics component is the effect of radiation. Very simple models of the greenhouse effect – like the model developed by Arrhenius we explored in Chapter 2 – calculate this as the balance between incoming solar radiation and outgoing infra-red radiation from the Earth. And Arrhenius's model could, in principle, be plugged into a modern dynamical core as a parameterization of radiation for each grid cell.

But the absorption of radiation by the atmosphere depends not just on how much of each greenhouse gas is present, but also the pressure and temperature of each parcel of air it passes through. A much more accurate calculation of the greenhouse effect can be created in a global circulation model by computing both the downward (solar) and upward (infra-red) radiation in each grid cell, for each layer of air, at each timestep, taking into account the properties the air in that cell.

At the Met Office, I spoke to John Edwards, who originally developed the radiation code, now named after him, that is used in the UM. John started work on this in 1990, and it took 13 years to develop a version suitable for both weather and climate models – and it's still undergoing further improvement today.[46] John's radiation code uses a detailed dataset of the absorption coefficients for each greenhouse gas, at each wavelength, to analyze how much radiation at that wavelength would be absorbed by the gases currently in the grid cell. Because the model has many layers of atmosphere, this automatically provides a multi-level analysis that – as we saw in Chapter 2 – is essential for representing how the greenhouse effect actually works. The latest version of this radiation code even includes the effects of metals in the atmosphere, for scientists simulating other planets, like "hot Jupiters" – the first exoplanets to be discovered orbiting other stars.

The code development and the research go hand-in-hand. The two cannot easily be separated, because working out the equations and writing the code that implements them are part of the same thought process. John tells me he likes to work with small chunks at a time, developing the equations and the code together, and using the code to check his equations make sense.

My conversation with John echoed a theme I heard from many of the scientists I met at the UK Met Office. A modern climate model is an incredibly complex thing, with different parts of the model developed by different experts across the lab. And the model itself is always evolving because it is a crucial part of the research conducted at the lab – researchers are always coming up with ways to improve some part of the model. Coordination of everyone's efforts can be tricky, as the model emerges organically out of all these research contributions. And making all the parts of an atmosphere model – the dynamics and the physics – work together efficiently on the supercomputers takes just as much time as building the individual components in the first place.

Models as Ongoing Research Projects

So, as with all climate models, work on the Unified Model can be characterized as an ongoing process of making better models. The current model is simultaneously a scientific laboratory used every day for science experiments, an experimental testbed for trying out new ideas for model improvements, and a forecasting tool used to produce short-term (weather) and long-term (climate) predictions for a variety of external customers. These external customers never run the model themselves – they want the forecasts, not the models that produce them. So the only people outside the lab who also use the model are other scientific collaborators, also engaged in research and model development.

Those aspects of the atmosphere the models can directly simulate – the dynamics – are captured very well in today's models, while the processes that work on smaller scales than the model grid – the physics – are less accurate. The latter are represented in the model by *parameterizations* – code that captures the typical or average effect within each grid cell. The set of things requiring parameterization has changed over the years, as the resolution of the models has improved. Still, a major research project at the Met Office has been to find better ways of representing these *sub-grid scale* processes, which often have a fine-grained structure. For example, convection currents within each grid cell aren't really independent – they have a systemic structure, creating patterns on many scales, from thunderstorms to monsoons that bring extreme weather and flooding to some parts of the tropics. Getting these systemic patterns right is a challenge, and is the focus of a lot of current research in climate modelling labs.[47]

The unification of weather and climate models helps, because the ability to explore a problem at multiple scales offers excellent insights. For example, in both 1-day weather forecasts and 20-year climate simulations, the UM tends to produce too much rain over the tropical oceans, because it generates low-intensity rainstorms too often. Knowing the same error occurs at very different timescales helps the modellers to identify which parts of the model are responsible, and allows them to correct for it when they interpret predictions from the model. Other errors only show up at specific scales. While I was visiting the lab in 2008, the Met Office had put together a cross-functional team to investigate how to improve the simulation of the Asian monsoons, which were running drier than they should be, but much worse in the climate model than in the weather forecast runs. By working together, the meteorologists and climate scientists pool their expertise to diagnose and fix these weaknesses in the model.

The investment the Met Office makes in additional supercomputing power just for testing newer model versions represents a strong commitment to keep improving the models. Two separate, identical supercomputers are used for the operational weather forecasting model runs, so that a new experimental version of the forecast model can be tested alongside the current operational model, and their results compared for each forecast. After many months of such testing, once it has proved itself, the newer version then replaces the operational model.

The opportunities to improve the models come from new research, analysis of the current performance of the models, and the demand from customers for steady improvements in forecast accuracy (see Figure 5.14). But over the years, the biggest improvements to climate models[48] have come from faster and faster machines – due to Moore's Law – and the changes needed for the current generation of supercomputers, which use massively parallel architectures to

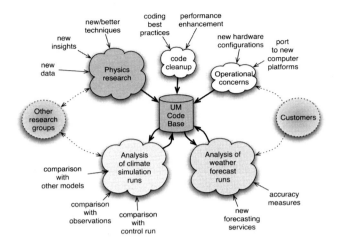

Figure 5.14 Sources of change for the UM Code base. Originally based on a sketch by Damian Wilson at the UK Met Office. (Adapted from Easterbrook and Johns (2009))

deliver more speed. Each new generation of supercomputers has enabled big advances in climate modelling – allowing scientists to increase the grid resolution, add more physical processes, and use ensembles to explore variability in the models. These improvements steadily add more detail to the models and improve their accuracy, while ensembles allow scientists to assess uncertainty in the chaotic processes that characterize weather and climate by doing many runs of a model, each with slight variations.

Since the early models in the 1960s, global climate models have grown from simulations of the atmosphere to complex coupled modelling systems, incorporating atmosphere, ocean, vegetation, hydrology, chemistry, and ice sheets. The most remarkable thing about these models is the amount of work that goes into them. Each model is the result of innumerable design decisions – the decisions described in this chapter barely scratch the surface. And this is certainly "big science." Hundreds of scientists have contributed to the development of the Unified Model over more than three decades, regularly revisiting each aspect of the design, looking for ways to improve its accuracy, speed up its algorithms, and fix its weaknesses. The results are impressive. The Met Office's weather forecasts are among the most accurate in the world, and its climate models are remarkably good at simulating the variations of climate across the planet, and the observed changes in climate over the past century. These simulations give climate scientists a way to run a huge variety of experiments that deepen our understanding of the Earth's climate – experiments we can't do on the real planet Earth, but which are essential for assessing future climate change. In Chapter 6, we will explore the kinds of experiment scientists run with these models.

Notes

1   Sadly, the weekly briefing in The Street ceased a few years ago, and is made available on the Met Office internal web instead.
2   Shortly before my visit, a review commissioned by the UK government concluded "No other single body has a comparable breadth of climate change science, data analysis and modelling, or has made the same contribution to global climate science and current knowledge." See Baker (2007).
3   In the past few years, several other labs have begun to merge their weather and climate models, but the UK Met Office remains the only one with a daily operational weather forecast model built from the same code. See Hurrell et al. (2009) for other examples.
4   See Brown et al. (2012) for an overview of the history of the UM and the advantages of the unified approach.
5   For a description of the configuration management tools in use when I first studied the UM, see Matthews et al. (2008).
6   The component models are known as Global Atmosphere (GA), Global Ocean (GO), Global Land (GL), and Global Sea Ice (GSI). See Williams et al. (2018) for an up to date overview.
7   The Software Engineering Institute in Pittsburgh promoted the approach from the early 2000s onward, but its first published case study of a successful SPL approach didn't appear until the mid-1990s. See Brownsword and Clements (1996).
8   The appendix to Brown et al. (2012) provides two case studies of the benefits of a unified approach.
9   The Met Office uses a state-of-the-art automated overnight testing process for this, to check if the latest changes break anything. See Chapter 8 for more on how climate models are tested.
10   One scientist I spoke to estimated 80%–90% of the code is used in both weather and climate models. But I haven't attempted to measure this.
11   In 2022, the Met Office started using a coupled atmosphere-ocean model for 5-day weather forecasts. Model improvements are continuous!
12   Staniforth and Thuburn (2012) define a dynamical core as the component that "solves the adiabatic and frictionless governing equations on resolved scales."
13   At least in terms of the time of all the scientists who have contributed to building it. It's hard to figure out the cost of building a climate model, because the code development is tightly entwined with the job of doing science. We'll return to this point in Chapter 7.
14   Moore predicted the number of components on a computer chip would grow a thousandfold from 1965 to 1975, and was spot on. See Moore (2006) for a retrospective.
15   In case you're curious, it runs Linux.
16   Or 8 petaFLOPS. Computer speeds are measured in FLoating Point OPerations per Second (FLOPS). The prefix peta- means 10^{15}.

17 A ranking of the fastest machines in the world is maintained by the TOP500 group. See www.top500.org/lists/2017/06/

18 Modern supercomputer companies use terms such as clusters, nodes, sockets, and cores, but not always consistently. A "node" is the basic unit of computing – basically a box with sockets into which individual circuit boards can be inserted, and wires to connect it to a shared network. Each circuit board in a node can contain one or more cores, where a core corresponds roughly to what we would once have called a Central Processing Unit – the part of the computer that can actually run a program.

19 See Dennis and Loft (2011) for a summary of the challenges involved in parallelizing climate models, and Lawrence et al. (2018) for other challenges as today's supercomputers evolve.

20 See Walters et al. (2017), Figure 1 for an analysis of how this scaling works in practice, on two generations of the Met Office's dynamical cores.

21 This is known as Wirth's Law, after Niklaus Wirth, who wrote a 1995 paper "A Plea for Lean Software."

22 A nano-second is a thousand millionth of a second, or 1×10^{-9} seconds.

23 These kinds of rhythm turn out to be important in collaborative scientific work. See Jackson 2010 for a fascinating study.

24 In practice, modellers don't increase the vertical resolution as often. But doubling the horizontal resolution plus the associated shorter timestep can still eat up nearly an order of magnitude gain in computer speed.

25 This is the Courant Condition, which we met in Chapter 3.

26 Both the ND and ENDGame dynamical cores use this scheme. For a good introduction, see Walters et al. (2017).

27 The Met Office's older models such as HadCM3 required atmosphere and ocean models to use the same grid, but the newer models allow more flexibility, and have a separate coupler component to do the re-gridding.

28 Yes, I'm deliberately avoiding some of the mathematical jargon. If you're fluent in the terminology, feel free to mentally translate as you read.

29 In the mid-2000s, spectral methods were used in 11 out of 14 weather forecasting models used around the world, and 10 of the 16 climate models used in the IPCC's 4th Assessment Report. See Williamson (2007).

30 The series of functions that express these harmonics is known as the Legendre polynomials.

31 See Lenhard and Winsberg (2010). Unfortunately, they have no evidence to support this assertion, other than a shallow reading of documents describing early model intercomparison projects, and even admit to this in their paper (p. 259). My field studies of different modelling centres suggests there is no entrenchment in Earth system models.

32 The full name of the project is ENDGame, which stands for "Even Newer Dynamics for General Atmospheric Modelling of the Environment." It was adopted into the Unified Model in 2014.

33 Gungho stands for "Globally Uniform Next Generation Highly Optimized."

34 See Staniforth and Wood (2008), for a more detailed account.

35 The full set of equations for the Met Office's New Dynamics core are given in Davies et al. (2005).

36 See White and Wood (2015), for a more detailed account of how the term "primitive equations" has been used in atmospheric sciences.

37 Models based on the Lat-Lon grid still need some filtering at the poles, to deal with the grid convergence problem. Also, most models still use the hydrostatic

approximation, which filters out sounds waves and gravity waves in the vertical dimension, by assuming air pressure at any point is determined only by the weight of air above it. The UK Met Office dynamical cores do not use this approximation.

38 At the Met Office, the global forecasting model now extends to 70 km, and the climate models go up to 85 km.

39 Folks at the Met Office told me a story, which may be apocryphal, of a model that didn't properly account for this, and over a long run, the atmosphere slowly disappeared, as a little bit of it was lost at each timestep into the gaps between the grid cells higher in the atmosphere.

40 Air pressure is conventionally measured in millibars (mbar) in meteorology, a unit first introduced by Bjerknes. However mbar is not an SI unit, so often scientists use the Pascal (Pa) instead. 100 Pa is a hectoPascal (hPa) and is equal to 1 mbar.

41 Taken strictly, this is the hydrostatic approximation. Models – such as the UM – which don't use this simplification, stick to using height as the vertical coordinate, with a terrain following adjustment in the lower atmosphere.

42 If each grid cell sets its terrain at the average elevation for that cell, mountainous regions will look like giant staircases, instead of the gentle slopes of Figure 5.12. These would mess up the airflow in the dynamical core, so usually a smoothing is applied to remove these effects.

43 The stratosphere and troposphere are defined by their temperature profiles. In the troposphere, temperature reduces with height. But in the stratosphere temperature increases with height. The boundary between them is lower towards the poles.

44 John Thuburn.

45 See Teixeira (2014) for more detail on how to calculate the effects of mountain waves.

46 It's now known as SOCRATES – Suite Of Community RAdiative Transfer code based on Edwards and Slingo.

47 See, for example, Slingo et al. (2009). More recent research is exploring the use of Machine Learning techniques to improve model parameterizations (Schneider et al., 2017).

48 For weather forecasting, big improvements have also come from having better observational data, particularly from more advanced satellites.

6

The Well-Equipped Physics Lab

Climate models provide a "virtual laboratory" for experiments that cannot be done on the real planet. A large community of scientists runs their own experiments on these models, and collects observations from the real world to see if these match what happens in the experiments. In climate science, the sharing of computer models helps build such a community by making it easier for scientists to develop their own experiments. Shared models also remove any mystery around an experiment, because the program code in the model is a precise, unambiguous statement of what the experiment does. The development of such a community was a crucial step forward for climate science, and, as we shall see, the National Centre of Atmospheric Research, in Boulder, Colorado played a central role in the development of this community.

The Mesa Lab

The city of Boulder nestles into the foothills of the Rocky Mountains in Colorado. From the airport in Denver, the mountains appear as a dark ribbon on the horizon. In the hour it takes to drive up to Boulder, they gradually grow in size – by the time you reach the outskirts of Boulder, the mountains dominate every view. Up above Boulder, on a plateau overlooking the city, sit the bold salmon-coloured turrets of the Mesa Lab, the headquarters of the National Center for Atmospheric Research (NCAR). The building was designed by the renowned architect I. M. Pei, who – inspired by the ancestral cliff dwellings of the Pueblo peoples – used a cubist design and salmon-coloured concrete to give the impression it was carved out of the mountain[1] (see Figure 6.1).

Inside the lab, Pei wanted to create an interesting space for an interdisciplinary group of scientists, to support the messy work typical of doing science. He designed the offices with lots of wall space for scientists to pin up notes and diagrams. Each office is a slightly different size, to allow for different

Figure 6.1 The NCAR Mesa Lab, in Boulder, Colorado. (Photo: Steve M. Easterbrook)

needs. In each tower, a set of "crows nest" offices can be reached – each by its own spiral staircase – and these offices open out onto rooftop patios, where the scientists can step outside to think while they contemplate the amazing view. Throughout the building, the corridors twist and turn, to avoid any sense of repetition. This makes the building more interesting – and almost impossible for new visitors to find their way around without help.

In Boulder, virtually everyone embraces a mountain sport, so naturally there's a steep hiking trail straight up the mountainside to the Mesa Lab and bike lanes on the long circuitous approach road. The lab sits a thousand feet higher than the city, so both routes involve working up a major sweat, and I find the air is noticeably thinner at the top. It takes me a few days to get acclimatized each time I visit, and I often have to stop for breath even just on the steps up from the parking lot.[2] So, while I did manage the bike trail a few times, most mornings I used the free shuttle bus, which has plenty of bike racks, and enjoyed the long freewheel bike ride back down in the evenings.

NCAR is America's leading centre for research on atmospheric sciences and climate change. Although it is funded primarily by the federal government, NCAR is not part of any federal agency. It's purely a research lab – it doesn't issue commercial weather forecasts, although it does have an excellent visitors' centre. It's funded primarily by the National Science Foundation, operated by a non-profit consortium of universities,[3] and employs over 1,000 staff, of whom nearly half are scientists, along with another 150 technical and engineering support staff.

A Community Model

NCAR's main climate model is known as the *Community Earth System Model (CESM)*. As the name suggests, the model is intended as a resource for the broader scientific community. The scientists at NCAR offer regular training workshops for scientists who want to learn how to work with the model, and NCAR provides user support and detailed descriptions of the design of each version of the model. As a result, the model is probably the most widely used climate model in the world today.

It also has one of the longest pedigrees. Computational modelling of the atmosphere began at NCAR in 1963. While the first models worked only on NCAR's computers, the intention was always to build a model that university-based researchers could run their own computational experiments on. This goal was reached in 1983, with the first public release of the *Community Climate Model*, offering the program code freely to anyone. At first, it was just a global atmosphere model, but it has undergone many improvements since then,[4] with ocean, land, and sea ice components added in the mid-1990s, and components to simulate glaciers, ocean waves, and rivers added more recently.

It isn't strictly accurate to call CESM "NCAR's model," because many other labs contribute substantial effort to developing the model, and funding comes from a number of US federal agencies. Both the ocean model (known as POP, the Parallel Ocean Program[5]) and the sea ice model (CICE, pronounced "C-ice") were originally developed at Los Alamos National Labs. Ongoing improvements to all the component models are managed by teams of scientists with representatives from government labs and university research groups.

More than 300 scientists show up every June for an annual workshop to hear about new improvements to the model and its components, coordinate plans for future work, and to discuss the latest science being done with the model. These workshops were traditionally held in Breckenridge, high in the Colorado Rocky Mountains, although recently they've moved to a larger venue in Boulder itself. In the summer of 2010, I arrived at NCAR just in time to attend that year's Breckenridge workshop, which gave me a rapid introduction to the community and how it works, and an opportunity to sit down with many of the lead scientists associated with CESM, and find out more about their work.

A Suite of Models

CESM is not really a single model. It's an integrated modelling suite, with seven separate model components – atmosphere; oceans; ocean waves; land surfaces; rivers; land ice; and sea ice – each developed by its own community of experts. These component models each have their own community of users, who often just run their component on its own. Oceanographers might run ocean simulations without worrying about interaction with the atmosphere; glaciologists might run just the ice sheet model on its own to study the movement of glaciers, and so on. Climate scientists often move back and forth between running an individual component to study specific processes, and running CESM as a whole, to study what happens when those processes interact with other parts of the Earth system.

The host for my visits to NCAR was Mariana Vertenstein, manager of the CESM software engineering group, a team of a dozen scientists who support the various working groups to ensure the software for the models is well-designed and properly tested. Over the years, Mariana's team has been responsible for transforming the component models that make up CESM from a disparate set of stand-alone models into an integrated modelling system. Mariana likens this approach to a well-equipped physics lab, with all the right equipment in place to do different kinds of experiments.

CESM weighs in at over a million lines of code, meaning considerable software engineering effort is required to coordinate the work of the community. But such effort is often invisible when it's done well. So I was surprised and delighted when I arrived at the Breckenridge workshop in 2010, to learn that the community was awarding Mariana the annual CESM distinguished achievement award,[6] an acknowledgement of both the central importance of good software engineering to scientific modelling, and the key role Mariana has played in managing the technical challenges of a large and complex engineering project.

A community model must also run on a wide variety of different machines. NCAR is unusual among climate modelling labs for designing the model to be relatively easy to port to different kinds of computers, and for guiding users across the world who want to run it on their own machines. When I visited in 2010, I noticed my own laptop, a MacBook Pro, was on the list of target machines, but wasn't yet officially supported, which meant nobody had yet built and tested a version of CESM for it. I decided to try installing it myself.[7] It took me a couple of days to get the code compiled and running before I had a successful test run on my laptop, largely because – like most modern scientific software – CESM is built on top of many existing scientific software packages, and I needed to make sure I had compatible versions of all these packages installed on my laptop first.

Of course, full-scale simulations of the climate in CESM would require a supercomputer. In the early days at NCAR, the supercomputers were housed

Figure 6.2 Two generations of NCAR's Supercomputers at the Facility in Cheyenne, Wyoming. Left: Yellowstone, a 73,000 core IBM iDataPlex cluster, installed in 2011 and decommissioned in 2017. Right: Cheyenne, a 145,000 core Hewlett Packard cluster, installed in 2016. (© 2022 UCAR)

in the basement of the Mesa Lab. But its needs have grown so much, it now operates a dedicated supercomputer facility in Wyoming. Two generations of its supercomputers are shown in Figure 6.2. When it was first installed, NCAR's latest supercomputer, Cheyenne, was ranked as the 20th fastest machine in the world.

Open Source

Most scientific software is developed by scientists themselves, for use in their own labs – tools for organizing and analyzing data from field studies, tools for displaying data and scientific results in different formats, and so on. Sometimes, a software tool used in one lab is useful to many other scientists, and the scientists who built it will often share it freely, making the code available on one of several popular code sharing websites.[8] Occasionally, these tools acquire a broader community of users, who build upon the original tools, often evolving them into a large software *libraries* – suites of useful tools – that the scientific community comes to rely on. Shared software libraries simplify much of the grunt work in doing science, from working with raw data all the way through to preparing papers for publication.

The idea of *open source* software is very attractive to scientific communities. Making your program code available to anyone who wants to adapt and modify it to their own needs reflects a core value for most scientists. Science is a community endeavour, and scientists need other scientists to replicate their work, to check their results are valid, and to build on their contributions. But most science is done on a shoe-string budget, held together with a patchwork of grants from government agencies, which never have enough funding to go around. Scientists usually have very little budget to pay for specialized software tools, and the demand for such tools is often too small to support commercial companies trying to sell them. Freely sharing the software is usually the only approach that works.

The vast majority of open source software, however, turns out not to be useful to anyone other than the people who built it. A lot of the software on open source code sharing sites has, in effect, no community of users at all.[9] A very small handful of projects have thousands of users, while thousands of projects have only a very small handful of users.[10] In this context, CESM is clearly a runaway success. The few hundred scientists who come each year to the annual CESM workshop represent only the tip of an iceberg. Over 6,000 scientists have registered to download and use CESM, and the number is growing rapidly – in the last couple of years, this number grew by about 900 per year. Many of these users register so they can download and install CESM on a shared computing facility, where many other scientists will have access to it. The CESM online discussions groups regularly attract tens of thousands of participants.

It took a long time to grow a community of this size. By regularly publishing newer and better versions of the model, documenting its design in detail, and training new users, NCAR has established CESM as the preferred climate model for a large and disparate community of scientists – atmospheric physicists, oceanographers, paleoclimatologists, ecologists, glaciologists, marine biologists, environmental scientists, chemists, and more. These scientists use the model to study the climate of the distant past, to make sense of recent or current data on global environmental change, and to explore future scenarios of how the climate might be further affected by both human activities and natural processes.

The Blue Book

It didn't used to be like this. When climate modelling first began at NCAR in the 1960s, there was no such community. The first generations of models could only be used at NCAR, and while NCAR was quite happy for scientists to come and visit and work with the models, in the early days very few scientists ever did.[11]

Perhaps surprisingly, the study of climate was not even part of NCAR's mission when it was founded in 1960. At the time, there was really no such thing yet as *climate science*. The idea that the climate was changing due to human activities was only known to a handful of scientists, and their work was largely ignored as implausible by the mainstream atmospheric science and meteorology communities. The study of climate was largely the preserve of descriptive geographers, who would create maps and collect statistics showing regional variations in climate, to explore the effect of local climate on human health, agriculture, and so on.[12] They assumed the climates they described were unchanging, and they concerned themselves only with what happens in the first few metres of air above the ground – the space in which humans live. Meanwhile, the role of physics in moving weather systems around was left to (theoretical) meteorologists and geophysicists.

The rationale for creating a US national centre for the study of the atmosphere was laid out in a 1959 report[13] – known at NCAR as "the blue book" – written jointly by a consortium of 14 universities for the National Science Foundation. The blue book argued a national centre could provide a coordinated, inter-disciplinary approach to the study of the atmosphere, on a scale not possible in individual universities, and suggested a research agenda covering four main areas of research, which I might re-label as: *motion*, *heat*, *water*, and *other things*. Atmospheric *motion* would encompass motion at all scales – from small-scale phenomena such as wind gusts and convection currents, through storm systems such as cyclones, up to global-scale circulation patterns. Atmospheric *heat* would include incoming solar radiation, energy exchanges between atmosphere and the Earth's surface, and the thermodynamics of cloud systems. Atmospheric *water* would require a complete analysis of the water cycle: how water passes between soils, rivers, lakes, and oceans, evaporation, air humidity, clouds of all different types, and precipitation.

And finally, under "other physical processes," the blue book identified things whose effect on the atmosphere was poorly understood at the time, including sound waves, electrical currents, and chemical reactions in the atmosphere. It is only here that the report acknowledges the possibility of a human impact – noting the "unsolved question of whether the carbon dioxide content of the atmosphere is increasing as a result of combustion processes and the even more elusive question as to possible changes in the Earth's electrical field as a result of nuclear explosions."[14]

The blue book only mentions climate in a brief section on climate control. Like von Neumann, the authors of the blue book expected advances in our understanding of the atmosphere would enable us to *control* the climate. "Finally, the physical linkage between the heat budget and the general circulation of the atmosphere is such a close one that any hope of effective climate control is likely to lie in alteration of some aspect of the heat budget." Nevertheless, the report made a powerful argument that the time was ripe for a massive push to improve our understanding of the atmosphere, given the vast improvements in data collection and computational power available in the postwar period.

The First NCAR Model

In the summer of 1963, shortly after approving I. M. Pei's design for the Mesa Lab, and before construction began, NCAR recruited two young atmospheric scientists (see Figure 6.3) who quickly discovered they shared an interest in building their own general circulation model (GCM) – a computer model of the entire atmosphere that could become a testbed for analysis of all four of the areas described in the blue book: motion, heat, water, and physical processes.

The more senior of the two, Akira Kasahara had studied at the University of Tokyo, earning a PhD on the structure of typhoons, and had moved to the United States where he spent six years as a research scientist at the University of Chicago, developing numerical models of hurricanes. Meanwhile, Warren Washington had just completed his PhD at Penn State University, focusing on the problem of how to transform meteorological observational data onto the regular grids needed for computer modelling. Both scientists had plenty of experience working with computer models, and were very familiar with the breakthroughs in the 1950s in the development of numerical weather forecast models.[15]

Figure 6.3 Warren Washington and Akira Kasahara in the early 1970s. (© 2022 UCAR)

The management in the early days at NCAR tended to view it as their job to hire the very best scientists, give them the resources they needed, and let them decide for themselves what research problems they should tackle – as long as they were big bold problems. Building a computer model of the global atmosphere certainly fit the bill. So when Kasahara and Washington described their desire to build their own GCM at NCAR over lunch one day in a Boulder restaurant, their boss, Phil Thompson, was delighted.[16] Thompson ensured they would have access to the new supercomputer NCAR had just ordered – a CDC 3600 – on which to develop the model.

Thompson believed this was the type of project that NCAR was created for, and had written an article[17] earlier that year for the NCAR Quarterly Newsletter arguing an investment in general circulation modelling was an "important gamble" for NCAR. Thompson described the effort as basic research, with an unknowable outcome. He argued such modelling would certainly expand our understanding of the atmosphere, and suggested a research program in which scientists working on different aspects of atmospheric science could express their ideas in mathematics, and then "plug in" those equations into a GCM to test them out. Among the potential applications for such research, he suggested a set of imagined weather-modification experiments that would be hard or impossible to do for real, but could be studied in a simulation: spreading a chemical film on the ocean to reduce evaporation; covering the polar ice sheets with black carbon to create a warming effect; or damming the Bering Strait to change patterns of sea temperatures.

The Birth of a Community

When they first got started, Kasahara and Washington were aware of several existing efforts to build similar models, all inspired by the 1955 breakthrough by Norman Phillips, described in Chapter 4. Phillips's GCM was ridiculously simple, with a cylindrical Earth and the state of the atmosphere expressed using air pressure as a single variable, but still developed its own stable jet stream, under the influence of the equations that describe the effect of heat from the sun and rotation of the Earth. The remarkable success of that model inspired a generation of atmospheric scientists to develop their own long-term global circulation models in this style.

Already, there was plenty of expertise in numerical methods and computational modelling among the meteorological community. Numerical weather forecasting had taken off rapidly, and by 1960, three countries – the United States, Sweden, and Japan – had operational numerical weather forecasting services up and running. But starting the model with the atmosphere at rest and seeing what patterns emerged makes global circulation modelling radically different from how models are used in weather forecasting.

A weather model only has to simulate a few days starting from data about current conditions. In contrast, a GCM has to simulate long-term stable patterns – which means the simplifications to the equations of motion that worked in early weather forecasting models don't work in GCMs. The weather models in the 1950s all used versions of Charney's equations. These smooth out fast moving waves that don't affect short-term weather forecasts but make the model unstable over longer runs. Over long runs in these models, the atmosphere would steadily lose energy – and sometimes air and moisture too – so realistic climatic patterns wouldn't emerge. The small group of scientists interested in general circulation modelling began to diverge from the larger numerical weather forecasting community, choosing versions of the equations with conservation of mass and energy built in, to give stable long-range simulations.

At von Neumann's urging, the US Weather Bureau established a General Circulation Research Laboratory, specifically to build on Phillips's success. It was headed by Joseph Smagorinsky, one of the original members of the ENIAC weather modelling team. Originally located just outside Washington DC, the lab has undergone several name changes and relocations, and is now the Geophysical Fluid Dynamics Lab (GFDL), housed at Princeton University, where it remains a major climate modelling lab today.

In 1959, Smagorinsky recruited the young Japanese meteorologist Syukuro Manabe from Tokyo, and they began work on a primitive equation model. Like Phillips, their first model represented only one hemisphere. Manabe concentrated on the mathematical structure, while Smagorinsky hired a large team of programmers to develop the code. By 1963, they had developed a nine-layer atmosphere model which exchanged water – but not heat – between the atmosphere and surface. The planet's surface, however, was flat and featureless – a continuous swamp from which water could evaporate, but with no internal dynamics of its own. The model could simulate radiation passing through the atmosphere, interacting with water vapour, ozone, and CO_2. Like most of the early GCMs, this model captured realistic larger global patterns, but had many of the details wrong.

Meanwhile, at the University of California, Los Angeles (UCLA), Yale Mintz, the associate director of the Department of Meteorology, recruited another young Japanese meteorologist, Akio Arakawa, to help him build their own GCM. From 1961, Mintz and Arakawa developed a series of models, with Mintz providing the theoretical direction, and Arakawa designing the model, with help from the department's graduate students. By 1964, their model represented the entire globe with a two-layer atmosphere and realistic geography.[18]

Computational limitations dominated the choices these two teams had to make. The GFDL team modelled only the northern hemisphere, with a featureless surface, so they could put more layers into the atmosphere, while the UCLA team chose the opposite route: an entire global model with realistic layout of continents and oceans, but with only two layers of atmosphere.

One other early model was developed single-handedly by Cecil "Chuck" Leith in 1960, at the Lawrence Livermore National Labs in California, on what was, at the time, the fastest computer in the world.[19] Leith had spent much of that year in Sweden, studying at Carl Rossby's atmospheric sciences institute in Stockholm, and while there, he designed his own five-layer hemispheric GCM. Leith never published his work – he built his model mainly to satisfy his own curiosity, and rapidly moved on to other research problems, although he later moved to NCAR and became a strong advocate of the effort to build a community model in the late 1970s. But his model became widely known because he made movies from the model outputs, through a laborious process of transferring static images of the state of the atmosphere at each timestep to photographic plates, and colouring the plates separately to illustrate different variables (see Figure 6.4). Leith enlisted a Hollywood production company to help create the films, and his movies were so effective in illustrating what the model could do that Warren Washington immediately adopted the idea at NCAR.

NCAR's Early Models

When they arrived at NCAR, Kasahara and Washington already knew these other research groups very well. Kasahara had spent time with Smagorinsky's group in the early 1960s, making use of their computer, and Washington had met with Leith several times to find out more about how his model worked. When they designed their own model, they drew on the experience of these other groups, but also wanted to do something different. Inspired by NCAR's mission to support the broader scientific community, they decided to build a model that would be easy for other scientists to understand and work with – basing their design on Lewis Fry Richardson's original formulation of the primitive equations, as described in his widely read 1922 book.

Their guiding design principle was to build a model to be sufficiently general so other scientists could *"incorporate their findings in the model and test*

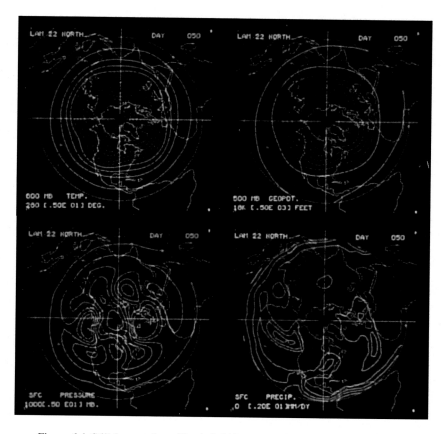

Figure 6.4 Still images from Chuck Leith's video of his model in action. The images show, clockwise from top left: temperature, geopotential height, precipitation, and surface air pressure. The images are centred over the North Pole, and the outer blue circle represents the limits of the simulation, at the equator. (Lawrence Livermore National Lab)

their hypotheses."[20] It's hard to run experiments on the real atmosphere. But hypothesis testing can be done in a simulation model by setting up different conditions, running the model for each condition, and comparing the results – a *virtual* experiment. In this way, computer models extend the range of practical scientific investigation to things that were previously hard to study. A virtual experiment won't necessarily tell us what will happen in the real world, but it often gives a very useful clue. By running virtual experiments many times in a simulation, under slightly varied conditions, scientists can learn a lot about why the real atmosphere behaves as it does. All scientific experiments are somewhat artificial like this[21]: biologists experiment on specially bred strains of mice and fruit flies that do not occur in the wild; chemists experiment on purified forms of chemicals, and psychologists run experiments on people in an artificial laboratory setting, rather than the social world in which they live. Even physics experiments are artificial: idealized objects sliding down smooth inclined planes do not generally occur outside the lab. Science thrives on simplified or idealized versions of reality.

Kasahara and Washington's first model was extremely simplified. It was a two-layer global model, using a standard Latitude–Longitude grid,[22] with grid points spaced out at 5° intervals, making them about 550 km apart at the equator. Each layer in the atmosphere was 6 km thick, giving a total atmosphere height of only 12 km. The first version of the model assumed the Earth's surface was a uniformly flat swamp, and it ran as a "perpetual January" – with the surface temperatures fixed using data for a typical January average. It did, however, include a radiation scheme.

Over the next 15 years, Kasahara and Washington steadily refined their models.[23] The second version, developed from 1968 onwards, fixed many of the limitations: the model included mountains, an active water cycle with realistic evaporation and condensation, and it used energy balance equations to calculate surface temperatures for the land areas, although ocean surface temperatures were still provided as fixed values. These later models could be set up to experiment with many different variants – changing the number of layers in the atmosphere (6 or 12 layers, each 3 km thick), the resolution of the grid (5° or 2.5°), with seasonal changes switched on or off, and so on. The model could even be run as a limited area regional model at a very high resolution of 0.625°, and 24 layers. Experiments with these models showed that increasing the resolution in the model dramatically improved how realistically it captured the patterns of the real-world atmosphere, so a steady improvement in resolution became a central goal for the team.

Then and Now

So by 1965 three major research labs[24] had working global circulation models and ongoing research efforts to refine and improve them, each with their own approach to the modelling (see Figure 6.5). Each of these labs consisted of two lead scientists and a handful of programmers to help with the coding. The entire general circulation modelling community consisted of no more than around two dozen scientists.[25] By sheer coincidence, each of the three labs was headed by a partnership between an American and a Japanese scientist: Washington

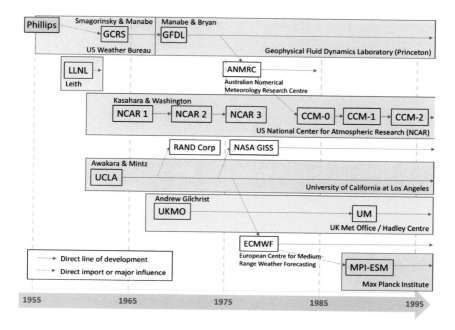

Figure 6.5 The early development of general circulation models. (Adapted from Edwards (2000))

and Kasahara at NCAR; Smagorinsky and Manabe at the US Weather Bureau, and Mintz and Arakawa at UCLA. The Japanese members of these teams had all trained at the same lab in the University of Tokyo,[26] and many of them had come to the attention of the American research labs at the first international conference on numerical weather prediction[27] in Tokyo in 1960.

The scientists building these models in the 1960s didn't think of themselves as climate scientists, and none of them referred to what they were building as *climate models*. When Kasahara and Washington set out to build their first model, their focus was on basic research in atmospheric science. Their models would support experiments that could test scientists' understanding the physical principles of the atmosphere, but the models could not simulate changes in the climate.[28]

Today, the research community working with these models is very different. In the early 1970s, with their models growing in sophistication, these atmospheric modellers suddenly found themselves at the forefront of an emerging new field. The models became a critical tool to study the likelihood and implications of future climate change. But when did this shift happen, and why?

Early Warming Signals

In Chapter 2, we noted that Arrhenius's 1894 climate model – and his theories about CO_2 and climate change – were largely dismissed by the broader scientific community, and ignored for more than half a century. There were occasional exceptions. For example, in the 1930s, the English engineer Guy Stewart Callendar analyzed CO_2 and temperature trends, and became convinced that there was a discernible rise in both, caused by the use of coal for energy. In a 1938 paper, he provided graphs showing both had risen slowly over the previous 50 years,[29] and gave a detailed analysis of the carbon cycle, to show that human emissions would accumulate in the atmosphere. He argued Arrhenius had been right all along.

Like Arrhenius before him, Callendar's work was also largely dismissed at the time – his paper was widely cited, but usually to disagree with it. There were plenty of counter-arguments.[30] Early attempts to measure the wavelengths of infra-red that water vapour and CO_2 absorbed suggested their absorption bands overlapped completely – so it wasn't obvious how adding more CO_2 would make a difference. And anyway, wouldn't the extra CO_2 just dissolve in the ocean, keeping the CO_2 levels in the atmosphere constant? Besides, the rise in CO_2 and temperatures in Callendar's charts was relatively small compared to the short-term variations in the data, and didn't show up in other records at the time.

In the 1950s, these arguments were demolished one by one. The first was due to a Canadian physicist, Gilbert Plass, who worked in the mid-1950s for Lockheed Martin on detecting the infra-red signatures of missiles. Plass had access to much more accurate data on how the atmosphere absorbs infra-red radiation than his predecessors, and realised the CO_2 and water vapour absorption bands don't completely overlap after all. Plass had also published results[31] showing the infra-red absorption bands change at different heights in the atmosphere, because gas molecules behave differently at different air pressures. He realized this removed the argument that the absorption effect is saturated in the lower atmosphere: the absorption bands sharpen with height, reducing the overlap between CO_2 and water vapour. The amount of CO_2 in the upper atmosphere would matter, even if it didn't matter lower down.

Plass became convinced that CO_2 from fossil fuel emissions would warm the planet, and he wrote extensively about it in both the scientific and popular literature.[32] His most widely cited paper,[33] in 1956, provided a detailed account of the absorption properties of CO_2, concluding that a doubling of CO_2 in the atmosphere would raise global average temperatures by 3.8°C, about midway between Arrhenius's original result of 5.7°C and Callendar's estimate of 2°C.

A naive reading of all these results would suggest they were steadily homing in on a correct answer, which the IPCC currently puts as likely between 2.5°C and 4°C.[34] But we now know that all of them made too many simplifying assumptions and ended up with (roughly) the right answers for the wrong reasons.[35] Callendar and Plass's models were in some ways a step backwards. While Arrhenius's model was conceptually correct, but suffered from very poor data, the converse was true for Callendar and Plass. Both had access to better data, but missed something that was obvious to Arrhenius: when the concentration of greenhouse gases changes, the calculation that matters is the balance between heat flows at the top of the atmosphere – the whole atmosphere will change temperature until incoming and outgoing energy flows to space match again. Both Callendar and Plass tried to do the calculation for the ground level, assuming the temperature of the atmosphere itself is fixed. But that makes no sense: if the ground warms, the air above it must also warm, and so on up throughout the atmosphere, until the upper atmosphere radiates enough extra infra-red to space to restore the balance.

Unfortunately, none of the errors in their models were discovered at the time. All of these scientists lacked an essential ingredient for scientific modelling: a community of other scientists willing to construct their own models and compare results carefully enough to identify and correct their errors.

Oceanographers Wade In

It would take another 20 years before such a modelling community emerged, when the global circulation modelling community turned their attention to the question of climate change. But meanwhile other scientists were investigating what happens to CO_2 in the atmosphere.

Carbon dioxide readily dissolves in water – that's how carbonated beverages are made. But if you try to dissolve too much, the water emits CO_2 again – the bubbles of CO_2 escaping gives our drinks their fizz. Left open, our drinks go flat,[36] when CO_2 in the drink reaches equilibrium with CO_2 in the air. So while CO_2 readily dissolves in the oceans, it wasn't clear for a long time whether it would stay there. Several groups of oceanographers in the 1950s began to investigate this question, as they sought to understand better how the ocean circulation works. And they had a new tool to explore it: *radiocarbon dating*.

The idea behind radiocarbon dating was developed in the 1940s by Willard Libby, an American chemist who went on to win a Nobel prize for his work. Libby discovered that cosmic rays occasionally hit nitrogen atoms in the upper atmosphere, mutating them at a slow but predictable rate into a mildly radioactive form of carbon, called carbon-14, which slowly decays back to nitrogen again, emitting faint radiation that can be detected with a Geiger counter. When living plants absorb carbon dioxide from the air, it includes some of this carbon-14. The plants don't absorb any more after they die, and the carbon-14 trapped in the dead vegetation slowly decays over thousands of years. So the relative proportion of carbon-14 in a fossilized plant can be used to calculate how long ago the plant died. Today, carbon dating is a standard technique for calculating the age of a fossil, but it can also be used to explore where else atmospheric carbon ends up, and how long it stays there.[37]

In the early 1950s, oceanographers at the Scripps Institute for Oceanography in California, under the leadership of their new director, Roger Revelle, were investigating the spread of radioactive fallout in the oceans from nuclear weapons testing. Their work was funded by the US military, who needed to know how quickly the oceans would absorb these contaminants, to assess the risks to human health. But Revelle had many other research interests. He had read Callendar's papers, and realized radiocarbon dating could be used to measure the age of dissolved carbon at different depths in the ocean. Just as carbon-14 trapped in fossil plants slowly decays, so does carbon-14 dissolved in the ocean. Revelle understood the importance of a community effort, so he persuaded a number of colleagues to do similar analysis, and in a coordinated set of three papers,[38] published in 1957, the group presented their results.

They all found a consistent pattern: the surface layer of the ocean continuously absorbs CO_2 from the atmosphere – on average, a molecule of CO_2 molecule stays in the atmosphere only for about seven years, before being dissolved into the ocean. But the surface waters also release CO_2, especially when they warm up in the sun. So the atmosphere and surface waters exchange CO_2 molecules continuously – and any extra CO_2 ends up shared between them.

All three papers also confirmed the surface waters don't mix much with the deeper ocean. So it takes hundreds of years for dissolved carbon to pass down into deeper waters. The implications were clear – the oceans weren't absorbing CO_2 anywhere near as fast as we were producing it.

There was worse news still. Seawater acts as a *buffered solution*. When CO_2 dissolves in the ocean, the water becomes more acid. But in a buffered solution, small changes in acidity trigger chemical reactions that "push back" against further absorption of CO_2 – big changes in atmospheric CO_2 cause only relatively small changes in the amount dissolved in the ocean.[39] Two years later, two oceanographers from Stockholm, Bert Bolin and Erik Eriksson, published a followup paper, analyzing the implications.[40] The buffering effect means a 10% increase in CO_2 in the atmosphere only causes a 1% increase in carbon uptake in the surface layer of the ocean. This, combined with the

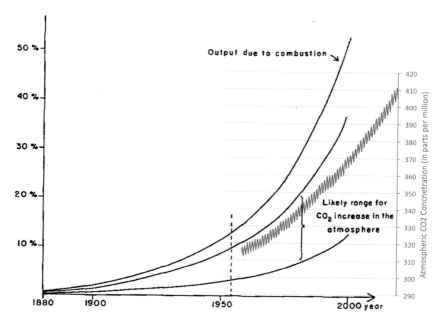

Figure 6.6 Bolin and Eriksson's prediction for increasing atmospheric concentrations of carbon dioxide (black lines), overlaid with Keeling's observed monthly
data[41] (blue line) and annual averages (orange line). The highest curve is a hypothetical, if all emissions were to stay in the atmosphere, while the lower curves
show the expected range given their calculations of likely ocean uptake. The
dashed line marks the year the prediction was made. Keeling's data shows the
characteristic annual sawtooth pattern, as the forests across the northern hemisphere take in carbon dioxide each spring, and release it in the fall. (Adapted from
Bolin and Eriksson (1958) with permission from Rockefeller Institute Press)

slow rate of ocean over-turning, means that about half of all human emissions
of CO_2 remain in the atmosphere for centuries. Bolin and Eriksson include a
startling graph at the end of their paper, predicting an exponential rise in atmospheric CO_2 over the second half of the twentieth century from the burning of
fossil fuels (see Figure 6.6). It was a bold prediction, given that, at the time,
there were no reliable measurements of rising CO_2 levels. And when the data
started rolling in, it was clear their prediction was correct.

Alarming Data

These findings set alarm bells ringing among the geosciences community. If
Bolin and Eriksson's forecast was correct, the effects of climate change would

be noticeable within a few decades. But without data, it would be hard to test their prediction. At Scripps, Revelle was already working to correct this, hiring a young chemist, David Charles Keeling, to begin detailed measurements. In 1958, Keeling set up an observing station on Mauna Loa in Hawaii, and a second station in the Antarctic, both far enough from any major sources of emissions to give a reliable baseline measurement of CO_2 in the atmosphere. Funding for the Antarctic station was cut a few years later, but Keeling managed to keep the recordings going at Mauna Loa, where they are still collected regularly today. Within two years, Keeling had enough data to confirm Bolin and Ericsson's analysis: CO_2 levels in the atmosphere were rising sharply. Figure 6.6 shows their prediction, compared with the data from Keeling's observatory.

Keeling's data helped to spread awareness of the issue rapidly among the ocean and atmospheric science research communities, even as scientists in other fields remained unaware of the issue. Alarm at the implications of the speed at which CO_2 levels were rising led some scientists to alert the country's political leaders. When President Lyndon Johnson commissioned a report on the state of the environment, in 1964, the president's science advisory committee invited a small subcommittee – including Revelle, Keeling, and Smagorinsky – to write an appendix to the report, focusing on the threat of climate change. And so, on February 8, 1965, President Johnson became the first major world leader to mention the threat of climate change, in speech to congress: *"This generation has altered the composition of the atmosphere on a global scale through ... a steady increase in carbon dioxide from the burning of fossil fuels."*

The report, released later that year, included the following conclusion about climate change: "By the year 2000 the increase in atmospheric CO_2 ... may be sufficient to produce measurable and perhaps marked changes in climate ..." and "At present it is impossible to predict these effects quantitatively, but recent advances in mathematical modelling of the atmosphere, using large computers, may allow useful predictions within the next 2 or 3 years."[42] This prediction also proved correct, but perhaps not surprisingly. As head of the largest of the three labs developing global circulation models, Smagorinsky was describing a project already underway in his lab.

Climate Modelling Takes Off

Awareness of the CO_2 problem was spreading rapidly through the scientific community just as the general circulation modelling community was getting established. At first, it wasn't clear GCMs would be suited to the task.

Computational power was limited, and it wasn't yet possible to run the models long enough to simulate the decades or centuries over which climate change would occur. Besides, the first generation of GCMs had so many simplifications, it seemed unlikely they could simulate the effects of increasing CO_2 – that wasn't what they were designed for.

To do this properly, the models would need to include all the relevant energy exchanges between the surface, atmosphere, and space. That would mean a model that accurately captured the vertical temperature profile of the atmosphere, along with the process of radiation, convection, evaporation, and precipitation, all of which move energy vertically. None of these processes are adequately captured in the primitive equations, so they would all need to be added as extra calculations in the models.

Smagorinsky's group at GFDL was the only group anywhere near ready to run experiments in their model to test the effect of different levels of CO_2 in the atmosphere. Their nine-layer model already captured some of the vertical structure of the atmosphere, and Manabe had built in a detailed radiation code from the start, with the help of a visiting German meteorologist, Fritz Möller. As an expert in radiative absorption, Möller was fascinated with Plass's work, and had tried to replicate Plass's model. But he found the results depended on assumptions about how the warming affected humidity and clouds.[43] Möller and Manabe agreed that the only way to resolve the problem was to build a better model of all the relevant heat exchanges in the full height of the atmosphere.

Manabe had such a model working by 1967, and together with his colleague, Richard Wetherald, published what is now recognized as the first accurate simulation of climate change,[44] work that eventually earned Manabe a Nobel prize in 2021. Running the global model for this experiment was still too computationally expensive, so instead they built a model of just *a single column* of atmosphere – a one-dimensional model that ignores horizontal movement of heat. The model could be run with 9 or 18 layers of atmosphere, and included the effects of upwards and downwards radiation through the column, exchanges of heat through convection, and the latent heat of evaporation and condensation of water. Manabe and Wetherald first tested this model with current atmospheric conditions, to check it could reproduce the correct vertical distribution of temperatures in the atmosphere, which it did very well. They then doubled the amount of carbon dioxide in the model and ran it again. They found temperatures rose throughout the lower atmosphere, with a rise of about 2°C at the surface, while the stratosphere showed a corresponding cooling. This pattern – warming in the lower atmosphere and cooling in the stratosphere – is a key fingerprint of greenhouse gas warming, and shows up in all modern global climate models, but wasn't confirmed by satellite readings until the 2000s. We'll return to this story in Chapter 8, as correct predictions like this offer strong evidence the models are correct.

By the mid-1970s, a broad community of scientists were replicating Manabe and Wetherald's computational experiment in a variety of simplified models, although it would take nearly a decade before anyone could run the experiment in a full three-dimensional GCM. But the community was beginning to use the term *climate modelling* to describe their work – a term given much greater impetus when it was used as the title of a comprehensive survey of the field by two NCAR scientists, Steven Schneider and Robert Dickinson in 1975. Remarkably, their paper charts a massive growth of research,[45] citing the work of over 150 authors who published work on climate modelling the in period from 1967 to 1975, after Manabe and Wetherald's original experiment.

The field had grown fast enough for Schneider and Dickinson to identify seven different types of climate model being used to understand the climate system. As well as Manabe and Wetherald's single-column model – a one-dimensional vertical model – there were various one- and two-dimensional horizontal models, which ignored the vertical structure, focusing instead on variations across latitudes, longitudes, or both. The most complex models were the three-dimensional GCMs, some of which included just the atmosphere, while others also modelled atmosphere–surface interactions.

It took some time, however, before these three-dimensional GCMs could run climate change experiments. Perhaps unsurprisingly, Manabe and Wetherald were again the first to do this, in 1975. Their GCM produced a higher result for when atmospheric CO_2 was doubled – an average surface warming of 3°C – and they attributed this to the snow-albedo feedback, which is included in the GCM, but not in their original single column model.[46] Their model showed an effect first noted by Arrhenius: a much greater warming at the poles than towards the equator – because polar temperatures are much more sensitive to changes in the rate at which heat escapes to space. And their model predicted global warming would speed up evaporation and precipitation, and hence produce more intense rainfalls. This prediction has already been demonstrated in the rapid uptick of extreme weather events in the 2010s.

The Birth of the Community Model

By the late 1970s, a large community of climate modellers had emerged, with a remarkable variety of different kinds of model. The GCMs were the heavyweights, requiring supercomputers to run on. They were still difficult to use, and rarely used outside the labs that developed them. In the meantime, a plethora of simpler models grew up to fill the void, until the next generation of GCMs appeared in the 1980s.

NCAR's climate models have come a long way since those days. Washington and Arakawa's original series of models had helped establish a pool of expertise at NCAR. But by the late 1970s, the design limitations in their early models were becoming clear. With the growth in speed of computers, and the arrival of parallel computing, alternatives to the Lat-Lon grid were needed, to avoid the polar convergence problem we discussed in Chapter 5. Washington began inviting experts in other numerical methods to visit NCAR, including Kamal Puri from the Australian Numerical Meteorology Research Centre, where they had already built a new model using spectral methods. At NCAR, Puri helped adapt the Australian model to run on NCAR's machines, and the NCAR team then studied it before building their own spectral model – the first Community Climate Model (CCM1) – taking the time to document the all their design decisions,[47] and to write a user's guide. By the early 1980s, the need for such a model was clear among the rapidly growing climate science community at NCAR's affiliated universities, as well as the meteorological community interested in long range (seasonal) weather forecasting.

With such a large and diverse community of users, a clear, modular design was essential. By making the components of the model modular, more choice can be offered to the users. For example, in the current atmosphere model in CESM, users can choose between three different dynamical cores, representing different ways of implementing the primitive equations, and between two different grids – Lat-Lon or cubed sphere. Users can also select how, at each timestep, the dynamical core calculations are interleaved with the physical parameterizations. Many users won't care, and will just use the defaults. But some need this flexibility when designing new kinds of experiment.

Where's the Fruit Fly?

Today's climate modelling community is large and diverse. Tens of thousands of scientists around the world make use of climate models to investigate a huge variety of research questions about the climate of planet Earth – and other planets too. More than two dozen research labs around the world run their own GCMs, although they vary in how much support they offer to the broader community of scientists interested in using their models. NCAR is untypical in this respect, as it is one of the only labs that makes community support such a high priority.

But there is also a large community of climate scientists for whom the GCMs are overkill. The leading-edge models are – and have always been – expensive to run, requiring access to multi-million dollar supercomputers. And setting up CESM to run for any given experiment is hard, because there are so many configuration choices, and a huge number of variables to deal with.[48] Scientists can simplify things by turning off some of the component models of CESM, but many important questions about climate change arise from interaction between components. So a large subset of the community needs simpler models for their experiments.

On my most recent visit, I met with another of NCAR's scientists, Isla Simpson, to talk about the work she's doing to adapt CESM to fill this need. Isla studies how climate change affects the variability of large-scale atmosphere patterns, such as the jet stream. She also studies what happens if we attempt to use *geoengineering* to try to slow down climate change – for example, by seeding the stratosphere with tiny particles that would reflect some of the incoming sunlight back to space. For the kinds of work Isla does, a single big run of CESM doesn't tell her much. What she really needs is a set of simpler models, where she can do a large number of different runs, while systematically varying the conditions. She calls these *parameter sweeps*. For example, she might take a parameter like water vapour, and slowly increase it in each run, to find out how it affects storm formation.

Isla's work builds on a long-standing tradition in climate science of working with simpler models to get a better understanding of the importance of specific parameters. There has been a long running debate in the field between those who believe in pushing for ever greater realism in GCMs versus those who think working with simpler models is a better route to improving our understanding of the climate system.[49] On the one hand, higher resolution models – incorporating more of the Earth system in their simulations – have gotten steadily better at reproducing observed climactic patterns of the recent past. But today's GCMs are now so complex it can be hard to pick out the effects you want to study from everything else that is going on in the model. So while they offer increasingly realistic simulations of the climate system, they become less useful for understanding what is going on in those simulations. An alternative is to look for the simplest model that exhibits the behaviour you're trying to study. The dishpan experiments we met in Chapter 4 are a great example of this – the characteristic pattern of Rossby waves was seen to occur just from rotation and localized heating in a dish of water.

In the early days of the field, scientists needing simpler computer models would construct their own, and the choices they made about what to include in their models were fairly ad hoc. In an influential 2005 essay,[50] Isaac Held at GFDL argued this makes it hard to develop a comprehensive understanding of how the atmosphere works. He compared this situation with human genomics, where rapid progress is possible not just because of a hierarchy of simpler

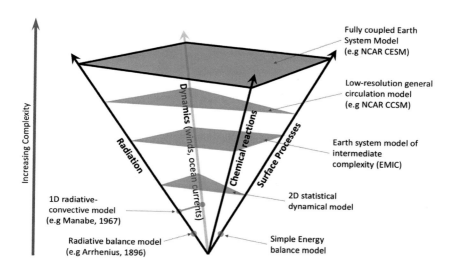

Figure 6.7 A visualization of the climate model hierarchy. The top of the inverted pyramid represents the most comprehensive, and hence the most complex of the models – today's Earth System Models. The edges of the pyramids represent four key elements of a model that might be simplified to get something simpler (and hence faster) than an ESM. Any given model might have a different combination of simplifications, represented here conceptually as the blue surfaces and dots. (Adapted from McGuffie and Henderson-Sellers (2005))

models to experiment with, but because of an agreement across the community to focus on specific models from this hierarchy. The models he's talking about, of course, are organisms – from the relatively simple, such as bacteria, through to the extremely complex, such as humans. A common evolutionary history ensures that humans still share many attributes of simpler organisms. Molecular biologists work with a few representative species from this hierarchy – including fruit flies. That's not because fruit flies are inherently important to study, but because they work as a simpler proxy for more complex creatures, they're relatively easy to breed and study in the lab, and because if a large community of scientists use the same species, they can build on each other's findings more easily. Many of the genes in a fruit fly that determine how it will develop and grow correspond to similar genes in humans, so the study of fruit fly genes has led to many important breakthroughs in understanding human genetics.[51]

What would be the equivalent of fruit flies in climate science? Schneider and Dickinson offered a way to think about this in their 1975 survey. Imagine the hierarchy of models as an inverted pyramid,[52] with the most complex – GCMs – at the top, and simpler models lower down (see Figure 6.7). Just below the GCMs are a class of models known as EMICs – Earth System Models of

Intermediate Complexity. These models simulate the carbon cycle, but use simplified atmosphere and/or ocean models to make them very fast to run. For example, the EMIC developed at the University of Victoria in Canada has detailed ocean, land, and ice sheet and carbon cycle components, but a very simplified one-layer atmosphere, and is used to study climate change over very long time periods, such as during the ice ages.

Each edge of Schneider and Dickinson's pyramid represents a different way of simplifying things. You could simplify how the model simulates winds and ocean currents – the dynamics – by having a coarser resolution grid. You could simplify the radiation by ignoring the fact that greenhouse gases absorb different amounts of energy at different wavelengths, and just calculate the average absorption for each greenhouse gas across all wavelengths – this is known as a *grey radiation* model. Or you could simplify how chemical reactions are represented, either by ignoring them completely, or by assuming they always happen at a constant rate.

Waterworld

Simplifying what happens at the surface of the planet offers some interesting choices. Early models represented the Earth's surface as a flat featureless landscape. Later versions distinguished ocean from land, and included height of the land, because hills and mountains strongly shape local weather and global circulation patterns. Today's models capture a lot more surface detail – including biological and chemical processes in plants, soils, and water. This allows the model to simulate regional climate patterns more accurately, but makes the model a lot more complex, and hence harder to understand. Scientists who want to study interactions in other parts of the model – for example, how sea surface temperatures affect atmospheric circulation – need something simpler. A good choice for them is to use an *aquaplanet* model, which simply removes all the land altogether.

The continents shape the ocean currents on planet Earth, and these in turn shape wind and weather. By removing the continents, scientists can ask more basic questions about how oceans and atmosphere interact. Scientists have been experimenting with aquaplanet models for many years. At NCAR, Isla explained there are many variants. The simplest have no ocean, just a planet-wide wet surface with fixed temperatures, from which water can evaporate. Slightly more complex versions use a "slab" ocean, in which there are no ocean currents – just a layer of water that can exchange heat with the atmosphere. More complex aquaplanets use a full dynamical ocean model to capture ocean

Double Drake

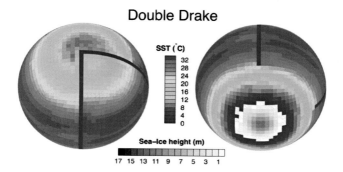

Figure 6.8 A Double Drake aquaplanet model. The model places two walls in the ocean stretching from the North Pole down to the middle of the southern latitudes. These simulate the way the two main land masses – the Americas and Eurasia – create a poleward heat transport in ocean currents that would otherwise just circulate in each latitude band. In this simulation, sea ice forms in the Antarctic, but the arrangement of walls drives more heat to the Arctic, preventing ice forming. (Reproduced from Ferreira et al. (2010). © American Meteorological Society. Used with permission.)

currents, which, like the winds, are shaped by heat from the sun and the rotation of the planet.

If you just remove the continents in an aquaplanet simulation, the oceans don't transport heat to the poles anywhere near as much as on planet Earth. However, Isla told me of a simple modification – known as a "Double Drake" aquaplanet (see Figure 6.8) – which does an excellent job of simulating this heat transport. In this model, two walls are placed in the ocean, running from the North Pole down to a point about 55° south of the equator. The walls run the full height of the ocean, and are placed about 90° apart longitudinally. The model is named after the Drake Passage – the gap between South America and Antarctica that allows the waters of the Atlantic and Pacific oceans to mix. So a Double Drake model simulates a planet with two distinct ocean basins, one much larger than the other – separated by two long skinny continents – connected via a southern ocean that circles the globe around the Antarctic. With just these walls, and with accurate heating and rotation, the Double Drake model provides a remarkably good simulation of the rate at which the oceans transport heat towards the poles on the real planet Earth, without the complexity of realistic continents.

Isla and her colleagues have now released an aquaplanet as a standard configuration of the latest version of CESM, so that the broader community can use it for their experiments. They have also released an even simpler configuration – just the dynamical core of the atmosphere model running on its own. The advantage of standardizing these is that everybody can now run their experiments in the same configurations, which are fully documented by NCAR, making it much easier to compare and reproduce each others experiments. And along with these two configurations, the team have started a broader discussion with the CESM community to identify further examples of standardized simple models that would be valuable for the community to share.

A Multitude of Experiments

The scientific community can run CESM as a fully featured Earth system model, or run any of the component models of CESM on its own, or they can configure CESM to run a simplified model. But what kinds of computational experiment do scientists run in this "well-equipped physics lab"?

Perhaps the best known is the doubled Carbon Dioxide experiment that Manabe and Wetherald pioneered in the 1960s and 1970s. As we saw in Chapter 1, Charney used this same experiment in 1979 to assess uncertainty in climate models, and it has since become known as a measure of the *Charney Sensitivity* – the sensitivity of the average surface temperature to a doubling of carbon dioxide.

There are several ways to do this experiment. The original involved two separate runs of the model, one with current concentrations of CO_2, and one with doubled concentrations. In each case, the model is run until surface temperatures settle into an equilibrium, to allow time for the "fast" feedback effects to play out, from water vapour, cloud cover, and ice albedo. The difference between the equilibrium temperatures in the two runs is the model's Charney Sensitivity.

This experiment doesn't tell you what happens to the planet *during* a period of climate change, because it doesn't simulate the transition between the two states. So an alternative is a single long simulation run, starting with the current – or, more usually, the *pre-industrial* – concentration of CO_2, and then steadily increasing it. Warren Washington and his colleague Gerald Meehl developed one of the first versions of this experiment on the Community Climate Model, in 1989. They ran the model with constant CO_2 for an initial spin up period,[53] and then increased the amount of CO_2 in the atmosphere by 1% per year for a 30-year period, comparing it with a run in which CO_2 stayed constant, and another in which CO_2 was instantly doubled at the beginning of the 30 years. With faster computers, today's modellers run this experiment for much longer, allowing CO_2 to reach a doubling – which takes about 70 years at 1% per year – and then holding it constant to allow the model to settle into a new equilibrium, for a total run of at least 150 years.

The 1% experiment is somewhat artificial, because on planet Earth, CO_2 levels haven't risen quite that fast.[54] But by standardizing on a 1% annual increase, scientists can compare models, explore how quickly the climate might change in response to rising CO_2 levels, and see what else might happen along the way in different parts of the world. For example, because the oceans contain so much water, it takes a long time for them to heat up, so there's a delay between adding CO_2 to the atmosphere, and the surface warming it causes. In the 1% experiment, when the model reaches a doubling of CO_2 the planet has only warmed partway. Scientists call the amount of warming at that point the *transient climate response*. With CO_2 levels then held constant, the warming continues for several more decades, until it reaches its new equilibrium temperature. So while CO_2 levels are increasing, there's a difference between the warming already experienced at that point, and the amount of delayed warming still to come. In the model experiments, the *transient* response is roughly half of the eventual *equilibrium* response. This is often interpreted as meaning that at any moment – while CO_2 levels keep rising – we've only experienced half of the warming we are "owed," although in reality it's a little more complicated, as we shall see.

The experiments measure the Charney sensitivity of each model, and the models each give slightly different values. Unfortunately, there is no direct way to measure climate sensitivity[55] for planet Earth. Experiments with the models – along with analysis of recent and prehistorical data – haven't pinned this number down any more than Charney was able to. In the 40 years since the Charney report, the range of likely values for climate sensitivity across the models has barely changed, leaving a frustratingly wide range of possible answers.[56] This is because the models still don't agree on the strength and timing of various feedbacks that kick in as the climate warms.

So it would be useful to measure the strength of each feedback in each model. Experiments to do this make it easier to understand the root causes of disagreement between models – although they don't necessarily tell us how strong each feedback is in reality. Manabe developed a simple experiment to measure each feedback effect on its own. The idea is identify which variable drives each feedback process, take values of that variable from the doubled CO_2 state, and insert them into the baseline climate model, to measure how much the temperature then changes. For example, Manabe would take the average values for humidity at each grid point in the doubled CO_2 experiment, and use them as prescribed values for humidity in a run of the model with normal CO_2 levels, to measure the water vapour feedback. He would then do similar experiments for cloudiness, to measure the cloud feedback, and for the extent of ice sheets to measure the ice-albedo feedback.

Unfortunately, Manabe's feedback experiments assume feedbacks are independent of one another, which is unlikely – for example, thick clouds will mask the effect of water vapour below them. So today's modellers take a different approach. For example, at NCAR, scientists run a series of experiments that introduce small changes in the model for each of these key variables, and measure how this alters the balance of incoming and outgoing radiation at the top of the atmosphere – a set of measurements known as a *radiative kernel*.[57] Scientists working with CESM can then measure how much each variable changed in their own experiments, and use the radiative kernels to estimate the strength of each feedback loop. They can also experiment with turning off specific feedback loops in CESM, by substituting an active component with a pre-computed set of values – a *data component* – which cannot react to what other components are doing.

As well as measuring climate sensitivity and feedbacks, climate scientists also use models to experiment with other things that can affect the climate, beyond greenhouse gases. Changes in the sun's heat output, eruption of volcanoes, and dust and smog in the atmosphere can all affect the climate. Because a climate model includes the physics of all these factors, each can be turned on or off in the model to see how much of the current observed global warming can be attributed to greenhouse gases. Scientists call these *attribution studies*.

A simple attribution experiment simulates what happened to the climate over the past century, using observational data on each possible cause of climate change. This also provides a basic test of the model – given measurements of all these factors over the twentieth century, can the model reproduce the observed surface temperature changes? The model can then be run again with each factor turned off in turn, to see how much difference each makes. Figure 6.9 shows the result of a set of such experiments for the twentieth century, with the models run to simulate surface temperatures given all known forcings (upper chart), and the same runs with human emissions of CO_2 turned off (bottom chart). The models produce *typical* short-term (year-to-year) variations in temperature, even though they cannot predict the actual temperature in any given year. The models all show the cooling effect of major volcanoes – from ash and sulphate particles[58] blocking out sunlight, until they wash out of the atmosphere after a few years. The models also show a warming in response to human emissions corresponding with the actual warming trend over the twentieth century. And all of the models show a slight cooling trend when human emissions are turned off.

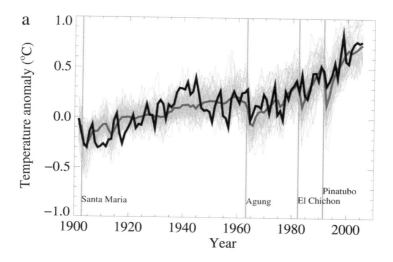

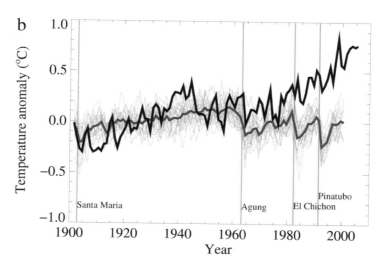

Figure 6.9 An experiment to test the effect of human versus natural causes of climate change. The charts show actual global surface temperatures (thick black line), plotted against twentieth-century simulations from a number of different climate models (thin coloured lines). Grey vertical lines mark the major volcanic eruptions of the twentieth century, each showing an abrupt cooling followed by a recovery over several years. The top chart shows 58 simulations from 14 different models. Each individual model is a thin yellow line, and the average of the models is shown in red. The bottom chart shows 19 simulations from 5 different models, with human emissions of greenhouse gases turned off. Individual model runs are thin blue lines, and the model average is the thick blue line. Temperatures are shown as deviations from the 1901–1950 average. (IPCC AR4 WG1 Figure 9.5)

All these experiments offer insights into what is happening in the models, and improve our confidence that the models are correct. But they don't give us a forecast for the future unless the levels of CO_2 in the experiments match what will actually happen. Long-term projections of likely climate change and its impacts are based on a kind of "what if" experiment. Scientists create different scenarios for how CO_2 levels might change over the coming century and beyond, using different assumptions about future global energy use – and therefore carbon emissions – over the coming decades. In Chapter 9, we'll examine how this approach works. Such projections are more for the benefit of policymakers and the general public than for the scientists themselves – who are more interested in understanding how the climate system works, rather than predicting the future.

What If?

Climate models are particularly useful for these "what if" experiments. For example, what if human emissions of greenhouse gases suddenly stopped tomorrow? This is merely a thought experiment, as it would take many years – decades, even – under the most optimistic scenarios to replace all our current use of fossil fuels with clean energy sources. So it's a kind of "world without us" scenario.[59] In a climate model, you can just turn off all human emissions and see what happens. Are we still owed further warming from past emissions, and if so how much? Climate scientists call this the *committed warming*.

Damon Matthews at Concordia University was one of the first researchers to try this particular experiment, using the University of Victoria's EMIC model. In his experiments, Damon set up the model to simulate 700 years from the year 1800. For the first 200 years (from 1800 to 2000) he provided the model with actual CO_2 emissions for each year. From then on, the model used steadily rising annual emissions – a "business as usual" pathway – until the total, cumulative, emissions reached some pre-specified level, after which CO_2 emissions were set to zero, and the model allowed to continue running to the year 2500. The experiments showed the same thing, no matter what point in the future emissions were zeroed out: while CO_2 emissions keep rising, the world keeps warming. *And then it stays at whatever temperature it has reached when emissions are zeroed out.*

The result of this experiment appears to contradict the 1% increase experiments, in which temperatures keep rising after hitting doubled CO_2. But these experiments aren't testing the same thing. The 1% experiments hold the amount of CO_2 constant after it has doubled, while Damon's experiment allows natural processes to slowly remove CO_2 from the air. The question is, how fast does this happen? Carbon dioxide is a very stable chemical, and doesn't break down naturally in the atmosphere – hence it's referred to as a *long-lived greenhouse gas*. The oceans and plants and soils rapidly absorb some of it, so the atmosphere initially keeps around half of any new emissions.[60] In Damon's experiments, this then slowly drops to just under a third by the end of 500 years. Measurements of the rate at which carbon enters the deep ocean show it will take thousands of years for CO_2 levels in the atmosphere to get back down to the levels they were at before the industrial revolution.

Meanwhile, the oceans have a large thermal inertia – it takes a lot of energy to heat them even by a small amount. So it takes centuries for the oceans to warm up, and it takes centuries for our extra CO_2 to disappear from the atmosphere. Damon's experiment suggests these two delays roughly cancel out, keeping temperatures the same for centuries. In other words, zeroing out human emissions does not reverse climate change, it merely stops it changing further.[61] So climate change is probably irreversible, at least on human time scales. And the only way to *stabilize* the climate is to get to zero emissions globally.

Damon's initial experiments left out a lot of detail, so other researchers have repeated the experiments in a variety of different models. Complications arise when you add in the effect of other greenhouse gases, especially the *short-lived* greenhouse gases such as methane. Methane is a much more powerful greenhouse gas than CO_2 – about 100 times more powerful – but is chemically unstable, so it doesn't contribute so much over the longer term.[62] Damon's initial experiments ignored short-lived greenhouse gases – adding these in produces a decades-long spike in temperatures before they stabilize. However, if we're imagining a scenario in which human emissions of greenhouse gases stopped instantly, then logically, other forms of pollution would also stop. The burning of coal and oil produces a lot of sulphur dioxide, which breaks down into sulphate particles in the atmosphere, and, like volcanoes, block some incoming sunlight to produce a cooling effect. This cooling effect partially offsets some of the warming from greenhouse gases. But sulphate particles wash out in rainwater fairly quickly – on the timescale of a few weeks. So more recent experiments[63] have explored how much difference short-lived greenhouse gases and sulphate particles would make to the initial temperature change in the first few years after zeroing out all emissions. The two together may balance each other out, but a lot depends on how fast each disappears from the atmosphere.

The relative contribution of each of these pollutants to warming or cooling is an important scientific question, and the rates at which each is naturally removed from the atmosphere can have important implications for policies aimed at limiting or banning them. So while the "world without us" experiment is interesting as a thought experiment, it also helps scientists explore how well the models capture what we know about the lifecycle of each of these pollutants, and helps identify where further data might be needed to ensure we fully understand the interactions between them.

Emergency Measures

The fact that sulphate particles – from both volcanoes and industrial pollution – have a cooling effect on the planet has led several people to suggest they could be used as an emergency measure to offset global warming. The Nobel prize-winning chemist, Paul Crutzen, called for a major research effort on this, in an essay in 2006, where he argued they might offer an important "escape route" if global warming started to spiral out of control.[64] There's a big downside: sulphate particles in the atmosphere already cause a huge global health problem, killing half a million people per year around the world, and the acid rain they cause has devastated forests and farmland around the world. Since the 1970s, clean air legislation in Europe and North America has required factories and power stations to scrub the sulphur from the smoke they produce before it enters the atmosphere.[65]

For many years, climate scientists chose *en masse* not to study such emergency measures, concerned that it would create a distraction from the work of preventing climate change. Besides, such research may create a kind of moral hazard – if politicians realize they can use stopgap solutions like this to delay the warming, it increases the chances they will further delay taking any action to reduce emissions. Crutzen argued we should at least run experiments to find out what is possible. His proposal suggests injecting the sulphur dioxide into the stratosphere, where it would stay in place longer – up to two years – so we would need a lot less of it, reducing the bad effects. So what if climate change became so bad we felt we had to try it? Would it work?

This is another "what if" question for the models. At NCAR, Isla showed me results of a recent experiment that uses an ensemble of 20 runs of CESM – to ensure any results aren't a fluke – in which sulphate aerosols are injected at four different places into the stratosphere, with the amounts automatically adjusted each year of the simulation to exactly balance the warming from greenhouse gases.[66] The model includes a detailed representation of atmospheric chemistry and the carbon cycle, to ensure the models simulate the chemical reactions and the impact on plant photosynthesis. The experiment suggests the idea will work, keeping global average temperatures stable, by steadily increasing the amounts of sulphur to keep pace with carbon emissions. But the amounts needed grow rapidly. If carbon emissions keep growing as they have in the past, by 2100, more than 50 trillion grams of SO_2 would be needed *every year* – about five times the amount released by the eruption of Mount Pinatubo in 1991. But the experiment shows that it's also remarkably difficult to control for regional differences in climate impacts. So while global average temperature was stable, the northern hemisphere still warmed, and the southern hemisphere cooled.[67] And the regional changes weren't small – Brazil and Australia cooled by between 0.5°C and 1°C, while northern Europe and Russia warmed by between 1°C and 2°C. More worryingly, the team found rainfall patterns across the tropics were severely disrupted, with an increased chance of monsoon failures in India.[68]

The political implications of these experiments are huge. If we ever decide we need to do this for real, it will be difficult to reach international agreement on what the "ideal" temperature should be. Other scientists have run a version of this experiment to see what happens if, after several decades of injecting SO_2 into the stratosphere, the sulphur injections are suddenly turned off completely – perhaps because of an international dispute about the impacts. In such experiments,[69] all the warming that had been masked during those decades occurs almost immediately, resulting in a sudden and dramatic shift in temperatures across the entire planet – an event known as *termination shock*. The implications seem clear: if we start down this road, and fail to address the underlying causes of global warming while we're busy geo-engineering the planet, we could make the problem far worse. On the other hand, we may need such emergency measures to buy us more time to get greenhouse gas emissions under control. Experiments on this with climate models will be vital in helping us weigh up the risks and understand the consequences.

Community Matters

I've used the term "experiment" to describe attempts to answer each of these questions using climate models. This may seem a strange use of the word, because there's no guarantee that what happens in the model would happen on the real planet Earth. But that's exactly how experiments often work in science: to test a hypothesis, you set up in the laboratory a simplified version of the phenomenon you are trying to understand, eliminating as many superfluous variables as possible. Such experiments cannot prove the same results would occur in the real world – for that, scientists have to find a way to repeat the experiments "in the field." Clinical trials are like this: a new vaccine that shows promise in lab experiments still has to be tested on real patients. But in some cases, repeating an experiment under real-world conditions isn't possible – it could be dangerous, unethical, or just too hard to control all the variables.

Science has an answer for that. If a laboratory experiment produces an interesting result, other scientists replicate the experiment, to make sure the results weren't a fluke. And the scientific community collectively explores whether observations from the real world match what was seen in the experiments. Gradually, over time, if no contradictions are found, the community comes to accept that the experimental result also applies to the real world.

As we've seen, the climate modelling community has grown dramatically over the past 50 years, and the models have grown in scope and complexity. Dozens of labs around the world now build their own climate models, and thousands of scientists run experiments on NCAR's Community Earth System Model. But the only people who run climate models are climate scientists themselves. When policymakers want to know what the science says about a policy-related question, they don't run a climate model – they rely on climate scientists to run the experiments. And while the program code for many of today's models are freely downloadable on the web, the amount of expertise needed to do anything useful with them means that nobody outside the climate science community ever does use them.

So a climate model like CESM is developed *by* the climate science community *for* the climate science community. To ensure the model continues to meet the needs of the community, NCAR established a set of working groups, which give the users a voice in how the model is developed and supported. There is a working group for each major part of the Earth system (atmosphere, ocean, land, ice sheets, biogeochemistry, atmospheric chemistry), and further working groups for the major scientific questions that the model is used to study (polar climate, climate variability, paleoclimate, societal dimensions). And last, but by no means least, a working group for software engineering, responsible for making sure the overall model is well-designed, well-tested, and easy to use. Each working group is co-chaired by one scientist at NCAR, and at least one scientist from another research lab, to ensure the needs and expertise of the broader community are included in all aspects of model development.

Each working group typically gets together for workshops twice a year, once at the annual CESM workshop in Breckenridge, and once during the winter. These meetings help the groups to plan new developments for each model component, develop new ideas for experiments, and run working sessions to resolve design challenges or address weaknesses in the model. The workshops play a vital role in developing consensus on where to focus their efforts, especially for deciding which of the simplifications and assumptions in their models most need to be corrected.

The face to face meetings are excellent for this, but also mean it can be hard for a scientist elsewhere in the world to contribute to the development of CESM. On my visits to other labs in Europe, I met a couple of scientists who had written code to plug into CESM for their own experiments, and felt it would be useful to others, but had been unable to get NCAR to accept that code into the official versions of CESM. They only succeeded when one of them went to NCAR as a visiting scientist. The phenomenon is common in many open source projects too – outsiders to the core team submit what they believe are useful additions to the project, only to have them persistently rejected by the project leaders.

While large software projects seem like they ought to accept contributions from anywhere, in practice a hierarchy of control is essential to keep the code coherent. Open source projects largely rely on volunteers to keep the project going, and volunteers offer very different kinds of help, from the occasional bug report, through to taking on development of a major new code (see Figure 6.10). Large community climate models like CESM are similar. Scientists contribute varying amounts of effort to the project, with a handful

General Open Source Project   CESM Community

Figure 6.10 The various different roles that contributors to an open source project can make are often described as like the layers of an onion. Individual coders might move towards the centre over time, if they have sufficient interest and technical know-how, and might move away from the centre if their interest wanes. CESM has a more stable core, as the Scientific Steering Committee and Working Group leaders are appointed by NCAR and its partner institutes. Contributions to the outer layers rely similarly on people having the appropriate expertise and interest.

of core developers employed by NCAR and partner institutions to build and maintain the model, and a much larger group of scientists who contribute to the project because they find the code useful for their scientific work.

The number of scientists who contribute code to CESM is relatively small compared to the size of the broader CESM community, but that can still mean 50–100 scientists contributing in any given year. Coordinating these contributions is hard because new code that enables one scientist's experiments to run might completely mess up those of another scientist. And testing new contributions to CESM is a complex process because every addition to the code has to work in all the different configurations of the model – long runs are usually needed to evaluate the overall effect on the climate states simulated in the model. We'll explore how the testing process is managed in more detail in Chapter 8. But the result is an ongoing tension between the goals of accepting everyone's contributions, versus maintaining a very high quality model.

Why Build a Climate Model?

The goals of the scientists who built the first GCMs were relatively simple. As curiosity-driven research in atmospheric dynamics, their aim was to see if it was possible to build a model that could maintain a *statistical equilibrium* – an atmosphere in which average conditions (for temperature, pressure, and so on) would remain stable, even as heat and air masses moved around the planet. The first models could only maintain such a stable climate for a few week's worth of simulation, but gradually the models improved until they could be run indefinitely in such a stable state, limited only by the amount of computer time available.[70] Getting such a stable state requires careful attention to the numerical approximations chosen for the core equations of the model, to ensure they don't violate the laws of conservation of mass and energy.

Once the model can produce a stable run, the questions start to multiply: does the model reproduce the vertical structure of the atmosphere, with a steady reduction in temperature with height, up to the top of the troposphere? Is the model still stable if you add the complete water cycle – evaporation of water vapour from the surface, transport of moist air from one place to another, and production of rain? Such questions drove the early work in the 1960s.

But the goals of the modellers changed rapidly in the late 1960s and early 1970s, as climate change became a major concern across the atmospheric sciences. By the mid-1980s, GCMs – along with their simpler variants – were being used for a huge variety of experiments,[71] which we could divide into three groups. The first group runs the models to simulate conditions in the distant past, such as the variation of the climate during the ice ages. This work requires very long simulation runs, so typically uses simplified models or lower grid resolutions. The second group focuses on understanding long-term predictability of weather, on the scale of a few months to a few years. This work simulates longer-term patterns in weather such as El Niño in the eastern Pacific, or the monsoon rains in the tropics, and needs very high resolution grids, to capture the dynamics of these phenomena. The third group works on identifying the causes and consequences of modern climate change, including the detection and attribution studies we met earlier. These experiments use a range of models, often moving back and forth between simpler and more complex models, to explore cause and effect relationships. And since the 1990s, the modellers are often asked to run a fourth group of experiments: long-term projections of future climate change, to be used for assessments such as the IPCC reports.

Today's models are used for a much wider set of purposes. For example, a climate model can be used to fill the gaps in weather data from the past. Collection of weather data over the twentieth century slowly improved as more observing stations were set up, and from the mid-1970s, coverage improved dramatically with the dawn of the satellite era. But studying how the weather patterns changed over the twentieth century is hard if each instrument only collected data for some parts of the period. A climate model can help when run in *data assimilation* mode. All the available weather data over the course of the twentieth century is fed into the model as it runs, nudging it so that the simulation mirrors as closely as possible what actually happened. Meanwhile, the model outputs all the important weather variables for every grid point at every timestep. Meteorologists call this a *reanalysis product* – a complete, gridded, three-dimensional time series of atmospheric data over some period of time that is consistent with the available data from that period. The approach works because the equations of the model produce plausible weather patterns from the incomplete data, like generating a mini weather forecast at each timestep. Reanalysis products then make an interesting test for all climate models – can each model produce a statistically similar climate when run with just the boundary conditions, without feeding in any of the observational weather data?

Climate models are also frequently used to help debug other climate models. When the model does something strange or obviously wrong – for example, if it contradicts observational data – it can be hard to trace where in the model the problem lies. So scientists will ask colleagues in other labs if they can run experiments to see if their model exhibits the same problem. And if one model gets something right, and another gets it wrong, the modellers can compare the program code to help identify the problem and correct the erroneous model.

In the last decade or so, another urgent use of climate models has emerged. As the impacts of climate change are felt around the world, people need to know more about what to expect in their own regions as climate change worsens. Regional and city governments need to know, for example, how to prepare for extreme weather, flooding, drought, or wildfires. Utility companies need to predict how changing temperatures will affect demand for power – for air-conditioning, for example – and how extreme weather will put stress on the infrastructure of the power grid. The insurance industry needs to know how climate change will increase the risks of large claims for damage from extreme weather, especially as these have already skyrocketed over the last decade.

To serve these needs, new organizations are springing up offering *climate services* that take the results of climate models and interpret them for specific customers, advising these customers how to assess the likely local impacts of climate change, and how to adapt existing infrastructure to cope with the expected changes. These organizations use projections of future climate change produced by global climate models, usually without running the models themselves. But the grids used in global climate models are still typically tens of kilometres between grid points, which does not give enough detail for local planning and decision-making. So these climate services organizations often develop and run *regional* climate models, which work in a similar way to global climate models, but for a limited area, allowing them to have a much higher resolution grid. Data for the edges of the region being simulated are taken from a suitable run of a global climate model, so the effect is like nesting a high resolution model for one specific area inside a lower resolution global model, although the two are normally run separately. An alternative is to *downscale* the outputs of a global model, using statistical models of local conditions to predict how changes at the grid points in the global model would vary at other nearby locations.

All of these uses of climate models depend on a community of experts to interpret the outputs of the models. Just as the raw outputs of a weather forecast model would mean little to us without the benefit of a weather reporter to interpret the forecast, the outputs of a climate model really only make sense to a climate scientist. The modelling centres regularly publish data output from their models for a large number of standard model experiments, but making sense of this data can be as hard as understanding how the models work in the first place. So a large community of scientists work with this data to understand what it tells us about climate change, and what it tells us about the models that have been designed to simulate it.

Notes

1 For a detailed history of the building and its architecture, see Warner (1985).
2 The lab is 6,200 feet (1,900 m) above sea level, about 1,000 feet higher than the town of Boulder itself. At that height, a lungful of air has about 20% less oxygen than at sea level. I sometimes get headaches from mild altitude sickness on my first day or so when visiting NCAR.
3 Confusingly, the consortium is called UCAR – the University Consortium for Atmospheric Research. So a university can join UCAR, but an individual can visit NCAR.
4 Including two changes of name. The original atmosphere-only model was known as the Community Climate Model (CCM), and it was renamed the Community Climate System Model (CCSM) in the mid-1990s, when further components were added. It became the Community Earth System Model (CESM) in the late 2000s, in recognition of its broader scope beyond the climate system itself.
5 As I write this, there are plans at NCAR to switch to a different ocean model, the Modular Ocean Model (MOM), originally developed at the Geophysical Fluid Dynamics Laboratory (GFDL) at Princeton University. Ocean modelling in the United States could be described as a MOM and POP operation!
6 After accepting the award, Mariana gave a talk entitled "Better Science through Better Software." A summary of her talk is at www.easterbrook.ca/steve/2010/07/ better-science-through-better-software/
7 In the process, I even found and reported a bug in the Fortran compiler I was using! If you're interested in the details of what it takes to install on a laptop a complex software system intended for supercomputers, my installation notes are available at www.easterbrook.ca/steve/2010/07/a-portable-climate-model/ #comment-3451
8 Nowadays, that generally means Github. In 2018, CESM version 2.0 was released via GitHub at https://github.com/ESCOMP/cesm
9 See, for example, Madey et al. (2002), whose study of software projects on the then-popular code sharing site SourceForge found that a quarter had only a single participant – presumably the person who first posted the code – and a further 10% had only two or three participants. This observation has been replicated recently, for newer open source sharing sites such as Github, by Allaho and Lee (2015).
10 See Xu et al. (2005).
11 Warren Washington estimates that around 20 scientists in total from outside NCAR used the early versions of the models, in the period from 1963 to about 1980 (Washington, Personal communication).
12 This point is made strongly in Weart's (1989) interview of Joseph Smagorinsky, along with a detailed description of the goals of the early work on General Circulation Models. See also Weart (2013).
13 UCAR (1959).
14 UCAR (1959, p. 45).
15 Kasahara and Washington had already met, briefly, at the Courant Institute in New York, where Kasahara worked as a research scientist. Washington would travel there to use their computers while he was studying at Penn State. The Courant Institute had a tradition of afternoon tea each day at 4 pm on the top floor of the building, where the scientists could gather, gaze out at the view over New York, surrounded with blackboards and plenty of chalk, and chat about whatever they liked. At these teas, Kasahara and Washington met with many of the mathematicians who had worked on the Manhattan project, and the institute's founder, Richard Courant, who had established much of the mathematics of solving

differential equations by approximate methods in the 1930s, and for whom the Courant Condition was named, which we met in Chapter 3.

16   When I chatted with Warren Washington recently about this meeting, he pointed out that Thompson had a very low-key way of doing things. It was an era when scientists didn't have to write big proposals to get the resources they needed for a project. Akira Kasahara describes Thompson's signal of approval at the end of the lunch as merely raising his eyebrows twice. See Kasahara (2015) and Edwards (1998).

17   The article doesn't carry a byline, but Washington is sure that Thompson was the principal author. See Anonymous (1963).

18   See Arakawa (2000).

19   Known as the LARC, for Livermore Automatic Research Calculator (it features as one of the high points in the graph of computer speeds in Chapter 5). When it first arrived, Leith had the machine virtually to himself, which led some of his colleagues to start calling it the Leith Atmospheric Research Calculator. His model used the primitive equations, with a 5-minute timestep, and a 5° grid. It would take about an hour to compute a day's worth of simulation. See the interview with Chuck Leith in Edwards (1997).

20   Kasahara (2015, p. 14).

21   Some of these examples are from Frigg and Reiss (2009).

22   To reduce computational load, and avoid the grid convergence problem we described in Chapter 5, some grid points were skipped around the latitude bands towards the poles.

23   Details of all three generations of models from this period are described in Bretherton et al. (1975), along with details of experiments on the models that test their sensitivity to different kinds of changes.

24   Around 1968, a team at the UK Met office led by Andrew Gilchrist also began working on a GCM but they published little until the 1970s. Gilchrist's group didn't have a running model until the Met Office acquired a new IBM machine in the early 1970s.

25   A much larger community of meteorologists, likely numbering in the hundreds, was already engaged in building numerical weather forecasting models in the 1960s, in a number of different countries, as national weather services were rapidly adopting these models into their operational forecasting.

26   They were all trained by Professor Shigikata Syono. Many of Syono's students emigrated to the United States during the postwar period, as job opportunities in Japan were poor. See Lewis (1993) for an account of 11 meteorologists from Syono's lab who emigrated to the United States.

27   In his memoir, Akira Kasahara (Kasahara, 2015) includes a photo from a dinner party at the conference, featuring Jule and Elinor Charney, Norm and Martha Phillips, and scientists who were – or would shortly become – principal researchers in each of the three research groups: Smagorinsky, Kasahara, and Arakawa.

28   Warren Washington tells me that nobody at NCAR used the original Washington-Kasahara models for climate change experiments; such experiments didn't start until after the switch to the first generation of community climate models in the 1980s. Early climate change model experiments at NCAR in the 1970s used simpler energy balance models.

29   See Callendar (1938). Interestingly, Callendar, like Arrhenius, thought global warming would be a good thing. See p. 236: "the combustion of fossil fuel [...] is likely to prove beneficial to mankind in several ways."

30   Callendar published further papers dealing with all of these objections, but the available data at the time were too weak to convince most scientists.

31 See Strong and Plass (1950).

32 Plass does appear to be the first to worry about the negative impacts. In a 1956 paper, he describes it as a "a very serious problem over periods of the order of several centuries," but then is unable to decide which would be worse: switching to nuclear power or sticking with fossil fuels (see Plass, 1956). Writing in an article for Scientific American in 1959, after (incorrectly) concluding that sea life will be unaffected, he offers the throwaway line: "Perhaps only man will be uncomfortable" (see Plass, 1959).

33 See Plass (1956). This paper is reproduced in the volume "The Warming Papers" (Archer and Pierrehumbert, 2011), but note that the reproduction of Plass's Figures 5 and 7 in that volume incorrectly label both the upward and downward radiation curves and the absorption bands.

34 See IPCC (2021, p. SPM-14).

35 Despite their errors, both Callendar and Plass made important advances in our understanding of climate change – Callendar on the nature of the carbon cycle, and Plass on the absorption properties of CO_2.

36 Extra energy speeds this up, for example, if you warm your drink, or give the can a good shake before you open it.

37 Similar analysis is used to show the CO_2 added to the atmosphere over the last century must be from fossil fuels, as it contains less carbon-14.

38 See Craig (1957), Revelle and Süess (1957), and Arnold and Anderson (1957).

39 Revelle and Süess's (1957) paper mentions this effect but doesn't explore the implications. In the paper, it's mentioned only in one paragraph, which reads as though it was added at the last minute. In his analysis of the history of this paper, Weart points out the manuscript, preserved in Revelle's papers, has this additional paragraph scotch-taped onto the original draft, likely in response to a reviewer's comment. See Weart (2007, footnote 2).

40 See Bolin and Eriksson (1958).

41 See Keeling et al. (2018). Keeling's data has been normalized to an 1880 baseline of 289 ppmv.

42 See Revelle et al. (1965, p. 127).

43 By varying these assumptions, he found Plass's model would give almost any result for doubled CO_2, from a slight cooling, to warming of over 10°C. See Möller (1963).

44 See Manabe and Wetherald (1967). This paper is now widely viewed by climate scientists as the most influential paper in the field. The type of model they used is now referred to as a *radiative-convective* model.

45 See Schneider and Dickinson (1974). The explosion of work since 1967 in the reference list at the end of this paper is remarkable.

46 See Manabe and Wetherald (1975).

47 See Williamson et al. (1987).

48 At a meeting I sat in on during my most recent visit to NCAR, one of the software engineers relayed a request from scientists outside NCAR to change the default configuration of the models to output less data. The atmosphere model, for example, was outputting 900 different variables while the ocean model was outputting another 400. Multiply this by the number of grid points in the model, and the number of timesteps in a long simulation, and you get many terabytes of output data from a century-long simulation. At NCAR, this isn't a problem – the supercomputer centre handles it, and their preference is to have the model output all its variables. At a university, this amount of data makes the model almost unusable, but it's hard work to go through the list and decide which variables not to output. If the default was instead a minimal set, that would shift the burden

of effort onto the NCAR scientists who would then need to choose which extra variables to turn on.

49 See Katzav and Parker (2015).

50 See Held (2005).

51 See Mohr (2018). Mohr's book "First in Fly" explores this research in great detail. She points out at least five Nobel prizes have been awarded to scientists who study fruit flies.

52 See Schneider and Dickenson (1974). They actually described it as a regular pyramid, but I've inverted it, as I think that better illustrates the ongoing development of more complex models.

53 The spin up is needed to allow the model to settle into a realistic climate from a steady state starting point. For this experiment, they separately spun up the ocean model for 50 years and atmosphere model for 15 years, then coupled them together for a further 16 years before starting the experiment. See Washington and Meehl (1989).

54 Although it has accelerated in recent decades. From Keeling's data at Mauna Loa, CO_2 concentrations rose at about 0.3% per year in the 1960s. That rate has steadily increased, so by the 1980s, it was rising by 0.5% per year, and in the 2010s, it rose by 0.6% per year.

55 Strictly speaking, planet Earth doesn't have a Charney Sensitivity. It's an artificial measure, in which we assume some feedbacks exist while others do not.

56 See Knutti et al. (2017) for an overview of what scientists have learned over the years in the quest to pin down a more precise figure for climate sensitivity.

57 More precisely, a radiative kernel is the partial derivative of the Radiative Flux at the top of atmosphere with respect to one of the variables (water vapour, cloudiness, etc.). A kernel can then be multiplied by the size of the change in that variable in any run of the climate model to assess the size of that feedback. See Soden et al. (2008).

58 Volcanoes produce a lot of sulphur dioxide (SO_2). This oxidizes rapidly in the atmosphere to produce sulphate aerosols, high in the atmosphere, which scatter enough of the incoming sunlight to create a global cooling effect. These eventually dissolve in rain water, to produce acid rain.

59 Alan Weisman's book "The World Without Us" explores the implications of this scenario in a lot more depth, looking at how long it would take for the planet to absorb all the other things human society has created. See Weisman (2007).

60 See Solomon et al. (2013) for a summary of how we know how fast CO_2 and other greenhouse gases will hang around in the atmosphere.

61 See Matthews and Caldeira (2008) for a detailed description of these experiments.

62 Methane oxidizes to produce CO_2. Its half-life in the atmosphere is about nine years. So if emissions stopped entirely, the amount of methane left in the atmosphere would reduce by half roughly every nine years.

63 See, for example, Armour and Roe (2011).

64 See Crutzen (2006).

65 In the global temperature records of the twentieth century, global warming seems to suddenly accelerate in the 1970s. In part, this is because the clean air acts of the late 1960s and early 1970s began to have an effect, removing the cooling effect of sulphate particles that was counter-acting the warming the in previous few decades.

66 See Tilmes (2018) for a description of the experiment.

67 The experiment tried to control for this by injecting different amounts in each hemisphere, but was only partially successful at this.

68 See Simpson et al. (2019).
69 See, for example, McCusker et al. (2014), who used CCSM 4, an older version of CESM, for their experiment. This is also a central plot point in the novel "Termination Shock" by Neal Stephenson.
70 von Neumann dubbed this the "infinite forecast," and the term featured prominently in his memo to the US Weather bureau, arguing for the creation of what became GFDL. See Smagorinsky (1983).
71 See, for example, Schlesinger (1986).

7

Plug and Play

To fully understand climate change – its causes and consequences – you need a grasp of many different fields of science. Bringing together multiple experts can be hard because researchers are increasingly specialized, don't understand each other's jargon, and aren't encouraged to explore how their knowledge inter-relates. But in climate science, computational models overcome these barriers. Today's climate models are assembled from many pieces, built by different research groups, each capturing a different aspect of the overall climate system. This isn't easy – like a jigsaw puzzle where the pieces weren't designed to fit together. But once the pieces are assembled, the models support a new kind of collaboration. They allow scientists from very different fields to combine their knowledge to answer big questions, and work together on shared experiments. In this chapter, we'll explore this process of coupling climate models, find out why it's so challenging, and meet another of our case studies, the Institut Pierre Simon Laplace (IPSL) in Paris, France.

The Jussieu Campus

On the left bank of the river Seine in the centre of Paris, a few hundred metres downstream from the Notre Dame Cathedral, sits the modern architecture of the Jussieu campus, home to many of the science labs of the Sorbonne University. The buildings of Jussieu form an elevated grid of six-storey office blocks, suspended above the ground so that only the cylindrical stairwells at each grid intersection reach the ground (see Figure 7.1). The research labs inhabit the suspended buildings – like the bars of a grill – that span between these stairwells.

When I first visited more than a decade ago, the structure looked more like a prison than a university campus. To enter the campus you crossed a dry concrete moat guarded with wire security fencing. The wind whipped across the

202

Figure 7.1 The Jussieu campus, showing (a) the original elevated structure with cylindrical stairwells, (b, c) examples of how the original architecture has been adapted by re-skinning the structure, to roof in the open squares and to enclose some of the spaces below the grill to create new study spaces for students. (Photos by Steve M. Easterbrook)

open paved ground floor space, and there was graffiti, vandalism, and decay everywhere. To add to the effect, many of the research labs kept the doors to the stairwells locked for security, and I often found it hard to move through the building without descending to the ground level, crossing the windy concrete slab, and heading up another stairwell.

Despite the bleakness of the Jussieu campus, I enjoyed my visits, partly because I could hang out in the cafes and markets of Paris's Latin Quarter, but more importantly because the university is home to the research labs of the Institut Pierre Simon Laplace (IPSL), one of the world's leading centres for Earth Systems science.

Since my first visit, a major renovation of the campus has reconnected the campus with the streets around it, and improved the environment for the students. Greenery has been added to the courtyards, and many of the open spaces underneath the buildings have been enclosed with glass and steel to create elegant new study spaces, including a new library, an auditorium, and several enormous glass-roofed plazas. By adding new walls and covers – a new skin to the building – the campus looks welcoming again.

Coupling

I first visited Jussieu in the summer of 2008, when I travelled to Paris, to meet the team who built NEMO, one of the most widely used ocean models in Europe.

I was intrigued by the problem of *coupling* – building a comprehensive climate model by connecting together existing models that simulate different parts of the climate system. Many climate scientists I met talked about wanting to make their models "plug and play." The idea is that scientists studying different parts of the climate system should be able to plug new components into the model easily. For example, a soil scientist studying how soils store and release carbon might want to plug in a new soil model to improve the simulation of the carbon cycle; a chemist studying the formation and decay of ozone might want to plug in a new atmospheric chemistry module to explore how ozone is affected by a warming climate. But how hard is it to plug in new components like these?

That summer, the scientists at the UK Met Office were busy incorporating the ocean model NEMO into their Unified Model, to replace their original ocean model. This gave me an opportunity to witness "plug and play" in action. How do you switch out the old ocean model and plug in a new one? And is it similar to plugging in other components of a climate model?

At the time of my visit, things were not going smoothly. The scientists at the Met Office were struggling to adapt NEMO to work with the rest of their model, and were frustrated that the NEMO team in Paris seemed to be ignoring suggestions to make NEMO run faster within the Met Office models. The rivers in their land surface model weren't putting water into NEMO's oceans in a realistic way, and there were disagreements about how to handle the tides. I realized they were suffering from a problem I'd seen at NASA: if the software teams don't communicate well, neither will their software. So I decided to take the train to Paris to meet the ocean modellers at IPSL, learn more about how ocean models are built, and find out why coupling these models was proving so hard.

Since that original visit, things have gotten much better. The Met Office scientists now participate in a regular series of workshops that bring together all users of the NEMO ocean model, to coordinate work on the model, and to plan changes for the next release of the code, which now happens annually. But what I learned on that visit was a glimpse into the long struggle to get ocean and atmosphere models to work together, and the importance of coordination between different labs in making this happen.

Finding NEMO

I arrived in Paris on a blistering hot day in the summer of 2008, to meet with Claire Lèvy, manager of the NEMO development team, who then introduced me to the rest of the team: ocean modeller Rachid Benshila,

Marie-Alice Foujols, who leads IPSL's software engineering team, and lead scientist Gurvan Madec, who arrived on his rollerblades while we were drinking coffee.

NEMO,[1] which stands for Nucleus for European Modelling of the Ocean, is actually a collection of several distinct models, each of which captures a different aspect of the oceans. The NEMO team describe it as having three parts: blue ocean, white ocean, and green ocean. Blue ocean refers to the properties of the water itself, particularly the ocean circulation patterns – how water moves around the planet under the influence of heat from the sun and the effect of gravity and the Earth's rotation, while constrained by the shape of coastlines and seabeds. White ocean refers to sea ice in the ocean, which grows and shrinks over the seasons, and alters ocean circulation patterns in the process. And green ocean refers to ocean life and its nutrients – particularly plankton – and how these impact the ocean chemistry and the density and clarity of the water.

The blue ocean model is the oldest part of NEMO. It is based on OPA (Ocean PArallèle), which calculates the movement of water within the oceans in much the same way an atmosphere model calculates the movement of air. OPA was developed in the 1980s, and originated out of work Gurvan did for his PhD thesis, but has been substantially re-written since then by the NEMO team. It's a primitive equation model, with the key variables being velocity of the water (in three dimensions), temperature, salinity, and sea-surface height. It uses a tri-polar grid,[2] with grid lines converging to two points over the continents in the Northern Hemisphere, rather than at the North Pole, to avoid the numerical problems we explored in Chapter 5 (See Figure 7.2).

The NEMO team is remarkably small, compared to most other modelling teams I have visited. So they share their program code freely, and rely on a broader community of scientists to contribute their own improvements to the model. But the work of testing these additions and folding them back into the core model sometimes overwhelms the team in Paris. As team manager, one of Claire's key goals is to build a stronger sense of community across this broad group of NEMO users, for example, by bringing them together for workshops where they can also have meals together and get to know one another. The more they get to know each other, the better they are at shared decision-making.

This need for a shared understanding is central to the challenges the UK Met Office was facing in its attempts to couple NEMO to the Met Office models. But before exploring these challenges, I should explain a little more how an ocean model works.

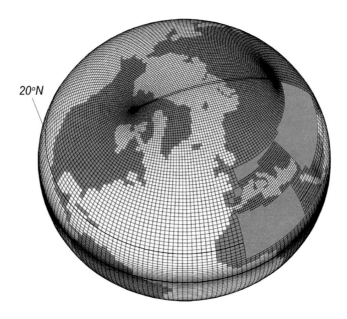

Figure 7.2 The tri-polar grid system used in the NEMO ocean model at a resolution of 2°. The singularity at the North Pole is replaced with two convergence
points over Asia and North America. South of 20°N, it uses a regular Lat-Lon
grid. (IPSL, courtesy of Gurvan Madec)

Ocean Modelling

At its core, an ocean model is very similar to an atmosphere model. Air and
water both obey the same laws of physics, and are subject to the same forces.
So the primitive equations[3] that describe the movement of heat and mass in the
atmosphere can describe ocean currents. As with atmosphere modelling, you
start with a three-dimensional grid and a set of numerical algorithms to calculate
how the key variables change at each grid point, from one timestep to the next.

At first sight, ocean modelling might seem simpler than atmosphere modelling, because water doesn't expand and contract like air, and ocean models
don't have to deal with clouds and precipitation. However, ocean boundaries
are more complex. While the atmosphere covers the whole planet to a relatively uniform height, the ocean depth varies dramatically across the planet,
with complex shapes at the seabed and the coastlines. Ocean life – algae and
plankton – makes a big difference to the clarity of the water, and hence the
depth to which sunlight, and hence heat, penetrates.

Water is much denser than air, so things happen on very different scales. In the atmosphere, areas of high and low pressure spanning hundreds of kilometres develop and propagate in a matter of days. In the ocean, it would take months for water to move similar distances, and the typical size of ocean turbulence is much smaller – swirls or *eddies* in ocean currents are no more than a few tens of kilometres across. So an ocean model needs a much higher grid resolution, and must be run for much longer timescales to allow disturbances to propagate. When you spin up an atmosphere model from a state of rest, realistic weather patterns will appear within a month or so of the simulation. But in an ocean model, you have to simulate several centuries before realistic, stable ocean circulation patterns appear.

And salt content matters, because it affects the density of the water. Saltiness varies across the oceans – rivers inject fresh water into coastal waters, while saltier water can be found in the Arctic where the formation of sea ice leaves more salt in the surrounding waters. Water that is colder and saltier is denser, so it tends to sink, drawing in warmer, fresher water from the south to replace it. In the North Atlantic in particular, this flow of water from the south cools rapidly under the subarctic air, generating a persistent downward flow, feeding cold salty water into the deep ocean. These flows in the North Atlantic are one part of an engine that drives a planet-wide pattern of ocean currents (see Figure 7.3), dubbed the *great ocean conveyor belt* – although scientists prefer to call it the *overturning* or *thermohaline circulation*, from *thermo-* meaning heat, and *haline* meaning saltiness.

The ocean conveyer is a slow moving flow – it can take water 1,000 years[4] to do the full circuit. But any given parcel of water might not make the full trip, as ocean currents are much more complex than simplified diagrams of the ocean conveyor would suggest. In the last decade or so, sophisticated arrays of instruments have given us a much richer picture of the ocean flow, especially in the deep ocean.[5] In many parts of the world, local winds affect surface currents, and these change a lot from season to season. It's only in the Atlantic that the slow overturning of the ocean depicted in the conveyor diagrams is persistently strong. This means that the North Atlantic is the only major site in the world where large amounts of dissolved carbon – from human emissions – regularly flow from the surface waters into the deep ocean.[6]

The full complexity of ocean currents only shows up in very high resolution ocean models. Coarse resolution models – with grid cells 50–100 km across – cannot capture ocean eddies. But when you increase the resolution of the grid cells to around 10 km, the full pattern of flow and eddies start to emerge in the models (see Figure 7.4). These higher resolution simulations are known as *eddy-permitting models*. But the computational power needed to run an ocean

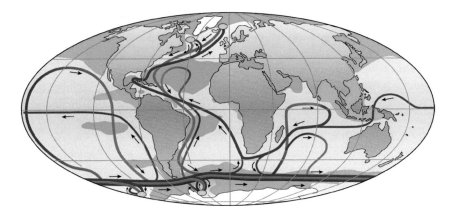

Figure 7.3 Simplified diagram of the thermohaline circulation, sometimes called the Great Ocean Conveyor Belt. Red shows the flow of warmer surface waters, while blue shows the flow of colder deep ocean, and purple shows bottom currents. Areas shaded green are the saltiest waters; areas shaded blue are the least salty. Yellow circles mark the main sites where surface waters flow down into the deep ocean – in the northern North Atlantic, the Ross Sea, and the Weddell Sea. (Reproduced from Rahmstorf (2002) by permission of Springer Nature, © 2002)

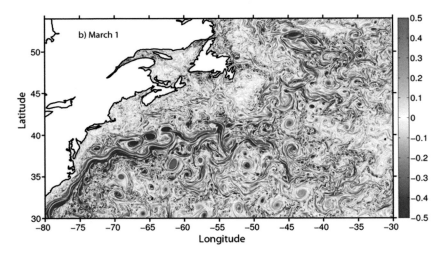

Figure 7.4 Ocean eddies in the North Atlantic, as simulated in an ocean model, with a resolution of 1/12° (roughly 10 km). Blue shows water that is moving clockwise, and red shows water that is moving anticlockwise, with the intensity of the colour indicating rotational speed. This image is a snapshot from the simulation for March, when the vorticity patterns are stronger than in the summer. (Reproduced from Chassignet and Xu (2017). © American Meteorological Society, used with permission.)

model for long simulations of the whole planet at this resolution is still beyond today's computers. Ocean modellers who want to study a specific region often use two different setups of the same model, one nested inside another.[7] For example, a high resolution eddy-permitting model of just the North Atlantic might be nested inside a lower resolution global ocean model.

With models set up in this way, oceanographers can run experiments to explore what causes the ocean circulation patterns, and how they change under different conditions. In the distant past, the overturning circulation in the North Atlantic sometimes stopped almost completely, leading to dramatic changes to the global climate. For example, 13,000 years ago, as the world was warming up from the last ice age, melting glaciers suddenly poured huge amounts of fresh water into the North Atlantic, shutting down the Atlantic circulation, in a period known as the *Younger Dryas*.[8] Temperatures over Greenland plunged by around 10°C in the space of a few decades, leading to a temporary return of an ice age for another 1,000 years. Whether such a shutdown could occur again as Greenland's ice sheets melt remains an open question,[9] as does the impact it would have on global climate. Most of today's models predict a slow-down of the North Atlantic circulation under greenhouse gas warming – which may mean cooler climates for Northern Europe,[10] even as the rest of the planet warms. But it's not yet clear whether another Younger Dryas-like shutdown is even possible.

Ocean models can be used for many other experiments. Some of these are specific to the oceans, while others, such as the relationship between ocean circulation and climate require the ocean model to be coupled to an atmosphere model to study how they affect one another.

An Open Ocean

From the start, Gurvan and his colleagues set out to make their ocean model, OPA, available to other scientists to conduct these kinds of experiment. They realized that sharing the code widely would help improve it, but the code would have to be easy for other scientists to understand. In the 1980s, most scientific code was, to put it bluntly, disposable – built quickly to run a specific experiment, without any thought for longer-term needs. Gurvan explicitly rejected this approach, and chose instead to make good design a priority.

So the team focused on writing high quality program code – code that is clearly structured, easy to read, and designed to work on many different computers. In the early days of the project they produced an extensive programming style guide[11] to ensure everyone in the project shared the same ideas of good design practice. Claire Lèvy, the manager of the NEMO team, calls this approach *code sustainability*, to emphasize that looking after the code should never be separated from doing the science.

This careful attention to good design can mean model development is slower.[12] When scientists at other labs write useful additions to OPA, the team at IPSL often re-write the code according to the style guide. And the decision to ensure the code is portable to different computers means they may reject changes designed to make it run faster on one specific supercomputer, if that makes it harder to run on other machines.

This approach makes NEMO an attractive model for weather forecasting agencies, where reliability and sustainability of well-engineered code is particularly important. In the 1990s, the French national weather forecasting agency, Météo-France, and a new ocean forecasting company, Mercator, both chose to incorporate OPA into their operational forecasting models. When the UK Met Office followed suit in the early 2000s, they proposed a consortium to give all the major users a stake in looking after the model – each consortium member would dedicate one full time scientist to contribute to improving the model. The consortium chose the new name, NEMO, to express the idea that this was now a Europe-wide project. Today, the consortium has grown to five agencies from France, Italy, and the United Kingdom.

Around the time the consortium was formed, the Paris team added several new components to OPA. The first of these – the green ocean – is a model of ocean plants and the nutrients they depend upon, known as PISCES.[13] The ocean ecosystem is an important part of the global carbon cycle, and hence needed for longer-term simulations of the climate. PISCES computes the growth rates of four types of plankton, based on the relative abundance of key nutrients on which they depend – nitrate, ammonium, phosphate, silicate, and iron – as well as the availability of carbon and oxygen.

Then, in the early 2000s, they added a white ocean – the Louvain Ice Model[14] (LIM), developed at the University of Louvain-la-Neuve in Belgium. LIM computes the annual growth and decline of sea ice in both the Arctic and Antarctic waters, calculating the thickness of the ice, and its movement under the influence of gravity, the Earth's rotation, and ocean currents. LIM also keeps track of salt content, as it alters the freezing point of water.[15] The saltier the water, the colder it has to be before it freezes, because salt molecules get in the way when water molecules combine to form crystals of ice – ice crystals themselves are pure water.

So overall, NEMO is the collective name for all three components (OPA, PISCES, and LIM). It is a sophisticated, state-of-the-art ocean model, with a well-deserved reputation for good engineering. But that doesn't necessarily mean integrating NEMO into other agencies' weather and climate models is easy. To see why, we need to go back in time to the first attempt to couple an ocean model to an atmosphere model, and understand the challenges involved.

AO-Coupled Models

While computational modelling of the atmosphere took off rapidly in the 1950s, oceanography lagged behind, mainly because of lack of data. Meteorologists around the world had collected detailed observations of the state of the atmosphere since the nineteenth century, but observational data from the oceans were scattered and sporadic, relying on ships to record measurements of the waters they moved through. In the 1950s and 1960s, a series of missions to systematically measure the state of the oceans began to provide the overall picture of ocean currents and temperatures. This new data inspired a concerted effort to model the ocean, by adapting the numerical techniques being used in atmospheric models.

Much of the initial modelling was done at the Geophysical Fluid Dynamics Lab (GFDL) at Princeton in the 1960s. In the previous chapter, we met the work of Manabe and Wetherald at GFDL, and their pioneering experiments on climate sensitivity in their global circulation model. Given their lead in developing atmospheric models, it's not surprising they were also pioneers in ocean modelling. Joe Smagorinsky, the head of GFDL, realized the importance of the interaction between the atmosphere and ocean, in 1961, he hired an oceanographer, Kirk Bryan, to develop an ocean model, with the goal of eventually coupling it to the atmosphere model.

By the late 1960s, Bryan had a working ocean model. His first model was greatly simplified – a single, rectangular ocean with flat walls and a flat seabed. It could be configured to run with just horizontal (two-dimensional) ocean currents, or full three-dimensional flows, and had just enough detail for experiments on the large-scale overturning patterns of the ocean, and the role of winds and temperature differences in driving ocean currents.

Manabe and Bryan then set about coupling their ocean and atmosphere models together. For their first experiments, they used a very simplified world, representing only one third of the planet – the fat slice shown in Figure 7.5 – of which half was ocean and half was land. This simplification allowed them to run the atmosphere and ocean models on the same grid, to make data exchanges at the grid points simpler. If the grids and timesteps match, connecting the models is easier – at each timestep, exchanges of heat, water, etc. can be passed

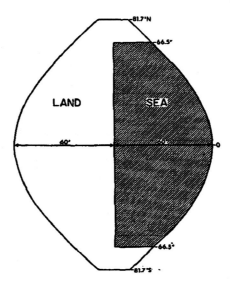

Figure 7.5 The slice of the planet used in Manabe and Bryan's 1969 first coupled Atmosphere-Ocean model. The slice spans 120° of longitude. Between 66.5° North and South, the planet is half ocean and half land. The grid convergence problem at the poles is avoided by slicing them off at 81.7° North and South. (Reproduced from Manabe and Bryan (1969). Published 1969 by the American Meteorological Society.)

directly from each grid point at the ocean's surface to the corresponding grid point at the bottom of the atmosphere, and vice versa.

While using the same grid helps, reconciling the time scales is harder. The ocean and atmosphere continuously exchange heat and mass (mainly water and salt spray). But when this exchange happens in the coupled model on a coarse grid, the models send each other large amounts of heat or mass at individual grid points, which then rapidly mess up the simulations. Each model needs time to absorb these changes. And while heat added to the atmosphere dissipates to other grid points over a matter of days, in the ocean it can take months to spread across the grid, during which the atmosphere keeps delivering more heat at those grid points.[16] So the ocean simulation rapidly becomes unstable. Manabe and Bryan solved this problem in their first coupled model by slowing down the atmosphere model to give the ocean more time to absorb changes.

In their first experiment, they spun up the atmosphere and ocean models separately, without any coupling, to allow each model to settle into a stable climate. For the ocean model, this took a 60-year simulation – long enough for a characteristic temperature gradient to form in the ocean, and for an ice sheet

Figure 7.6 The slightly more realistic ocean topography used in Bryan and Manabe's 1974 Ocean Model. The contour lines represent ocean depth, labelled in kilometres. (Reproduced from Bryan et al. (1975). Published 1975 by the American Meteorological Society.)

to form around the North Pole. Next, they ran a program to couple the models. This would run the atmosphere model to simulate 3 hours, and then the ocean model to simulate 12 days. It would then transfer data between the two models at the ocean surface, and repeat the cycle. In effect, the ocean had a timestep 100 times longer than the atmosphere. The technique worked well enough for Manabe and Bryan to run their experiment for an entire year of atmosphere simulation – 100 years for the ocean – to see how the ocean would redistribute heat from the atmosphere. Although celebrated as the first successful coupled model, Bryan later wrote that this first experiment was really a failure, as the ocean never reached equilibrium, even after a century of simulation.

Over the next few years they developed a series of improvements, including a slightly more realistic geography (see Figure 7.6). The atmosphere and ocean models still used the same grid, but to give the ocean even more time to react, Manabe and Bryan increased the time differential even further – running the ocean for 320 years for each year of simulated atmosphere. Again, they started the models from a state of rest, to see what patterns would emerge. By the end of the simulation, a realistic distribution of sea surface temperatures emerged, with a rough approximation of the Great Ocean Conveyer – surface waters moving towards the poles, and deeper waters moving back towards the equator. However, the model also had many inaccuracies, including too much build-up of ice at the North Pole, and an overly weak Gulf Stream in the North Atlantic, likely because the model didn't get the salt content right in the waters around Greenland.

More than anything, these experiments showed how challenging it would be to build a coupled model. Oceans move much more slowly than air, and the shape of the seabed and coastlines strongly affect the patterns of ocean circulation – so ocean models need a much higher grid resolution and take much longer to reach equilibrium. There's a trade-off – scientists must choose a grid resolution that works best for their experiments, within the available computing time. Getting the balance wrong means the simulation either takes too long to run, or will fail to accurately simulate the processes of interest.

Today's coupled models put the atmosphere and ocean on the same timescale, but provide more flexibility by allowing mismatching grids – each model can run on its own grid. A separate component, a *coupler*,[17] does the necessary calculations to convert the data from one grid to the other each time the models need to exchange data. When the geometry of the grids is different, like NEMO's tri-polar grid, these *regridding* calculations can be complicated, but it's still faster to re-grid the data exchanged at each timestep than to use the same (high) resolution grid for both ocean and atmosphere. With a coupler to handle the data exchange, scientists have much greater flexibility in their choice of grids and grid resolutions for each component model.

The Flux Correction Problem

However, Manabe and Bryan discovered another problem that was much harder to solve. Their atmosphere and ocean models were developed and tested separately. On their own, each could run indefinitely, and produce a stable climate, with realistic patterns of winds (in the atmosphere model) and ocean currents (in the ocean model). But when coupled together, the simulation was no longer stable – each model would tend to cause the other to drift over time.

Each model separately captures the key physical equations needed for a stable simulation when the boundary conditions – for example, temperature and water exchanges at the sea surface – are fixed. But when you couple them together, each model's boundary conditions are no longer fixed. Each can only produce a stable simulation if disturbances introduced by the other model balance out over time. In the real world, these disturbances vary a lot from year to year. For example, in El Niño years, the warm surface waters of the Eastern Pacific push heat into the atmosphere causing a distinct change in weather patterns across the Americas, while in La Niña years, the heat flows in the opposite direction, into the ocean. In the real world, these disruptions balance out over decades, so that the climate is stable in the long term – or at least it would be if we were not adding more greenhouse gases to the atmosphere.

But in a numerical model, with its many simplifications, these heat exchanges can destabilize the simulation entirely.

That's exactly what happened in the early atmosphere-ocean coupled models. Inaccuracies in the separate models – particularly in the movement of heat towards the poles – meant each model was continually reacting to disturbances in the heat balance at the ocean surface. When coupled together, both models would steadily drift away from a stable climate, reaching climate patterns that were implausible on the real planet Earth.

To fix the problem, Bryan and Manabe came up with a clever, but controversial solution. They would artificially correct the amount of heat and moisture crossing the boundary at the ocean's surface to counteract any long-term drift away from the mean values[18] for these variables. These *flux corrections* continually nudge the models back into a stable climatic pattern.

This approach is reasonable if you're using the models for short-term simulations to study weather patterns. It *may* even be reasonable over longer-term simulations, for experiments that simulate periods of stable climate in the Earth's history. But flux corrections undermine any claim that these atmosphere-ocean coupled models could simulate a changing climate in response to human activities. In a flux-corrected model with increasing greenhouse gases, you cannot tell if the flux corrections are interfering with any resulting change in the climate.[19]

Throughout the 1970s and 1980s, all coupled atmosphere-ocean models used flux corrections, and the community was sharply divided on whether this was scientifically acceptable.[20] I've met climate scientists who still argue that climate change projections provided to governments during this time were ill-advised, as the modellers couldn't say for sure their models were accurately simulating a changing climate, particularly as the size of the overall drift the flux corrections were removing was similar to the size of the climate change the models produced in response to increasing greenhouse gases.

Today's climate models don't use flux corrections. And it turns out flux corrections in the early models didn't matter after all – recent experiments[21] show both flux-corrected and uncorrected models show similar amounts of warming when you increase greenhouse gases.

IPSL was one of the first labs in the world to build a coupled climate model that didn't need flux corrections, and, as we'll see, it required a big shift in thinking. It helped that the IPSL team had a very different goal from Manabe and Bryan's – instead of trying to produce a stable simulation to study current climate patterns, they wanted a model that could simulate the large changes in climate that occurred in the distant past, such as during the ice ages. For this, the model had to get more of the science right, and had to capture more than just the interaction of ocean and atmosphere.

A Federated Model

Two years after my first visit to the NEMO team, I went back to Paris for a longer visit to learn how IPSL's climate model was developed. The structure of IPSL's coupled model reflects the structure of IPSL itself, which operates as a federated set of research labs – so I think of it as a *federated* model.

At the time of my visits, IPSL had six distinct research labs, although this has since grown to nine. These labs all use computational models of various kinds for a wide range of research areas, including molecular physics, astrophysics, oceanography, and meteorology. An interest in atmospheres is common to several labs, as they study atmospheres of Earth, other planets, and even the sun's atmosphere – the *heliosphere*.[22] Each lab is a large research enterprise in its own right: many of these labs have well over 100 staff scientists, and some as many as 200.

For my second visit, I was hosted by two scientists who have spent many years grappling with the challenges posed by IPSL's federated structure. One of my hosts, Sylvie Joussaume, is lead scientist at the Laboratory for the Science of Climate and the Environment (LSCE), one of IPSL's newer labs. When Sylvie's lab was founded in the early 1990s, there was very little collaboration between the various labs at IPSL. The meteorology lab LMD (Laboratorie de Meteorologie Dynamique) had developed a global atmosphere model. And we already met the ocean model, OPA, developed at the oceanography lab, LOCEAN.[23]

In the 1990s, LMD and LOCEAN had quite different cultures. LMD's atmosphere model was developed purely for use in-house by the scientists who needed to run it for various experiments. In contrast, as we saw earlier, LOCEAN put a lot more emphasis on good engineering practices and shared their model with other ocean scientists around the world, to help make it even better.

Resolving such differences in engineering practices is tricky. Most of the centres I've visited have now created a distinct role and career path for software engineers, although this is a relatively new development since the mid-2000s. The engineers in these roles are all deeply engaged in the science, having either trained as climate scientists or numerical modellers – it appears to be easier for a climate scientist to learn good software practices, than it is for a programmer to learn the complexities of climate modelling. My other host at IPSL, Marie-Alice Foujols is one of the few scientists I met who had followed the latter path. She has a degree in computer science and applied math, and joined an oceanography research lab early in her career, out of a fascination with ocean modelling. She has worked with climate scientists ever since, and has developed a deep expertise in how climate models are put together.

Marie-Alice leads a team of about 20 software engineers tasked with looking after the diverse parts of IPSL's coupled climate model, to ensure these components work together.[24] The scale and complexity of modern coupled climate models is large enough that it demands such a team to keep things coordinated. Marie-Alice's software engineering team is independent of any of the individual labs, and instead is part of an IPSL-wide global climate modelling team, dedicated to coordinating the modelling work of all of the labs.

Adapt or Start Over?

When Sylvie's new lab, LSCE, was created the goal was to study climate change across different timescales, with a particular interest in climates of the distant past – *paleoclimate* – to provide a better understanding of why the climate changes. Sylvie and her team needed a way to experiment with very long simulations of the Earth's climate, over thousands or even millions of years. Such a model would need to capture the full carbon cycle – how carbon is exchanged between the atmosphere and ocean, and how it is absorbed and released over time by plants and soils on the land and by plankton and sedimentation in the ocean – because, as we saw in Chapter 2, the flows of carbon in and out of the atmosphere, oceans, soils, and permafrost play a central role in the cycle of ice ages and warmer periods.

So the new team faced a dilemma. Could they take an existing coupled atmosphere-ocean global circulation model – an *AO-GCM* – and adapt it for these long-term simulations? Or should they develop a new model from scratch?

Over lunch one day in a street cafe in Paris, I asked Sylvie and Marie-Alice how much a state-of-the-art climate model would cost to develop from scratch. Sylvie told me she had already given this question some thought. She suggested it would take a team of 50 scientists working for 20 years – around 1,000 person-years – plus the cost of running a dedicated supercomputer facility.

After discussing it a little more, we came up with a price tag of about $300 million.[25] Why so much? What Sylvie was describing is typical of how most of today's climate models came about. These models have been under steady development for decades, in large research labs. In the early days, at labs like NCAR and GFDL, climate models were built by much smaller teams – say two lead scientists and a few assistant programmers. And you can still build a basic climate model that way. But a state-of-the-art model today requires a much wider range of expertise. At IPSL, around 100 people contribute to the climate modelling work – about 80 scientists, plus Marie-Alice's team of software engineers. These scientists think of their work as *doing science*, rather than *developing models*, but their work is still an essential part of developing, testing, and then improving the model.

The supercomputers are also expensive. Our hypothetical team would need a faster machine every few years to keep up with Moore's Law, and it costs a lot to run these machines, especially for the energy needed to keep them cool.[26] Testing the models takes a lot of computer time – in labs that run their own dedicated supercomputing facilities, around a quarter of the time on the machine might be reserved for developing and testing new versions of the models, while the rest is used for science experiments. This is indeed "big science," with research budgets to rival fields like high energy physics and genomics.

So building a new climate model from scratch would be slow and expensive. But adapting an existing model from another lab might not help either. Sylvie's colleague, Olivier Marti – who helped build the first version of the coupled model at LSCE in the early 1990s – talked me through the decision-making they went through.

At the time, several other research labs around the world already had coupled climate models, but none of these included the full carbon cycle. The team at LSCE could have taken one of these existing models and tried "plugging in" their own model of the carbon cycle. They would still need to make lots of changes to the adopted model, for example, to adjust the seasonal cycle to represent changes in the Earth's orbit over the period of the ice ages, and to optimize the model for very long runs. And for millennium-scale simulations, you have to be a lot more careful to ensure that when air and water move around the planet, the amount of each substance – water, air, carbon, salt, etc. – is conserved globally. Even tiny changes could matter: you don't want to find that after tens of thousands of years of simulation, all the air has disappeared due to rounding errors at each timestep. Yet, at the time, none of the existing models ensured this.

That wasn't the only thing missing. The early AO-coupled models were coupled only via exchanges of heat and moisture at the ocean's surface. But other interactions matter too. Take, for example, what happens to water in the atmosphere. When it forms into clouds and produces rain, that water leaves the atmosphere. If it falls on the ocean, we just calculate the mass of water to be given back to the ocean in each grid square. If it falls on the land, some of this water will return to the ocean – via rivers. Some will be absorbed by soils and plants, and some evaporates straight back into the atmosphere without taking a trip to the ocean.

In early models, much of this was handled by including simple rules to specify what should happen, on average, at the land surface. For example, in

Bryan and Manabe's original models, the land surface was treated as a large bucket that could hold water. When rain falls in a grid square containing land, that bucket fills. Fixed parameters would then determine how much water spills over into neighbouring squares, and how fast water would evaporate back into the atmosphere, at any given temperature. Getting this right is important because evaporation plays a key role in determining local climates, by taking heat energy with it – evaporation cools the land and warms the air.

Plants were represented in these models only to the extent that they affect the physics. For example, dark forests reflect less sunlight than bright deserts, and trees have a small friction effect on surface winds. The early models captured this with two parameters – albedo and roughness – selected based on typical vegetation in each grid cell. But this means you can't study other important interactions in the climate system, such as how changes to the land – growth or decline of forests, deserts, and farmland – alter water and carbon retention over time.

The feedback loops that drive changes in the climate over long timescales don't respect simple physical boundaries between atmosphere, ocean, and land. So to study climate change, you need to simulate the land surface processes explicitly – the route that rivers take to get the water back to the ocean, moisture in different levels of soil, the effect of different kinds of vegetation, and so on. In this respect, the modellers at IPSL were well ahead of the field, in the early 1990s. LMD's atmosphere model already had a sophisticated multi-layered soil model,[27] which simulated how moisture moves between different layers of the soil and plant roots, how water evaporates from different types of leaves, and the ways in which rainwater is absorbed by the soil or runs off horizontally in heavy rainfalls. But they didn't yet have a model of how plants grow and decay – thus storing and releasing carbon. And they couldn't yet simulate how these processes interact with the atmosphere and oceans over very long time periods.

Sylvie and her team decided to rethink how coupling works, taking a holistic view of how all the parts – atmosphere, ocean, ice sheets, vegetation, and so on – interact. They needed a coupled model that didn't rely on artificial fixes. And they needed access to experts in atmosphere and ocean modelling, to help them put it all together.

Their solution was to bring together components that had already been developed in other labs at IPSL, and use these as the building blocks for a new coupled model, tailored to their needs. By using components that already existed at IPSL, the expertise they needed would also be nearby.

The dilemma over whether to adopt another centre's model or build your own is common to all climate science labs. Most labs end up with a mix of both strategies – some components built in house, while others are borrowed from elsewhere. I think of it as a kind of *bricolage* – a style of art, architecture, or music created by bringing together existing things: whatever happens to be available at hand. In art, bricolage aims to achieve a unifying theme while combining unexpected elements. Similarly, the art of creating a coupled climate model is to unify a disparate set of existing models of the various parts of the climate system, to reveal new insights about how the whole climate system works in reality. So on my visits to IPSL, while I was marvelling at Paris's juxtaposition of traditional and modern architecture, I was also starting to understand how the software of climate models themselves mimic this mix of old and new components.

Fixing the Flux Problem

In 1994, Sylvie, Olivier, and their colleagues began work coupling LMD's atmosphere model to LOCEAN's ocean model, adding the missing biological processes to capture how carbon cycles into and out of plants, soils, and oceans. When I asked Olivier what the biggest challenge in this process was, his answer surprised me. He pointed out the scientists are actually very good at communicating and coordinating their work. But the key challenge is to convince them to adopt a new scientific goal – different from the one they've been working on for years. At the time, the scientists at IPSL were skeptical about the value of coupling their models together. And it's natural for scientists to want to keep working within their own specialized fields.

The tension between scientists' goals shows up if a component model causes problems in the coupled model. Each component works well on its own, because the scientists who understand it best have tested it thoroughly – with prescribed boundary conditions. When their model is coupled to other models, and problems occur, it's natural for each team to want to blame other components. So the big challenge is social – building a community of people across the different labs who are committed to a common goal of developing and using a coupled model, rather than focusing on their own specialism. In the end, IPSL created a new cross-functional team – the *Pôle de Modelisation* – with representatives from each of the labs to help build such a community.

The solution to the *flux correction* problem illustrates this challenge very well. In the early 1990s, all coupled atmosphere-ocean models would show a steady drift in sea surface temperatures without these artificial corrections – the atmosphere and ocean models would continually push each other out of equilibrium. When they first coupled their atmosphere, ocean, sea ice, and land surface models together, the IPSL team also observed this same tendency to drift.[28] But because their goal was to build a realistic coupled model, they chose not to add flux corrections. Instead, they ran a series of experiments to explore the cause of the drift. It helped that computers had gotten much faster over the 20 years since Manabe and Bryan's first coupled model. This allowed them to run higher resolution models where the exchanges of heat between atmosphere and ocean was spread out over more grid points – reducing the problem of big changes at any single grid point, and making it easier to study how the model was moving heat around the planet.

In hindsight, the solution to the flux correction problem now seems obvious. The early modellers had assumed that if the atmosphere and ocean models each work well on their own, the problem must be in how they are coupled together. But this is exactly backwards. In the real world, the atmosphere and the ocean are never isolated from each other. Together, they move heat around the planet – from the tropics, which receive a lot of energy from the sun, towards the poles, where more heat is lost again to space.

So it's not possible to accurately test an atmosphere model in isolation – we don't know what the real atmosphere would do if there were no oceans. The same goes for an ocean model. While we can be reasonably confident that the parts of the model based on physical laws are correct, there's wriggle room in the empirical parts of the model – parameterizations for things like clouds that cannot be directly simulated. Modellers calibrate their models[29] by adjusting these parameters to best match observed climate patterns, and keep the model stable. And if you calibrate an isolated atmosphere (or ocean) model, you're tuning it to a condition that never occurs in reality – the model will end up with the right results for the wrong reasons.

By the mid-1990s it was clear that all atmosphere models exhibited the same problem. A study[30] published in 1995 compared 15 atmosphere models from different labs around the world with the best available data about north-south heat flows in the atmosphere and oceans, at specific points on the planet. None of them were getting it right. The study suggested possible causes, but in hindsight it's now obvious that the atmosphere models were overcompensating for the lack of an ocean to help move heat around. In some models, the overcompensation was so strong that when you add up all the flows of heat, it was as if the atmosphere assumed the oceans move heat in the wrong direction – back towards the equator. It's not surprising these models went wrong when coupled to oceans that also move heat polewards.

The same study offered an important clue to fixing the problem. Comparison between atmosphere models showed they disagreed most on how they represent clouds.[31] Clouds trap heat below them, and reflect sunlight back into space, so play an important role in vertical movement of heat. If the models were messing up the horizontal movement of heat at the surface of the planet, it was likely because heat wasn't arriving where it was supposed to – the vertical movement of heat up and down through the atmosphere and oceans must be wrong. So clouds were the culprit, and the problem could be fixed by re-visiting how the parameters for clouds and heat diffusion were tuned in the atmosphere model.[32] Re-tuning these for the coupled model was fairly easy – far easier than convincing the atmospheric physicists at LMD that such re-tuning was necessary. In the end, a few minor tweaks to the atmosphere code removed the problem entirely.

Closing the global water budget – making sure that the total amount of water in the entire model was constant – proved to be a bigger challenge. This required better simulation of rivers and ground-water flows to ensure precipitation that doesn't evaporate still finds its way back to the ocean. Getting growth and decline of sea ice was tricky too. There was no sea ice module in the ocean model at the time – the addition of the LIM came later – and none of the existing sea ice models supported the long runs they wanted to do. It took the IPSL team several years to build an accurate simulation of ground-water, rivers, and sea ice.

Still, the work proceeded faster than if they had started entirely from scratch, and having ocean and atmosphere experts available at IPSL was crucial. By 2000, they had the first successful coupled model to incorporate a complete carbon cycle, with no artificial flux corrections, which they released as IPSL-CM1.

In the two decades since then, the model has become increasingly sophisticated, with the addition of the LIM in the ocean; a more sophisticated land surface model, known as Orchidee,[33] to compute how vegetation changes over time from things like forest fires and changing local climates; and improvements in how carbon is taken up by in the ocean by plankton – microscopic sea creatures and plants. IPSL now releases a new, improved version of the model every few years, along with a detailed description of what has been added, and how the new elements affect the ability of the model to simulate climates of the recent and distant path.

Portraits of a Climate Model

When I first started visiting climate modelling labs, I wanted to familiarize myself with the models before I visited. As a software engineer, what I really wanted was a set of high-level architectural diagrams of the software structure.

The diagrams[34] I use when I teach software engineering consist of lots of boxes and arrows – boxes to represent the major blocks of program code, and arrows between them representing relationships between these code chunks. Such diagrams play a similar role to the detailed architectural plans used when constructing buildings – they help everyone on the team to understand what goes where, so their work remains coordinated. I teach my students to sketch these diagrams as their own personal roadmaps, to help them make sense of code that other people have written.

But climate scientists rarely draw architecture diagrams. When they do document their models, they write extensive accounts of the science expressed in the models – sets of equations, along with commentary on the numerical algorithms that implement them. But very few diagrams, or at least not the kinds of diagram a software engineer might expect.

That's not to say climate modellers don't like visualizations. On the contrary, in the climate labs I visited, every desk and wall is papered with graphs and charts showing the output of climate models. Some of these are very colourful – maps of the planet coloured to show how a variable changes across the globe, and often multiple sets of the same chart placed side-by-side to make it easier to compare the results of different model experiments. But these are visualizations of the *science*, rather than the *software*.

The closest I could find to a software architecture diagram is the Bretherton diagram, dating back to a workshop[35] on climate modelling in 1985 (see Figure 7.7). Originally termed the "wiring diagram," it shows boxes representing processes that need to be simulated, and wires representing fluxes of matter and energy exchanged between them – and hence data that needs to be passed from one module to another. When it was first made, this diagram represented a very ambitious blueprint for future models, as the existing models only covered a small fraction of these processes. But since then, the models have steadily grown to incorporate more and more of the processes included in the Bretherton diagram. The most advanced of today's Earth system models include detailed simulations of nearly all the terrestrial and marine biogeochemical processes shown on the Bretherton diagram.

The Bretherton diagram is what software engineers sometimes call a *reference architecture* – a standardized view of how a climate model *ought* to be structured. But it doesn't show how today's models differ from each other, nor how they implement this architecture. Over the years, climate models have become steadily larger and more complex, and the days when a single scientist could write the code for an entire model have long gone. But that also means it's harder and harder to find anyone who understands the whole of any of today's models.

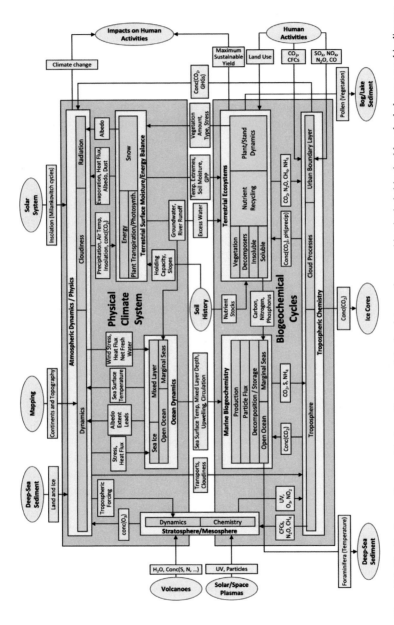

Figure 7.7 The Bretherton diagram. Modern climate models simulate nearly everything included in the blue shaded areas on this diagram, while the beige ovals around the edge represent their inputs and outputs. (Adapted from NASA (1986) and Fisher (1988))

So to help get a sense of the actual architecture of modern climate models, I challenged one of my students, Kaitlin Naughten (née Alexander), to find a way to compare the structures of the current generation of models. At the time, Kaitlin was an undergraduate in applied mathematics at the University of Manitoba. Her analysis of climate models began as a summer research project, and grew from there. She ended up working with eight different climate modelling centres, getting the program code from each centre, and analyzing the structure of the code. As a result of her work, Kaitlin produced visualizations of the main structure of many leading climate models, showing some fascinating similarities and differences between the models.[36] Four of her diagrams are shown in Figure 7.8.

The bubbles in Kaitlin's diagrams are scaled according to the number of lines of program code. The relative sizes of the various model components vary greatly – in terms of lines of code – both within each model, and between models. The size of a program can be used as a rough estimate[37] of how much effort it took to write the code and how complex it is. So the relative size of a module in these diagrams gives us a measure of how much scientific work went into producing it.

Not surprisingly, the atmosphere component is the largest in all these models. This reflects the much longer history atmospheric modelling – compared to other components – and the emphasis all these labs place on getting the behaviour of the atmosphere right.

In other respects, the models differ greatly. Some of the models have substantial code modules devoted to atmospheric chemistry, reflecting a growing concern that pollution, air quality, and climate change are closely inter-related, and must be adequately modelled to understand their impacts on climate and human health. Other models, such as IPSL's, place more emphasis on capturing the effect of land processes (particularly vegetation) and ocean biogeochemistry (abbreviated to BGC), because they model the full carbon cycle.

The diagrams also show many of the components have distinctive names, because they are also used as stand-alone components by the scientific communities who build them. Some of these names are amusing. IPSL's vegetation model is Orchidee, while the UK Met Office's is called Triffid. The two original ocean models developed in the United States were known as MOM and POP.[38] CESM still uses POP, but is considering switching to MOM. HadGEM2 uses an older version of MOM, while newer versions of HadGEM use NEMO.

Finally, Kaitlin's diagrams show the distinction between *scientific code*, which implements the scientific equations, and *infrastructure code*, shown in grey. Think of it as the glue that holds the parts of the model together and makes sure they work properly. The couplers[39] – which are rarely shown in

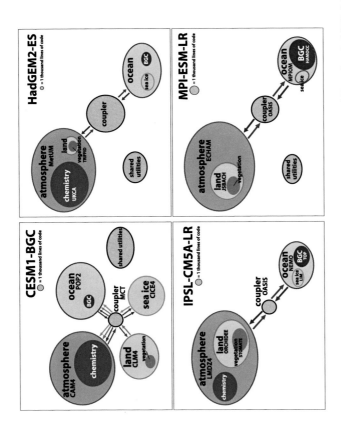

Figure 7.8 The high level architecture of modern climate models (Reprinted from Alexander and Easterbrook, 2015). Model components are scaled according to the number of lines of code in the configurations used for each centre's main submission to the IPCC Fifth Assessment Report. These models are from the four major centres described in this book. (a) CESM is the Community Earth System Model developed at NCAR, in Boulder, Colorado; (b) HadGEM2 is the Hadley Global Earth System Model developed at the UK Met Office, in Exeter, United Kingdom; (c) IPSL-CM5A is Climate Model 5 developed at the Institut Pierre Simon Laplace, in Paris, France; (d) MPI-ESM is the Earth System Model developed at the Max Planck Institute, in Hamburg, Germany. Note that the diagrams are not to scale with one another – see Figure 7.9 for relative size. (Figure by Kaitlin Naughten, CC BY 4.0)

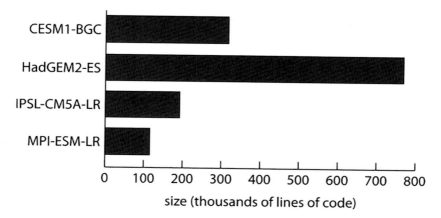

Figure 7.9 The relative size of the four models shown in Figure 7.8, in lines of code. Note that these measurements are of the number of lines of code after extracting and building these specific model configurations – each lab maintains a larger code base from which a whole family of models can be built. (Figure by Kaitlin Naughten, CC BY 4.0)

scientific presentations of the models – have grown to be substantial programs in their own right. Coupling software passes data between the component models at each timestep as the simulation runs, and processes this data in various ways. If the atmosphere and ocean models use different grids, the coupler must convert data from each model to the other's grid at each timestep. Couplers also handle data archiving, and often carry out sanity checks on the simulation, such as checking that the total mass of air and water in the model doesn't change over time, even as it moves around between the different parts of the Earth system.

Architectural Styles

It should be clear by now that for large complex software systems, a good structure is essential to keep everything coordinated. The architecture of buildings is a good analogy. As we've seen in the last few chapters, the buildings that house the climate research labs I visited are each unique, with design flourishes where architects have asserted their particular styles. And yet the basic functions of these buildings are the same. Each houses a community of scientists doing similar kinds of scientific work – analyzing data, building and running computer models, presenting their work to each other, and so on.

Likewise, the climate models built in these labs all look different, but their basic function is the same: simulate the various parts of the climate system on planet Earth well enough so that scientists can run experiments in the model to help them understand how the climate system works. There are at least two dozen other labs around the world each with their own global coupled climate model, each approaching the task in their own way. And hundreds more research groups build separate models of specific parts of the climate system.

After visiting a number of different labs, I began to realize these labs have quite different goals for their climate models, shaped by the interest and expertise of their scientists and the goals of the funding agencies providing the resources. Each lab likes to demonstrate its value by differentiating itself from other labs. For example, the emphasis on biological processes in IPSL's model reflects its history as the first climate model to include an active carbon cycle – and the model's original purpose for paleoclimate experiments.

In contrast, UK Met Office distinguishes itself as the only lab to have integrated its climate modelling with operational weather forecasting, and HadGEM2 dominates in size because of this – the weather forecasting code requires a lot more detail than other atmosphere models. As the shared code is run every day for weather forecasting, the models are extensively tested and improved, and benefit from advances in meteorology as well as climate science.

Meanwhile, the architecture of NCAR's model, CESM1, reflects its status as the world's first community climate model. While other models more clearly show their history as Atmosphere-Ocean GCMs, with additional components subsumed into either the atmosphere or ocean code, CESM has a distinct star-shaped architecture, reflecting a deliberate choice to keep all major components – including the sea ice and land modules – fully separate. This makes the model very modular, minimizing how much each component must know about the other components it is interacting with, and making it easier for other scientists to plug in their own experimental versions of these components.

Architecture and Change

The analogy between buildings and software goes further. Buildings have complex structures, and those structures shape what we can do with them. The needs of the people inhabiting a building tend to change much faster than the building itself, so we end up putting up with awkward room layouts, or we get creative in adapting the building to our needs. Even the best architects cannot foresee how their buildings will be used and adapted in the future – extensions get added, the internal layout gets changed, and the cladding on the building gets updated.

Sometimes, either through luck or foresight, architects create adaptable structures that work well, even as different occupants come and go. More often, the bold flourishes that win architectural awards end up becoming a liability for the people who have to live or work in the building, because they make it harder to modify the building when needs change.

In his book "How Buildings Learn," Stuart Brand popularized the idea that buildings adapt to keep up with the needs of their occupants[40]. Brand views a building as a set of *shearing layers* – each of which might be sheared off and replaced over time. He identifies six distinct layers for a building: Site, Structure, Skin, Services, Space plan, and Stuff. At one end of the scale, the *Site* of a building is fixed and unchanging,[41] while at the other end, our *Stuff* – furniture and belongings – can be moved around as often as we like.

The layers in between adapt at different speeds. The *Structure* of a building is slow to change, enduring for many decades, usually until the entire building is torn down and replaced, or a major extension added. But a building's *Skin* might change several times during the life of the structure, as for example, in the enclosure of the ground floor spaces of the elevated buildings on the Jussieu campus in Figure 7.2. *Services* – heating, cooling, plumbing, wiring – tend to wear out and are often upgraded, usually without affecting the Skin or Structure of the building. The *Space plan* – the interior layout of the building – changes more frequently, when we add or remove partitions to reconfigure rooms. To future-proof a building, the design should allow each layer to change independently.

The same principle applies to software, but it is largely invisible. Complex software systems need a structure – an architecture – to keep them from becoming an unworkable mess, and their initial architecture tends to get less and less suitable as the software evolves. Today's climate models have particularly long lifetimes (decades!), and are continually updated to take advantage of faster computers, improvements in our understanding of the climate system, and new components representing additional parts of the Earth system.

It may seem that software structure can be changed at will – after all, it's just program code. But software has its own equivalent to load-bearing walls, which you tear down at your own risk. These are the interfaces between program modules, and they embody many design decisions and assumptions about what each part of the program is supposed to do, and how it is supposed to do it. When software that used to work well suddenly starts misbehaving, it's often because someone made a change that breaks the interface between components, and as a result, bad data gets passed from one part of the program to another.

So what are the equivalents of Brand's shearing layers in the architecture of climate models, and how well do they support the changing needs of scientists? And how well do they support the goal of "plug and play"?

Modularity

One of the founders of the field of software engineering, David Parnas, wrote a playful essay[42] comparing software aging to human aging. Like people, old software gets slower, less able to do what it used to do, and more forgetful – more likely to crash and lose our data. With tongue firmly in cheek, he suggested a research program into *software geriatrics*.

The problem is that the world keeps changing. Our needs and expectations from computer systems change, as does the hardware our programs run on, and the other systems they have to interact with. Changes to a complex software system rarely fit nicely within the original design, and each change can introduce new problems. So there are two root causes of the symptoms of software aging: a failure to modify software to keep up with a changing world, and the mess we cause when we do modify it.

Parnas was also the first software researcher to demonstrate how important it is to choose a modular design to fend off software aging. By dividing the software into separable chunks, or *modules*, programmers can hide the details about how each module works from the rest of the program, with a simplified interface for other modules – a list of the functions it can carry out, the kinds of data it will need, and the kinds of data it will provide. Like fire doors in a building, these interfaces stop errors from spreading – if you change details inside one module, it should not affect other modules. A well-chosen set of modules and interfaces can simplify future changes by isolating them to just one module. But a poorly chosen architecture can lead to a cascade of problems, as each change in the software causes more changes to be needed to other modules. So a core competency of a software engineer is the ability to anticipate future needs and select an architecture that's flexible enough to accommodate them.

When you replace a model component in a coupled climate model, even minor things like the values used for physical constants can matter. One scientist told me of a model showing strange discrepancies, which they eventually tracked down to the ocean and atmosphere models using slightly different values for the radius of the Earth.[43] Component models often use different calendars too. Some models simplify things by ignoring leap years, and others simplify things further by using a 360-day year with all the months of equal length. For many experiments, this works fine, unless you need to integrate real-world data into the model as it runs. A good choice, then, is to hand responsibility for many of these things to a coupler, so each component doesn't have to define constants and keep track of dates itself.

Speaking the Same Language

Early programming languages were structured around *procedures* – lists of instructions grouped according to the order they had to be carried out. Slightly better is to think in terms of *functions*, grouping chunks of code together that do similar things, while the detail of how they do it can be hidden from the rest of the program, and changed when needed. Newer *object-oriented* programming languages are organized around *objects*, representing the things a program has keep track of – bank accounts, data files, or the state of the atmosphere – as this set of objects is much less likely to change than the kinds of calculation we want to perform on them. So *objects* are a lower shearing level than the *functions* and *procedures* that do things to them.

Climate models have been around long enough to have lived through all of these eras in programming practice. The models are written in what many people now see as an antiquated programming language – Fortran. When IBM created Fortran in the 1950s, it was the ideal language for translating mathematical formulas into computer instructions – hence the name, FORmula TRANslation. Over the years, new versions of Fortran have appeared that include newer concepts such as functions and objects, and if you study the code in most climate models, you'll see a mix of older and newer styles of Fortran, reflecting the fact that parts of the program are always being updated.

I've asked many climate scientists whether they'd be better off ditching Fortran entirely and adopting a modern programming language. Some like the idea, but most think it won't happen, for several reasons. One is the cost of starting over, which we talked about earlier. Another reason is *conservation of familiarity*. It's a self-reinforcing feedback loop: climate scientists have to learn Fortran because all the current models are written in it, and climate models have to be written in Fortran because that's the language everyone in the field knows. But that's not the whole story, because climate scientists frequently pick up new programming practices and tools when they see obvious advantages in them.

So another reason is efficiency. Fortran code tends to be fast, as it is very similar to the low-level steps – the machine code – that a computer uses when executing a program. Modern, object-oriented programming languages add a lot more structure to a program at the cost of efficiency, relying on the fact that modern computers are so much faster anyway. But when you have to wait weeks for a climate simulation to run on one of the world's fastest supercomputers, efficiency really does matter. A lot.

But perhaps the most compelling reason is that it would make very little difference. Climate models already have a well-thought out architecture, based on the scientific domains they represent. Much of the code consists of a few lines of program to calculate a mathematical formula, wrapped in a lot of nested loops, to apply the formula over and over again for each grid cell at each timestep. Fortran compilers are very clever at optimizing such code for efficiency, executing the repeated code in parallel on the supercomputer, rather than in a fixed order. So the code would look very similar, no matter which programming language it was written in. There is no compelling reason to ditch Fortran.

Divide Nature at Its Joints

Besides, programming languages are far too low a level to think about software architecture – like trying to design a building by focusing on how bricks can be put together. For very large programs you need better ways of thinking about structure.[44]

In the early days of atmosphere and ocean models, each model was built by a very small team – small enough that each team member could understand the whole thing, and they could get around a table regularly and take design decisions together. But today's models take things to a whole new level. When you have dozens – or even hundreds – of scientists contributing to the model, you need a structure to organize their work, not so much for technical reasons, but because of human limitations. It's simply not possible for every contributing scientist to participate in every design decision, and it's not possible for them all to understand every aspect of the model.

Good software architectures use natural divisions in the problem domain, so that a complex problem can be divided into more manageable chunks – often expressed in textbooks as *"divide nature at its joints."* For climate models, this can be applied quite literally – for example, the ocean's surface is a natural boundary between the atmosphere and oceans, and this boundary shows up as a distinct interface in the software of all global climate models.

But look more closely, and a second organizing principle can be seen at work. As well as the physical distinctions, such as atmosphere versus ocean, there are distinctions between scientific fields – physics vs. biology, for example – and further distinctions between subfields. And as scientists working in these different subfields are organized into separate research groups, or even separate labs, the architecture of the model tends to match the organizational structure of the labs that build it.

This pattern is so common in software engineering, it has a name – *Conway's Law*.[45] If you have a very large software development team, you have to break it into smaller teams, so each team can focus on a different software module. The software architecture simplifies the interaction between modules, to minimize how much coordination is needed between teams. The effect works both ways: software companies tend to organise their teams according to the structure of the software they're building, and the structure of the software is shaped by the way the company is organised.

For scientific software, Conway's Law reduces the amount that different scientists need to know about each other's field before they can work together. Scientists can contribute to the model without having to learn every detail about each other's work. In an inter-disciplinary field like climate science, this is important. The computational models play a central role in allowing scientists with very different kinds of expertise to work together. The architecture of the model divides *scientific work* at its joints.

Models Organize Scientific Work

In the academic world, we often refer to each subject as a *discipline*, and we train students in each field to learn a specific set of rules – a disciplined approach – for how to tackle problems in that field. Specialist knowledge and training from one discipline don't necessarily help a researcher to understand what scientists in other disciplines do.

This is a recent thing. Up until the mid-nineteenth century, most scientists would happily tackle a variety of problems ranging from pure mathematics to applied sciences and engineering. With rapid progress in science and engineering from the nineteenth century onwards, a researcher would need to learn ever more background to become expert at anything, so an era of specialization began, with each scientist training for work in ever narrower areas of study.

Each discipline has its own set of research methods, and its own ideas for what counts as progress. This means each discipline has a set of problems it can study – problems for which these methods are well-suited – and a set of problems it cannot study because the methods don't work well, or don't work at all. Because scientific training focuses on mastering the methods from one discipline, many scientists will ignore problems for which their methods don't work, rather than have to learn a whole new set of methods.

However, some problems are so big that they require an inter-disciplinary approach. Climate change is certainly one of these.[46] Inter-disciplinary research can be hard in many research labs, because the various disciplines have evolved apart. Each has amassed such a large body of tacit knowledge and technical vocabulary – jargon – that it can be hard for scientists even to talk to experts from other disciplines. Even within the same field, scientists don't always agree on the meaning of key terms[47] – I once sat in on a workshop for geologists who were trying to create a unified geological map of Europe, who realised each country's geological surveyors had defined "bedrock" in a different way.

Computational models don't prevent such problems, but a shared computer model helps overcome them. In most of science, we're not very good about explaining our jargon, because we assume other scientists in our field already understand it. So scientific papers are hard to read for people outside the field. But when you create a computer model, you have to be explicit about everything, because the computer knows nothing. Each concept encoded into the model has to be spelled out in series of explicit steps to tell the computer exactly how to compute it. There cannot be any ambiguity.

This means a computational model acts as an important intermediary in inter-disciplinary work, forcing scientists to make everything explicit. Rather than trying to explain an abstract theoretical idea, you can show someone the model running and explain what it's doing. And if you want to know exactly how a particular calculation is carried out, you can look at the program code. Or you go and find the relevant scientist, and ask them why the model does what it does – and use the model as a shared reference.

Comparing two models is a lot easier than comparing two theories. I observed this a lot in every lab I visited – scientists would compare two different models (e.g., from two different labs) to understand how each has interpreted and implemented a particular piece of the science differently. This turns out to be a crucial technique when testing and debugging the models, as we'll see in the next chapter. The program code helps scientists realize when they need to ask such questions, and acts as the ultimate source for precise answers.

Avoiding Forks

So sharing the program code and data openly improves communication between scientists from disciplines who have to work together to understand the climate system as a whole, and it helps to have a software architecture that matches the structure of the scientific work. But what happens when you want to plug in a new component? If each component has a solid scientific basis, and works well on its own, in theory, you shouldn't need to change any code when you incorporate it into a global climate model. But if the models are built by different teams, using different assumptions and simplifications, changes are always needed when you couple them together.

This introduces another risk – *code forking*. This is a perennial problem in large open source software projects. Because the program code is freely available, anyone can take a version of the code and modify it for their own needs. If the modifications are useful, they can be incorporated into the shared code so that everyone gets them. The community remains unified. But if a particular subgroup doesn't share their changes, the two versions of the software diverge, until they are so different it is impossible to merge them again – the development of the software has forked into two separate paths. Such splits are usually bad for everyone. The community itself fragments into smaller groups, and each loses access to crucial expertise. And because code forks are often the result of unresolved disagreements, the fragmentation of the community creates confusion and distrust, and many people stop participating altogether. The leaders of open source projects strive to avoid code forks.

Climate modelling labs face the same challenge, and use the same tools[48] as open source software communities to keep everyone's contributions to the program code organized. *Version control* tools allow scientists to create many different variants of the program. These tools view the evolving program code like a tree, with branches representing experimental variants created by each scientist. Anyone can create their own branch – thus risking a fork – but the tools allow them to merge their branch back into the main trunk whenever they have changes that work well and are useful. And overnight, every night, a whole series of automated tests run on the trunk, to check that the model still works with any new code merged into the trunk that day. If any of these tests fail, the merge can be rolled back, and whoever contributed that code can continue to work separately on their branch, until the problem is identified and fixed. If a scientist prefers to continue working on an experimental branch, they can also incorporate new contributions from the trunk, or even from other branches, so they don't miss out on the latest developments.

These tools allow a very large team of scientists to build their own experimental variants of a climate model, without the whole project descending into chaos. Even so, code forks do still sometime happen, especially when one lab adopts a significant module from another lab. For example, the UK Met Office has always relied on using ocean models developed elsewhere. For many years, they used the MOM ocean model, which was originally developed at GFDL in the United States. When they first adopted it, it was a state-of-the-art ocean model. But in adapting it to work with the rest of the Met Office's unified model, they inadvertently forked it from the original. So while the GFDL team kept MOM up to date with the latest science, the modified version used at the Met Office was stuck in the past.

By the early 2000s, the Met Office scientists realized they were missing out on the latest developments in ocean modelling. They needed an up-to-date ocean model, and were determined not to make the same mistake again. When they chose to adopt NEMO – or rather, OPA as it was at the time – they didn't want just a copy of the code. Instead, they pushed for a consortium agreement among NEMO's main users, so that ongoing improvements to the ocean model would be shared with the whole community, and a code fork avoided.

When I first visited IPSL in 2008, the Met Office had just signed on to the NEMO consortium agreement. The UK Met Office wanted changes made to NEMO to couple it to the Met Office models, and to make it run faster on their supercomputers. They were frustrated that the NEMO team wouldn't accept those changes into the standard version of NEMO. And meanwhile, the small NEMO team in Paris – just four scientists – was struggling to handle requests from across the consortium for updates to the model – changes that were not only incompatible with the NEMO team's engineering guidelines, but were sometimes also incompatible with each other. The NEMO team focused on changes they thought improved the model, and set aside any changes they felt broke the good engineering practices that made NEMO such an attractive model in the first place.

But the real problem wasn't these decisions, it was the lack of communication between the groups. By the summer of 2008, both groups felt the consortium agreement was failing, and convened a set of meetings to decide what to do. When I visited IPSL two years later, in 2010, I was delighted to find that the communication problems had been fixed. The partners in the consortium had instituted an annual "merge workshop," where they all came together for a couple of days to merge all the changes each of them had made into NEMO, and to decide together how best to handle each one. In addition, the NEMO team had built a *validation toolkit* – a series of standard tests to run on the ocean model, so that each consortium member could do their own testing, rather than relying on IPSL to do it for them.

Plug and Participate

So today's climate models have grown far beyond the atmosphere and ocean models of the 1960s and 1970s. They've grown in detail and scope, often through accumulation of new components. Each component model is built by

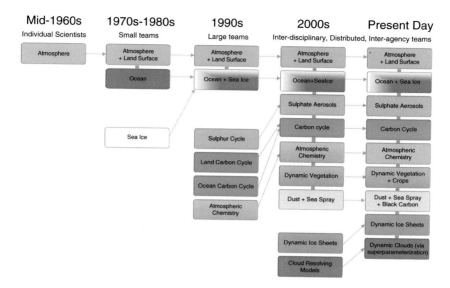

Figure 7.10 The development and growth of coupled climate models. Many components started as separate models, built by different communities of researchers, and were incorporated into coupled climate models when they were seen as mature. (Adapted from Washington et al. (2009) and National Academies (2016))

a community of experts from a particular discipline, usually for their own purposes – to simulate the processes they study – and these separate models have been incorporated into coupled climate models over the years (see Figure 7.10).

As the models have grown, they've become an essential connection between scientists working in different disciplines. Maintaining today's models requires the collaboration of many different experts, and the models support this collaboration by allowing scientists from different disciplines to combine their knowledge, forcing them to be precise and explicit about their understanding of the processes they study.

Today's climate models have evolved well beyond the point where any one scientist fully understands the entire model. Hence, large distributed teams and inter-agency agreements are needed to keep everything coordinated, and a good choice of architecture reduces the amount of communication. The scientists who work on these models share an understanding of the overall architecture of the models, expressed in diagrams such as the Bretherton wiring diagram. Even within a coupled model, the modellers work to keep the model components as distinct as possible, to retain the link to the community of experts who build each piece, and prevent code forking.

Coordinating the work of these large inter-disciplinary teams isn't easy, and today's climate modelling labs rely on sophisticated open source software tools to manage their shared program code. And in most cases, they use these same tools to release their code as open source, so that other scientists around the world can download them, experiment with them, and contribute improvements back for the community to share. Coordinating this work is hard, but reaching agreement on shared goals among very disparate scientific teams is even harder – many of the key milestones in developing coupled models occurred only once different groups of scientists were persuaded that the goal of combining their work into a single model was worthwhile.

But what about that goal of making the models "plug and play"? In a perfect world, different scientists should be able to plug new elements into the coupled models without making substantial changes to their own model, nor to the coupled model system. But as the example of flux corrections showed, testing a model on its own won't show how well the model will work in a coupled system, because of complex interactions between components. So incorporating new elements into the coupled model relies on inter-disciplinary expertise to make the coupled system work and to chase down unexpected behaviours. While plug and play is a lovely idea, the climate system is sufficiently complex that it's probably impossible in practice.

And anyway, scientists don't want to blindly plug in any new component. Details matter to them – they want to know what the model is doing as it runs. Their goal isn't to keep everything neat and tidy. It's to learn things they didn't already know about how the various parts of the climate system affect one another.

Notes

1   See Madec (2008).
2   The original OPA model used the stretched grid shown in Figure 5.4a of Chapter 5, but the current version uses the tri-polar grid.
3   Some changes to the basic equations are needed, for example, because water does not compress like a gas does, so the ideal gas laws don't apply.
4   Or longer, if it makes several trips around the Antarctic. Deep ocean water upwelling in the southern ocean is about 1,000 years old, on average.
5   See, for example, Lozier (2010). Oceanographers prefer the term Meridional Overturning Circulation (MOC) as it is easier to define based on the net flow in the north-south direction at each height in the ocean. The AMOC – the Atlantic portion of the MOC – is where the pattern is strongest.
6   The Southern Ocean also dissolves a lot of carbon, but ocean circulation patterns prevent much of this reaching the deep ocean. See, for example, Frölicher et al. (2015).
7   See Talandier et al. (2014), for an example experiment with NEMO set up in this way, to explore the impact on AMOC.

8 Named after the Arctic wildflower, White Dryas, whose leaves in the fossil record mark the changing temperatures. There was also an Older Dryas period about 1,000 years earlier, although the fossil records for this are less well defined.

9 Broecker (1987) was one of the first to point to this as a potential tipping point in climate change. It was also the key plot point of the movie The Day After Tomorrow, although nearly all the science in that movie is completely wrong. See https://climatesight.org/2012/04/26/the-day-after-tomorrow-a-scientific-critique/

10 The United Kingdom, for example, is much further north than Toronto, but enjoys a milder climate because of the heat driven up from the equator by the ocean currents and the gulf stream system. If these weaken, the United Kingdom could see winters as cold as those of southern Ontario.

11 See www.nemo-ocean.eu/doc/node135.html

12 Programmers refer to the opposite approach as "fast and dirty." You might get something basic working quickly, but the code is usually hard to understand, hard to modify, and full of subtle errors.

13 PISCES stands for Pelagic Interactions Scheme for Carbon and Ecosystem Studies. See Aumont et al. (2015).

14 See Rousset et al. (2015) and Vancoppenolle et al. (2009) for a description of the model.

15 We often talk about salt being used to melt ice, but at the molecular level, that's not really what happens. On the surface of any chunk of ice, water is continually melting and refreezing. If you add salt, it doesn't make ice melt faster, but it slows the refreezing. This shifts the balance between melting and freezing, so there is less ice at a given temperature.

16 The problem is really an artifact of having a very coarse resolution grid. It goes away in higher resolution models, because the heat added is spread over many more grid points.

17 The NEMO coupler is known as OASIS, and can be seen in two of the four coupled model systems in Figure 7.8. See Craig et al. (2017).

18 The normal approach is to subtract the long-term trend from the fluxes at each timestep.

19 Some centres would run their model with the flux corrections turned off for climate change experiments. If you compare the baseline and doubled CO_2 runs, and they have the same underlying drift, the drift disappears when you subtract one run from the other. However, this assumes the drift doesn't interfere with any feedback loops that affect the climate response.

20 See Shackley et al. (1999) for a detailed discussion of the controversy, and how different scientists responded to it. They identify two distinct groups of scientists depending on their attitude to the use of flux corrections: "pragmatists" and "purists." But note that the research described in this paper was conducted in the early 1990s, and Shackley et al. were unaware that by the time their paper was published, several research groups had already solved the flux correction problem.

21 See description in Stocker (2011, p. 146 onward). These experiments show no substantial difference between flux corrected and non-flux corrected models, for moderate climate change scenarios. For extreme climate change, the comparison is more complex, as it's not clear what the flux corrections should do.

22 Much of this work is done in the lab LATMOS (which stands for Laboratoire ATmosphères, Milieux, Observations Spatiales), which studies the atmospheres of Earth and other planets.

23 LOCEAN stands for Laboratoire d'Océanographie et du Climat: Expérimentation et Approches Numérique.

24 And that they will run correctly on different supercomputers. Of the climate mod-
    elling centres I visited, IPSL is the only one that doesn't have access to its own
    dedicated supercomputer, so the model needs to be portable enough to run on
    whichever borrowed machines they have access to, such as the long-term arrange-
    ment for use of the supercomputers at France's Centre for Atomic Energy.
25 Let's say $150 K annual salary × 50 scientists × 20 years. That's $150 million for
    salary, plus about the same again for the supercomputing facility. See www
    .easterbrook.ca/steve/2010/09/whats-the-pricetag-on-a-global-climate-model/
26 Climate scientists are very aware of the energy footprint of their computing cen-
    tres. Some of them use the heat from the supercomputers to heat nearby buildings,
    while others have relocated their computer centres to colder climates, to reduce
    the energy needed to cool them.
27 See Dahan (2010) for a detailed history of these developments, and the corre-
    sponding shift to inter-disciplinary thinking.
28 See Braconnot et al. (1997).
29 See Hourdin et al. (2017). We'll return to the issue of model calibration (aka tun-
    ing) in the next chapter.
30 See Gleckler et al. (1995). I'm grateful to Matt Huber at Purdue University for
    alerting me to this paper. Matt was also working on paleoclimate analysis (using
    CESM) and also solved the flux correction problem around the same time as
    the IPSL team. Note that this paper is an important early example of the value
    of Model Intercomparison Projects, which we will examine in more detail in
    Chapter 8.
31 Clouds have remained the biggest source of uncertainty in climate modelling for
    the last 40 years. See Bony et al. (2013) for a retrospective.
32 See Laurent et al. (1998) for a list of all the parameter changes needed to stabilize
    the IPSL model.
33 ORCHIDEE stands for ORganizing Carbon and Hydrology In Dynamic
    EcosystEms.
34 The Unified Modelling Language (UML) standardizes a lot of these different
    kinds of diagram. Some software engineers love UML and others hate it. So its
    use across the software industry is very patchy.
35 See Fisher (1988). The original diagram was constructed on a wall over the
    course of a workshop at Jackson Hole in Wyoming. Francis Bretherton, who at
    the time was a scientist (and ex-director) at NCAR, eventually had to pay to re-
    paint the wall after the workshop was over.
36 Kaitlin's full analysis is available in Alexander and Easterbrook (2015).
37 Programmers can always contrive examples where a program can be improved by
    making it shorter, the obvious example being to remove modules that are never
    used. Sometimes a more efficient algorithm uses fewer steps. But in practice,
    these happen rarely, and number of lines of code has been shown to correlate well
    with sophistication and complexity of a program. See, for example, Herraiz et al.
    (2007).
38 The acronyms are Modular Ocean Model and Parallel Ocean Program, while
    TRIFFID stands for Top-down Representation of Interactive Foliage and Flora
    Including Dynamics. Climate modellers like good acronyms.
39 See Valcke et al. (2012).
40 See Brand (1995). The original idea is from the architect Frank Duffy, although in
    Duffy's original descriptions, he only identified four layers.
41 Except in the rare case where an historical building is moved to another site, to
    ensure preservation.

42 Parnas (1994).

43 This turns out to be trickier than you might think, as there is no correct answer. We cannot measure the radius of the planet directly, so we have to calculate it from other things, and each way of calculating it produces slightly different answers. It even matters how many significant digits you include when putting it in the program.

44 See Shaw and Garlan's classic 1996 book "Software Architecture" for a compelling version of this argument.

45 Named after Melvin Conway, who explored the idea in his 1968 paper "How Do Committees Invent?" (Conway, 1968)

46 Climate scientists recognised this early. For example, when Stephen Schneider founded the journal Climactic Change in 1977, he gave it a deliberately interdisciplinary focus, despite his director advising him that this would hamper his career. See Weart (2013).

47 The sociologist Susan Leigh Star pointed out many examples of this in her work on boundary objects – shared tools like taxonomies that can be used in different ways in different scientific fields, without any agreement over meaning. See Star (2010).

48 See Matthews et al. (2008) for a detailed description of these tools – as they were when I first started studying climate models – and how scientists adapted them to their own needs.

8

Sound Science

Our confidence in climate science depends to some extent on our confidence that the models are valid. But a computational model can never be perfect, because a model cannot capture everything. What do we mean by "valid"? In this chapter, we will examine how climate modellers test their models, and what they do when they find errors. One surprising result is that climate models appear to be less buggy than almost any other software ever produced. More importantly, climate modellers have adapted the tools of science – hypothesis testing, peer review, and scientific replication – in remarkable new ways to overcome the weaknesses in any individual model, to ensure their scientific conclusions are sound. A study of the Max Planck Institute for Meteorology, in Hamburg, Germany will show how they do this.

An Adapted Model

The Max Planck Society is one of the world's top institutions for scientific research. Since it was founded more than a century ago, its scientists have won 33 Nobel prizes. Funded primarily by the German federal government, it runs more than 80 different research labs across Germany and beyond. In Hamburg, Germany's second largest city, there are three Max Planck labs, and the largest of these is the Max Planck Institute for Meteorology (MPI-M). Housed on the campus of the University of Hamburg, MPI-M is now at the heart of a large-scale partnership with the University and the City of Hamburg, known as *Klimacampus* – a network of institutions engaged in research and education on climate change and its impacts.

MPI-M itself occupies one wing of a lightning bolt-shaped building on the leafy Bundestrasse (see Figure 8.1), next door to the University's Institute for Meteorology, a few doors down from the German national climate computing centre, DKRZ,[1] which houses the supercomputers and provides expertise to

Figure 8.1 Bird's-eye view of the Zentrum für Marine und Atmosphärische Wissenschaften (ZMAW) building in Hamburg, Germany. The wing on the right houses the Max Planck Institute for Meteorology, while the wing on the left houses the University of Hamburg's Institute for Meteorology. (MPI-M)

help develop and maintain the climate models. The researchers work in the wedge-shaped wings of the MPI-M building, around a central atrium that runs the entire height of the building, criss-crossed by walkways, under a glass skylight. As well as being the quickest route to the break room for coffee, I found the walkways served another important function in a research lab: they gave me a glimpse of the entire building from within – an instant overview of who is around, and judging from the open office doors, who might be willing to let me interrupt them for a chat.

The research teams at MPI-M are divided into three divisions, matching the three main components[2] of their models: Atmosphere in the Earth System, Ocean in the Earth System, and Land in the Earth System. The host for my visits, Reinhard Budich, is responsible for ensuring the model components from these three divisions work together properly. Reinhard has led a number of European funded research projects to build shared software infrastructure, and tools for sharing climate data with scientists around the world.

I first visited for a month in August 2010. The weather was glorious, so on my first evening, Reinhard and I sampled the local beer at a rooftop bar overlooking Hamburg's harbour, while he filled me in on the history of the lab and its climate models. MPI-M itself dates back to the 1970s, but the climate modelling work really got underway in 1988, when DKRZ was created as a joint project between the University and the Max Planck Society. They began by experimenting with an existing atmosphere model – from the European Centre for Medium-range Weather Forecasts (ECMWF) – rather than building their own from scratch.

MPI-M now runs two major coupled Earth system models. The older of the two, MPI-ESM,[3] was adapted from the original program code of the ECMWF atmosphere model, but has gone through many decades of evolution, and today it bears few traces of its origins. The newer model, ICON, began in 2001 as a research project – in partnership with the German Weather Forecasting Service – to explore how to build a unified weather and climate model with an icosahedral grid.[4] In the two decades since, ICON has grown to become a fully coupled Earth system model, with its own atmosphere and ocean components. Despite having radically different dynamical cores, these two coupled Earth system models do share some components – for example, they both use the same land surface and vegetation model.

My first visit in 2010 happened during a busy time for the lab. The computing centre had just moved to a brand new building, and was expanding its staff of programmers to play a bigger role in testing the models and sharing climate data. The ICON team had just doubled in size and was starting work on coupling their new dynamical core with other components of the climate system. The earth system modelling team was busy testing the latest version of MPI-ESM, ready to run a set of experiments as the lab's contribution to the next major assessment report of the UN's Intergovernmental Panel on Climate Change (IPCC).

So it was an excellent opportunity for me to see first-hand how scientists test their models, and to discover how good today's models actually are. Climate scientists have developed a remarkably effective set of practices for ensuring the scientific quality of their work, even as they are continually frustrated by the technical barriers that get in the way of making their ambitious simulations work. Building and assessing a climate model is woven into the scientific work of the labs, so any flaw in a model becomes a topic for scientific investigation. More importantly, the climate modelling community has created a formidable, worldwide process for evaluating climate models to ensure sound scientific results – and advice for policymaking – even when each individual model has obvious weaknesses. It's a remarkable example of global collaboration.

Prepping for the IPCC

During that first visit to Hamburg, Reinhard invited me to sit in on the weekly meetings of the Coupled Model Steering Group, a team Reinhard chaired at the time, which included one representative from each of MPI-M's divisions: atmosphere, ocean, and land. The team was making sure the latest models would be ready to complete a set of experiments for the upcoming IPCC Fifth Assessment Report (AR5), working to a tight deadline to share their model results before work began on the assessment report itself. The experiments would take enormous amounts of computer time, so the team had reserved a large block of time on DKRZ's supercomputers for much of the rest of the year. I didn't realize it then, but what I was witnessing was one small part of what may well be the largest set of coordinated computational experiments ever conducted.[5] More on that later.

When I arrived, the team was behind schedule. They had picked an ambitious, high-resolution configuration of the model for these experiments, but it had not yet passed all its tests. Some model runs were already underway, but many of the experiments were held up while the team tracked down remaining bugs. In fact, all the climate modelling centres I visited that year were in a similar state: trying to get their experiments finished for the IPCC deadline,[6] while watching their schedules slip as they tracked down software problems and technical glitches.

In the previous IPCC report, the Max Planck model had been rated as one of the most accurate,[7] but they had been late getting their model experiment results submitted, and as a result, some studies had omitted their model. Nobody wanted a repeat of that.

This time round, the team had chosen to use two new configurations of MPI-ESM. The more ambitious of these would use a much higher resolution than before, with the ocean on a 0.4° grid, equivalent to about 50 km grid squares at the equator, chosen to give the most accurate simulation of the twentieth-century climate. This model needs to be run for a simulated 1,500 years to create a realistic ocean circulation state as a starting point for other experiments – which takes several months on the supercomputer. This run was already well underway when I began my visit, but other decisions were still needed, such as whether to include the full carbon cycle in the experiments. The carbon cycle would be the biggest advance in their models since the previous IPCC report, and very few other labs had active carbon cycles yet. But the chlorophyll scheme in the ocean model and the dynamic vegetation scheme in the land surface model were still being tested, and still encountering bugs. And both still needed to be validated against observational data.

Fixing these would delay the start of the main experiments. To make matters worse, other problems were surfacing. The atmosphere team had re-written their shortwave radiation code to make it run twice as fast, but were also now finding bugs in their new code. The lab had a backup plan – switch to a lower resolution model, which would shorten the run times, allowing them to delay the start of the runs. But the lower resolution versions hadn't been fully tested either, and time was running out.

Protection from Errors

In all the labs I have visited, scientists have told me they spend a lot of time fixing errors in the models, and they feel their software should be better. But should it? What I was witnessing in Hamburg was exactly what I expect for any complex software project preparing a major new release of their code – every programmer knows it's almost impossible to get the code correct on the first attempt. So we test and test and test to find errors, and fix them before releasing the software for others to use – or before running the big experiments that might guide international climate policymaking. So I wasn't particularly concerned that the scientists were finding errors in the code. What I really wanted to know was whether they miss any, and if so, what happens then. When large software teams face a time crunch, they often take shortcuts on the testing. And that's when the trouble starts.

When I began my research into climate models a decade ago, I came up with several key research questions: How do scientists check whether their program code is correct? How do they ensure experiments can be reproduced? How does a large team of scientists from different disciplines maintain a shared understanding of the model? How do they prioritize what to work on next? And how do they detect and prevent errors in the software?

The last question is particularly important. In my work at NASA many years ago, I studied the causes of engineering disasters. In 1986, the Space Shuttle Challenger exploded shortly after take-off, killing all seven astronauts on board. It was a national tragedy, and a massive shock for NASA. It was also the main reason why my job there existed. The investigation report from the Challenger accident led to an agency-wide effort to improve its engineering processes, including the creation of what is now the Katherine Johnson Independent Verification and Validation Facility in West Virginia, where I worked in the 1990s. The facility's job is to work with all NASA centres, to ensure software errors will not cause disasters.

Humans make mistakes, miss vital signs, and overlook hidden defects. So engineers use multiple layers of fault protection to prevent such mistakes leading to an accident – often described as the Swiss cheese model.[8] Each step in the engineering process might have mistakes – human errors – like the holes in a slice of Swiss cheese. But if you stack enough slices on top of each other, there is no hole all the way through. The more layers you add, the less the chance of this happening. So we add lots of layers of protection: each design decision is reviewed by multiple teams, tests are repeated under different conditions, and redundancy is built in by including multiple versions of critical components, so that if one fails, another can take over. The goal is to understand what kind of errors can occur, and ensure they cannot lead to an accident.

So when an accident does occur, it's never due to a single error. Holes must have aligned in all the layers of Swiss cheese together to allow a mistake to get all the way through. Accident investigations don't stop when they discover the root cause of failure – they have to investigate how and why each layer of protection failed. After major accidents, the investigations typically reveal a whole series of poor decisions throughout the organization, where known risks were ignored and fail-safes built into the design were over-ridden.[9] The key problem is not that there are errors in the design, but that the *process* of finding and correcting errors itself fails. All major engineering disasters share this in common – multiple interacting failures in the human organization end up *removing* safety margins.[10] And communication failures between engineering teams are always a factor, as people fail to communicate *risk* clearly.

Take, for example, NASA's Mars Climate Orbiter, which in 1998 crashed into Mars on arrival, rather than entering orbit around the planet. The newspapers reported that the spacecraft confused Imperial and Metric measurements. And while that's (sort of) true, it's only a tiny part of the story. After all, doesn't NASA test its software before sending spacecraft to Mars?

It turns out the software with the error wasn't even on the spacecraft – it was in a data file of rocket thruster performance used by mission control back on Earth[11] to track the position of the spacecraft on its nine-month voyage to the red planet. Unfortunately, NASA treats ground software as less risky, and tests it less thoroughly than the flight software. This particular data file was supposed to help the ground crew calculate how much the spacecraft's trajectory is affected each time the spacecraft fires a thruster. And on the journey to Mars, thrusters occasionally have to fire to counter the tendency for the spacecraft to spin[12] due to solar wind – pressure from the sun's photons bombarding the solar panel on one side of the spacecraft. But the program to do these calculations didn't work at all for the first few months of the mission, due to formatting errors in its data files. So at first, the ground crew computed their course corrections by hand.

Three months into the mission, when the ground crew finally got the program working, they noticed immediately the results differed from their hand calculations, but they didn't log this in their issue-tracking system. The ground crew were stressed, running two other missions to Mars at the same time, and didn't investigate why the thruster on this spacecraft fired more often than the previous mission, which had solar panels on both sides – and hence was less prone to spin. And the engineers who designed the spacecraft weren't included in the critical design review meetings for the navigation software. If they had investigated any of these issues while the spacecraft was on its way to Mars, the navigation team could have corrected the trajectory. As the spacecraft approached Mars, each new calculation put it closer and closer to Mars for its first approach. But each time, the ground crew chose to believe the most optimistic of their calculations. So they never used the emergency course corrections designed for exactly this kind of problem. In the end, the spacecraft grazed past the planet at less than 60 km above the surface, far below the safe threshold of 85 km needed to swing into orbit, rather than crashing into the planet.

I use case studies like this when I teach software engineering, to show errors like this are common, and the danger comes when you ignore the symptoms. No matter how good you are at testing, it's impossible to eliminate every possible error. This is where the layers of Swiss cheese come in – each missed step was a layer that could have caught the error: including the right people in review meetings, keeping track of each time the system doesn't behave as expected, investigating *all* anomalies, using appropriate safety margins when approaching orbit, and providing relief when staff are stressed. Accidents occur when people ignore signs of a system not behaving as it should.

So for my study of climate modellers, I wanted to know whether they ever ignore evidence of errors in their models. It turns out the climate modellers I have met are obsessive about tracking down errors, and devote considerable effort to it. They even publish papers in peer-reviewed journals describing new techniques for testing their models, and the kinds of error these tests find.[13] As we'll see, this obsession pays off.

Remarkably Few Bugs

Software testing is quite an art – it requires a methodical approach and the creativity to ask good "what if" questions to expose errors that only show up in unusual situations.[14] And it needs a skeptical mindset. Instead of trying to show the program works, it's better to assume the errors are there in the program, and make it your job to hunt them down. Climate scientists are good at this. After all, they already know their models are imperfect, and they spend most of their time studying all the ways in which their models fail to match reality. They treat hunting for errors as part of the scientific process, running experiments to pin down each source of error.

To assess how effective a testing strategy is, we need to know how many errors it misses. Unfortunately, when we're done testing, we know how many errors we found, but not how many we missed. But if we wait a few years, we can investigate how many more errors were discovered and reported *after* the software was put to use. That's too late to help improve the software, but it tells us something important about the organization that built it. In the software industry, companies use this approach to assess their *defect density* – the average number of errors found after release, per thousand lines of code.

The gold standard is NASA's Shuttle flight software,[15] which had the lowest defect density ever measured, at around 0.1 defects per thousand lines of code. With about 400,000 lines of code, that still means around 40 errors made it through testing. Software errors were often reported during flights, but none of these ever caused an accident, because of all the fault protection – each Shuttle had four identical flight computers, plus a fifth running a completely independent version of the flight software. After each flight, NASA engineers would analyze every reported software error, and they would release a new, corrected version of the flight software about every 18 months. It was probably the most expensive software ever produced, in terms of dollars per line of code.

Other safety-critical software systems – such as air traffic control systems – have been measured at 1–3 errors per thousand lines of code. These systems rely heavily on other safety measures to avoid accidents. In industries where software errors are less likely to cause significant harm, quality standards are much lower. Less than 5 errors per thousand lines is generally considered very high quality software, and many companies report error rates between 10 and 30 per thousand lines. For everyday computing, this is frustrating, but we've learned to tolerate it – we just reboot our computers when they go wrong.

How do climate models compare to these numbers? A few years ago, one of my graduate students, Jon Pipitone, set out to find out. Jon interviewed many climate scientists and collected examples of bugs they had found while testing their code, to give us a sense of where the key problems lay.[16] But the most interesting – and surprising – result of his work came when he measured the defect density of climate models once they had been built and tested.

The labs Jon contacted were happy to give him access to the program code for their models, along with access to their logs of bug reports, and the complete history of every change made to the program code over time. This in itself is remarkable – commercial software companies rarely provide us with this kind of information. Openness about errors is an important layer of protection – another slice of the Swiss cheese.

As Jon found out, counting defects is hard. Each new version of a climate model contains many changes from the previous version. Some add new scientific capabilities or make the code run faster, while others fix errors. But it's not always clear which is which, and sometimes someone fixes an error in the code even though nobody reported a bug, perhaps because it was spotted while making other changes. To simplify things, Jon adopted a broad definition of defect as *any problem that was fixed* – whether anyone had reported it or not. This corresponds to a definition often used in the industry to distinguish defects – things that *have* to be fixed – from things that can be left as potential future improvements.

Jon's results surprised us all. The three climate models he assessed all had a defect density less than 1 defect per thousand lines of code – lower than all the comparison open source projects we assessed, and certainly lower than any commercial software reported in the literature. These results put climate models into the extremely high quality range, rivalling the quality of mission-critical flight code used in NASA's manned spacecraft, although more work is needed to confirm these results, and check whether they apply to other climate models.

If Jon's results are correct, there are several likely explanations. First, climate modellers are the experts, and tend to write all their own code, so they avoid the misunderstandings that occur when programmers have to talk to *other* experts to find out what the software is supposed to do. Second, climate models are run only within the climate science community, usually on the supercomputers they are designed for, so they avoid the kinds of error that show up when novice users try installing and running software on all sorts of different computers, with all sorts of bad data. Software is much more likely to crash if users do weird and wacky things with it.

I also think climate modellers are more cautious than other kinds of programmer, spending longer testing their code before releasing it. Because a climate model must run successfully for very long simulations, most defects in the program code will show up during such a run – the model crashes, or the simulation becomes unstable. Or the simulation is stable, but the results are scientifically implausible. Such errors may be hard to diagnose and fix, and will hold up the release of a new version of the model. But they also get in the way of doing the science, so there's no point releasing the model until they are fixed. In all the labs I visited, testing was a high priority, and I observed a huge number of different types of test being applied.

Jon's analysis is encouraging, as it shows all the effort spent tracking down errors pays off, and the strategies the modellers use to test their code work well. During my visits to Hamburg, I was able to see first-hand what those testing strategies look like.

Testing a New Model

Good testing strategies rely on a hierarchy of tests,[17] starting with simpler ones, and building up to the most sophisticated. In Hamburg, I met with Marco Giorgetta, the project leader for ICON, who told me that after nearly a decade of work, the dynamical core was complete, having passed a rigorous series of tests. Marco had just been given the go-ahead to hire eight more people, doubling the size of his team, to build a coupled model using this new icosahedral core. Building a new coupled model from scratch is a rare among the climate modelling labs, and given the amount of work involved, I can see why. To cut down on the effort, Marco's team use parts of the old model whenever they can – anything that doesn't depend on the grid geometry, such as the radiation code and the whole of the land surface model, JSBACH.

As we saw in Chapter 5, building a new dynamical core is hard. So is testing it. The full equations cannot be solved analytically – so there is no "correct solution" to use as a test case. Meanwhile comparison with observational data is hard to do until the coupled model is complete, once all the complexity of the real planet Earth has been included. So Marco's team uses two main strategies.[18] The first is to run simplified tests where the correct answer can be computed in advance, or where a reference solution is available in other published papers. Such tests include airflow over an isolated mountain, and the ability to simulate stable planetary waves – like the Rossby waves we met in Chapter 3.

The second strategy is to use the old atmosphere model, ECHAM, as a reference, running the same test in both models and comparing the results. That doesn't mean ECHAM is assumed to be correct. Rather, the idea is that differences in the two models should be *predictable*. If they disagree when they should agree, or vice versa, that's a clue there's an error in one of the models. The team supplement these with many other tests where subjective judgement is needed to figure out if the model gets the fine structure in the atmosphere correct, and that things happen in the right places.

During my visit, Marco walked me through one of the automated tests they use – the *baroclinic wave test*.[19] This sets up ICON for a dry atmosphere with a known steady state – one in which if no other disturbance occurs, the atmosphere would stay in that state indefinitely. The test then inserts a single disturbance in the wind in the Northern Hemisphere, which should lead to a predictable pattern of cyclones over a period of 10 days or so. The entire test runs for 30 simulated days, to see if the pressure waves propagate realistically. The test automatically compares the result with a standard solution, and reports any deviations, so it can be re-run every time changes are made to the model.

Hypothesis Testing

At the time of my visit, Marco's team were well into the next stage of testing, running the model for longer simulations as an aquaplanet – ocean everywhere and no continents. For these tests, the team add the physics code for convection and radiation to the dynamical core, and run the model with fixed sea-surface temperatures, to compare the results with a reference solution from ECHAM. While these tests are good at finding remaining errors in the numerical algorithms, they work more like a scientific experiment than a conventional software test, because they start with a hypothesis about how the atmospheric patterns in the ICON model should differ from ECHAM, due to differences in their designs. Running both models as an aquaplanet allows the team to test these hypotheses.

This hypothesis testing approach reminded me of something I had observed two years previously at the UK Met Office. Every run of the climate model is set up as a controlled experiment, with an earlier run of the same model – or a reference model – providing the control. In Exeter, every model run was documented in a kind of electronic lab notebook, or *validation note*. This records the purpose of the run and what results were expected (the hypothesis), and automatically produces a set of graphs and charts to visualize the model outputs, comparing the experimental version of the model with the reference version. If the experiment indicates that the hypothesis is correct – that the change really does improve the model – it still has to be reviewed by others at the lab before it can be accepted into the next release of the model.

A similar approach is used in all the labs I have visited. Modellers treat each change to the code as a controlled experiment, with a hypothesis about how a specific improvement to the model should affect the model's behaviour – even if the proposed change is only a few lines of code. They typically use an existing model as a control and compare the outputs of their experimental version against it to see if the hypothesis was correct. Other scientists at the lab then review these experiments, similar to how scientific papers are subject to peer review before they can be published. It's a slow, painstaking process, but it works.

The way climate models are built most closely resembles an approach in the software industry known as *agile development*.[20] In settings where customers don't yet know what they really need, or don't know what's possible, it's hard to make detailed project plans and specify in advance what the software must do. In such cases, it's best to start by building some simple prototypes, get users to try them, and then keep improving them in small steps, with lots of user feedback. In the past two decades, an entire "agile" methodology has grown up around this approach, emphasizing small teams that communicate well, and rejecting the reliance on detailed specifications and project plans.

Climate modellers have two huge advantages over the agile methods used in the software industry. First, they are their own users, so they avoid the communication difficulties that occur when people try to explain to programmers

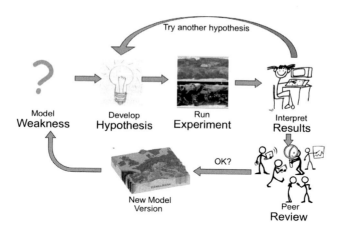

Figure 8.2 Hypothesis-driven software development. Each change to the model originates from studying a weakness in the model and creating a hypothesis for an improvement that would change the model in a specific way. The modellers then run experiments in the model to test this hypothesis, and their results are peer-reviewed by other scientists in the lab.

what they need. More importantly, treating each code change as a scientific experiment brings a lot more rigour to the process. Each lab I visited has developed tools to assist with this, and the tools make the modellers think more carefully about what they are trying to achieve – for example, by deciding in advance what to use as the reference case, and which variables they need to look at when comparing the models. In the agile development world, a similar strategy, known as Test-Driven Development[21] has the programmers write test cases in advance, before making any change to the code, to clarify their thinking about what they are trying to do. So I like to call the practice used in climate labs *Hypothesis-Driven Development*, as it has the same underlying philosophy (see Figure 8.2).

Reproducibility, Down to the Last Bit

When you make changes to a complex piece of software, there's always the possibility of introducing new errors. A change to the model might pass the hypothesis testing process I just described, but still introduce subtle errors elsewhere. Running full-scale simulations to (re-)test all the different model configurations takes a huge amount of computer time. So climate modellers use an automated early warning system to identify new errors.

A climate model runs the same code run over and over again for each grid point, at each timestep in the simulation. This means nearly every line of code is executed many times over during the first few timesteps of a simulation. If there are errors, they tend to show up early. So every night, overnight, an automated testing suite runs a few timesteps of each of a large number of different model configurations. If anyone introduces new code that breaks things, they'll usually find out when they arrive at work the next morning. In Hamburg, one of the application support scientists, Thomas Jahns, showed me how this works, via a tool called Buildbot – which is widely used across the software industry for this kind of automated testing.

Thomas and I also chatted about how these automated tests help ensure scientific reproducibility. If you make a change to the model, one of the most important questions to ask is whether the change alters the climate in the model – if you re-run a scientific experiment in a different version of the model, would you get the same results? As we saw in Chapter 4, chaos theory tells us that tiny differences eventually lead to very different states in the model. For climate science, this should not matter, as long as the overall patterns are the same – long-term statistics such as average rainfall and temperature, and the frequency of extreme weather. After all, the climate does not determine what weather we'll get on any specific day. But checking for this is expensive – you would need to run long simulations and check they are statistically similar.[22] This would tie up a lot of computing resources for a very long time.

Luckily, there's a clever shortcut. If you run two different versions of the model for just a few dozen timesteps, and the results are *exactly* identical, that's a good sign they won't diverge later on. These tests must look at every single *bit* – the ones and zeros used to store numbers in the machine. The match must be perfect, down to the last bit of every variable – hence these are known as *bit-comparison* tests. These tests are very fast, and can easily be automated and run every night, overnight.

Bit-comparison tests are used a lot in climate labs. One such test checks that if a run is interrupted and then restarted from the saved state, the results are identical to the uninterrupted run. Other tests check that different configurations of the model also produce identical results. This includes configurations that vary how many processors to use – for example, spreading the computation over a lot more nodes in the supercomputer – and configurations that change which diagnostic outputs the model produces.

It's also possible to use bit-comparison tests to check whether a new version of the model is still able to reproduce older runs. Most model improvements will fail to bit-reproduce, because that's the whole point – if the model is better at simulating some aspect of the climate, it won't be identical to the old version. But these types of improvement can be designed to be turned on or off, so the new version can still mimic the old model. A bit-comparison test then checks the new version of the model can still give identical results on old experiments.

The land surface team in Hamburg showed me an example of this in action. The land surface model, JSBACH, began life in 2002, when the team extracted the rudimentary land surface representation from the ECHAM atmosphere model, and developed it further by adding a detailed leaf model with photosynthesis. The new leaf model changes how water and energy are handled in the model. Water transport changes because of transpiration from the leaves, and the energy balance changes because evaporation from the leaf surfaces cools them down. The atmosphere team was nervous these changes would mess up the overall climate in ECHAM, so they asked that the entire leaf model be designed to be turned on or off, to test how it impacts the atmosphere.

Thomas and I also spent some time discussing the drawbacks of bit-comparison tests. First, they don't catch all errors – it's possible that further along in the simulation, a programming error messes things up. So they represent a kind of "minimum standard" a model must pass before other tests are done. But insisting that newer versions of the model must bit-compare with old versions also limits what kinds of change can be made. Big improvements to the way the Earth system is represented in the model will nearly always break this test, and it doesn't always make sense to have them "turn off."

Some labs I've visited use *double-call* tests in situations like this. For example, the atmosphere model might be set up to be coupled to both the old and the new version of the land surface scheme. At each timestep, outputs from the atmosphere model are fed to both the old and the new vegetation model, although data from only one of them would be fed back to the atmosphere. This allows a detailed comparison of how the old and new component react to the same atmospheric conditions.

Sometimes, maintaining bit reproducibility is impossible, for example, when there is a change of compiler, change of hardware, or optimizations that make the code run faster. The decision about whether to insist on bit repro-ducibility – from one version of the model to the next – is a difficult trade-off between flexibility and ease of testing. It also depends on when the change is being made. Thomas pointed out that while the lab is getting ready for IPCC runs, changes that break bit comparison wouldn't be allowed. But at other times, especially in the early stages of planning a major new release of a model, such changes would be acceptable, as long as there's a scientific justification.

Testing the Whole System

On one of my later visits to Hamburg, I met Christian Hovy, who wrote his entire PhD thesis[23] on how climate models are tested. Christian compared the testing strategies used in Hamburg with those used at other labs, including GFDL in Princeton, NJ, and two climate modelling labs in Japan. He found that all of the labs use similar approaches, and all make extensive use of automated tools for testing. But they varied a lot in how much they rely on any specific methods, like bit-reproducibility tests.

Christian's PhD thesis explores a surprising omission in the testing techniques used in climate modelling labs. For most software, the ideal testing strategy is to write automated tests for each routine in the program, which can be re-run whenever that part of the program has to be altered. This is known as *unit testing*, because it tests one program unit at a time, separately from the rest of the program. Climate modellers use very few of this kind of test, and Christian set out to find out why. One reason is that it's very hard to set up the input data needed for each routine within a climate model without running the entire model. Also, in many cases, it's not clear what the "correct" results should be for each unit in isolation from the rest of the model, because the ability to simulate a stable realistic climate is an emergent property of the entire model. Hence, climate modelling teams build up their models incrementally, relying primarily on end-to-end tests of the entire model at each stage. And instead of testing individual routines in isolation, they probe for correctness in other ways, using bit-reproducibility tests, and runs of simplified versions of the model, such as the aquaplanet setup.

In the end, the tests that matter most are integrated simulations over long timescales. For example, in Hamburg, the toughest test for the dynamical vegetation model is a millennium-scale simulation, starting with conditions as they were in 800 AD, to see whether the model reaches a realistic state for the twentieth century. The dynamic vegetation model doesn't simulate human activity – such as changes in farming and forestry – over that period of time, so it needs to be told how humans have altered the land during the thousand-plus years of the run. The model must correctly simulate how the climate and vegetation change in response. Comparison with observational data is tricky, because the model is designed to get the overall climate conditions right, but there is very little data on carbon and nitrogen fluxes at any specific site. So instead, the test focuses on whether the model correctly captures how vegetation patterns alter – for example, changes in the treeline and the growing season – when climate conditions change in different regions of the world.

Latent Errors

As with any software, testing can never eliminate errors completely. There is always a chance of undiscovered errors in the code, where the climate model runs and gives plausible results, but isn't doing what the modellers designed it to do. Such defects can only remain hidden if their effects are small, with no obvious disruptions in any of the output variables collected during a model run. But this makes them indistinguishable from the expected imperfections because the model is only an approximation of the real planet Earth.

This is well illustrated by one of the errors that the Max Planck teams missed during their extensive testing the year I visited in 2010. The previous generation of climate models simulated the observed warming of the planet over the last few decades reasonably well, but they all underestimated the impact of this warming on Arctic sea ice – the ice has melted faster than the models predicted. There are several possible reasons for this, the most likely of which is the simulated sea ice was too simplistic – usually represented as a single layer of ice, with no variation in thickness within each grid cell. So these models fail to simulate what happens when sea ice starts to melt. During the Arctic summer, the heat from the sun tends to melt the top of the ice surface. Some of the resulting water flows back into the sea, but some is trapped in *melt ponds* on the top of the ice. These melt ponds are darker than the white ice, so they absorb more of the sun's energy than the surrounding ice, creating a feedback effect – once a melt pond forms, the ice underneath it melts even faster.

Melt ponds are much smaller than the grid cells used in climate models, so their effects are usually captured in sea ice models by making a small overall adjustment to ice albedo when the ice is close to its melting point. But it's not that simple. Older ice – which has survived for multiple years – tends to be thicker and colder, and so less prone to melt ponds than newly formed ice from the most recent winter. Studies of the Arctic sea ice confirm this. Melt ponds on new ice tend to be shallower and broader, covering a wider area than melt ponds on old ice. This could explain why the models underestimated the loss of Arctic sea ice – as the planet warms, more of the old ice is lost, and the pattern of melt ponds changes. To test this hypothesis, the Max Planck team added a new parameterization for melt ponds into their model that takes into account how the depth and spread of ponds is affected by the age of the ice.

Unfortunately, a bug in the code meant that the new parameterization was ignored, so ice albedo was calculated in the model as though there were no melt ponds at all – and the bug was present for all their IPCC experiments. When the team later discovered this bug, they set about investigating the impact on their model runs. Using the buggy version of the model as a control, they fixed the errors and ran the model again with the same setup, to compare the effects.[24] Their experiments showed that with the melt ponds active, the Arctic sea ice does melt slightly faster in a warming world – although still not as fast as it has in reality. However, the overall effect on the rest of the climate system is negligible, so the bug doesn't invalidate other climate studies that use data from their model.

Small errors like this do occasionally slip through testing. But the way this is handled is important. When the modellers discover such errors, they run more experiments to analyze the impact, and publish the results so that the rest of the community will be aware of them. The journal paper[25] describing the official release of ECHAM6, describes the melt-pond error and its impact, along with several other small errors that were found after the IPCC runs were complete. Analyzing these mistakes – and sharing them with the community – adds another layer of the Swiss cheese by reducing the chance that such errors will lead to incorrect scientific conclusions.

Models and Truth

All this testing offers some confidence that the models are well-constructed, and that the modellers have a robust process for finding and investigating errors. But it still doesn't tell us whether climate models are scientifically valid. In other words, does a climate model represent the truth?

Computational models don't fit the traditional view of the scientific method taught in high schools. But the notion of a single "scientific method" is itself a myth.[26] The day-to-day work of scientists involves a variety of tools and approaches, with lots of dead-ends and mistakes, and only appears as a logical sequence from hypotheses to conclusions when written up afterwards.[27] Computational models are like other models scientists use as simplified versions of the world which they can study to gain insights on how the world really works.

It would be nice to be able to say a model is "true," and have a method for verifying this. But as the historian Naomi Oreskes pointed out in a widely cited paper[28] in 1994, no computational model can ever pass this test. In fact, the point holds more broadly – no scientific theory, model, or hypothesis can ever be proven true in this way, because the world is always more complex than our scientific explanations.

In the 1930s, the philosopher Karl Popper suggested good science should focus on trying to disprove – or *refute* – theories. Indeed, he argued a theory is only scientific if there is a critical test that *could* refute it. Each time an experiment or observation fails to disprove the theory, that increases our confidence in it. But only after a long process of failing to refute it do scientists accept a theory as correct. Today, most scientists follow some version of this approach.[29]

A strict interpretation of Popper would have us throw out any scientific theory as soon as we encounter a situation it doesn't work for. So, technically speaking, we should have thrown out Newton's Laws when astronomers noticed things they couldn't explain – like the anomalies in the orbit of planet Mercury that were later explained by Einstein's theory of relativity.[30] Today, Newton's Laws are still regarded as true – *even though Einstein refuted them* – because they explain how forces such as gravity work in *nearly* all cases. So scientific theories are like computational models – they simplify things, but don't always work in all situations.

If Popper's approach doesn't guarantee truth, what distinguishes (good) science from just making things up – that is, *pseudoscience*? The Hungarian philosopher Imre Lakatos tackled this question by focusing on entire programmes of research, rather than individual theories.[31] To Lakatos, a programme of research is scientific if it is making progress by generating novel predictions from its theories, and having those predictions confirmed by observation. A field that is not able to do this is regressing – encountering more and more difficulty in applying its theories to the world.

Lakatos observed that in any given field of study, there is a core body of theory accepted as correct, and hence not open to the kind of refutation Popper advocated. Around these core theories are a set of ancillary hypotheses that help to connect the core theories to things we can observe in the real world. These ancillary hypotheses are treated as tentative, and can be adjusted – or replaced – if the evidence refutes them. A scientific field can make progress by adjusting these ancillary hypotheses so that the core body of theory can explain more and more observed behaviours of the world. For example, Newton's laws don't tell you directly how the planets will move, but his laws can be used to develop methods to predict their orbits. If any of these predictions fail, we adjust *how* we're using Newton's Laws rather than throwing out the laws altogether.

This means all scientific knowledge is, to varying degrees, *contingent*. New evidence may come along that requires scientists to adjust their theories, and they tend to do this not by discarding the core theories, but by adjusting how theories are interpreted and applied. Lakatos's approach says as long as we can keep doing this to expand the set of things we can successfully explain and predict, we are doing science. But if the contradictory evidence starts to outweigh the things that can be explained by the theory, the field should no longer be considered scientific. In such cases, a new set of core theories may emerge to explain more of this contradictory evidence.

Lakatos's view matches what I observed in the climate modelling labs I visited. Some parts of a climate model – most notably, the dynamical core and the physics of radiation – are fully understood, thoroughly tested, and accepted as correct. These parts of the model are based on well-established physical laws, and are trusted because we know these laws work well at the scales of time and space that the models operate.

Other parts of the model are more tentative, especially the *parameterizations* of processes that happen on smaller scales than the model grid – things like clouds, convection currents, and the melt ponds we met earlier in this chapter. These cannot be simulated directly, either because of computational limits, or because they are not yet sufficiently understood. So instead, parameterizations capture the average effect of these processes under different conditions in the model. Parameterizations play the role of ancillary hypotheses, to be confirmed or refuted by comparing them with real-world data. Most of the ongoing work in climate modelling labs focuses on improving these parameterizations. And all the while, the field can be seen to be progressing, because the set of successful predictions from climate models continues to grow.

Model Tuning

Choosing the values for model parameters is difficult, and requires some subjective judgment. Ideally, values for these parameters should be determined from observations, but they are often things that are hard to measure with any certainty. Sometimes all we have is a statistical analysis of the range of likely values. *Cloud fraction* in each grid cell is a good example – it's needed when calculating how much of the sun's radiation is absorbed by the atmosphere. But cloud fraction depends on many different things going on in a grid cell – humidity and temperature certainly, but also convection currents, dust particles, and so on. There is no obvious way to calculate it, and reliable measurements of all these factors are hard to come by.

As is often the case at the leading edge of a scientific field, a lot of trial and error is needed to pick good values for these uncertain parameters. Climate modellers call this *model tuning,* although statisticians more commonly call it *parameter estimation.*[32] You could also think of it as calibration, like setting the zero point on your bathroom scales. As we saw in Chapter 7, parameter choices that work in an ocean or atmosphere model running on its own might not work when you couple the model components together, because model tuning also compensates for things still missing from the model. Take, for example, the ocean chlorophyll scheme in the Max Planck models. Chlorophyll exists in the ocean in plankton and algae. It absorbs carbon dioxide and produces oxygen through photosynthesis. Older versions of the ocean model didn't calculate how much chlorophyll there would be in each ocean grid cell, so its overall effects were accounted for by *tuning* other parameters to compensate.

Adding a dynamic calculation of ocean chlorophyll *should* improve the model. But it's rarely that simple. In Hamburg, Helmuth Haak told me that when they added the new chlorophyll scheme, it worked fine in the standalone ocean model. But in the high resolution coupled model, it slowed the ocean overturning circulation, creating regions that were too cool over Europe and the Northern Pacific. Tracking down why this happened was hard.

In principle, it's possible to *over-tune* a climate model, continually adjusting all the parameters until the model perfectly matches a specific set of historical observations – say, observed surface temperatures over the twentieth century. But doing this makes no sense, because overfitting to one set of observations will decrease the model's skill at reproducing other observed climates, such as the pre-industrial era, or ice age climates. It's also impossibly hard, because the parameters interact, and their connection with the overall behaviour of the model is incredibly complex. The number of experiments you would have to run to find the optimal combination of parameters would be huge.

So instead, most modelling centres do a limited amount of tuning to satisfy one or two specific goals, and document how they do this, so it can be taken into account when comparing models. Most often, the chosen goal is to get the correct energy balance at the top of the atmosphere or the correct average surface temperature for a historical period when the climate was stable. And they do this only for a handful of parameters, most often those relating to clouds and albedo, as these have the biggest uncertainty ranges. Increasingly, modellers use an approach known as *Uncertainty Quantification*, which seeks to measure each source of uncertainty in the model, to guide the choice of parameters.[33]

For Helmuth's problem with the ocean chlorophyll, it seemed likely one of the ocean parameters needed to be adjusted for the coupled model. By reasoning about what connects chlorophyll to ocean temperatures, and running a number of experiments, Helmuth tracked it down to the parameter for how deeply sunlight penetrates in ocean – known as *shortwave attenuation* – which plays a similar role to cloud parameters in the atmosphere, and is just as hard to measure with any certainty. Helmuth told me the most important part of this was to document his decision process in tuning this parameter, so that other scientists can see what he did, and evaluate its validity.

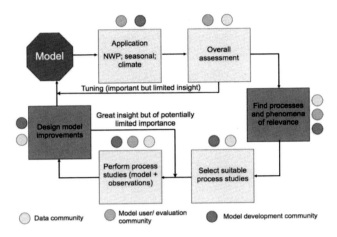

Figure 8.3 Model improvement process. (Reproduced from Jakob (2010). © American Meteorological Society. Used with permission.)

Another way of looking at model tuning is that it helps pin down the remaining sources of uncertainty in climate models, guiding the research community to areas where more research is needed. Since the early 2000s, this work has been organized around Climate Process Teams, which bring together climate scientists from different labs for a focused campaign to assess a specific source of uncertainty in the models, and to collect data to help improve the relevant model parameterizations. Coincidentally, I first learned about climate process teams while I was in Hamburg, in the coffee room one day, when I bumped into Christian Jakob, a visiting researcher from Monash University in Australia. Christian had just published an essay[34] setting out a vision for accelerating model improvements, which captured some of my own observations on the process of model improvement (see Figure 8.3).

Predicting the Future

In Chapter 4, we noted that climate scientists don't actually build their models to predict the future, but rather to understand the past and present. But the models *can* make predictions, and one of the biggest sources of confidence in climate models is that their predictions keep turning out to be correct. Sometimes we have to wait for many decades before such predictions are confirmed by observations. In many cases, the predictions were also warnings that were never acted on – much of the damage now being caused by climate change could have been avoided if we had developed climate policies based on the early models.

The oldest successful climate model predictions are, of course, from Svante Arrhenius, in 1894. As we saw in Chapter 2, his model predicted the climate would warm in response to humans burning fossil fuels. And despite errors in his data and flaws in his model, he was able to correctly predict the poles would warm faster than the tropics,[35] the land would warm faster than the oceans, and nighttime temperatures would rise faster than daytime. Arrhenius also correctly predicted that reduced carbon dioxide caused most of the global change in temperature during the ice ages, although it was nearly a century before this was confirmed by analyzing bubbles of air trapped in ancient Antarctic ice.

One of the most important predictions from climate models is that rising greenhouse gases will warm the lower atmosphere and cool the stratosphere. This pattern shows up in all modern climate models, and was first noted by Manabe and Wetherald in 1967, in their original single-column model, which we met in Chapter 6. Manabe and Wetherald's model was the first to capture in detail the vertical structure[36] of the atmosphere under greenhouse gas warming. If carbon dioxide slows the rate at which heat from the surface passes up through the atmosphere, the warming in the lower atmosphere must be accompanied by cooling in the upper atmosphere – because the upper atmosphere still loses heat to space, but now receives less from below. Manabe and Wetherald's model predicted this cooling would start at about 20–25 km above the surface, and would be more pronounced at around 40 km. The model also predicted that the stratospheric cooling would be much bigger than the corresponding surface warming.[37]

The prediction of stratospheric cooling is important, because it distinguishes greenhouse gas warming from other possible explanations for global warming. For example, if global warming was caused by the sun, we would see warming in all levels of the atmosphere. But at the time of Manabe and Wetherald's work, there were no reliable long-term measurements of the stratosphere to confirm their prediction. And indeed, for several decades, attempts to assess stratospheric temperatures from satellite data seemed to show no change at all. This apparent failure of prediction led some skeptics to dismiss climate models entirely.

Checking this prediction was complicated because in the 1980s, the ozone layer in the lower stratosphere was thinning – due to pollutants such as chlorofluorocarbons[38] (CFCs) – leading to an "ozone hole" over the Antarctic each winter. Loss of ozone *also* cools the stratosphere, because less ultraviolet light from the sun is absorbed in the ozone layer, although this cooling occurs lower – at the bottom of the stratosphere, at around 20 km. In 1987, the UN's Montreal Protocol regulated the use of CFCs, leading to a measurable recovery[39] in the ozone layer by the mid-1990s. So the stratospheric cooling predicted by climate models wasn't confirmed until the early 2000s, once a long enough record of stratospheric temperatures had been collected, and newer satellite instruments were better able to distinguish changing temperatures at different heights.[40]

Climate models also correctly predict what happens when a major volcano erupts. Active volcanoes spew clouds of ash and sulphur dioxide, and the winds spread these widely across the planet. The ash tends to wash out within a few months, but the sulphur dioxide remains for several years. Both block incoming sunlight, so major volcanoes cool the planet slightly, for 2–3 years after they erupt. A climate model cannot predict *when* a volcano will erupt, but if you add an artificial volcano to the model – by including a short burst of ash and SO_2 – the model shows exactly the kind of cooling observed from real volcanoes.

Simulating the Past

Interestingly, volcanic eruptions offer another important test for climate models. When the planet warms from increasing CO_2, it triggers a feedback effect, as warmer air holds more moisture, and water vapour is also an important greenhouse gas. This amplifies any warming, so getting the feedback effect right is important for accurate predictions of climate change. With volcanoes, you get the same effect in reverse. The cooling from volcanoes reduces the amount of moisture in the air, triggering a feedback that cools the planet even more. In the late 1990s, at GFDL, Brian Soden and colleagues ran a simulation[41] in their model to see if it would match the water vapour feedback effect seen after the 1991 eruption of Mount Pinatubo in the Philippines, one of the largest volcanic eruptions of the twentieth century. Global cooling from Mount Pinatubo lasted for about three years, as can be seen in Figure 8.4. Not only did the GFDL model get the overall amount of cooling correct, but the decrease in water vapour was correct too, matching measurements from satellites.

Hindcasts like this help to answer the question we began with at the beginning of this book – how accurate are climate models? But each run of a climate model only shows one possible pathway through the chaotic system that is the Earth's climate system. You need to run a model many times over to understand the full range of its behaviour. Such an *ensemble* of runs allows modellers to ignore any specific weather patterns in their simulations, and focus instead on the average of all the weather – that is, the climate. Each run uses the same settings, but starts from a different initial state. The Max Planck team has recently created the largest of these ensembles.[42] It consists of 100 runs of the model using known *forcings* – changes in greenhouse gases and other factors that cause the climate to change – to simulate the years 1850–2005. Each run was initialized using a different year from the spin-up run, and they have added several different scenarios for the future to extend these runs over the years 2006–2099. In total, the ensemble includes more than 60,000 simulated years.[43] Such an ensemble takes a huge amount of computational time, but provides a sophisticated way of comparing the model to reality – does the average of all of these runs match the average observed temperature over the last 150 years?

Figure 8.4 shows how this looks. The red line is the observed average global surface temperature, and the black line is the average of the Max

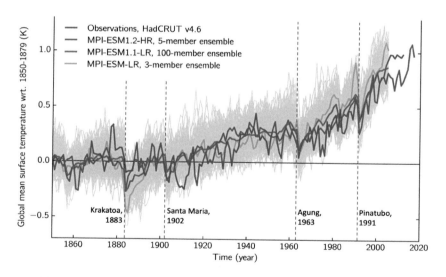

Figure 8.4 Historical simulations of three versions of the Max Planck Institute's Earth System Model for the period 1850–2005, compared with the surface temperature record, HadCRUT,[44] which is shown in red. Each model was run multiple times, from different initial states, to produce an ensemble of runs. Each individual run gives one thin grey line, while the average for each ensemble is shown as the thicker coloured line. Major volcanic eruptions of this period are marked with vertical dashed lines. (Adapted from Mauritsen et al. (2019). Used with permission.)

Planck large ensemble. The other coloured lines show the results of two, smaller ensembles using different versions of the model.[45] Thin grey lines show each individual run. The warming from increasing carbon dioxide over the twentieth century can clearly be seen in both the temperature record and the models, as can the short-term cooling effect of major volcanoes. Notice, however, the simulations all over-react to the eruption of Krakatoa in 1883 – the models start from a state with no background volcanic activity, so Krakatoa represents the first major injection of volcanic aerosols into the models. In reality, regular eruptions of smaller volcanoes mean there is always some volcanic ash in the atmosphere.

Getting It Right

Accurate hindcasts still don't guarantee accurate predictions. While weather forecasters can check how well they did every day, climate modellers have to wait a long time to test their predictions. By now, enough time has elapsed since the early climate models in the 1970s and 1980s to assess their predictions over the last 30 years, and it turns out most of them did very well indeed, especially considering how simplified they were. For example, in Manabe's original climate change experiments in 1967, which we met in Chapter 6, he predicted a temperature rise of about 0.8°C by the year 2000, assuming a 25% increase in CO_2 over the course of the twentieth century. Manabe's assumption about the rate that CO_2 would increase was almost spot on, and so was his calculation for the resulting temperature rise.[46]

One of the most famous projections of climate change among these early models was produced by Jim Hansen in 1988. At the time, Hansen was the director of NASA's Goddard Institute for Space Studies. Amid growing political concern about climate change, Hansen was invited to testify to the US Congress in the summer of 1988, which was, at the time, the hottest year on record. In the middle of a sweltering heatwave, Hansen told Congress "It is time to stop waffling so much and say that the evidence is pretty strong that the greenhouse effect is here." He presented to congress three projections of climate change from NASA's model, based on three different scenarios for greenhouse gas emissions, as shown in Figure 8.5. The dashed vertical line marks 1988, so the model projections to the right of this are his prediction. Note that today, climate scientists would use an ensemble of runs, to smooth out year-to-year variability, like the analysis in Figure 8.4. At the time, however, computers weren't powerful enough to make ensemble runs feasible.

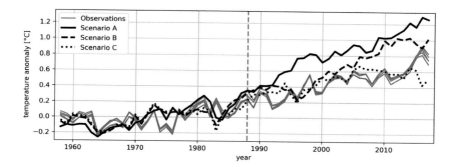

Figure 8.5 Comparison of Hansen's 1988 model projections with 30 years of observational data. The blue lines are annual average global surface temperatures from five different datasets. The three black lines are Hansen's model runs, under three different scenarios for greenhouse gas emissions. Scenario A assumed much higher growth in CO_2 levels than occurred in reality, and as a consequence, substantially overestimates the warming. (Reproduced from Hausfather et al. (2020). Used with permission.)

At first sight, it looks like Hansen's scenario C was a fairly accurate projection. But we should dig deeper.[47] A climate model can only give an accurate prediction of climate change if it's given the right forcings. In Hansen's experiments, scenarios A and B included a projected rise in CO_2 that matches almost exactly what happened, while scenario C had CO_2 levels stabilize from the year 2000, which of course didn't happen. But scenario A greatly overestimated the rise in other greenhouse gases, such as methane and CFCs – the latter of which did indeed start to fall in the 1990s, in response to the Montreal protocol. Over the 30-year period, scenario A represents almost double the total greenhouse forcing compared to what actually happened, while the true forcings were somewhere between scenarios B and C.

Volcanic eruptions also matter. Hansen's model could not have predicted the eruption of Mount Pinatubo in 1991, which shows up clearly in the observations, nor the abnormally large El Niño year in 1998, which shows up as a spike in the observations. However, he did include a large volcanic eruption in 1995 in scenarios B and C, which is why these two model runs show a large dip in temperature in the mid-1990s. And in the 2000s, the correspondence between observations and scenario C is somewhat of a coincidence, as the model is responding to a flattening of the curve of greenhouse gas emissions, while the slower warming in the observations is largely due to a shift in ocean currents. Coupled climate models often produce such multi-year shifts, but cannot predict *when* they will occur.[48]

Better than Data

There's a proverb, often attributed to the Swiss army, which says "When the map and the terrain disagree, believe the terrain." Or, in our case, if the models and data disagree, believe the data. However, many of the climate scientists I've spoken to tell me nowadays, when the models and data disagree, it's often the data that turn out to be wrong. This seems counter-intuitive, until you consider how global climate data are put together.

An example will help. In the 1990s and early 2000s, climate scientists were unable to explain a dramatic drop in global surface temperatures in August 1945, which appeared to put a sudden end to several decades of warming (see Figure 8.6). The temperature drop in 1945 could not be explained as the result of a volcanic eruption, and could not be reproduced in any of the climate models. Nor was it associated with any known patterns such as El Niño, which releases heat stored in the oceans in some years, making the land surface warmer. Initial hypotheses focused on the nuclear bombs dropped on Hiroshima and Nagasaki that summer, but analysis showed these deadly explosions did not affect global temperatures.

The puzzle was finally solved in 2008 by David Thompson from Colorado State University, while he was on sabbatical in the United Kingdom, visiting the lab that compiled the dataset. Most climate scientists thought there must be a missing physical cause for the sudden cooling, but Thompson wondered if the problem was how the data was collected. He noticed the cooling only affected the oceans. Up until the late twentieth century, most sea surface temperatures were collected by ships, so he set about quizzing shipping experts. The crew of each ship would measure the temperature of the water they were moving through, and record the result – with time, date, and location – in the ship's log. After the voyage, readings from the ship's logs would be collated to build an overall picture of ocean temperatures.

Traditionally, this meant a sailor had to throw a bucket over the side, draw up some water, and insert a thermometer. By mid-century, however, many ships had started measuring water temperature at the engine room intakes, where it is used to cool the engines. The problem is that the two methods give different results – bucket readings tend to be cooler, as the water cools in the bucket before the temperature is read. To make matters worse, some ships used insulated buckets and others didn't. Thompson realized that over the course of the war, European shipping largely came to a halt, and more than 80% of the wartime data was provided by US ships alone, almost all of which used the engine intake method. At the end of the war, British merchant shipping resumed, contributing almost half the readings over the rest of the decade.

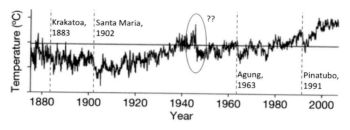

Figure 8.6 An early version (v3) of the HadCRUT temperature record, after removing multi-year variabilities such as the El Niño Southern Oscillation (ENSO). The vertical dashed lines show the major volcanic eruptions shown over this period. (Adapted from Thompson et al. (2008). Used by permission of Springer Nature.)

And British ships still used buckets. If you correct for the type of shipping, the temperature drop disappears entirely. The models were correct – it was the data that were wrong.

As well as temperature data collected on the ground and ocean, we also have measurements of temperatures higher in the atmosphere, from two sources. The first of these are *radiosondes* – instruments such as thermometers – attached to weather balloons, released once or twice a day in different parts of the world. The second is satellites, which cannot measure the temperature of the atmosphere directly, but can measure microwave radiation emitted by oxygen in the atmosphere, from which the temperature of a cross-section of the atmosphere can be calculated. Satellites with these *microwave sounding units* were first launched in 1979.

In the mid-1990s, two scientists from the University of Alabama in Huntsville (UAH), John Christy and Roy Spencer, published an analysis of the first 15 years of this satellite data, showing that the lower atmosphere – up to about 8 km – appeared to have cooled over this time rather than warmed. This contradicted the models, which showed greenhouse gas warming would heat the lower atmosphere, while cooling the stratosphere. Worse still, Christy and Spencer found no evidence of any stratospheric cooling either. Both scientists were fêted by those who didn't believe in climate change, and regularly invited by right-wing politicians to testify in the US congress, whenever climate policy was up for debate. The implication was clear – satellites can't lie, so the models must be wrong.

However, these satellites were never designed to provide long-term temperature records, and suffer from a number of problems that make it hard to compare temperatures over time. In order to measure a change in temperature, you have to decide what baseline to use for comparison, and Christy and Spencer had chosen a particularly warm baseline. But that's not all. Over the years, satellites lose altitude as they slow in their orbits, and their orbits tend to drift laterally – to the east or west – which messes up the timing of their measurements with respect to the Earth below. Satellite measurements have to be adjusted for these problems. When other research groups attempted to replicate Christy and Spencer's work, they found many errors in how these adjustments had been applied, as well as a blending of temperature trends from different heights that cancelled each other out. Over the decade after their original paper, the pair published a series of corrections to their dataset,[49] which gradually revised the temperature trend upwards, until it eventually agreed with the trends predicted by the models.

Pause for Thought?

Data errors are also partially responsible for a widespread belief in the mid-2010s that global warming had stopped completely over the previous 15 years, despite the models predicting a steady increase. After a particularly hot year in 1998, driven by a release of stored ocean heat in an unusually strong El Niño, temperatures over the next decade seemed to settle down, with nothing to rival the record-shattering year of 1998. Climate scientists generally don't regard any trend over the period of a decade or shorter as significant, because multi-year variability – the fluctuations shown in Figures 8.4, 8.5, and 8.6 – bring short-term temperature swings that are much larger than any short-term warming trend.

Climate change skeptics showed no such reticence, and headlines such as "Global Warming Over" started appearing in newspapers before the end of the decade. By 2014, some climate scientists were also acknowledging an apparent pause – or "hiatus" – in the warming trend, and reasons for it were discussed at length in the IPCC assessment reports released that year. Over the next few years, more than 200 scientific papers[50] were published that discussed some aspect of this hiatus.

But it turns out climate change didn't pause after all. Only one dataset at the time – the HadCRUT surface temperature record – showed flat temperatures over the 15 year period from 1998. A sharp eyed statistician might immediately be suspicious of the choice of a particularly warm year, 1998, as the starting point for a trend analysis, and indeed several statisticians at the time pointed out that focusing on this year in particular is a kind of selection bias. And the additional heat from climate change doesn't just show up at the surface – the oceans and lower atmosphere heat up too, so a surface temperature record only shows part of the picture. But these weren't the only problems.

Surface temperature records are pieced together from weather monitoring stations all over the world, along with the ocean temperatures record from ships and buoys. This data doesn't match the regular, gridded data points in the models, nor does it cover the world evenly, as there are a lot more data from some parts of the world than others – the Arctic, for example, has very few surface monitoring stations. So the data must be processed to make sure areas of equal size contribute equally to the overall average – through a process of *spatial averaging*.

Complicating matters further, most of this data is collected by meteorologists, to use in weather forecasting. Weather forecasters generally don't worry about long-term data consistency, so it doesn't matter much if some of their instruments drift out of calibration over the years, or fail and get replaced by a different instrument, or end up getting moved from one site to another. But to a climate scientist, consistent measurement over time is crucial. So to compile consistent long-term records, all sorts of corrections are needed in the data.[51] For example, one technique compares each weather station with its neighbours, so sudden changes or long-term drifts that don't show up in neighbouring stations can be detected and corrected. Compiling these consistent long-term datasets is difficult and time consuming.[52]

So surface temperature records compiled by different teams differ slightly from one another, depending on what sources of data they used, and how they processed them to remove errors and fill gaps. It turns out older versions of the HadCRUT dataset did a poor job of filling in missing data from the poles, where there are very few direct measurements to rely on. And yet the poles have been warming at a much higher rate than the rest of the planet. So if you omit them, you miss a lot of the recent warming. A major update of the HadCRUT dataset in 2012 partially corrected this, showing temperatures had indeed been rising over the previous decade. And then, in 2020, a further update did a much better job of correcting for the missing Arctic measurements, and showed there was a significant warming trend throughout the period after all (see Figure 8.7).

These corrections bring the observational data much closer to the model projections for the 2000s and 2010s, although the observed surface warming was still slower than the models had predicted. Two additional factors explain this gap. One is that there was a lot more volcanic activity in this period than were included in the models. The second is to do with how heat moves around in the Pacific Ocean. If you initialize the models from the state of the ocean in the 1990s, and run a decadal simulation, the models do indeed match the observed rate of surface warming.[53]

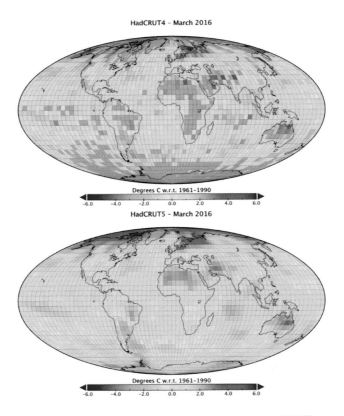

Figure 8.7 An example of gaps in the older versions of the HadCRUT temperature data for one particular month, March 2016. The top image shows missing data as grey cells in HadCRUT4. The lower image shows how these were filled in using statistical techniques for HadCRUT5. Note the prevalence of warmer, red cells in the infilled data. (Reproduced with permission from Carbon Brief)

Model Intercomparison

Climate models go through a rigorous testing process, and are regularly compared with data from the past to assess their accuracy. The models often help scientists find errors in this observational data, and predictions from the models have largely proven to be correct. But there is one more crucial test any scientific work must pass: Can scientists from other labs reproduce the results?

In the early days of climate modelling, this wasn't possible. As we saw in Chapter 1, the first systematic attempt to compare climate models from different labs was the Charney Report in 1978. Charney asked two different modelling teams to run the same climate sensitivity experiment in several of their models, and to provide him not just with the results, but with a description of the design choices they had made. The result was far more valuable than any one experiment. It was a detailed analysis of how differences in the models affected their results. The models agreed the planet would warm in response to a doubling of CO_2, but they disagreed on precisely how much.[54] And the main source of disagreement was how feedback effects were captured in the models – especially cloud feedbacks.

As more modelling groups developed Global Circulation Models in the 1980s, such comparisons became harder. Most centres didn't have fast enough computers to run the long simulations needed for climate sensitivity experiments. The models also differed in which parts of the climate system they simulated, and how they were initialized. But demand for a more coherent approach was growing. In 1988, amidst a wave of alarm about the implications of climate change, the United Nations created[55] a new international body, the IPCC, to assess the research on climate change and to publish regular reports that could guide policymaking.

For the IPCC's first assessment report, published in 1990, one of the lead authors, Robert Cess, came up with a way to replicate Charney's assessment, without the need for very long simulations.[56] In a normal climate sensitivity experiment, you change the amount of CO_2 in the atmosphere, and let the model run until surface temperatures stabilize again. Cess's experiment reverses this. He created three sets of sea surface temperature data – one that mimicked modern day temperatures, one that was consistently warmer by 2°C and one cooler by 2°C. He invited 12 different climate modelling labs in seven different countries – United States, Canada, United Kingdom, France, Germany, China, and Japan – to use these in their models[57] and report the resulting energy imbalance at the top of the atmosphere. Cess also asked the teams to run each experiment twice – once with a clear sky (no clouds), and once for normal cloudiness, so the size of the cloud feedback could also be compared.

Cess's experiment asks the climate change question backwards – how big an energy imbalance[58] does a surface temperature difference of 2°C (or 4°C) correct for? The results showed the models largely agreed for their clear-sky experiments, but disagreed widely for cloudy skies, confirming Charney's observation that clouds were the biggest source of disagreement. Today's models agree about many aspects of climate change, but they still disagree about the size of the cloud feedback in response to CO_2 warming.

While Cess's experiment was valuable, it lacked a crucial ingredient – nobody outside each modelling lab could see what was happening in the models during the runs. So the World Climate Research Programme (WCRP) brought together lead modellers from different centres for a workshop at NCAR in August 1989 to brainstorm other ways of comparing models. They realized what they needed were standardized experiments that could run on any model, with a required list of outputs to be collected from the models. These outputs would then be made freely available so that the entire research community could study them.

The first project to take this approach was the Atmosphere Model Intercomparison Project (AMIP), launched in 1992. AMIP used Cess's idea of prescribing sea surface temperatures. The experiment focused on a recent decade, 1979–1988, for which excellent observational data was available, and provided a gridded dataset of daily sea surface temperatures and sea ice distributions. Each participating centre was asked to report the values for 39 specific variables in the models, at both 6-hourly intervals and as monthly averages[59] – a detailed account of what happened in each model during the run.

The idea was a huge success, and very soon, other model intercomparison projects were established. A paleoclimate project (PMIP) coordinated by IPSL in Paris asked modelling groups to run their atmosphere models to simulate the climate conditions of the mid-Holocene (6,000 years ago) and the peak of the last ice age (21,000 years ago). And a seasonal prediction intercomparison project (SMIP) explored how well the models simulated seasonal patterns – such as monsoons – when started from observed sea surface temperature data. Today, there are more than 40 active model intercomparison projects underway around the world, and another 30 or so that have completed their work.[60]

The Biggest Experiment

By far the most ambitious of these projects are the Coupled Model Intercomparison Projects (CMIPs) – the experiments that Reinhard and the team were preparing for when I first visited Hamburg. The first CMIP launched in 1996, and involved 21 different coupled models from around the world – every coupled model that existed at the time.[61] CMIP1 asked each team to simulate a steady-state climate, to investigate the impact of flux corrections, which about half the models at the time were still using. CMIP2 then asked them to run a climate change scenario with carbon dioxide increasing by 1% per year. Initially, the project only captured a small selection of data from the model runs, mainly focusing on monthly means. But capabilities for storing and sharing the data over the web were improving steadily, so some of the modelling groups re-ran their experiments and shared every single variable from every single component of their models.

By 2003, when planning started for the IPCC's fourth assessment report, it was clear that model intercomparison projects were crucial to evaluate the models and analyze their results, and CMIP3 was scaled up accordingly. The project defined 12 different experiments, including a simulation of the twentieth century, three different scenarios for future climate change up to 2100, extensions of these to the year 2200 with constant conditions, and a doubled CO_2 experiment. Seventeen modelling groups took part, with a total of 23 different models, yielding more than 30 terabytes of data. Each group submitted their data by sending disks in the mail, as internet upload speeds were too slow at the time. This data was then shared freely, and scientists around the world published more than 200 papers based on analysis of this data.

The scale of the CMIP[62] projects has grown remarkably since then. CMIP6, which is currently underway (in the early 2020s) involves 49 climate modelling labs, with more than 100 different models, 287 different experiments, and will collect an anticipated 50 petabytes of data from all the model runs.[63] The CMIP projects are now so big that most labs cannot run every experiment, so there is a minimum set of experiments that every participating team must run. CMIP6 includes five benchmark experiments that all participating models must run.[64] The remaining experiments are coordinated by a federated set of 21 more specific model intercomparison projects, shown in Figure 8.8.

When they have completed their runs, each modelling centre submits its data to a distributed data storage system called the Earth System Grid Federation,[65] which makes it easier for anyone to find and download this data for free. Scientists around the world spend years analyzing the results, comparing performance of the models, discussing findings at conferences and workshops, and publishing their analysis. These papers then form an important source of evidence about the science of climate change for the IPCC reports, alongside observational studies, studies of paleoclimate data, and so on.

The IPCC assessment reports themselves take a huge amount of work. The IPCC produces a new set of assessment reports approximately every 6–7 years, which evaluate and summarize all the latest climate science. The reports are published in three massive volumes – each well over a thousand densely packed pages – plus a shorter summary for policymakers. Hundreds of scientists contribute to the writing process, and being picked to join one of the writing teams is considered a huge honour. None of the scientists are paid to do it, and they fit the writing effort around their regular jobs in universities and research labs.[66] It takes several years to complete each assessment report, with drafts circulated for expert review, while the summary for policymakers is subjected to line-by-line review and approval by governments around the world.

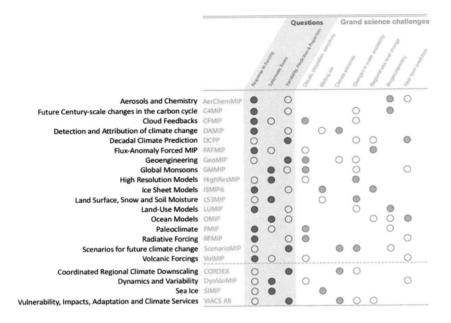

Figure 8.8 The 21 federated model intercomparison projects of CMIP6. The first three columns are the three key scientific questions for CMIP6 ("How does the Earth system respond to forcing? What are the origins and consequences of systematic model biases? How can we assess future climate change given internal climate variability, climate predictability, and uncertainties in scenarios?"). The remaining columns correspond to seven grand science challenges from the World Climate Research Programme, where greater understanding is needed. (Reproduced from Eyring (2016). CC-BY 4.0.)

To maintain the integrity of the assessment reports, the author teams can only refer to work already published in the peer-reviewed literature,[67] and there are strict deadlines for when papers have to be published in order to be included. Naturally, this leads to a busy few months in the climate science community as scientists scramble to get their work published by the deadline so it can be included in the assessment reports.

All the Latest Science

It is a matter of pride for each climate modelling centre to ensure data from their models contributes to the IPCC reports. But to do that, their data has to be ready long before the IPCC's publication deadline. So the CMIP project sets a much earlier deadline by which each climate modelling team must complete their experiments and submit the results to the Earth System Grid. The modelling teams are highly motivated to use their latest and best models for these experiments, to show the broader community what they can do, even though the simplest way to get the runs done would be to use an older, lower resolution, more stable model.

None of the labs I've visited take the easy way out, hence the scramble I witnessed to get the newest models ready during my first visit to Hamburg, an experience that was repeated at each of the other labs I visited that year. So the IPCC assessments induce a (roughly) seven-year rhythm on the work of climate modelling labs, as each lab strives to prepare a new, state-of-the-art version of their model in time for each CMIP. As well as spending nearly a year planning and completing all the CMIP experiments, the labs then spend another year or two publishing papers that describe the design of their latest model and assessing its capabilities.

Publishing papers to document each new release of a model is now standard practice in climate modelling, and the field has at least two peer-reviewed journals[68] dedicated to this. In the 1970s and 1980s a single paper would suffice to announce a new model, but nowadays the models are so complex it takes a whole set of papers. The work I observed in Hamburg during my visit eventually led to a set of 20 papers – describing each component of the models in detail – published in a special issue of the Journal of Advances in Modelling Earth Systems in 2013. These papers are an important source for scientists who want to analyze the data from these models, to understand how the models were designed.

Model Intercomparison Projects bring a number of important benefits to the modelling community. They bring the community together with a common purpose, and hence increase awareness and collaboration between different labs. More importantly, they require the participants to reach a consensus on a standard set of model scenarios, which often entails some deep thinking about what the models ought to be able to do. Likewise, they require the participants to define a set of standard evaluation criteria, which then act as benchmarks for evaluating the strength and weaknesses of each model. Finally, they also produce a consistent body of data representing a large ensemble of model runs, which is available for the broader community to analyze. This approach is not unique to climate modelling – other fields of computational science such as bioinformatics[69] use a similar approach, although none do it on quite the same scale as the climate modelling community. Quite simply, CMIP is the largest internationally coordinated computational experiment ever conducted in any branch of science.

The Best Model Is All the Models

Despite all these successes, all the climate scientists I have spoken to will readily agree that each model still has many weaknesses – things they get wrong, and things they miss out altogether. The IPCC's fifth assessment report has a long list of examples. Some models show an anomalous and persistent band of rain across the Pacific just south of the equator,[70] some have air too dry over land areas such as the Amazon, and others can't get right the timing and magnitude of South Asian monsoons and the cycles of El Niño and La Niña in the Pacific. All of these are areas of ongoing research in the modelling centres.

Because each individual model has *different* weaknesses, the average of all the models ends up being better than any single model[71] – any weaknesses in an individual model is compensated for by other models that do better in that area. So the most accurate climate simulation is simply the average of all the available runs from all the available models. We call this a *multi-model ensemble* – a collection of runs from as many models as possible, all run under exactly the same conditions, which is what the model intercomparison experiments provide.

For policymakers, a multi-model ensemble offers the best summary of the science. For the modellers, it allows comparisons to be made between models, and provides an estimate of how much uncertainty remains for any given climate variable. It is also an excellent way to identify weaknesses in each model, and to put them into context. Finally, multi-model ensembles give us the basis for two strong conclusions about the accuracy of climate models. First, for the basic questions about the physical processes that drive climate change, the models get it right – they are able to simulate both recent climate change and the longer-term changes that have occurred in the pre-history of planet Earth. But for detailed high-resolution predictions about local effects of climate change – say on the scale of an individual farm or town – the models are simply not good enough yet, because the models sometimes still disagree on how much climate change we will experience in our own neighbourhoods.

Quality Is Fitness for Purpose

In trying to answer the question of how good climate models are, we've explored the question from several angles – how the models are tested, whether any errors slip through this testing process, whether the models make successful predictions, and how climate scientists themselves compare and evaluate their models.

Climate scientists have several important advantages over programmers who build the commercial software that inhabits the computers around us. The development of the program code is tightly embedded in their scientific work, and they treat each change to their model as a science experiment. Many other scientific teams around the world are all building their own models of the same phenomena, but they are not commercial competitors, so they regularly compare their models to identify errors, and share ideas for how to improve the models. And most importantly, these comparisons are carried out in the open, on a carefully defined set of experiments, with all the data shared freely with anyone who wants to analyze it. This comparison process, on a standard set of benchmark experiments, is unusual, even for scientific fields, and it holds climate modellers to a very high standard.

Climate modellers use an extensive battery of tests to find errors in their models. This takes a lot of time and effort, but by the time they are done, there are fewer errors in their software than almost any other software in the world. Occasionally a software error slips through this process, but the modellers are diligent about documenting these errors and reporting them in their published papers, to alert anyone using their models or data. Occasionally, a version of the model used in experiments reported in a published paper has later been found to contain a software bug. But I have yet to find any case where such a bug invalidates any of the conclusions of the paper.

The key point is that climate models are not treated as "truth machines" by the climate science community – the conclusions scientists report in their published papers are not the outputs of a model, but the result of careful analysis of how a model experiment alters (or not) our understanding of how the climate system works. The modellers know that the models are imperfect approximations of very complex physical, chemical, and biological processes. Conclusions about key issues such as climate sensitivity are based not on individual model runs, but on many different experiments with many different models over many years, and the extent to which these experiments agree or disagree with other sources of evidence. It's this interpretation of the science by experts who understand the models that really matters.

There is, however, a danger that climate models are treated as truth machines when their results are presented to others outside the field. The cultural anthropologist Myanna Lahsen raises this concern in her 2005 study of the cultural practices of climate modellers. Myanna argues that people who are several steps removed from the climate modelling labs are much more likely to accept model outputs uncritically as "the truth," and indeed, charts showing future projections of climate change from climate models are often shared on social media in this way. This danger is exacerbated by the politicization of climate discourse in the media, which can make climate modellers reticent about discussing any weaknesses of their models with those outside the field. However, in this respect, climate science seems no different from any scientific field, as nearly all scientific results are presented as truth in the media, without any of the caveats that scientists express in their papers.

As we saw, "true" or "false" is the wrong way to label scientific theories and computational models. Rather, each can be thought of as having a scope of applicability – aspects of the world where it applies very well and can be used to successfully explain and predict what will happen. The real question for climate models is whether they are being used to answer scientific questions to which they are well suited. When they are being used to explore our current understanding of the climate system, and to guide scientists to areas where more study is needed, climate models do an excellent job. When used to predict future climate change, more caution is needed, as we'll see in the next chapter. While climate models give us tremendous insight into the scale of climate change we're likely to see in the next few decades, the further we move away from the stable climate in which human civilization arose, the less sure we can be that climate models will give us accurate predictions. And there is one area in particular where current climate models are relatively weak – telling us what climate impacts are likely to be at the scale of an individual town or community. The grid cells in the models are too big for such fine-grained analysis. Climate models are excellent at giving the big picture, but still leave us in the dark about exactly how each of us will be affected.

Notes

1   DKRZ stands for Deutsches KlimaRechenZentrum, the German Climate
    Computing Centre.
2   See the discussion on Conway's Law in Chapter 7.
3   Which stands for Max Planck Institute – Earth System Model. Its three major
    components are an atmosphere model, ECHAM, an ocean model MPI-OM, and a
    land surface model, JSBACH. The "Ham" in ECHAM is short for Hamburg, so it's
    not really an acronym, which confuses journal editors, who often ask for it to be
    spelled out. JSBACH stands for Jena Scheme for Biosphere Atmosphere Coupling,
    named after Jena, the city in Germany where some of the early vegetation model-
    ling originated.
4   The name ICON comes from the term ICOsahedral Nonhydrostatic. For an expla-
    nation of Icosahedral grids, see Chapter 5, particularly Figure 5.8b.
5   Particle physicists have a coordinated set of (physical) experiments on the Large
    Hadron Collider that rivals this in scale, in terms of data generated. And other
    fields of computational modelling do run smaller model intercomparison projects.
    But CMIP is certainly the largest of them all.

6 As we'll see later in the chapter, it's not technically an IPCC deadline, but rather a deadline the modelling community sets itself in advance of the IPCC timeline.

7 See, for example, Connolley and Bracegirdle (2007).

8 See Reason (1997).

9 The book Normal Accidents, by Charles Perrow, published two years before Challenger, in 1984, uses the nuclear accident at Three Mile Island to illustrate this point.

10 For a set of case studies, see Leveson (1995).

11 Specifically, in a data file called Small Forces, which gave the force of the spacecraft thruster in pounds-seconds (Lbf-s) while the program was expecting Newton-seconds (Ns). So the force was underestimated by a factor of about 4.45. But the force perpendicular to the spacecraft's trajectory is very small (hence the name) so the net effect on the spacecraft trajectory was very hard to measure.

12 It's called an angular momentum desaturation maneuver. The spacecraft has an internal flywheel with an electric motor that it can spin in the opposite direction to keep itself stable, so that it doesn't need to use its limited supply of fuel. But when the flywheel can't go any faster, there's no choice but to fire a thruster to counter the spin and slow the flywheel. Ideally, the thruster would do nothing other than de-spin, but there's always some small effect on the spacecraft's trajectory too. This has to be taken into account when doing course corrections during the approach to Mars.

13 See, for example, Williamson et al. (2009) for an analysis of the tests that found two major errors in an early version of the NCAR dynamical core.

14 Engineers refer to these as "corner cases" – situations where several variables are outside the range of normal operations, so that testing one condition at a time will cause you to miss the fault.

15 See Fishman (1998) for a very readable summary of the Shuttle flight software development process.

16 A summary of Jon's results are available in Pipitone and Easterbrook (2012).

17 See, for example, Pope and Davies (2002) for a description of a similar hierarchy of tests used at the UK Met Office.

18 See Wan et al. (2013) for a detailed description of the ICON core and how it was tested, and Williamson et al. (1992) for a detailed list of the simplified tests.

19 These standard tests for a dynamical core were first proposed by scientists at NCAR, who report on their effectiveness at finding errors. See Williamson et al. (2009).

20 See the Agile Manifesto, https://agilemanifesto.org

21 See Beck (2002).

22 With increasing computing power, some limited statistical testing like this is now feasible. See, for example, Baker et al. (2015).

23 See Hovy (2020).

24 The resulting study is written up in Roeckner et al. (2012).

25 See Stevens et al. (2013).

26 The idea that there is no such thing as "a scientific method" was argued forcefully by Feyerabend, in his 1975 book Against Method, and observed in scientific practice by Latour and Woolgar, in their 1979 book Laboratory Life: The Construction of Scientific Facts. Both remain controversial among the scientific community, but are relevant to the broader question of how scientific knowledge is produced and evaluated. But that's a topic for another book entirely.

27 Lakatos, whom we'll meet shortly, dubbed these "rational reconstructions."

28 Oreskes et al. (1994). Oreskes also points out that the terms verify and validate are used to mean very different things in different communities. Confusingly,

software engineers switch the meaning of these two terms, compared to their everyday meanings.

29 With the acknowledgement that accepted theories might still prove to be wrong. In the 1960s, Thomas Kuhn pointed out that a field of science sometimes experiences a revolution in thinking, when a whole body of theory has to be discarded and replaced.

30 Briefly, Mercury's perihelion – the point of its orbit where it comes closest to the sun – gradually moves around the sun faster than predicted by Newton's laws. Einstein explained this as the result of the sun's mass bending spacetime, and his theory of relativity predicts the observed precession.

31 See Lakatos (1976).

32 See, for example, Hourdin et al. (2017) for an overview of model tuning, and a survey of how different labs do this. See also Schmidt and Sherwood (2015) and Mauritsen (2012) for details of how specific labs approach model tuning.

33 More specifically, UQ uses a Bayesian approach that starts with best guesses, and then systematically alters several parameters simultaneously to find optimal combinations.

34 Jakob (2010).

35 Confirmed by recent measurements. See, for example, Serreze et al. (2009).

36 Some early models in the 1970s and 1980s omitted the stratosphere, and hence missed this pattern.

37 Which makes sense – there's a lot less air in the stratosphere, so a lot less thermal mass. A change in energy will therefore induce a much larger temperature change than in the lower atmosphere.

38 CFCs are also powerful greenhouse gases. So while the ozone hole and climate change aren't directly related, eliminating the use of CFC has helped avoid some additional warming from these trace gases.

39 Unfortunately, the ozone layer is likely to thin again as climate change worsens, because in a colder stratosphere, less ozone forms – which is why the ozone hole tends to appear during the winter and early spring months, and recover during the summer.

40 See Seidel et al. (2011).

41 See Soden et al. (2002).

42 See Maher et al. (2019).

43 It also includes 100 runs of a 150-year scenario where CO_2 rises by 1% per year.

44 HadCRUT is a global surface temperature record produced by combining the sea surface temperature record (HadSST) maintained by the Hadley Centre and the land surface temperature record (CRUTEM) maintained by the Climate Research Unit at the University of East Anglia. A number of versions of this temperature record are available, as both teams regularly publish improved datasets with better error correction.

45 The newest version, MPI-ESM1.2 does best, partly because it is a higher resolution model, and partly because it has been tuned the observed twentieth-century climate sensitivity, to correct the over-sensitivity of the older models. As climate sensitivity is assumed not to change, this tuning should also give the most accurate projections over the twenty-first century.

46 CO_2 levels rose from about 300 ppm in 1900 to 370 ppm in 2000, a rise of 23%. The change in temperature over this period, calculated as the change in decadal means in the HadCRUT5 dataset was 0.82°C. See Hausfather et al. (2020) for a more detailed analysis.

47 More detailed comparison are available in Hausfather et al. (2020) and at www .realclimate.org/index.php/archives/2007/05/hansens-1988-projections/

48 See England et al. (2015).
49 See Karl et al. (2006).
50 See Lewandowsky et al. (2018) for an extensive discussion.
51 The so-called "Climategate" scandal relates to this work. In 2008, hackers took email records from a server at the Climate Research Unit (CRU) at the University of East Anglia, which compiles the land surface part of HadCRUT, one of the most well-known global surface temperature records. While selected quotes taken out of context from these emails appeared to show the scientists hiding their data, in fact, all the data was freely available from other sources, and the scientists were found to have done nothing wrong. See Russell et al. (2010).
52 For a brief overview of this work, see Santer et al. (2011). Scientists now use sophisticated algorithms to detect errors in these datasets, and test their algorithms using benchmarks with deliberately seeded errors. For a detailed description of this work, see Willett et al. (2014).
53 See Meehl et al. (2014) for a detailed discussion.
54 Cess and Potter (1988) give results from five different models ranging from 2.8°C to 5.2°C.
55 Specifically, the IPCC was created jointly by the World Meteorological Organisation (WMO) and the UN Environment Program (UNEP). Membership is open to all nations that are members of the WMO and the UN. Four years later, at the Rio Summit in 1992, the UN agreed a new treaty, the UN Framework Convention on Climate Change (the UNFCCC), which now guides an annual meeting, the Conference of the Parties (COP), where new international agreements on climate policy are negotiated.
56 See Cess et al. (1989). Cess reports that only 3 of the 14 GCMs they studied had been used for climate sensitivity experiments at that point. The first IPCC assessment report, published in 1990, lists climate sensitivity experiments in 26 models, although only four of them are full atmosphere-ocean GCMs.
57 The models were run in "perpetual July" mode, to remove seasonal variation. This switches off the change in sunlight received at different latitudes over the course of the year.
58 At the top of the atmosphere. The experiment assumes the models don't disagree on the relationship between CO_2 levels and radiative forcing, which is mostly true. See Section 3.6 of Cubasch and Cess (1990) for more detail on this experiment.
59 See Gates (1992).
60 See the list at www.clivar.org/clivar-panels/former-panels/aamp/resources/mips Model output data is available freely from www-pcmdi.llnl.gov/projects/pcmdi/index.php
61 See Meehl et al. (2000).
62 Curiously, there never was a CMIP4. The CMIP projects weren't originally designed to contribute so directly to the IPCC assessment reports, but CMIP2 ended up forming the basis for the third IPCC report and CMIP3 for the fourth. To avoid confusion, the community agreed to renumber the projects so that CMIP5 would coincide with the fifth assessment report, AR5.
63 See Eyring et al. (2016).
64 The five benchmarks are: The original AMIP experiment with prescribed sea surface temperatures; experiments with CO_2 rising by 1% per year; an abrupt quadrupling of CO_2; a "pre-industrial" control run, with CO_2 levels as they were before the industrial revolution; and a hindcast of the last 150 years.
65 See Cinquini et al. (2014).

66 For a glimpse into what it's like to be a volunteer author for the IPCC, see Schulte-Uebbing et al. (2015).

67 The IPCC does sometimes draw on what is known as "grey literature" – work that has been published, for example, by nongovernmental organizations (NGOs), but not subject to peer review. However, this only done for reports that are publicly available for expert review, and the preference is always to rely on reputable scientific journal publications. See IPCC (1998, Appendix A).

68 The two journals are Geoscientific Model Development (GMD), and the Journal of Advances in Modeling Earth Systems (JAMES). I served as an associate editor for many years on the editorial board of GMD.

69 See, for example, the Critical Assessment of protein Structure Prediction (CASP) projects at predictioncenter.org, which began in 1994.

70 Known as a double ITCZ. The Intertropical Convergence Zone is a natural phenomenon where the trade winds from the northern and southern hemispheres meet, near the equator, typically producing a distinct band of cloud across the Pacific. But some models persistently produce a double band, which does not occur in reality.

71 See Reichler and Kim (2008).

9

Choosing a Future

Scientists have been building computational models of the climate and study-ing the consequences of our use of fossil fuels for more than a century. In the twenty-first century, these consequences are all around us, and the need for urgent action has become clear. In this chapter, we show how experiments with climate models give us a clear picture of the choices we face, and how the cli-mate system will respond to those choices. We'll show how advice from climate models shapes policy targets, such as the 2 °C limit and goal of reaching net-zero emissions. In the political arena, scientific advice has to compete with many other sources of information and misinformation, which has slowed meaningful action, so we'll also examine the political processes by which we collectively make decisions, and the role each of us plays in those processes. Ultimately, climate models can guide us on how to tackle climate change, but only if we find the wisdom to understand and act on that guidance.

Wisdom from Models

The most important question about climate change is: what will we do about it? Climate models have been predicting global warming as a result of human activities for more than a century. Since the 1980s, the connection between fossil fuels and climate change has not been in any doubt in the scientific com-munity.[1] But there *has* been much debate about how soon the effects would play out, how bad those effects would be, and what the world should do about it. Uncertainty on these questions – along with deliberate misinformation by industry lobbyists – has delayed the world from taking effective action on climate change for nearly three decades.

At the 1992 Earth Summit in Rio de Janeiro, the United Nations established the Framework Convention on Climate Change (UNFCC), which included an agreement to achieve *"stabilization of greenhouse gas concentrations in the atmosphere at a level that would prevent dangerous anthropogenic interfer-ence with the climate system."*[2] The agreement was an important step forward, but it didn't specify what constituted "dangerous," and left the details to be negotiated at an annual series of international summits.[3]

Climate models cannot tell us what counts as "dangerous," as they do not make value judgments.[4] Nor can they make policy recommendations. To com-plicate the picture, the models show climate impacts vary in their speed and severity in different regions of the world. What counts as dangerous depends on where you live and whether you have the resources to adapt. The worst impacts are likely to occur in many of the poorest regions, while the richest nations are responsible for the vast majority of historical carbon emissions, making climate change an enormous equity issue.

Still, policymakers need specific targets to focus international negotiations. Over the years, a number of different targets have been proposed. The most widely adopted is the United Nation's agreement to limit climate change to no more than +2°C over pre-industrial global average temperatures. This limit traces back[5] to an influential report from the Stockholm Environment Institute in 1990 which concluded that beyond 2°C of warming, *"the risks of grave damage to ecosystems, and of non-linear responses, are expected to increase rapidly."*[6] Whether this is the right limit is still hotly debated, as is figuring out how to achieve it.

However, the question of *what it would take* to meet the 2°C limit has become much clearer over the last few decades. Through the use of model intercomparison projects – which involve a huge number of coordinated experiments on models from many different climate modelling labs – the cli-mate modelling community has arrived at a remarkably consistent picture of how quickly we have to curb global greenhouse gas emissions to meet any specific limit on global temperature rise. This work is regularly assessed by the UN's Intergovernmental Panel on Climate Change (IPCC), whose reports summarize the science and provide a set of pathways for the future, to guide national and international climate policymaking and to allow us to assess progress.

In this final chapter, we'll explore what that guidance looks like. We'll identify the most important lessons from climate modelling, and see how they feed into policymaking. We'll also explore the implications of the 2°C limit, along with other ways of setting and interpreting goals for limiting climate change. We'll consider what the models can and cannot tell us, and how likely we are to encounter nasty surprises. Finally, we'll discuss why the world has been so slow to respond to the threat, despite the clear warnings from climate scientists, and we'll end with some thoughts about what we ought to do now.

The Trillionth Tonne

After my first study of how climate scientists build and test their models, my colleagues at the UK Met Office encouraged me to present my work at the annual conference of the European Geosciences Union, normally held every April in Vienna, Austria. The conference is huge. That year, 2009, there were more than 10,000 scientists attending. Since then, the conference has only grown. There are so many sessions happening in parallel you have to browse the online program ahead of time, and download your own schedule of the talks you want to attend.

My talk was scheduled for the last day of the conference, so I had the rest of the week free to take in as much of the conference as I could.[7] As this was my first time attending a geosciences conference, I wasn't sure where to start. My co-author, Tim Johns, acted as my tour guide, steering me towards talks he felt represented the cutting edge of climate science. I learned about how climate scientists measure uncertainty and weigh up probabilities, heard about the potential for abrupt climate changes – or *tipping points* – as the planet warms, and discovered some scientists were already starting to model what would happen if we attempt emergency responses to climate change via *geoengineering*. I also attended many talks on technologies for sharing climate data across the scientific community.

But one talk that week stood out for me, both for the elegance of the modelling experiment, and the importance of its implications. I had already met the speaker, Chris Jones, the previous summer at the Met Office, and interviewed him about his work, so I knew a bit about what to expect. However, my interviews with Chris had focused on the technical challenges in his work, and I hadn't yet heard him talk about the bigger picture. Chris was presenting results from a collaboration with colleagues at the Universities of Oxford and Reading, to be published that same month in the prestigious journal Nature, on what the team called *the trillionth tonne*.[8]

The question Chris addressed in his talk is: how much coal, oil, and gas can we still use? The European Union had formally adopted the goal of keeping warming below the +2°C limit in the 1990s, and there was a widespread expectation this goal would be adopted by the UN at the Copenhagen summit in December 2009 – which it was. The work Chris presented that year was part of a larger effort within the climate science community to analyze this target and what it would take to meet it. Their answer turned out to be very simple – the world must not burn more than a trillion tonnes of carbon. Ever. The implications are profound, but before we discuss them, we'll explore how they arrived at this answer.

Why 2°C?

Ideally, policymakers need clear, evidence-based targets, backed by robust scientific results, as a basis for international treaties. But distilling the science down to useful – *actionable* – guidance is not easy. Take, for example, the +2°C limit. The 1990 Stockholm report from which this limit arises offered a traffic light approach.[9] The safe zone, green, is where temperatures stay below 1°C of warming. Beyond this, in the amber zone, the report anticipated *"rapid, unpredictable, and non-linear responses that could lead to extensive ecosystem damage."* The world passed the +1°C threshold in the early 2000s, and some of the impacts described in the report are already evident – widespread increases in extreme heat, flooding, and wildfires. The upper limit, +2°C, marked the red zone, where damage would become irreversible, and new feedback effects could be triggered that would further amplify the warming.

The risks described in the report for the amber zone include stress on ecosystems, because plants – especially trees – can't easily migrate to higher latitudes when climate zones shift polewards; the loss of farmland as sea levels rise, flooding fertile river deltas; sudden shifts in regional climate patterns as ocean circulation patterns change; and shifts in rainfall patterns, with many areas receiving considerable additional rainfall and flooding, while others experience more frequent droughts. The report also reviewed the potential for feedbacks to kick in at higher rates of warming, should we enter the red zone: sudden release of huge amounts of methane from melting permafrost and from undersea crystalline deposits known as *calthrates;* massive release of CO_2 from dying vegetation as the climate changes; and the potential for a warming ocean to start releasing CO_2 rather than absorbing it. The temperature limits were intended to guard against these risks.

The report also compared these limits with climates of the distant past. Warming of 2° to 2.5°C is comparable with previous inter-glacial periods 125,000 years ago, when early humans lived in hunter-gatherer groups and sea levels were 5–7 metres higher. Temperatures above 3°C take the Earth back to the Pliocene, 3–5 million years ago, long before humans evolved. Finally, warming of 5°C or more takes us to the "hothouse" Earth of 56 million years ago,[10] when there were no ice sheets or glaciers anywhere on the planet, and sea levels were at least 70 m higher than today. Transitions between these periods in the Earth's history were marked by mass extinctions, where the majority of species were wiped out.

This report established the idea of 2°C being an upper threshold for dangerous climate change, even while the rest of its warnings were largely ignored.

But this number itself was only a rough estimate, and reflects our preference for whole numbers and simple messages. The original Stockholm report – and subsequent analysis in the IPCC assessment reports – all make it clear there's no sudden change at 2°C. The risks get steadily worse with greater warming, as does the potential for unforeseen impacts to emerge. While there's clearly a need to set specific limits to guide the political process, there's no scientific way to decide exactly where these limits should be.

Within the climate science community there has been much criticism of the 2°C limit as far too high. In 2008, Jim Hansen, then director of NASA's climate modelling lab,[11] proposed instead a target of reducing CO_2 concentrations in the atmosphere. His work drew on extensive analysis of paleoclimate records, from which he concluded *"If humanity wishes to preserve a planet similar to that on which civilization developed and to which life on Earth is adapted, […] CO_2 will need to be reduced from its current 385 ppm to at most 350 ppm, but likely less than that."*[12] Hansen described the drastic action that would be needed to achieve this – phasing out all coal use, putting a price on carbon to limit the use of oil, and radically transforming agricultural and forestry practices to soak up past emissions. Hansen's proposal inspired a global protest movement called 350.org, which continues to push for this more ambitious target. But concentrations have continued to rise, surpassing 420 ppm in 2022 (see Figure 1.4).

The Association of Small Island States (AOSIS) has also long been critical of the 2°C limit, because at that temperature, sea-level rise may wipe them out completely. Projections from coupled climate models show in a +2°C world, sea-levels would continue to rise for centuries, as the Greenland and Antarctica ice sheets continue to melt.[13] It would also mean the loss of 99% of all coral reefs.[14] These consequences led AOSIS to lobby for years for a lower "guardrail" limit at 1.5°C, and this was finally adopted in the language of the Paris agreement in 2015, which agreed to *"pursue efforts"* towards it.[15] Unfortunately, the Paris agreement doesn't link these global limits in any way to the commitments made by each country to reduce emissions – analysis of the initial commitments under the Paris agreement project the world would still warm by around 3°C by the end of the century.[16]

Future Scenarios

It's not easy to translate a limit on rising global temperatures into specific actions or policies to ensure it. Future projections of climate change using a global climate model are always *"what if"* experiments. The model needs, as input, a detailed scenario for how much of each greenhouse gas – and other pollutants – humans will add to the atmosphere each year,[17] along with any major changes in land use, such as deforestation. Creating such a scenario requires a lot of thought. What if over the coming century, the global economy grows rapidly, with more international trade, higher consumption, and ever growing demand for energy? Or what if there are trade wars and the world fragments into more regional trade blocks? What if there is more emphasis on protecting the environment and development of renewable energy? What if the world agrees and enacts strict policies on climate change? Each of these factors will affect how fast emissions grow, and whether and when they then might peak and then decline.

Over the years, the IPCC has developed various scenarios to serve as inputs to climate models. These scenarios result from detailed analysis of economic, social, and technological trends[18] to understand how these trends interact, and how they would affect global greenhouse gas emissions. In 2000, the IPCC's Special Report on Emissions Scenarios (SRES) identified 40 different scenarios, grouped into six different families (see Figure 9.1). The scenarios labelled "A" describe a world more focused on economic growth, while those labelled "B" describe a world focused on environmental protection. Similarly, the scenarios labelled "1" assume greater globalization, with more international trade, while those labelled "2" assume more regionalization, in a world with trade wars and protectionism. For example, the B1 family represents a world marked by global progress towards sustainable development, while the A2 family describes regional competition for economic growth. The A1 family, which envisages a continuation of the trend for increasing globalization and rapid growth, was subdivided further according to the likely energy sources used to fuel that growth – FI for Fossil fuel Intensive, T for a Transition to renewable energy, and B for a Balanced mix of energy from different sources. A1FI was regarded as the "business as usual" scenario, as it continued the late twentieth-century trend of expanding fossil fuel extraction to drive rapid economic growth.

These scenarios are intended to be politically neutral – the IPCC takes no stance on which of these storylines is more likely, nor which is more desirable. The idea was to map out plausible futures for society, so that climate models could then calculate the consequences. There are, of course, likely feedback loops – for example, if rapid growth leads to environmental destruction, it could trigger famine, war, or even societal collapse.[19] And of course, if the world uses these analyses to enact strong climate change policies, that would change the storyline. But none of these potential feedbacks are included in the scenarios.

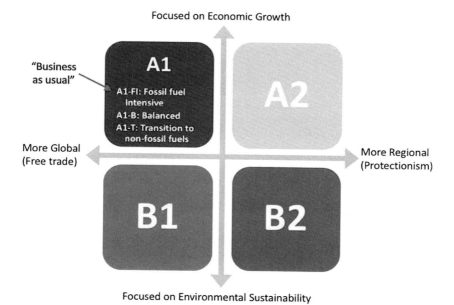

Figure 9.1 The six scenarios from the IPCC's 2000 Special Report on Emissions Scenarios (SRES).

The IPCC assessment reports show how climate models respond to these scenarios (see Figure 9.2). Figure 9.2a shows the expected warming under three of the SRES scenarios over the remainder of this century,[20] with hind-cast simulations of the twentieth century in black. Future projections use a different colour for each scenario. The shaded regions show the range of results from multiple models, while the darker lines show the average of all the models for each scenario. Running these simulations is computationally expensive, so not all climate modelling groups were able to run all the scenarios – the numbers in brackets show how many models participated in each scenario run.

The data used to compile these charts come from the Coupled Model Intercomparison Projects we met in Chapter 8, but this figure shows just one tiny part of that analysis – focusing on a single variable, global average surface temperature, and just on simulations of the twentieth and twenty-first centuries. Data from these intercomparison projects also allow scientists to analyze many other consequences of climate change – its effects on rainfall, seasonal norms and extremes, regional impacts, sea-level rise, melting sea ice and glaciers, and so on. Further experiments in CMIP focus on other things

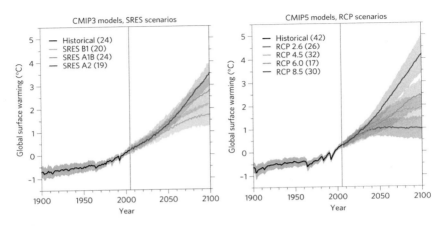

Figure 9.2 Projections of future global temperature change from (a) the IPCC Fourth Assessment Report in 2007, and (b) the IPCC Fifth Assessment Report in 2014. The black line shows simulated historical temperatures. Bold lines show the average of all the models for each scenario, while shading shows the range from different models. Numbers in brackets indicate how many models simulated each scenario. The temperature scale shows warming compared to the last quarter of the twentieth century. As the world had already warmed by about 0.75°C over pre-industrial conditions, all these scenarios exceeds the UN's 2°C limit, except for RCP2.6. (Reproduced from Knutti and Sedláček (2013). CC-BY 3.0.)

the models can be used for, including analysis of how well they simulate climates of the past, and hypothetical experiments that alter the atmosphere in other ways.

Updating the Scenarios

When planning began for the fifth IPCC assessment report, it was clear a new set of scenarios were needed. With growing pressure for international agreement on stronger climate policies, policymakers needed scenarios that reflected what such policies might achieve. None of the scenarios in the earlier assessment reports stay below the 2°C limit, so policymakers wanted to know what it would take. Was it even still possible?

The IPCC invited 130 climate scientists from around the world to a workshop in the Netherlands, in September 2007, to develop a new set of scenarios.[21] Scientists from three different research communities came together for this workshop: climate modellers; social scientists who build Integrated

Assessment Models (IAMs) representing economic and social trends; and scientists who study how climate change affects people – a field known as Impacts, Adaptation, and Vulnerability (IAV).

The previous approach was very slow – social scientists started with plausible storylines for how society might change, and used their socio-economic models to generate predictions for annual greenhouse gas emissions over the coming century. They then passed these to climate modellers as inputs to the physical climate models. To speed things up, the 2007 workshop focused on creating a set of plausible pathways for *concentrations* of greenhouse gases in the atmosphere, which each community could then analyze, in parallel, for plausibility. The community selected four *representative* pathways, chosen to be likely upper and lower limits[22] for global concentrations of greenhouse gases in each of two different future worlds – a world that enacts international climate policies, and a world that fails to do so.

The names chosen for these pathways are a little awkward. They are referred to as *Representative Concentration Pathways* (RCPs), because they focus on how concentrations of greenhouse gases in the atmosphere might change over time, but each is named after the total impact on the planet's energy balance – the *radiative forcing*,[23] in watts per square metre – by the end of this century, if we were to follow each pathway. In all but one of these scenarios, concentrations of greenhouse gases in the atmosphere continue to rise throughout this century, because we keep adding more each year. So in each case the total forcing – and hence the amount of warming – is bigger than today's. Figure 9.2b shows how global temperatures would rise for each pathway.

In the most optimistic pathway, RCP2.6, we start reducing annual greenhouse gas emissions immediately. Emissions drop to zero by the second half of the century, and then become negative – meaning we find a way to remove carbon from the atmosphere faster than we add it. This scenario would keep global temperatures below the 2°C threshold, but only just – and it would far exceed the 1.5°C limit. By contrast, in the worst-case scenario, RCP8.5, CO_2 concentrations keep increasing even beyond the end of the century. The models show this would lead to as much as 5°C of warming by 2100, with a lot more to come in the twenty-second century. Many parts of the planet would become uninhabitable.

There's much debate in the climate science and climate policy communities about whether these best- and worst-case scenarios are plausible. The worst-case scenarios (A1FI and RCP8.5) may depend on burning more fossil fuel reserves than actually exist. In the 2010s, the development of clean energy accelerated faster than the "business-as-usual" scenarios anticipated. Emissions cuts proposed under the Paris agreement would put us on track to do no worse than RCP4.5. On the other hand, the most optimistic scenario, RCP2.6, assumes large-scale removal of CO_2 from the atmosphere in the second half of the twenty-first century, using technologies that are largely still hypothetical. This doesn't mean the 1.5°C target is off the table. But as we'll see, it does require a much more radical approach.

Uncertainty

The spread of projections in Figure 9.2 can be interpreted as *scenario uncertainty* – we don't know which of these paths we will follow. Think of it as a choice. Humanity, collectively, must choose which of these paths to follow: will we continue on the upward trajectory of the recent past, or will we bend the curve downwards to avoid the worst impacts, and if so, how fast?

There's a second kind of uncertainty represented in this figure – within each scenario, the shaded region shows the spread of results from different models. Climate scientists call this *structural uncertainty*, as we cannot be sure how well each model captures all the relevant physical structure of the climate system. The Model Intercomparison Projects we met in Chapter 8 are an important tool for assessing this kind of uncertainty – many different models from different labs around the world are run on exactly the same inputs, for a huge range of experiments. Data from these *Multi-Model Ensemble* experiments provides a detailed view of how and why the models vary, allowing scientists to analyze how accurately each model can simulate climates of the past, including the relatively stable climate of the pre-industrial era, the more recent climate change over the twentieth century,[24] and the larger changes in climate during the ice ages.

As we saw in Chapter 8, these Model Intercomparison Projects have grown to become the largest coordinated computational experiments in the world. These projects – along with detailed analysis of observational data from the past and present – help to separate what we know about climate change from what we don't know. This is important because uncertainty is often used as an argument to delay implementation of climate policy.

Figure 9.2 also shows that for the first few decades of the projections, the disagreement between models – the shaded region – is much larger than the difference between the scenarios.[25] However by the end of the century, the converse is true – the difference between scenarios is much bigger. This illustrates a fundamental dilemma in climate policymaking. The choices we make in the next few years might not make a measurable difference to the climate change we experience until several decades have passed. But they will make a profound difference to the world we create by the end of the century, and in the centuries to come.

Where the models do disagree, it's usually because of the choice of empirical parameters that stand in for processes that cannot be simulated explicitly. To assess how much these parameter choices matter, modellers use another kind of ensemble, known as a *Perturbed Physics Ensemble*, which involves systematically varying individual parameters to measure their effect. The long-running Climateprediction.net project,[26] which began in 2001, uses crowdsourcing by allowing anyone to run parts of the experiment on their home computers when they are otherwise idle, and to display the results as a screen saver. Over the years, hundreds of thousands of people have signed up to participate, allowing the project to run as many as 10,000 versions of one of the UK Met Office models for a range of experiments: testing how variations in the land vegetation map affect the hydrological cycle; how variations in the sulphate aerosol parameters affect climate sensitivity[27]; and how parameters for cloud formation and water vapour affect the model's ability to correctly simulate observed ocean states.[28]

An additional source of uncertainty arises from variability within the Earth's climate system. Large-scale weather patterns often have a significant but temporary impact on regional climates, which in turn show up as year-to-year variations in climate indicators – temperature, precipitation, humidity, etc. Some of these patterns are big enough to show up at the global scale. For example, years where there is a strong El Niño have higher average surface temperatures than La Niña years, because they change how heat is stored and released from the oceans. This means accurate simulation of shorter-term climate change – over the scale of a decade or two – may depend heavily on the chosen starting state. Climate modellers assess this kind of uncertainty using *Initial Condition Ensembles*, like the Hamburg Large Ensemble we met in Chapter 8. Using many runs of the same model, each started from a slightly different initial state, the modellers can assess how much this internal variability affects short-term and long-term climate trends.

These various model ensembles provide some assurance that the models give reliable projections of future climate change. But they don't entirely eliminate the possibility that all the models may be missing unexpected feedback loops that could trigger as the planet warms. Such a possibility argues strongly for caution – keeping the limit as low as possible. The further we move away from the stable climate of the past 10,000 years, the more likely we are to encounter such surprises.

Our Carbon Budget

The scenario analysis shown in Figure 9.2 doesn't tell us *how* to stay within the UN's 2°C limit, nor the tougher 1.5°C limit. To answer this with a global climate model you would, in effect, have to run the model backwards to find scenarios that stay within a specific global average temperature. But simulation models can't run backwards like that. So it may take many runs – with hundreds of different scenarios – to identify the pathways that keep within these limits. If it takes a couple of weeks to run each simulation on a fast supercomputer, you'll wait a long time for an answer.

In his talk at the 2009 EGU conference, Chris Jones showed how to do this without needing a supercomputer. His conclusion – to stay below 2°C, we cannot ever burn more than a trillion tonnes of carbon[29] – builds on a remarkably robust result that emerged from climate models in the late 2000s. For all the complexity of the climate system, the peak warming we should expect largely depends on just one thing: the total amount of carbon humanity adds to the atmosphere over time – our *cumulative global emissions*. So the 2°C limit turns into a very simple rule.

Chris pointed out that if you add up all the carbon emitted since the dawn of the industrial revolution, it's already well over 500 billion tonnes – half a trillion. And existing known fossil fuel reserves are enough to put at least another trillion tonnes of carbon into the atmosphere. So to stay within the UN's limit, the majority of all current reserves of fossil fuels cannot be used.

The way Chris and his colleagues calculated this is interesting. Ideally, the analysis should use all the available climate models, as we know the average of all the models is better than any individual model, and the range of responses from the models gives a sense of the range of uncertainty. But the data from the CMIP experiments only cover a few scenarios, and Chris and his colleagues wanted to explore *all possible scenarios*.

They solved the problem by developing an extremely simplified model that can be calibrated to mimic the global temperature response of each of the big climate models, while sacrificing all other details. Their model expresses the energy balance of the planet as a single equation, and couples this to a simple carbon cycle model to calculate how quickly carbon is removed from the atmosphere by the soils and surface oceans, and the slower processes by which it is sequestered into the ocean depths. The parameters in these equations can be set to mimic[30] any fully coupled Earth System Model, or they can be varied systematically over a range of values likely to be plausible compared to observational data.

The team then generated hundreds of potential emissions pathways over the coming century, each representing a possible future (see Figure 9.3a). Each pathway starts with emissions rising as they have been over recent decades, and assumes that, at some point, annual emissions will peak and then decline again. So the pathways are generated by varying three things: when the rise in

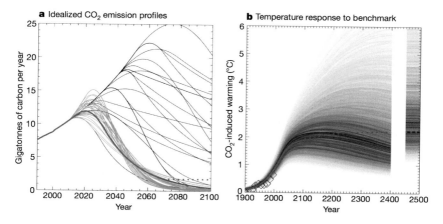

Figure 9.3 Potential emissions pathways, and plausible temperature responses: (a) each of the possible pathways generated for the experiment. Orange pathways are those where the total cumulative emissions is 1 trillion tonnes of carbon. The red pathway was then selected as an example to compute the expected warming over the coming four centuries shown in (b). Note the longer timescale! Shading in (b) indicates probability – darker means more probable – and the solid red line shows the most likely response. Dotted red lines (and the slice of responses towards the year 2500) show what happens if we maintain net-zero emissions to stabilize CO_2 concentrations in the atmosphere at 490 ppm. (Reproduced from Allen et al (2009) by permission of Springer Nature)

emissions begins to slow; how quickly it then peaks; and how steeply it then declines. The team put each of these pathways into their simplified model to compute the temperature response over the coming centuries. And because the model can be adjusted to mimic other models, the team computed the results for *every* plausible climate model, to give a spread of possible answers. The graph in Figure 9.3b shows all of these possible outcomes for just one selected pathway – the one shown in red in Figure 9.3a – with darker grey shading showing the more likely outcomes.

Every Tonne Matters

Studies by other climate scientists all confirm a similar result – no matter which pathway we follow, and no matter which model we use, the peak global temperatures depend primarily on the cumulative total of carbon we add to the atmosphere. The result is so strong that if you plot cumulative emissions against peak global temperature – from any scenario, in any climate model – you get

Every tonne of CO₂ emissions adds to global warming

Global surface temperature increase since 1850-1900 (°C) as a function of cumulative CO₂ emissions (GtCO₂)

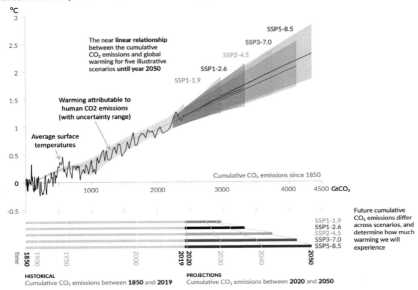

Figure 9.4 The relationship between cumulative emissions and surface temperature rise. The chart shows an almost linear relationship between cumulative CO₂ emissions and the rise in global surface temperature since the period 1850–1900. The five scenarios illustrated here for future warming are updated versions of the RCP scenarios, known as Shared Socio-economic Pathways (SSPs) – SSP1-1.9 was added after the Paris agreement, to represent a world that stays below the 1.5°C threshold. Note that all the scenarios are truncated at 2050. In all but SSP1-1.9, further warming continues in the second half of the century. (Reproduced from IPCC AR6 WG1 SPM figure 10)

almost a perfect straight line (see Figure 9.4). The steepness of the line varies a little between models, but the models all agree it is a straight line.

So it turns out it doesn't matter when and where greenhouse gas emissions occur. Carbon dioxide is a long-lived greenhouse gas – once we put it into the atmosphere, it stays there for hundreds of years. Every tonne we emit makes the problem worse, including every tonne already emitted in the past, and every tonne we will emit in the future.

This result also means you can convert any goal for limiting global temperatures into a cumulative emissions target, to give what has become known as the *carbon budget* – the maximum amount of carbon we can burn globally and stay within the desired temperature. The term carbon budget is a little unfortunate, as it sounds like this is an amount of carbon we can still safely spend. In reality, the size and severity of climate impacts grow, the more of the budget we use up. Going past a trillion tonnes will put us over 2°C, and into the "red" zone of dangerous warming – where the impacts of climate change will pose an existential threat to many ecosystems and communities around the world.

There is still some uncertainty – and disagreement between models – on exactly *how much* warming you get per tonne of carbon, as can be seen in the spread of the shaded area in Figure 9.3b. But we can use that to estimate the *probability* of success for achieving any given target. For example, a trillion tonnes only gives us a 50% chance of meeting the UN's 2°C limit. If we want better odds, the budget has to shrink accordingly. For a 66% chance, the remaining carbon budget shrinks to 250 billion tonnes of carbon. In the years since I saw Chris's talk, we've emitted another 100 billion tonnes. That cuts the remaining budget significantly, but it is still *possible* to stay below a trillion tonnes. The bad news is that global emissions are still rising.[31] Among the orange "trillion tonne" pathways in Figure 9.3a, the longer it take use to reach peak emissions, the more steeply the subsequent cuts have to be to stay on the path.

Some Serious Implications

These findings lead to three important facts about climate change, which together emphasize how hard climate change is to solve. The first is that global temperatures will keep on rising until we stop adding more carbon to the atmosphere. International climate negotiations have begun to acknowledge this, in the discussion about reaching "net-zero emissions" – the point when any ongoing emissions from human activities are balanced by processes that artificially remove carbon from the atmosphere. Because it will take years to build a replacement green energy infrastructure, we cannot cease all use of fossil fuels instantly. So the target date for reaching net-zero is typically set a few decades into the future, such as 2050.

Whether pushing off net-zero until mid-century is the right thing to do is hotly contested. On one hand, analysis from climate models shows that to keep the planet below 2°C of warming does require us to reach net-zero by the middle of this century. On the other hand, these studies also show net-zero alone isn't enough. Early deep emissions cuts will be needed in the 2020s, because it is the cumulative emissions over the years that determine how much the planet warms. So focusing on a long-term target for the middle of the century can also be a way of putting off making crucial large emissions reductions in the short term.

The second fact is that climate change is largely irreversible, at least on human timescales. As we saw in Chapter 6, model experiments where human emissions instantly cease show the temperature of the planet stabilizes at whatever level it had reached. It takes the planet several decades to warm up under its extra blanket of greenhouse gases, but this ongoing warming is roughly counterbalanced by the initial absorption of some of those greenhouse gases by oceans and soils. The planet's temperature will stabilize once we reach net-zero, but it will not cool down again.

For many people, this is counter-intuitive. Other kinds of pollutants wash out of the atmosphere fairly quickly. Heavy rains can clear many kinds of pollution from the atmosphere in a matter of hours – although they may then persist in soils and waterways. For such pollutants, once we stop producing them, the air clears relatively quickly. Clean air legislation usually leads to a rapid improvement in air quality. But greenhouse gases aren't like that.

Long-lived greenhouse gases take thousands of years before they disappear entirely from the atmosphere.[32] Roughly speaking, about half of each additional tonne of CO_2 disappears within a few decades, absorbed by soils and oceans. Plants, particularly trees, help in this process by breathing in carbon dioxide and turning it into organic matter which builds up layers of soil – although some of this returns to the atmosphere every winter when fallen leaves decompose, and forest fires release a lot more of it. Two slower processes remove the remainder. The first is the flow of ocean surface waters into the deep oceans via the overturning circulation, which, as we saw in Chapter 7, takes hundreds of years. The second is a process of rock weathering, in which carbon dioxide dissolved in water forms a weak acid (carbonic acid) which reacts with calcium in rocks to form limestone (calcium carbonate). This eventually ends up in new sedimentary layers at the bottom of the ocean. Natural rock weathering would take thousands of years to fully remove the billions of tonnes of carbon we have added to the atmosphere.

Much research is under way to develop technologies that can remove carbon dioxide from the atmosphere faster, using a variety of chemical and mechanical processes. Unfortunately, none has been shown yet to work well at a large enough scale to make any significant difference. And many of these technologies require massive amounts of energy – which would have to come from a source other than burning more fossil fuels.

The conclusion is inescapable. Our carbon emissions accumulate in the atmosphere, and cannot be easily removed. So climate change is, in effect, irreversible on the scale of human lifetimes,[33] unless we invent a way to remove

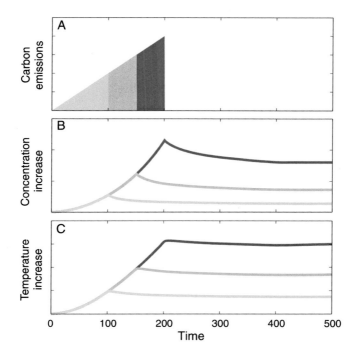

Figure 9.5 The long-term relationship between emissions, atmospheric concentrations, and global surface temperatures. The chart shows, schematically, the consequences of three different scenarios (yellow, orange, and red) where emissions rise steadily and then end abruptly. In each case the carbon accumulates in the atmosphere, with an exponential rise, and begins to fall again after emissions cease, but with a very long tail. Temperatures remain roughly flat after the peak. (Reproduced from Knutti and Rogelj (2015) by permission of Springer Nature)

carbon cheaply, on a massive scale. Most likely, whatever peak temperature we're at when we reach net-zero, we will be stuck at for generations to come (see Figure 9.5).

The third fact is a consequence of this. To prevent dangerous levels of global warming, we have to avoid burning the majority of current known reserves of coal, oil, and gas.[34] There is enough carbon locked up in existing fossil fuel reserves to take the planet through at least 3–4°C of warming. If, in the coming years, we extract and use the majority of coal, oil, and gas in these reserves, we will blow through any agreed ceiling on global temperatures. Keeping most of our existing fossil fuel reserves in the ground represents a significant challenge for society – the world has to find a way to forego the enormous financial benefits that could be made on such valuable natural resources. Oil and gas extraction has been the most profitable industry on the planet for the last 50 years.[35] Saying "no" to that will not be easy.

Is 1.5°C Still Possible?

In response to the agreement to make efforts towards the 1.5°C limit expressed in the Paris agreement, the IPCC produced a special report, in 2018, studying the implications of this lower limit, and analyzing scenarios that might achieve it. The report makes it clear the difference between 1.5°C and 2°C will affect some communities much more than others: "*Populations at disproportionately higher risk of adverse consequences with global warming of 1.5°C and beyond include disadvantaged and vulnerable populations, some Indigenous peoples, and local communities dependent on agricultural or coastal livelihoods.*"[36]

The report concludes that holding warming below 1.5°C will make a huge difference: ten million fewer people at risk from sea-level rise; several hundred million fewer people at risk from climate-related health issues and poverty; and significantly less stress on food security across equatorial regions. In many cases, dropping the limit from 2°C to 1.5°C means impacts are halved: half as many plants and animal species will be at risk, half as many ecosystems threatened, the loss to global fisheries will be halved, and the number of people affected by water stress halved.

To explore what it would take to hold to this limit, the report used a similar method to the trillion tonne analysis, running very simplified climate models[37] to test a large number of scenarios collected from existing published studies. All the scenarios require urgent deep emissions cuts. The report also discusses how to achieve this: completely replacing all fossil fuel energy production with clean energy alternatives by mid-century, reducing demand for energy across the board via energy efficiency measures, and changing people's behaviour to reduce demand. Buildings, transport, and industry would all have to consume less power. In each case, this would entail radical changes in how we do things – for example, in transportation, the majority of journeys would need to shift from planes and cars to (electric) buses and trains, and we would need to arrange our cities and neighbourhoods so less daily travel is needed. In agriculture, this would mean a dramatic reduction in the use of pasture land for farm animals, so that this land can be used for re-forestation, and a shift in what we eat – less meat – and big reductions in food waste.

The emissions scenarios[38] that keep below the 1.5°C limit all share two crucial features (see Figure 9.6). All would need to reach net-zero global

Global total net CO₂ emissions

Billion tonnes of CO₂/yr

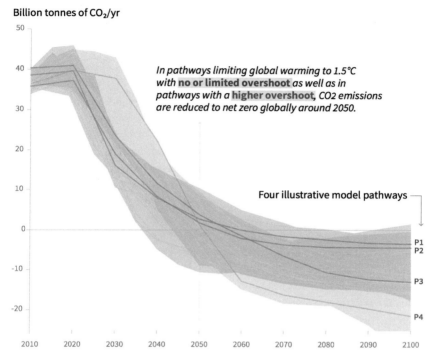

In pathways limiting global warming to 1.5°C with **no or limited overshoot** *as well as in pathways with a* **higher overshoot**, *CO2 emissions are reduced to net zero globally around 2050.*

Four illustrative model pathways

P1
P2
P3
P4

Figure 9.6 Rapid reduction in CO₂ emissions to stay below 1.5°C. In blue: scenarios that keep below this limit require emissions to drop by about half by 2030, and reach net zero by around 2050. In grey: scenarios that would overshoot the 1.5°C threshold, and then require very high carbon removal technologies in the second half of the century to cool the planet down again. These scenarios all assume rapid reduction in emissions of other greenhouse gases. (Reproduced from IPCC Special Report on 1.5°C, 2018, figure SPM3a)

emissions by mid-century, and all would require immediate rapid cuts throughout the 2020s – around 7% every year – so that emissions would halve by 2030, and then halve again by 2040. Scenarios (shown in grey) that fail to make these early rapid cuts would overshoot the 1.5°C target, and would then require large-scale deployment of technologies to suck carbon out of the atmosphere again in the second half of the century, to bring temperatures back down.

All of this would require a massive investment estimated at USD$2.4 trillion per year globally for two decades, or about 2.5% of global GDP. Such a massive investment for a rapid transformation of society is certainly possible – it would be akin to putting each country on a war footing,[39] to reorganize every industry. The biggest barrier is political – our political leaders are still unwilling to acknowledge the scale of change needed.

What the Models Can't Do

Climate models are excellent tools for improving our understanding of the climate system, allowing scientists to run computational experiments to test their hypotheses, and compare the results with observational data. They also allow us to make useful projections of likely future climate change, as they encapsulate so much of what we know about how the climate responds to various changes. And because they make theories about the climate system explicit and precise, they help to improve communication and collaboration across the scientific community.

While we can be sure the models get most aspects of global climate change right, the models still disagree on some impacts – especially on regional impacts – and cannot simulate fine-grained, local changes. More importantly, there are big gaps between what climate models do and what we really need, as a society, to comprehend the enormity and urgency of climate change.

First, climate models don't help us imagine what life will be like in a climate changed future. The charts and diagrams I have presented in this book give us plenty of numbers, but these don't really show us what a world warmed by say 2°C or 3°C will be like, and how different those worlds might be. And we're easily misled by our intuitions here – after all, a couple of degrees doesn't sound like much at all. In the 2010s, as the warming crossed the threshold of 1°C, some of the impacts started to become obvious: increased flooding from heavier rainfall, increased wildfires from hotter drier weather, and supercharged cyclones that pack more energy but move more slowly, leaving a lot more devastation in their wake. Seeing these impacts play out has clearly changed how the media reports climate change, and has energized climate activism. But when climate models predicted these impacts 30 years ago, it didn't capture the public imagination in the same way, perhaps because the predictions lacked any specificity – such as where and when the floods and fires would hit. And photographs of the impacts are much more visceral than line graphs. For the same reason, it's still very hard for us to picture the difference between a +1.5°C world and a +2°C, or between a +2°C world and +3°C world, no matter how much the models tell us this difference matters.

Climate models also don't tell us much about how climate change will affect us in the near-term – over the next few years. While seasonal to decadal forecasting has improved, it still remains much harder than both short-term weather forecasting and end-of-century climate prediction. We also need to know how conditions will change at a specific location, say a farm, a city, or the neighbourhood where we live. Such information is critical for farmers to plan what crops to grow, for city governments to prepare for extreme weather events, for insurance companies to calculate risks and potential losses, and for individual citizens to understand how climate change will affect them. The grid cells in global climate models – typically 30–50 km across, even in today's very high resolution simulations – are simply too coarse to provide such localized advice.

To fill this need, new organizations are beginning to appear, offering *climate services*. These organizations work with data from global climate models and observational data from satellites and weather stations, and add their own analysis, to offer more specific advice for governments, companies, and citizen groups. Climate services organizations make use of tools such as *downscaling*, which uses statistical techniques to fill the gaps between grid points in outputs of global models, and *regional modelling*, which specializes a climate model to simulate a specific region at a much higher resolution, using data from a global model to constrain what happens at the edges of the region.

Finally, climate models cannot give us precise answers about *tipping points* – thresholds where feedback effects kick in and turn a gradual change into a sudden shift in conditions.[40] Model experiments and data from the distant past tells us that such tipping points exist, and allow us to understand the mechanisms in detail. But uncertainties in the models make it hard predict precisely when these would occur.

Known tipping points include the melting of the Antarctic and Greenland ice-sheets, where, once the melting starts, flows of water under the ice lubricate the ice sheets causing them to slide much faster into the ocean, triggering instability in the ice further inland. Triggering these tipping points could add many metres to sea level rise over the next few centuries. Similarly, the melting of sea ice in the Arctic Ocean may reach a tipping point when the ice that routinely melts every summer never re-freezes again in the winter. Other tipping points affect the Earth's major ecosystems, including the loss of coral reefs due to warmer, more acidic oceans, and the loss of rainforests such as the Amazon, due to warmer, drier conditions. In such cases, the damage we're already seeing to these systems could become permanent, such that they never recover.

Each of these tipping points can in turn trigger further tipping points. Melting of the Greenland ice sheet could release enough fresh water into the Arctic Ocean to trigger a shutdown of the Atlantic Meridional Overturning Circulation, as we discussed in Chapter 7. This circulation pattern has already slowed by around 15% in the last few decades.[41] A full collapse of these ocean currents would bring sudden, dramatic climate shifts to many parts of Europe, Africa, and the Americas.

Predicting precisely when a tipping point will trigger is hard, due to the nature of chaotic processes – as we saw in Chapter 4 – which become less predictable as they approach a major shift in behaviour. But it's also due to lack of data. While there are examples of these tipping points in the geological record, long before the modern era, they are rare, and none of the shifts in climate happened as fast as modern climate change. One of the reasons to limit climate change to within the UN's target thresholds is to avoid triggering these kinds of tipping points.

In all of the scenarios described above, none of the climate models produce "runaway" global warming, where the planet just keeps heating up until it is entirely uninhabitable. Such a possibility is sometimes floated in the media, and by some climate activists, who worry about the possibility of human extinction. As we saw in Chapter 2, the planet only warms until it reaches a new thermal equilibrium – where outgoing heat lost to space balances incoming heat from the sun. So once we stop adding more greenhouse gases to the atmosphere, the warming stops too, although if we trigger any tipping points before then, they will greatly amplify the damage. Avoiding runaway warming shouldn't give us much comfort though – the worst-case scenarios will still cause widespread suffering across the planet, and will certainly make some parts of the world uninhabitable.

Why Haven't We Done More?

Climate models can show us the likely consequences of our choices, but they cannot make those choices for us. Many scientists I have spoken to assume given what we know about the science of climate change, it is obvious what we should do about it. Surely, they argue, a rational policymaking process would take rapid and decisive action to transition the world away from a dependence on fossil fuels, and away from destructive land management practices. And yet, despite more than 40 years of clear warnings from the scientific community, carbon emissions have continued to rise steadily, and very few countries have enacted the kinds of policy necessary to bring greenhouse gas emissions to a rapid halt.

Unfortunately, there is a significant gap between knowledge and action. Action on climate change doesn't flow from knowing what the models tell us – it also involves a value judgment. It requires us to weigh up future outcomes against current wants and desires. We're not very good at this. People who know that smoking causes cancer still smoke. And those of us who don't smoke still routinely ignore our doctors' advice on getting exercise and eating healthily. Partly, this is because we tend to discount the value of things that are far away in our futures, and put a high value on things we can enjoy right now.

Economists make these value judgments explicit by calculating a *discount rate* for future costs, to reflect the intuition that having some amount of money today is more useful than having that amount in several years' time. So while climate scientists drew on the laws of physics to build their models, economists built assumptions about discount rates and economic growth[42] into their analyses, which often then showed the cost of future damage from climate change would be smaller than the cost of taking action on it today. Today, most economists[43] agree the early economics models vastly underestimated the cost of damage from climate change.

We are also surrounded by social influences and systems that train us to certain behaviours, even if we know, rationally, they are poor choices. And we tend to bundle those influences and values into ideological systems that then filter how we see the world. Studies of science communication show people tend to reject scientific findings that clash with their political worldview, and readily accept those that don't.[44]

Combine this form of motivated reasoning with the allure of money, and you have a recipe for inaction. The oil companies whose profits derive from selling fossil fuels already knew about climate change in the 1970s and 1980s – their own scientists told them – just as the tobacco companies were aware of the link between smoking and cancer. But those companies exist in a capitalist society that values short-term profit over long-term sustainability, and they are led by (mostly) men who are entrenched in an ideological mindset that prioritizes individual freedom and unregulated enterprise over protecting the environment and ensuring long-term sustainability. So instead of making investments in alternative fuels, these companies doubled down, seeking to maximize the return on investment from fossil fuel extraction, while lobbying governments to delay any regulation on carbon emissions. They even paid some scientists[45] to promote the idea that the science was still too uncertain, and that action on climate change would be premature. Few people today would regard this as ethical behaviour. But we all tend to act based on our value systems, rather than what the science shows.

Worse still, we don't have appropriate ethical frameworks for these kinds of decision. The philosopher James Garvey describes[46] climate change as *ethics smeared out in space and time*. Our individual choices join with the choices of huge numbers of other people, to cause harm to people at some future time, most likely in some other part of the world. Our understanding of ethical behaviour doesn't generally extend that far. We can easily argue it's wrong to kill someone, but can we argue that it is wrong to live a comfortable life today, powered by forms of energy that everybody uses, if in the long term that might make life miserable for people yet unborn? And even when we do recognize we have a responsibility to future generations, it's not clear exactly how much that should restrict our actions today.

We also have difficulty seeing climate change as a problem of collective action, rather than individual action. For many years, the most common message – at least in Western cultures – focused on steps an individual could take to reduce their personal carbon footprints: save energy, fly less, eat less meat, and so on. While these things do matter, individual actions by concerned citizens are dwarfed by the global growth in emissions driven by government policies and corporate profit-seeking. All of our infrastructures – buildings, transportation, large-scale agriculture, manufacturing, shipping, etc. – are built on the assumption that fossil fuels are the dominant energy source and will continue to be. Until we dismantle and replace these infrastructures, it will be very hard for any of us to live a zero-carbon life. So the message that individuals must take responsibility for their own personal carbon footprints merely shifts the blame. The companies most responsible for carbon emissions have been happy to promote this message,[47] as it takes the onus away from them.

The final missing link is politics, and especially the question of how wealth and power influences our political processes. One of the reasons so little has been done about climate change in the last 40 years is that politicians are regularly funded and lobbied by the wealthy corporations who stand to lose the most from strong climate policies. As Machiavelli pointed out[48] anyone seeking change *"will have for his enemies all those who are well off under the existing order of things, and only the lukewarm supporters in those who might be better off under the new."* There will be many opportunities to profit from a massive global investment in zero-carbon infrastructures, but the companies who will benefit either don't yet exist, or are too small to wield political power. We don't have the political structures in place to take collective global action on climate change, and indeed, our current global institutions, such as the UN, are strongly biased towards business as usual, because they are dominated by the wealthy nations who have gained most from the current economic system.

So What Should We Do?

What should people do, in the face of all of this? I am often asked this question by journalists, and I usually try to steer them away from it, because the question itself tends to push us into thinking about our individual contributions to the problem, instead of the vital question of how to bring about political change. If I am challenged to offer guidance, I say the three most important things any of us can do about climate change are, first, to talk about it; second, to get political; and third, to make it your job.

Talking[49] about climate change – with friends, family, co-workers, and even strangers – is vitally important, because it helps to remind us all just how widespread our concerns are, and it helps reinforce our collective values around sustainability. Transformative change is hard. If we avoid talking about it, we'll never know how much other people around us share our concerns, and our political leaders won't know how much support there is for change. Plus, talking about climate change can be therapeutic – instead of bottling up our fears, we share them, which means we can start to help each other turn away from despair and start to galvanize action.

Getting political means joining with others in political campaigning, protest groups, putting pressure on politicians, and helping elect leaders who share our concerns. In a democratic system, change only occurs if large numbers of citizens get together and demand it. Most of the important steps we need to take are in the hands of our elected representatives, whether it's our national leaders, or our local city councillors. Politicians tend to act only on things for which they sense there is widespread support. So make sure local representatives know how you feel about climate change, and join a political organization campaigning for urgent climate action. Make your voice heard.

Finally, by making climate change your job, I mean look for ways to incorporate climate action into how you earn a living, no matter what kind of work you do – including vital but unpaid work such as parenting and volunteering in the community. Virtually every sector of the economy contributes to climate change, either directly through carbon emissions, or indirectly by how it consumes energy and resources, or how it affects people's behaviour. Many jobs will change dramatically over the next few decades, either because of the impacts of climate change, or because of the societal changes needed for a rapid transition to a sustainable world. If you work for a large organization, does it have a climate change plan? Can you get together with co-workers and create one? Can you push for changes in the workplace to make things more sustainable? For some, it might mean looking for a career change, to find a role where your skills and knowledge can be most effective. It might not be obvious where your skills are needed, but there's work to be done everywhere. Ask around, and see what other people are doing – your skills will be needed somewhere.

Most importantly, we must not give into despair, because despair tends to stifle action. There are plenty of people, some claiming to be experts, peddling the idea that we are doomed. Today's climate models – the work of a huge worldwide collaboration among thousands of scientists – show that unchecked climate change will change life on Earth for everyone, causing widespread death and suffering, and destroying many of the world's vital ecosystems. But the models also show us clear pathways to avoid these worst-case scenarios. By acknowledging the severity of the crisis, and then choosing to work for a rapid transition to a sustainable world – choosing hope – we can follow those pathways together.

Notes

1   The 1980s also saw the launch of a campaign funded by the fossil fuel industry, aimed at misleading the public into thinking there was no consensus among scientists. See Supran and Oreskes (2017).
2   See United Nations (1992, Article 2, p. 4).
3   Known as the Conference of the Parties (COP). COP3 in 1997 produced the Kyoto Protocol, which bound 36 industrialized nations to reduce their emissions to below their 1990 levels. Canada later withdrew, and the United States never ratified it. The other nations met the target, but largely through accounting tricks, and global emissions rose sharply through this period. See Grubb (2016) for a thoughtful discussion on what Kyoto did achieve. COP21 in 2015 produced the Paris Agreement, under which each country was free to determine its own commitments to reduce emissions, but encouraged to improve these commitments on a regular basis. Whether this approach will be more successful is yet to be seen.
4   For a recent discussion of the importance of acknowledging values in climate science, see Pulkkinen et al. (2022).
5   See Randalls (2010) and Gao et al. (2017).
6   See Rijsberman and Swart (1990).
7   I ended up liveblogging much of the conference. See www.easterbrook.ca/steve/topics/conferences/egu2009/
8   The full title of the paper is "Warming caused by cumulative carbon emissions towards the trillionth tonne." See Allen et al. (2009). It's one of a pair of papers in the same issue addressing this question. The other is Meinshausen et al. (2009).
9   See Rijsberman and Swart (1990).
10 Known as the Paleocene-Eocene Thermal Maximum (PETM).
11 The Goddard Institute for Space Studies, in New York.
12 See Hansen et al. (2008).
13 See, for example, Schaeffer et al. (2012), which concludes eventual sea-level rise for 2°C will be double that of 1.5°C.
14 Corals are not explicitly represented in global climate models, so this impact is assessed using sea surface temperatures from an ensemble of climate models to determine whether each reef around the world would cross the threshold for long-term degradation. See Schleussner et al. (2016).
15 In 2018, the IPCC published a special report on the 1.5°C limit, analyzing emissions pathways that could avoid breaching this limit. All require much more rapid emissions reductions than have been proposed under the Paris agreement.

16 See Rogelji et al. (2016). In the early 2020s, improved commitments under the Paris agreement bring this down closer to 2°C, although it remains to be seen whether many countries will achieve their commitments.

17 Technically, older GCMs need to be given as input the concentration of each gas in the atmosphere for each year. Newer Earth System Models, which have an active carbon cycle, only need to be told how much is added each year from human activities.

18 The models used for this work are known as Integrated Assessment Models (IAMs). They model the interaction of population, technology development, economic growth, trade, and so on, and produce estimations of pollution levels as a result. They are sometimes incorrectly called climate models, but are very different from the climate models we have discussed in this book, as they do not simulate the physical climate system. See Figure 1.4 in Chapter 1.

19 Climate models don't tell us anything about the likelihood of societal collapse. But other kinds of analysis have assessed the possibility, particularly if higher warming leads to widespread food shortages. See, for example, Kemp et al. (2022).

20 The report also shows the temperature increases when these scenarios are extrapolated over the twenty-second and twenty-third centuries, showing in each case, warming continues unabated.

21 See Moss et al. (2008) for a detailed summary of this workshop.

22 Roughly speaking, the selected scenarios are at the 5% and 95% confidence levels in each case, over the spread of results from all available IAMs.

23 The IPCC defines radiative forcing relative to pre-industrial times, using the year 1750 as a baseline. So RCPs are labelled by the *change* in forcing over 350 years, up to 2100. How quickly and how much the world will warm in response to this change in forcing is left to the models to calculate.

24 As an example, the CMIP6 ensemble shows a larger model spread than in CMIP5. A handful of the CMIP6 models had significantly higher climate sensitivity than the before, but analyses showed these models were also the poorest at reproducing past temperature changes. For a discussion see Tokarska et al. (2020).

25 For a detailed quantification of how the relative contribution of each source of uncertainty over the course of these future projections, see Lehner et al. (2020).

26 The project was inspired by SETI@home, which harnesses people's home computers to help Search for ExtraTerrestrial Intelligence. Climateprediction.net uses the same distributed computing platform as SETI@home. It uses an older version of the UK Met Office model, exploiting the fact that home computers today run as fast as supercomputers from previous decades.

27 See Ackerley et al. (2009).

28 See Sparrow et al. (2018).

29 Note that one tonne of carbon actually means 3.67 tonnes of carbon dioxide, because of the extra weight of the oxygen atoms. Measures of annual emissions are normally given in tonnes of CO_2, rather than tonnes of C.

30 For just the one variable: global average surface temperature. The simple model cannot compute any other climate indicators.

31 In 2020, the global pandemic caused a drop in annual emissions of around 5%, but they rebounded fully by 2021.

32 See Solomon et al. (2013).

33 In Chapter 6, we met Damon Matthew's "world without us" experiments, where he demonstrated this in a climate model. Ongoing warming as the oceans take time to reach equilibrium is roughly balanced by a slight cooling from natural greenhouse gas removal processes.

34 The fossil fuel industry puts of a lot of emphasis on carbon capture and storage (CCS) which they hope would allow us to keep burning fossil fuels for energy while capturing the carbon before it goes up the chimney. But this is largely an unproven technology, and would only work at large-scale power plants. It's also not clear whether the CO_2 can be reliably stored so it never reaches the atmosphere.

35 The Guardian estimated profits of nearly US$3 billion per day since 1970. See Carrington (2022).

36 IPCC (2018, p. 9).

37 The simplified models used were Model for the Assessment of Greenhouse Gas-Induced Climate Change (MAGICC) and Finite Amplitude Impulse Response (FAIR). See IPCC (2018, Chapter 2).

38 The report estimated the remaining carbon budget to be around 580 gigatonnes of CO_2, or about 11 years' worth of emissions at 2018's rate, when the report was published. For comparison with the trillion tonne study, that would imply a total cumulative budget of about 0.75 trillion tonnes of carbon.

39 A point made very well by Seth Klein in his book "A Good War." See Klein (2020).

40 See Lenton et al. (2019).

41 See Caesar et al. (2018).

42 See Stern (2016).

43 See, for example, Howard and Sylvan (2015) and Kikstra et al. (2021).

44 See, for example, Lewandowsky et al. (2013).

45 See Oreskes and Conway (2010).

46 See Garvey (2008).

47 See, for example, BP's personal carbon footprint calculator, which they heavily advertised in the early 2000s, helping to popularize the idea. See Doyle (2011).

48 From Machiavelli (1532).

49 See Hayhoe (2021).

References

Abraham, R., & Ueda, Y. (2000). *The Chaos Avant-Garde: Memories of the Early Days of Chaos Theory*. Singapore: World Scientific.

Ackerley, D., Highwood, E. J., & Frame, D. J. (2009). Quantifying the Effects of Perturbing the Physics of an Interactive Sulfur Scheme Using an Ensemble of GCMs on the Climateprediction.net Platform. *Journal of Geophysical Research Atmospheres*, *114*(1), 1–14.

Ackerman, F., DeCanio, S. J., Howarth, R. B., & Sheeran, K. (2009). Limitations of Integrated Assessment Models of Climate Change. *Climatic Change*, *95*(3–4), 297–315.

Alexander, K., & Easterbrook, S. M. (2015). The Software Architecture of Climate Models: A Graphical Comparison of CMIP5 and EMICAR5 Configurations. *Geoscientific Model Development*, *8*(4), 1221–1232.

Allaho, M. Y., & Lee, W. (2015). Analyzing the Social Networks of Contributors in Open Source Software Community. In P. Kazienko & N. Chawla (Eds.), *Applications of Social Media and Social Network Analysis* (pp. 57–75). Cham: Springer International Publishing.

Allen, M. R., Frame, D. J., Huntingford, C. et al. (2009). Warming Caused by Cumulative Carbon Emissions towards the Trillionth Tonne. *Nature*, *458*(7242), 1163–1166.

Anonymous. (1963, January). The General Circulation: A Testing Ground. *NCAR Quarterly*.

Arakawa, A. (2000). A Personal Perspective on the Early Years of General Circulation Modeling at UCLA. In D. A. Randall (Ed.), *General Circulation Model Development: Past, Present, and Future* (pp. 1–65). San Diego, CA: Academic Press.

Arakawa, A., & Lamb, V. R. (1977). Computational Design of the Basic Dynamical Processes of the UCLA General Circulation Model. *Methods in Computational Physics: Advances in Research and Applications*, *17*(1), 173–265.

Archer, D., & Pierrehumbert, R. T. (2011). *The Warming Papers*. Oxford: Wiley-Blackwell.

Armour, K. C., & Roe, G. H. (2011). Climate Commitment in an Uncertain World. *Geophysical Research Letters*, *38*(1), 1–5.

Arnlond, J. R., & Anderson, E. C. (1957). The Distribution of Carbon-14 in Nature. *Tellus*, *9*(1), 28–32.

313

Arrhenius, S. (1896). On the Influence of Carbonic Acid in the Air upon the Temperature of the Ground. *Philosophical Magazine and Journal of Science*, *41*(251), 237–276.

Arrhenius, S. (1896). Über Den Einfluss Des Atmosphärischen Kohlensäuregehalts auf Die Temperatur Der Erdoberfläche. *Appendix to the Papers of the Royal Swedish Academy of Sciences (Bihang till Konglig Svenska Vetenskaps-Akademiens Handlingar)*, *29*(1), 1–102.

Aspray, W. (1990). *John von Neumann and the Origins of Modern Computing*. Cambridge, MA: MIT Press.

Aumont, O., Ethé, C., Tagliabue, A., Bopp, L., & Gehlen, M. (2015). PISCES-v2: An Ocean Biogeochemical Model for Carbon and Ecosystem Studies. *Geoscientific Model Development*, *8*(8), 2465–2513.

Baker, A. H., Hammerling, D. M., Levy, M. N. et al. (2015). A New Ensemble-Based Consistency Test for the Community Earth System Model (pyCECT v1.0). *Geoscientific Model Development*, *8*(9), 2829–2840.

Baker, E. (2007). *Hadley Centre Review 2006 Final Report*.

Bauer, P., Thorpe, A. J., & Brunet, G. (2015). The Quiet Revolution of Numerical Weather Prediction. *Nature*, *525*(7567), 47–55.

Beck, K. (2002). *Test-Driven Development by Example*. Boston, MA: Addison-Wesley.

Bender, M. (2013). *Paleoclimate*. Princeton, NJ: Princeton University Press.

Bjerknes, V. (1904). Das Problem der Wettervorhersage, betrachtet vom Standpunkte der Mechanik und der Physik (The Problem of Weather Prediction, Considered from the Viewpoints of Mechanics and Physics). *Meteorologische Zeitschrift*, *21*(1–7), 663–667.

Bolin, B., & Eriksson, E. (1958). Changes in the Carbon Dioxide Content of the Atmosphere and Sea Due to Fossil Fuel Combustion. In B. Bolin (Ed.), *The Atmosphere and the Sea in Motion: Scientific Contributions to the Rossby Memorial Volume 1* (pp. 130–142). New York: Rockefeller Institute Press.

Bony, S., Stevens, B., Held, I. M. et al. (2013). Carbon Dioxide and Climate: Perspectives on a Scientific Assessment. In Ghassem R. Asrar & James W. Hurrell (Eds.), *Climate Science for Serving Society* (pp. 391–413). Dordrecht: Springer.

Braconnot, P., Marti, O., & Joussaume, S. (1997). Adjustment and Feedbacks in a Global Coupled Ocean-Atmosphere Model. *Climate Dynamics*, *13*(7–8), 507–519.

Brand, S. (1995). *How Buildings Learn: What Happens after They're Built*. New York, NY: Viking Press.

Bretherton, F., Fulker, D., Gille, J. et al. (1975). *Development and Use of the NCAR GCM*. Technical Report No. NCAR-TN/STR-101, National Center for Atmospheric Research.

Broecker, W. S. (1987). Unpleasant Surprises in the Greenhouse? *Nature*, *328*(6126), 123–126.

Brown, A., Milton, S., Cullen, M. et al. (2012). Unified Modeling and Prediction of Weather and Climate: A 25-Year Journey. *Bulletin of the American Meteorological Society*, *93*(12), 1865–1877.

Brownsword, L., & Clements, P. C. (1996). *A Case Study in Successful Product Line Development* (No. CMU/SEI-96-TR-016). Pittsburgh: Software Engineering Institute, Carnegie Mellon University.

Bryan, K., Manabe, S., & Pacanowski, R. C. (1975). A Global Ocean-Atmosphere Climate Model. Part II. The Oceanic Circulation. *Journal of Physical Oceanography*, 5(1), 30–46.

Caesar, L., Rahmstorf, S., Robinson, A., Feulner, G., & Saba, V. (2018). Observed Fingerprint of a Weakening Atlantic Ocean Overturning Circulation. *Nature*, 556(7700), 191–196.

Callendar, G. S. (1938). The Artificial Production of Carbon Dioxide and Its Influence on Temperature. *Quarterly Journal of the Royal Meteorological Society*, 64(1909), 223–240.

Carrington, D. (2022, July 21). Revealed: Oil Sector's 'Staggering' $3bn-a-day Profits for Last 50 years. *The Guardian*.

Cess, R. D., & Potter, G. L. (1988). A Methodology for Understanding and Intercomparing Atmospheric Climate Feedback Processes in General Circulation Models. *Journal of Geophysical Research*, 93(D7), 8305.

Cess, R. D., Potter, G. L., Blanchet, J. P. et al. (1989). Interpretation of Cloud-Climate Feedback as Produced by 14 Atmospheric General Circulation Models. *Science*, 245(4917), 513–516.

Charney, J. G., Arakawa, A., Baker, J., Bolin, B., Dickinson, R. E., Goody, R. M., … Wunsch, C. I. (1979). *Carbon Dioxide and Climate: A Scientific Assessment*. Washington, DC: US National Academies.

Charney, J. G., & Eliassen, A. (1949). A Numerical Method for Predicting the Perturbations of the Middle Latitude Westerlies. *Tellus A*, 2, 38–54.

Charney, J. G., Fjörtoft, R., & Neumann, J. Von. (1950). Numerical Integration of the Barotropic Vorticity Equation. *Tellus*, 2(4), 237–254.

Chassignet, E. P., & Xu, X. (2017). Impact of Horizontal Resolution (1/12° to 1/50°) on Gulf Stream Separation, Penetration, and Variability. *Journal of Physical Oceanography*, 47(8), 1999–2021.

Cinquini, L., Crichton, D., Mattmann, C. et al. (2014). The Earth System Grid Federation: An Open Infrastructure for Access to Distributed Geospatial Data. *Future Generation Computer Systems*, 36, 400–417.

Connolley, W. M., & Bracegirdle, T. J. (2007). An Antarctic Assessment of IPCC AR4 Coupled Models. *Geophysical Research Letters*, 34(22), L22505.

Conway, M. E. (1968). How Do Committees Invent. *Datamation*, 14(4), 28–31.

Craig, A., Valcke, S., & Coquart, L. (2017). Development and Performance of a New Version of the OASIS Coupler, OASIS3-MCT-3.0. *Geoscientific Model Development*, 10(9), 3297–3308.

Craig, H. (1957). The Natural Distribution of Radiocarbon and the Exchange Time of Carbon Dioxide between Atmosphere and Sea. *Tellus*, 9(1), 1–17.

Crawford, E. (1996). *Arrhenius: From Ionic Theory to the Greenhouse Effect*. Canton, MA: Science History Publications.

Crutzen, P. J. (2006). Albedo Enhancement by Stratospheric Sulfur Injections: A Contribution to Resolve a Policy Dilemma? *Climatic Change*, 77(3–4), 211–219.

Cubasch, U., & Cess., R. D. (1990). Processes and Modelling. In J. T. Houghton, G. J. Jenkins, & J. J. Ephraums (Eds.), *Climate Change: The IPCC Scientific Assessment: Report Prepared for Intergovernmental Panel on Climate Change by Working Group I* (pp. 69–91). Cambridge, UK: Cambridge University Press.

Dahan, A. (2010). Putting the Earth System in a Numerical Box? The Evolution from Climate Modeling toward Global Change. *Studies in History and Philosophy of Science Part B: Studies in History and Philosophy of Modern Physics*, *41*(3), 282–292.

Davies, T., Cullen, M. J. P., Malcolm, A. J. et al. (2005). A New Dynamical Core of the Met Office's Global and Regional Modelling of the Atmosphere. *Quarterly Journal of the Royal Meteorological Society*, *131*(608), 1759–1782.

Dennis, J. M., & Loft, R. D. (2011). Refactoring Scientific Applications for Massive Parallelism. In P. Lauritzen, C. Jablonowski, M. Taylor, & R. Nair (Eds.), *Numerical Techniques for Global Atmospheric Models* (pp. 539–556). Heidelberg, Germany: Springer-Verlag.

Diacu, F. (1996). The Solution of the N-Body Problem. *The Mathematical Intelligencer*, *18*(3), 66–70.

Doyle, J. (2011). Where Has All the Oil Gone? BP Branding and the Discursive Elimination of Climate Change Risk. In N. Heffernan & D. Wragg (Eds.), *Culture, Environment and Ecopolitics* (pp. 200–225). Newcastle upon Tyne, UK: Cambridge Scholars Press.

Dufresne, J.-L. (2008). La détermination de la constante solaire par Claude Matthias Pouillet. *La Météorologie*, *8*(60), 36.

Dufresne, J.-L. (2009). *L'effet de serre: sa découverte, son analyse par la méthode des puissances nettes échangées et les effets de ses variations récentes et futures sur le climat terrestre*. Université Pierre et Marie Curie, Paris.

Dyson, G. (2012). *Turing's Cathedral*. New York, NY: Pantheon Books.

Easterbrook, S. M., & Johns, T. C. (2009). Engineering the Software for Understanding Climate Change. *Computing in Science & Engineering*, *11*(6), 65–74.

Edwards, P. N. (1997). *Interview of Cecil Leith by Paul Edwards*. Niels Bohr Library & Archives. American Institute of Physics, College Park, MD. www.aip.org/history-programs/niels-bohr-library/oral-histories/31392

Edwards, P. N. (1998). *Interview of Akira Kasahara by Paul Edwards*. Niels Bohr Library & Archives. American Institute of Physics, College Park, MD. www.aip.org/history-programs/niels-bohr-library/oral-histories/32440-1

Edwards, P. N. (2000). A Brief History of Atmospheric General Circulation Modeling. In D. A. Randall (Ed.), *General Circulation Model Development: Past, Present, and Future* (Vol. 70, pp. 67–90). San Diego, CA: Academic Press.

Edwards, P. N. (2010). *A Vast Machine: Computer Models, Climate Data, and the Politics of Global Warming*. Cambridge, Massachusetts: MIT Press.

Ekholm, N. (1901). On the Variations of the Climate of the Geological and Historical Past and Their Causes. *Quarterly Journal of the Royal Meteorological Society*, *27*(117), 1–62.

England, M. H., Kajtar, J. B., & Maher, N. (2015). Robust Warming Projections Despite the Recent Hiatus. *Nature Climate Change*, *5*(5), 394–396.

Eyring, V., Bony, S., Meehl, G. A. et al. (2016). Overview of the Coupled Model Intercomparison Project Phase 6 (CMIP6) Experimental Design and Organization. *Geoscientific Model Development*, *9*(5), 1937–1958.

Feldman, D. R., Collins, W. D., Gero, P. J. et al. (2015). Observational Determination of Surface Radiative Forcing by CO2 from 2000 to 2010. *Nature*, *519*(7543), 339–343.

Ferreira, D., Marshall, J., & Campin, J. M. (2010). Localization of Deep Water Formation: Role of Atmospheric Moisture Transport and Geometrical Constraints on Ocean Circulation. *Journal of Climate*, *23*(6), 1456–1476.

Feyerabend, P. (1975). *Against Method: Outline of an Anarchist Theory of Knowledge.* London: New Left Books.

Finkbeiner, A. K. (2006). *The Jasons: The Secret History of Science's Postwar Elite.* New York, NY: Viking Press.

Fisher, A. (1988). One Model to Fit All. *Mosaic*, *19*(3).

Fishman, C. (1998). They Write the Wight Stuff. *IEEE Engineering Management Review*, *26*(4), 26–31.

Fleming, J. R. (1999). Joseph Fourier, the 'Greenhouse Effect', and the Quest for a Universal Theory of Terrestrial Temperatures. *Endeavour*, *23*(2), 72–75.

Foote, E. (1856). Circumstances Affecting the Heat of the Sun's Rays. *American Journal of Art and Science*, *23*(67), 382–383.

Fourier, J. (1827). On the Temperatures of the Terrestrial Sphere and Interplanetary Space. *Mémoires de l'Académie Royale Des Sciences*, *7*, 569–604.

Frenzen, P. (1993). *Interview of Dave Fultz.* American Meteorological Society Oral History Project. https://opensky.ucar.edu/islandora/object/archives:7598/

Friedman, R. M. (1993). *Appropriating the Weather: Vilhelm Bjerknes and the Construction of a Modern Meteorology.* Ithaca, NY: Cornell University Press.

Frigg, R., & Reiss, J. (2009). The Philosophy of Simulation: Hot New Issues or Same Old Stew? *Synthese*, *169*(3), 593–613.

Frölicher, T. L., Sarmiento, J. L., Paynter, D. J. et al. (2015). Dominance of the Southern Ocean in Anthropogenic Carbon and Heat Uptake in CMIP5 Models. *Journal of Climate*, *28*(2), 862–886.

Fultz, D. (1949). A Preliminary Report on Experiments with Thermally Produced Lateral Mixing in a Rotating Hemispherical Shell of Liquid. *Journal of Meteorology*, *6*(1), 17–33.

Gao, Y., Gao, X., & Zhang, X. (2017). The 2 °C Global Temperature Target and the Evolution of the Long-Term Goal of Addressing Climate Change – From the United Nations Framework Convention on Climate Change to the Paris Agreement. *Engineering*, *3*(2), 272–278.

Garvey, J. (2008). *The Ethics of Climate Change: Right and Wrong in a Warming World.* London, UK: Continuum International Publishing.

Gates, W. L. (1992). AMIP: The Atmospheric Model Intercomparison Project. *Bulletin of the American Meteorological Society*, *73*(12), 1962–1970.

Gleckler, P. J., Randall, D. A., Boer, G. et al. (1995). Cloud-Radiative Effects on Implied Oceanic Energy Transports as Simulated by Atmospheric General Circulation Models. *Geophysical Research Letters*, *22*(7), 791–794.

Gleick, J. (1987). *Chaos: Making a New Science.* New York, NY: Viking Books.

Grubb, M. (2016). Full Legal Compliance with the Kyoto Protocol's First Commitment Period – Some Lessons. *Climate Policy*, *16*(6), 673–681.

Hanel, R. A., Conrath, B. J., Kunde, V. G. et al. (1972). The Nimbus 4 Infrared Spectroscopy Experiment: 1. Calibrated Thermal Emission Spectra. *Journal of Geophysical Research*, *77*(15), 2629–2641.

Hansen, J. E., Sato, M., Kharecha, P. et al. (2008). Target Atmospheric CO2: Where Should Humanity Aim? *Open Atmospheric Science Journal*, *2*(15), 217–231.

Harper, K. C. (2008). *Weather by the Numbers: The Genesis of Moden Meteorology.* Cambridge, MA: MIT Press.

Harper, K. C., Doel, R., & Smagorinsky Thompson, T. (2006). *Interview of Margaret Smagorinsky.* American Meteorological Society Oral History Project. https://opensky.ucar.edu/islandora/object/archives%3A7644

Hausfather, Z., Drake, H. F., Abbott, T., & Schmidt, G. A. (2020). Evaluating the Performance of Past Climate Model Projections. *Geophysical Research Letters,* *47*(1), 2019GL085378.

Hayhoe, K. (2021). *Saving Us: A Climate Scientist's Case for Hope and Healing in a Divided World.* Atria/One Signal Publishers.

Hegerl, G. C., Zwiers, F. W., Braconnot, P. et al. (2007). Understanding and Attributing Climate Change. In S. Solomon, D. Qin, M. Manning, Z. Chen, M. Marquis, K. B. Averyt, … H. L. Miller (Eds.), *Climate Change 2007: The Physical Science Basis. Contribution of Working Group I to the Fourth Assessment Report of the Intergovernmental Panel on Climate Change* (pp. 663–745). Cambridge, UK: Cambridge University Press.

Held, I. M. (2005). The Gap between Simulation and Understanding in Climate Modeling. *Bulletin of the American Meteorological Society,* *86*(11), 1609–1614.

Herraiz, I., Gonzalez-Barahona, J. M., & Robles, G. (2007). Towards a Theoretical Model for Software Growth. In *Fourth International Workshop on Mining Software Repositories (MSR'07:ICSE Workshops 2007)* (pp. 21–21). IEEE.

Högbom, A. (1894). Om sannolikheten för sekulära förändringar i atmosfärens kolsyrehalt (On the probability of global changes in the level of atmospheric carbon dioxide). *Svensk Kemisk Tidskrift (Swedish Chemical Journal),* *6*, 169–177.

Hourdin, F., Mauritsen, T., Gettelman, A. et al. (2017). The Art and Science of Climate Model Tuning. *Bulletin of the American Meteorological Society,* *98*(3), 589–602.

Hovy, C. (2020). *Unittests für die Klimamodellentwicklung.* PhD thesis, University of Hamburg.

Howard, P., & Sylvan, D. (2015). *Expert Consensus on the Economics of Climate Change.* Institute for Policy Integrity, New York, NY: New York University School of Law.

Hurrell, J., Meehl, G. A., Bader, D. et al. (2009). A Unified Modeling Approach to Climate System Prediction. *Bulletin of the American Meteorological Society,* *90*(12), 1819–1832.

IPCC. (2021). Summary for Policymakers. In V. Masson-Delmotte, P. Zhai, A. Pirani, S. L. Connors, C. Péan, S. Berger, … B. Zhou (Eds.), *Climate Change 2021: The Physical Science Basis. Contribution of Working Group I to the Sixth Assessment Report of the Intergovernmental Panel on Climate Change* (pp. 3–32). Cambridge, UK: Cambridge University Press.

IPCC. (2018). Global Warming of 1.5°C, Summary for Policymakers. Geneva.

IPCC. (1998). Principles Governing IPCC Work. Geneva.

Jackson, S. J., Arbor, A., Ribes, D., & Arbor, A. (2010). Exploring Collaborative Rhythm: Temporal Flow and Alignment in Collaborative Scientific Work. In *iConference, 3–6 February, 2010* (245–254). Urbana-Champaign, IL.

Jakob, C. (2010). Accelerating Progress in Global Atmospheric Model Development through Improved Parameterizations. *Bulletin of the American Meteorological Society,* *91*(7), 869–876.

Jouzel, J., Masson-Delmotte, V., Cattani, O. et al. (2007). Orbital and Mmillennial Antarctic Climate Variability Over the Past 800,000 Years. *Science (New York, N.Y.)*, *317*(5839), 793–796.

Karl, T., Hassol, S. J., Miller, C. D., & Murray, W. (2006). *Temperature Trends in the Lower Atmosphere: Steps for Understanding and Reconciling Differences.* Washington, DC: US Climate Change Science Program.

Kasahara, A. (2015). Serendipity: Research Career of One Scientist. NCAR Technical Note NCAR/TN-507+PROC (Vol. 507).

Katzav, J., & Parker, W. S. (2015). The Future of Climate Modeling. *Climatic Change*, *132*(4), 475–487.

Keeling, R. F., Walker, S. J., Piper, S. C., & Bollenbacher, A. F. (2018). Scripps CO2 Program. Retrieved from http://scrippsco2.ucsd.edu

Kemp, L., Xu, C., Depledge, J. et al. (2022). Climate Endgame: Exploring Catastrophic Climate Change Scenarios. *Proceedings of the National Academy of Sciences*, *119*(34).

Kikstra, J. S., Waidelich, P., Rising, J. et al. (2021). The Social Cost of Carbon Dioxide Under Climate-Economy Feedbacks and Temperature Variability. *Environmental Research Letters*, *16*(9).

Klein, S. (2020). *A Good War: Mobilizing Canada for the Climate Emergency*. Toronto, Canada: ECW Press.

Knutti, R., & Rogelj, J. (2015). The Legacy of Our CO2 Emissions: A Clash of Scientific Facts, Politics and Ethics. *Climatic Change*, *133*(3), 361–373.

Knutti, R., Rugenstein, M. A. A., & Hegerl, G. C. (2017). Beyond Equilibrium Climate Sensitivity. *Nature Geoscience*, *10*(10), 727–736.

Knutti, R., & Sedláček, J. (2013). Robustness and Uncertainties in the New CMIP5 Climate Model Projections. *Nature Climate Change*, *3*(4), 369–373.

Lakatos, I. (1976). Falsification and the Methodology of Scientific Research Programmes. In *Can Theories be Refuted?* (pp. 205–259). Dordrecht, Holland: Springer Netherlands.

Lamb, W. F., Mattioli, G., Levi, S. et al. (2020). Discourses of Climate Delay. *Global Sustainability*, *3*, 1–5.

Latour, B., & Woolgar, S. (1979). *Laboratory Life: The Social Construction of Scientific Facts*. Beverly Hills: SAGE Publications Ltd.

Laurent, C., Le Treut, H., Fairhead, L., & Dufresne, J.-L. (1998). *The Influence of Resolution in Simulating Inter-Annual and Inter-Decadal Variability in a Coupled Ocean-Atmosphere GCM, with Emphasis Over the North Atlantic.* Paris: Université Pierre et Marie Curie.

Lawrence, B. N., Rezny, M., Budich, R. et al. (2018). Crossing the Chasm: How to Develop Weather and Climate Models for Next Generation Computers? *Geoscientific Model Development*, *11*(5), 1799–1821.

Lehner, F., Deser, C., Maher, N. et al. (2020). Partitioning Climate Projection Uncertainty with Multiple Large Ensembles and CMIP5/6. *Earth System Dynamics*, *11*(2), 491–508.

Lenhard, J., & Winsberg, E. (2010). Holism, Entrenchment, and the Future of Climate Model Pluralism. *Studies in History and Philosophy of Science Part B: Studies in History and Philosophy of Modern Physics*, *41*(3), 253–262.

Lenton, T. M., Rockström, J., Gaffney, O. et al. (2019). Climate Tipping Points – Too Risky to Bet Against. *Nature*, *575*(7784), 592–595.

Leveson, N. G. (1995). *Safeware: System Safety and Computers*. Reading, MA: Addison-Wesley.

Lewandowsky, S. (2020). Climate Change Disinformation and How to Combat It. *Annual Review of Public Health*, *42*, 1–21.

Lewandowsky, S., Cowtan, K., Risbey, J. S. et al. (2018). The 'Pause' in Global Warming in Historical Context: (II). Comparing Models to Observations. *Environmental Research Letters*, *13*(12), 123007.

Lewandowsky, S., Oberauer, K., & Gignac, G. E. (2013). NASA Faked the Moon Landing – Therefore, (Climate) Science Is a Hoax: An Anatomy of the Motivated Rejection of Science. *Psychological Science*, *24*(5), 622–633.

Lewis, J. M. (1993). Meteorologists from the University of Tokyo: Their Exodus to the United States Following World War II. *Bulletin of the American Meteorological Society*, *74*(7), 1351–1360.

Lewis, J. M. (1998). Clarifying the Dynamics of the General Circulation: Phillips's 1956 Experiment. *Bulletin of the American Meteorological Society*, *79*(1), 39–60.

Li, X., & Peng, X. (2018). Long-Term Integration of a Global Non-Hydrostatic Atmospheric Model on an Aqua Planet. *Journal of Meteorological Research*, *32*(4), 517–533.

Lorenz, E. N. (1963). Deterministic Nonperiodic Flow. *Journal of the Atmospheric Sciences*, *20*(2), 130–141.

Lorenz, E. N. (1993). *The Essence of Chaos*. Seattle, WA: University of Washington Press.

Lorenz, E. N. (2006). Reflections on the Conception, Birth, and Childhood of Numerical Weather Prediction. *Annual Review of Earth and Planetary Sciences*, *34*(1), 37–45.

Lozier, M. S. (2010). Deconstructing the Conveyor Belt. *Science*, *328*(5985), 1507–1511.

Lynch, P. (1993). Richardson's Forecast Factory: the $64,000 Question. *The Meteorological Magazine*, *122*, 69–70.

Lynch, P. (2008). The Origins of Computer Weather Prediction and Climate Modeling. *Journal of Computational Physics*, *227*(7), 3431–3444. https://doi.org/10.1016/j.jcp.2007.02.034

Lynch, P. (2014). *The Emergence of Numerical Weather Prediction: Richardson's Dream*. Cambridge, UK: Cambridge University Press.

Lynch, P. (2016). An Artist's Impression of Richardson's Fantastic Forecast Factory. *Weather*, *71*(1), 14–18.

Lynch, P., & Lynch, O. (2008). Forecasts by PHONIAC. *Weather*, *63*(11), 324–326. https://doi.org/10.1002/wea.241

MacDonald, G., Abarbanel, H., Carruthers, P. et al. (1979). *The Long Term Impact of Atmospheric Carbon Dioxide on Climate*. Technical Report No. JSR-78-07. SRI International.

Machiavelli, N. (1532). *The Prince*. Antonio Blado d'Asola.

Madec, G. (2008). *NEMO Ocean Engine*. IPSL Technical Report.

Madey, G., Freeh, V., & Tynan, R. (2002). The Open Source Software Development Phenomenon: An Analysis Based on Social Network Theory. In *Americas Conference on Information Systems (AMCIS)*, Vol. 247, pp. 1806–1813.

Maher, N., Milinski, S., Suarez-Gutierrez, L. et al. (2019). The Max Planck Institute Grand Ensemble: Enabling the Exploration of Climate System Variability. *Journal of Advances in Modeling Earth Systems*, *11*(7), 2050–2069.

Manabe, S., & Bryan, K. (1969). Climate Calculations with a Combined Ocean-Atmosphere Model. *Journal of the Atmospheric Sciences*, *26*(4), 786–789.

Manabe, S., & Wetherald, R. T. (1967). Thermal Equilibrium of the Atmosphere with a Given Distribution of Relative Humidity. *Journal of the Atmospheric Sciences*, *24*(3), 241–259.

Manabe, S., & Wetherald, R. T. (1975). The Effects of Doubling the CO_2 Concentration on the Climate of a General Circulation Model. *Journal of the Atmospheric Sciences*, *32*(1), 3–15.

Matthews, D., Wilson, G. V., & Easterbrook, S. M. (2008). Configuration Management for Large-Scale Scientific Computing at the UK Met Office. *Computing in Science & Engineering*, *10*(6), 56–64.

Matthews, H. D., & Caldeira, K. (2008). Stabilizing Climate Requires Near-Zero Emissions. *Geophysical Research Letters*, *35*(4), 1–5.

Mauritsen, T., Bader, J., Becker, T. et al. (2019). Developments in the MPI-M Earth System Model Version 1.2 (MPI-ESM1.2) and Its Response to Increasing CO 2. *Journal of Advances in Modeling Earth Systems*, *11*(4), 998–1038.

Mauritsen, T., Stevens, B., Roeckner, E. et al. (2012). Tuning the Climate of a Global Model. *Journal of Advances in Modeling Earth Systems*, *4*(3).

McCusker, K. E., Armour, K. C., Bitz, C. M., & Battisti, D. S. (2014). Rapid and Extensive Warming Following Cessation of Solar Radiation Management. *Environmental Research Letters*, *9*(2).

McGuffie, K., & Henderson-Sellers, A. (2005). *A Climate Modelling Primer. A Climate Modelling Primer* (Vol. 1). Chichester, UK: John Wiley & Sons, Ltd.

Meehl, G. A., Boer, G. J., Covey, C., Latif, M., & Stouffer, R. J. (2000). The Coupled Model Intercomparison Project (CMIP). *Bulletin of the American Meteorological Society*, *81*(2), 313–318.

Meehl, G. A., Teng, H., & Arblaster, J. M. (2014). Climate Model Simulations of the Observed Early-2000s Hiatus of Global Warming. *Nature Climate Change*, *4*(10), 898–902.

Meinshausen, M., Meinshausen, N., Hare, W. et al. (2009). Greenhouse-Gas Emission Targets for Limiting Global Warming to 2 Degrees C. *Nature*, *458*(7242), 1158–1162.

Mohr, S. E. (2018). *First in Fly*. Cambridge, MA: Harvard University Press.

Möller, F. (1963). On the Influence of Changes in the CO_2 Concentration in Air on the Radiation Balance of the Earth's Surface and on the Climate. *Journal of Geophysical Research*, *68*(13), 3877–3886.

Monnin, E., Indermühle, A., Dällenbach, A. et al. (2001). Atmospheric CO_2 Concentrations Over the Last Glacial Termination. *Science (New York, N.Y.)*, *291*(5501), 112–114.

Moore, G. E. (2006). Moore's Law at 40. In D. C. Brock (Ed.), *Understanding Moore's Law: Four Decades of Innovation* (pp. 67–84), Philadelphia, PA.

Moss, R. H., Babiker, M., Brinkman, S. et al. (2008). *Towards New Scenarios for Analysis of Emissions, Climate Change, Impacts, and Response Strategies: IPCC Expert Meeting Report*. IPCC. Geneva.

Moss, R. H., Edmonds, J. A., Hibbard, K. A. et al. (2010). The Next Generation of Scenarios for Climate Change Research and Assessment. *Nature, 463*(7282), 747–756.

NASA. (1986). *Earth System Science.* Washington, DC: National Academies Press.

National Academies. (2016). *From Maps to Models. From Maps to Models: Augmenting the Nation's Geospatial Intelligence Capabilities.* Washington, DC: National Academies Press.

National Academies of Sciences Engineering and Medicine. (2017). *Valuing Climate Changes: Updating Estimation of the Social Cost of Carbon Dioxide.* Washington, DC: National Academies Press.

Nebeker, F. (1995). *Calculating the Weather. International Geophysical Series* (Vol. 60). Academic Press.

Olson, S. (2014). The National Academy of Sciences at 150. *Proceedings of the National Academy of Sciences, 111*(Supplement_2), 9327–9364.

Oreskes, N., & Conway, E. M. (2010). *Merchants of Doubt: How a Handful of Scientists Obscured the Truth on Issues from Tobacco Smoke to Global Warming.* New York, NY: Bloomsbury Press.

Oreskes, N., Shrader-Frechette, K., & Belitz, K. (1994). Verification, Validation, and Confirmation of Numerical Models in the Earth Sciences. *Science, 263*(5147), 641.

Ortiz, J. D., & Jackson, R. (2022). Understanding Eunice Foote's 1856 Experiments: Heat Absorption by Atmospheric Gases. *Notes and Records: The Royal Society Journal of the History of Science, 76*(1), 67–84.

Parnas, D. L. (1994). Software Aging. In *Proceedings of 16th International Conference on Software Engineering* (pp. 279–287). IEEE Comput. Soc. Press.

Perrow, C. (1984). *Normal Accidents: Living with High Risk Technologies.* Princeton, NJ: Princeton university press.

Persson, A. O. (2006). Hadley's Principle: Understanding and Misunderstanding the Trade Winds. *History of Meteorology, 3*, 17–42.

Peterson, T. C., Connolley, W. M., & Fleck, J. (2008). The Myth of the 1970s Global Cooling Scientific Consensus. *Bulletin of the American Meteorological Society, 89*(9), 1325–1337.

Petit, J. R., Basile, I., Leruyuet, A. et al. (1997). Four Climate Cycles in Vostok Ice Core. *Nature, 387*(6631), 359–360.

Petrov, Y. (2012). Harmony: EEG/MEG Linear Inverse Source Reconstruction in the Anatomical Basis of Spherical Harmonics. *PLoS ONE, 7*(10).

Pfeffer, R. L., & Chiang, Y. (1967). Two Kinds of Vacillation in Rotating Laboratory Experiments. *Monthly Weather Review, 95*(2), 75–82.

Phillips, N. A. (1956). The General Circulation of the Atmosphere: A Numerical Experiment. *Quarterly Journal of the Royal Meteorological Society, 82*(352), 123–164.

Pierrehumbert, R. T. (2004). Warming the World. *Nature, 432*(December), 2004.

Pierrehumbert, R. T., & Archer, D. (2011). By the Light of the Silvery Moon. In *The Warming Papers: The Scientific Foundation for the Climate Change Forecast* (pp. 45–55). Oxford, UK: Wiley-Blackwell.

Pindyck, R. S. (2013). Climate Change Policy: What Do the Models Tell Us? *Journal of Economic Literature, 51*(3), 1–23.

Pipitone, J., & Easterbrook, S. M. (2012). Assessing Climate Model Software Quality: A Defect Density Analysis of Three Models. *Geoscientific Model Development*, *5*(4), 1009–1022.

Plass, G. N. (1956). The Carbon Dioxide Theory of Climatic Change. *Tellus A*, *8*, 140–154. https://doi.org/10.3402/tellusa.v8i2.8969

Plass, G. N. (1956). The Influence of the 15μ Carbon-Dioxide Band on the Atmospheric Infra-Red Cooling Rate. *Quarterly Journal of the Royal Meteorological Society*, *82*(353), 310–324.

Plass, G. N. (1959). Carbon Dioxide and Climate. *Scientific American*, *201*(1).

Platzman, G. W. (1979). The ENIAC Computations of 1950: Gateway to Numerical Weather Prediction. *Bulletin of the American Meteorological Society*, *60*, 302–312.

Pope, V., & Davies, T. (2002). Testing and Evaluating Atmospheric Climate Models. *Computing in Science and Engineering*, *4*(5), 64–69.

Poynting, J. H. (1907). On Prof. Lowell's Method for Evaluating the Surface-Temperatures of the Planets; with an Attempt to Represent the Effect of Day and Night on the Temperature of the Earth. *Philosophical Magazine*, *14*(84), 749–760.

Pulkkinen, K., Undorf, S., Bender, F. et al. (2022). The Value of Values in Climate Science. *Nature Climate Change*, *12*(1), 4–6.

Rahmstorf, S. (2002). Ocean Circulation and Climate during the Past 120,000 Years. *Nature*, *419*(6903), 207–214.

Randalls, S. (2010). History of the 2°C Climate Target. *Wiley Interdisciplinary Reviews: Climate Change*, *1*(4), 598–605.

Reason, J. (1997). *Managing the Risks of Organizational Accidents*. London, UK: Ashgate Publishing.

Reichler, T., & Kim, J. (2008). How Well Do Coupled Models Simulate Today's Climate? *Bulletin of the American Meteorological Society*, *89*(3), 303–311.

Revelle, R., Broecker, W. S., Craig, H., Keeling, C. D., & Smagorinsky, J. (1965). Appendix Y4: Atmospheric Carbon Dioxide. In J. W. Tukey (Ed.), *Restoring the Quality of Our Environment*. Washington DC.

Revelle, R., & Suess, H. E. (1957). Carbon Dioxide Exchange between Atmosphere and Ocean and the Question of an Increase of Atmospheric CO2 During the Past Decades. *Tellus*, *9*(1), 18–27.

Richardson, L. F. (1922). *Weather Prediction by Numerical Processes*. Cambridge, UK: Cambridge University Press.

Rijsberman, F. R., & Swart, R. (1990). Targets and Indicators of Climatic Change. Report of Working Group II of the Advisory Group on Greenhouse Gases. The Stockholm Environment Institute.

Rodhe, H., Charlson, R., & Crawford, E. (1997). Svante Arrhenius and the Greenhouse Effect. *Ambio*, *26*(1), 2–5.

Roeckner, E., Mauritsen, T., Esch, M., & Brokopf, R. (2012). Impact of Melt Ponds on Arctic Sea Ice in Past and Future Climates as Simulated by MPI-ESM. *Journal of Advances in Modeling Earth Systems*, *4*(9).

Rogelj, J., den Elzen, M., Höhne, N. et al. (2016). Paris Agreement Climate Proposals Need a Boost to Keep Warming Well below 2 °C. *Nature*, *534*(7609), 631–639.

Rousset, C., Vancoppenolle, M., Madec, G. et al. (2015). The Louvain-La-Neuve Sea Ice Model LIM3.6: Global and Regional Capabilities. *Geoscientific Model Development*, *8*(10), 2991–3005.

Russell, M., Boulton, G., Clarke, P., Eyton, D., & Norton, J. (2010). *The Independent Climate Change E-mails Review*. www.cce-review.org/.

Santer, B. D., Wigley, T. M. L., & Taylor, K. E. (2011). The Reproducibility of Observational Estimates of Surface and Atmospheric Temperature Change. *Science*, *334*(6060), 1232–1233.

Schaeffer, M., Hare, W., Rahmstorf, S., & Vermeer, M. (2012). Long-Term Sea-Level Rise Implied by 1.5 °C and 2 °C Warming Levels. *Nature Climate Change*, *2*(12), 867–870.

Schlesinger, M. (1986). Physically Based Modeling and Simulation of Climate and Climatic Change. *Eos, Transactions American Geophysical Union*, *67*(49), 1377.

Schleussner, C.-F., Lissner, T. K., Fischer, E. M. et al. (2016). Differential Climate Impacts for Policy-Relevant Limits to Global Warming: The Case of 1.5 °C and 2 °C. *Earth System Dynamics*, *7*(2), 327–351.

Schmidt, G. A. (2005). Water Vapour: Feedback or Forcing? Retrieved from www .realclimate.org/index.php/archives/2005/04/water-vapour-feedback-or-forcing/

Schmidt, G. A., & Sherwood, S. (2015). A Practical Philosophy of Complex Climate Modelling. *European Journal for Philosophy of Science*, *5*(2), 149–169.

Schneider, S. H., & Dickinson, R. E. (1974). Climate Modeling. *Reviews of Geophysics*, *12*(3), 447.

Schneider, T., Teixeira, J., Bretherton, C. S. et al. (2017). Climate Goals and Computing the Future of Clouds. *Nature Climate Change*, *7*(1), 3–5.

Schulte-Uebbing, L., Hansen, G., Hernández, A. M., & Winter, M. (2015). Chapter Scientists in the IPCC AR5-Experience and Lessons Learned. *Current Opinion in Environmental Sustainability*, *14*(June), 250–256.

Seidel, D. J., Gillett, N. P., Lanzante, J. R., Shine, K. P., & Thorne, P. W. (2011). Stratospheric Temperature Trends: Our Evolving Understanding. *Wiley Interdisciplinary Reviews: Climate Change*, *2*(4), 592–616.

Serreze, M. C., Barrett, A. P., Stroeve, J. C., Kindig, D. N., & Holland, M. M. (2009). The Emergence of Surface-Based Arctic Amplification. *Cryosphere*, *3*(1), 11–19.

Shackley, S., Risbey, J., Stone, P., & Wynne, B. (1999). *Adjusting to Policy Expectations in Climate Change Modeling: An Interdisciplinary Study of Flux Adjustments in Coupled Atmosphere-Ocean General Circulation Models*. Stockholm, Sweden: The Stockholm Environment Institute.

Shaw, M., & Garlan, D. (1996). *Software Architecture: Perspectives on an Emerging Discipline*. Upper Saddle River, NJ: Prentice Hall.

Simpson, I. R., Tilmes, S., Richter, J. H. et al. (2019). The Regional Hydroclimate Response to Stratospheric Sulfate Geoengineering and the Role of Stratospheric Heating. *Journal of Geophysical Research: Atmospheres*, *124*(23), 12587–12616.

Slingo, J., Bates, K., Nikiforakis, N. et al. (2009). Developing the Next-Generation Climate System Models: Challenges and Achievements. *Philosophical Transactions. Series A, Mathematical, Physical, and Engineering Sciences*, *367*(1890), 815–831.

Smagorinsky, J. (1983). The Beginnings of Numerical Weather Prediction and General Circulation Modelling: Early Recollections. *Advances in Geophysics*, *25*, 3–38.

Snyder, C. W. (2016). Evolution of Global Temperature Over the Past Two Million Years. *Nature*, *18*, 1–17.

Soden, B. J., Held, I. M., Colman, R. et al. (2008). Quantifying Climate Feedbacks Using Radiative Kernels. *Journal of Climate*, *21*(14), 3504–3520.

Soden, B. J., Wetherald, R. T., Stenchikov, G. L., & Robock, A. (2002). Global Cooling After the Eruption of Mount Pinatubo: A Test of Climate Feedback by Water Vapor. *Science*, *296*(5568), 727–730.

Solomon, S., Pierrehumbert, R. T., Matthews, H. D., Daniel, J. S., & Friedlingstein, P. (2013). Atmospheric Composition, Irreversible Climate Change, and Mitigation Policy. In G. R. Asrar & J. W. Hurrell (Eds.), *Climate Science for Serving Society: Research, Modeling and Prediction Priorities* (pp. 415–436). Dordrecht, NL: Springer.

Sparrow, S., Millar, R. J., Yamazaki, K. et al. (2018). Finding Ocean States That Are Consistent with Observations from a Perturbed Physics Parameter Ensemble. *Journal of Climate*, *31*(12), 4639–4656.

Stainforth, D., Allen, M. R., Tredger, E. R., & Smith, L. A. (2007). Confidence, Uncertainty and Decision-Support Relevance in Climate Predictions. *Philosophical Transactions. Series A, Mathematical, Physical, and Engineering Sciences*, *365*(1857), 2145–2161.

Staniforth, A., & Thuburn, J. (2012). Horizontal Grids for Global Weather and Climate Prediction Models: A Review. *Quarterly Journal of the Royal Meteorological Society*, *138*(662), 1–26.

Staniforth, A., & Wood, N. (2008). Aspects of the Dynamical Core of a Nonhydrostatic, Deep-Atmosphere, Unified Weather and Climate-Prediction Model☆. *Journal of Computational Physics*, *227*(7), 3445–3464.

Star, S. L. (2010). This is Not a Boundary Object: Reflections on the Origin of a Concept. *Science, Technology, & Human Values*, *35*(5), 601–617.

Stern, N. (2016). Current Climate Models Are Grossly Misleading. *Nature*, *530*, 407–409.

Stevens, B., Giorgetta, M., Esch, M. et al. (2013). Atmospheric Component of the MPI-M Earth System Model: ECHAM6. *Journal of Advances in Modeling Earth Systems*, *5*(2), 146–172.

Stocker, T. (2011). *Introduction to Climate Modelling*. Berlin, Heidelberg: Springer Berlin Heidelberg.

Strong, J., & Plass, G. N. (1950). The Effect of Pressure Broadening of Spectral Lines on Atmospheric Temperature. *The Astrophysical Journal*, *112*(4), 365.

Supran, G., & Oreskes, N. (2017). Assessing ExxonMobil's Climate Change Communications (1977–2014). *Environmental Research Letters*, *12*(8), 084019.

Tait, P. G., Buchan, A., Creak, E. W., & Renard, A. (1889). *The Voyage of the HMS Challenger: Physics and Chemistry* (C. W. Thomson & J. Murray, Eds.) (Vol. II). London, England: Morrison & Gibb.

Talandier, C., Deshayes, J., Treguier, A. M. et al. (2014). Improvements of Simulated Western North Atlantic Current System and Impacts on the AMOC. *Ocean Modelling*, *76*, 1–19.

Teixeira, M. A. C. (2014). The Physics of Orographic Gravity Wave Drag. *Frontiers in Physics*, *2*(July), 1–24.

Thompson, D. W. J., Kennedy, J. J., Wallace, J. M., & Jones, P. D. (2008). A Large Discontinuity in the Mid-Twentieth Century in Observed Global-Mean Surface Temperature. *Nature*, *453*(7195), 646–649.

Thorpe, A. J., Volkert, D. H., & Ziemianski, M. (2003). The Bjerknes' Circulation Theorem: A Historical Perspective. *Bulletin of the American Meteorological Society*, *84*(4), 471–480.

Tilmes, S., Richter, J. H., Kravitz, B. et al. (2018). CESM1(WACCM) Stratospheric Aerosol Geoengineering Large Ensemble Project. *Bulletin of the American Meteorological Society*, *99*(11), 2361–2371.

Tokarska, K. B., Stolpe, M. B., Sippel, S. et al. (2020). Past Warming Trend Constrains Future Warming in CMIP6 Models. *Science Advances*, *6*(12), 1–14.

Tyndall, J. (1861). I. The Bakerian Lecture.—On the Absorption and Radiation of Heat by Gases and Vapours, and on the Physical Connexion of Radiation, Absorption, and Conduction. *Philosophical Transactions of the Royal Society of London*, *151*(0), 1–36.

United Nations (1992) United Nations Framework Convention on Climate Change.

University Committee on Atmospheric Research. (1959). *Preliminary Plans for a National Institute for Atmospheric Research*. Technical Report, National Center for Atmospheric Research.

Valcke, S., Balaji, V., Craig, A. et al. (2012). Coupling Technologies for Earth System Modelling. *Geoscientific Model Development*, *5*(6), 1589–1596.

Vancoppenolle, M., Fichefet, T., Goosse, H. et al. (2009). Simulating the Mass Balance and Salinity of Arctic and Antarctic Sea ice. 1. Model Description and Validation. *Ocean Modelling*, *27*(1–2), 33–53.

Very, F. W. (1901). Knut Angstrom on Atmospheric Absorption. *Monthly Weather Review*, *29 June* (6), 268.

Walters, D., Boutle, I., Brooks, M. et al. (2017). The Met Office Unified Model Global Atmosphere 6.0/6.1 and JULES Global Land 6.0/6.1 configurations. *Geoscientific Model Development*, *10*(4), 1487–1520.

Wan, H., Giorgetta, M. A., Zängl, G. et al. (2013). The ICON-1.2 Hydrostatic Atmospheric Dynamical Core on Triangular Grids – Part 1: Formulation and Performance of the Baseline Version. *Geoscientific Model Development*, *6*(3), 735–763.

Warner, L. (1985). *The National Center for Atmospheric Research: An Architectural Masterpiece*. Boulder, CO: The University Corporation for Atmospheric Research (UCAR).

Washington, W. M., Buja, L., & Craig, A. (2009). The Computational Future for Climate and Earth System Models: On the Path to Petaflop and Beyond. *Philosophical Transactions. Series A, Mathematical, Physical, and Engineering Sciences*, *367*(1890), 833–846.

Washington, W. M., & Meehl, G. A. (1989). Climate Sensitivity Due to Increased CO2: Experiments with a Coupled Atmosphere and Ocean General Circulation Model. *Climate Dynamics*, *4*(1), 1–38.

Weart, S. (1989). *Interview of Joseph Smagorinsky by Spencer Weart*. Niels Bohr Library & Archives. American Institute of Physics, College Park, MD. www.aip .org/history-programs/niels-bohr-library/oral-histories/5056

Weart, S. (2007). Roger Revelle's Discovery. Retrieved June 18, 2018, from https:// history.aip.org/climate/pdf/Revelle.pdf

Weart, S. (2013). Rise of Interdisciplinary Research on Climate. *Proceedings of the National Academy of Sciences*, *110*, 3657–3664.

Weisman, A. (2007). *The World without Us*. New York: Thomas Dunne Books.

Weyant, J. P. (2009). A Perspective on Integrated Assessment. *Climatic Change*, *95*(3–4), 317–323.

White, A. A., & Wood, N. (2015). Dynamical Meteorology | Primitive Equations. In *Encyclopedia of Atmospheric Sciences* (Vol. 1, pp. 384–392). Elsevier.

Willett, K., Williams, C., Jolliffe, I. T. et al. (2014). A Framework for Benchmarking of Homogenisation Algorithm Performance on the Global Scale. *Geoscientific Instrumentation, Methods and Data Systems, 3*(2), 187–200.

Williams, K. D., Copsey, D., Blockley, E. W. et al. (2018). The Met Office Global Coupled Model 3.0 and 3.1 (GC3.0 and GC3.1) Configurations. *Journal of Advances in Modeling Earth Systems, 10*(2), 357–380.

Williamson, D. L., Kiehl, J. T., Ramanathan, V., Dickinson, R. E., & Hack, J. J. (1987). *Description of NCAR Community Climate Model (CCM1)* (No. NCAR/TN285+STR). NCAR.

Williamson, D. L. (2007). The Evolution of Dynamical Cores for Global Atmospheric Models. *Journal of the Meteorological Society of Japan, 85B*, 241–269.

Williamson, D. L., Drake, J. B., Hack, J. J., Jakob, R., & Swarztrauber, P. N. (1992). A Standard Test Set for Numerical Approximations to the Shallow Water Equations in Spherical Geometry. *Journal of Computational Physics, 102*(1), 211–224.

Williamson, D. L., Olson, J. G., & Jablonowski, C. (2009). Two Dynamical Core Formulation Flaws Exposed by a Baroclinic Instability Test Case. *Monthly Weather Review, 137*(2), 790–796.

Wirth, N. (1995). A Plea for Lean Software. *IEEE Computer, 28*(2), 64–68.

Xu, J., Gao, Y., Christley, S., & Madey, G. (2005). A Topological Analysis of the Open Source Software Development community. In *Proceedings of the 38th Hawaii International Conference on System Sciences – 2005* (Vol. 00, pp. 1–10).

Index